Y0-AHO-005

MODERN ELOQUENCE

A Library of the World's Best Spoken Thought

Edited by
ASHLEY H. THORNDIKE

NEW YORK
MODERN ELOQUENCE CORPORATION

Advisory Editorial Board

BRANDER MATTHEWS, Chairman
Professor Dramatic Literature, Columbia University

SIR ROBERT LAIRD BORDEN
Formerly Prime Minister of Canada

NICHOLAS MURRAY BUTLER
President, Columbia University

JOHN W. DAVIS
Formerly U. S. Ambassador to England

HENRY CABOT LODGE
Late Senator from Massachusetts

ELIHU ROOT
Formerly Secretary of State, Secretary of War, Senator

OSCAR S. STRAUS
Formerly Secretary of Commerce, Ambassador to Turkey

AUGUSTUS THOMAS
Playwright, Chairman Producing Managers' Association

HENRY van DYKE
Professor of English Literature, Princeton University
Formerly U. S. Minister to the Netherlands

NEW YORK

MODERN ELOQUENCE CORPORATION

MODERN ELOQUENCE
IN FIFTEEN VOLUMES

The outstanding After-Dinner Speeches, Lectures and Addresses of Modern Times, by the most eminent speakers of America and Europe.

VOLUMES I · II · III
AFTER-DINNER SPEECHES

VOLUMES IV · V · VI
BUSINESS · INDUSTRY
PROFESSIONS

VOLUMES VII · VIII · IX
PUBLIC AFFAIRS
Literary · Educational · Government · Citizenship
Lives of Great Men

VOLUMES X · XI · XII
HISTORICAL MASTERPIECES
European · American · World War

VOLUME XIII
FAMOUS LECTURES
Humorous · Inspirational

VOLUME XIV
ANECDOTES · EPIGRAMS

VOLUME XV
PUBLIC SPEAKING
Debates

INDEX

Introductory Essays by Eminent Authorities giving a Practical Course of Instruction on the Important Phases of Public Speaking

MODERN ELOQUENCE

VOLUME VII

Public Affairs
LITERARY · EDUCATIONAL

Edited by
ASHLEY H. THORNDIKE
Professor of English, Columbia University

NEW YORK

MODERN ELOQUENCE
CORPORATION

Copyright, 1928, by
MODERN ELOQUENCE CORPORATION

Entered at Stationers' Hall, London
All rights reserved

PRINTED IN U.S.A.

CONTENTS

                                               PAGE

INTRODUCTION: The Literary Address
    HAMILTON WRIGHT MABIE xiii

ADAMS, CHARLES FRANCIS
    A College Fetish 1

ADLER, FELIX
    Marcus Aurelius 14
    Nature and the Religious Mood 30

ALLENBY, LORD
    Opening the Hebrew University at Jerusalem . . 33

AXSON, STOCKTON
    The World and the New Generation 34

BALFOUR, ARTHUR JAMES
    The Pleasures of Reading 41

BANCROFT, GEORGE
    The People in Art, Government, and Religion . . . 55

BUTLER, NICHOLAS MURRAY
    Five Evidences of an Education 73

CARLYLE, THOMAS
    Inaugural Address at Edinburgh 83

CHAPMAN, JOHN JAY
    The Unity of Human Nature 102

DEBS, EUGENE V.
    On Receiving Sentence 110

DRUMMOND, HENRY
    "First!" 116

EGGLESTON, EDWARD
    The New History 124

ELIOT, CHARLES WILLIAM
    Defects in American Education 136

CONTENTS

	PAGE
The Durable Satisfactions of Life	151
On His Ninetieth Birthday	154

FRANK, GLENN
    A Welcome to the Freshmen 158

GALE, ZONA
    The Novel and the Spirit 162

GEDDES, SIR AUCKLAND CAMPBELL
    Commencement Address 176

GIBBONS, JAMES, CARDINAL
    Supremacy of the Catholic Religion 183

GILMAN, DANIEL COIT
    The Characteristics of a University 193

HADLEY, ARTHUR TWINING
    Modern Changes in Educational Ideals 207

HARRISON, FREDERIC
    The Choice of Books 213

HOLLAND, RUSH LA MOTTE
    The Order of the Elks 230

HOPKINS, ERNEST MARTIN
    An Aristocracy of Brains 235

JORDAN, DAVID STARR
    Higher Education of Women 244

LA FOLLETTE, ROBERT MARION
    Which Shall Rule, Manhood or Money? 252

LOWELL, ABBOTT LAWRENCE
    Scholarship 259
    The Ninetieth Birthday of Charles William Eliot . . 260
    The Art of Examination 261

MANNING, HENRY EDWARD, CARDINAL
    Persecution of the Jews 266

MILLIKAN, ROBERT ANDREWS
    The Atom 272

MORRIS, WILLIAM
    Art and the Beauty of the Earth 279

CONTENTS

ix

MOTT, JOHN R.
   Meditation 289
NEWMAN, JOHN HENRY, CARDINAL
   Knowledge Viewed in Relation to Learning . . . 297
NEWTON, JOSEPH FORT
   The Ministry of Masonry 304
NICHOLSON, MEREDITH
   The Sunny Slopes of Forty 316
PANKHURST, EMMELINE
   Militant Suffragists 324
PINKERTON, ALFRED S.
   Spirit of Odd-Fellowship 333
REDFIELD, WILLIAM C.
   First Get the Facts 340
ROBBINS, SIR ALFRED
   Freemasonry in England and America 352
ROOT, ELIHU
   Seventy-Fifth Anniversary of the Century Club . . 365
RUSSELL, BERTRAND
   How to Be Free and Happy 370
SPALDING, JOHN LANCASTER
   Opportunity 383
THORNDIKE, EDWARD LEE
   Education for Initiative and Originality 391
VAIL, THEODORE NEWTON
   Life on the Farm 403
VAN DYKE, HENRY
   Books, Literature, and the People 408
WILLARD, FRANCES
   Work for Humanity 414
WILSON, WOODROW
   The Course of American History 417
ZOLA, EMILE
   Appeal for Dreyfus 437

ILLUSTRATIONS

ARTHUR J. BALFOUR	41
NICHOLAS MURRAY BUTLER	73
CHARLES W. ELIOT	136
GLENN FRANK	158
JAMES, CARDINAL GIBBONS	183
JOSEPH FORT NEWTON	300

INTRODUCTION

THE LITERARY ADDRESS

By HAMILTON WRIGHT MABIE

THE literary address is generally stamped with distinction of form; it is often a classic in literature as well as in oratory. This touch of art is imparted to it in some cases by the material with which it deals, and in more by the skill of the speaker. As a rule, literary themes fall into the hands of men familiar with the best literary models and skilled in the art of writing. A glance at the list of contributors to these volumes brings to clear view the literary accomplishments of the speakers and the prominence of literary quality in their work. There have been many effective, successful, and eminently useful lecturers whose utterances have perished with them; men who used the platform for high ends, but who were concerned primarily with the content of their thought and conviction rather than with the expression; who addressed themselves to the immediate rather than the remote audience, and who endeavored to make the most of the moment, indifferent to the judgment of the future. Much of the most effective and characteristic work done on the platform has had this quality of immediate but ephemeral impressiveness; it was planned, shaped, and presented with nice adjustment to time, place, and hearers; and in touching deeply the feeling of the hour, stimulating its thought, awakening its conscience and dissipating its weariness, it served a wholesome and worthy end.

The literary address has had the advantage, as a rule, of dealing with subjects which lay outside the fierce discussions of the hour in the clear atmosphere of another century, or the quiet seclusion of a life devoted to art. If a man is speaking on the slavery question, at a time when the air is charged with passion, he is not likely to escape the heat and turbulence of debate; if he is speaking on Milton or Shakespeare or Burns he can hardly fail to touch some of the chords which vibrate in the soul of humanity beyond the reach of the emotions of the hour. It is true that even in dealing with matters which, in discussion, awaken the bitterest feelings the master speaker so relates them to universal principles and interprets them with such noble breadth of charity that the touch of literature gives the utterance of the moment the significance of a classic. This was what Lincoln did in the two Inaugural Addresses, and in the few imperishable sentences spoken at Gettysburg. But these are the supreme moments of the masters of speech; they come at long intervals, and they come only to the greatest spirits. Webster said with true insight that for the great speech three things were essential; a great man, a great theme, and a great occasion; and this conjunction of favorable conditions rarely occurs.

In dealing with literary themes, however, the speaker has the advantage of handling material which is essentially cultural in quality; it appeals to the imagination and lends itself readily to the shaping mind. A speaker need not be wholly great in order to feel the inspiration of a poet's life and thought; it is easier to be lifted into the region where thought carries the torch of imagination in its hand by the memory of Burns than by the need of municipal reform. In one sense subjects have little to do with literature, which always has its roots in temperament, individuality, manner and form; in another sense, however, they have much to do with the presence or absence of that quality in writing which we call literature. In suggestiveness, power to kindle emotion, and abiding human interest literary subjects have much to do with the making of literature.

The contents of these volumes are drawn largely, though not exclusively, from literature; one may find them in the libraries in the alcoves set apart to oratory, or in those set apart to literature. This could not be said of any other group of addresses selected by subject. Those who heard Mr. George William Curtis, on the last occasion in which he appeared in public, deliver the address on James Russell Lowell, spoken for the first time before the Brooklyn Institute on the seventy-third anniversary of the poet's birth, will never forget the exquisite harmony, one might say the complete identification, of oratory and literature which was accomplished in the speaker, the theme, and the manner. Something of the richness of the subject passed into the orator; in whom the charm of public speech was deepened and enhanced by the beauty of that art which speaks of and to the human spirit with voices as various as its experiences and as eloquent as its dreams. It was once said of this accomplished orator and high-minded man, whose melody of voice seemed to be the vibration of his own nature, that when he delivered his captivating address on Sir Philip Sidney, it was as easy to believe that Sidney was discoursing of Curtis as to believe that Curtis was speaking of Sidney. Mr. Curtis spoke often and effectively on themes of public interest, but he was never so happy as when he touched with delicacy, humor, and insight some subject which led him within the magical boundaries of literature.

The literary address has been heard in its perfection at the celebrations of the Phi Beta Kappa Society in Harvard University. The memory of an oration delivered by Buckminister in 1809 has become one of the traditions of the anniversary; it was on one of these occasions that Everett, in 1824, welcomed Lafayette in that stately and musical style which charmed two generations of critical listeners; that classic of American thought, Dr. Bushnell's "Work and Play," was spoken first before the Harvard Phi Beta Kappa; and it was in the presence of the same audience that Wendell Phillips made his last important address. The long line of distinguished speakers on these occasions has not been broken even in these later years, when oratory has lacked something of its earlier richness and influence; and if the addresses delivered before this Society were collected they would form a contribution to what may be called literary oratory of the first importance, not only as regards artistic form but content of thought.

A foremost place in this long list of literary addresses must be given to Emerson's oration on the "American Scholar," delivered on August 31, 1837, which Dr. Holmes has characterized as "the declaration of American intellectual independence."

That address was in the key of the best thought of the new world; it was an interpretation of opportunity and work in America which ought to be written in the heart of our great, restless, turbulent, active society. Not less notable was the address delivered by Emerson before the Harvard Divinity School in the following year, which became the subject of a fierce discussion in which Emerson remained significantly silent.

A full generation later Emerson spoke again before the Phi Beta Kappa, and Lowell has left a charming impression of his manner: "Emerson's oration was more disjointed than usual, even for him. It began nowhere and ended everywhere, and yet, as always with that divine man, it left you feeling that something more beautiful had passed that way—something more beautiful than anything else, like the rising and setting of stars. Every possible criticism might have been made on it but one—that it was not noble. There was a tone in it that awakened all elevating associations. He boggled, he lost his place, he had to put on his glasses; but it was as if a creature from some fairer world had lost his way in our fogs, and it was our fault, not his. It was chaotic, but it was all such stuff as stars are made of." Many of Emerson's most characteristic utterances are to be found in his addresses, and through them he spoke most directly and intelligibly to his contemporaries. Justice has never been done to the charm of his manner and the magic of his voice on the platform. In many of his hearers the love of poetry began with his reading of passages from Homer or Wordsworth.

Among Emerson's contemporaries in the field of American letters there were a number whose faces and voices were familiar on the platform, and whose work was first given to the public in the form of addresses. Dr. Holmes was for a time an industrious lecturer, and for many years a speaker on occasion. He has left a highly characteristic description of one kind of country audience: "I have sometimes felt as if I am a wandering spirit, and this great unchanging multi-vertebrate which I faced night after night, was an ever-listening animal, which writhed along after me whenever I fled, and coiled up at my feet every evening, turning up to me the same sleepless eyes

THE LITERARY ADDRESS xvii

which I thought I had closed with my last drowsy incantation."

James Russell Lowell, in the early years of his career as a man of letters, spoke to his contemporaries as well as wrote for them. At that time the interest in lectures was widespread and intelligent, but the means of transportation and the hotel accommodations brought hardship to the most experienced traveler. Even in that golden age of the Lyceum there were drawbacks and disappointments. "To be received at a bad inn," wrote Lowell, "by a solemn committee, in a room with a stove that smokes but not exhilarates, to have three cold fish tails laid in your hand to shake, to be carried to a cold lecture-room, to read a cold lecture to a cold audience, to be carried back to your smoke-side, paid, and the three fish tails again—well, it is not delightful, exactly."

In the face of these annoyances many men of light and leading, or of gifts of eloquence and humor, found the platform a vantage ground of great importance for the teaching of new ideas or the reform of existing conditions. Theodore Parker, "the deputy-sheriff of ideas," impressed his strenuous personality on many audience; Wendell Phillips brought literary skill of a high order as well as great gifts of eloquence and sarcasm and passionate conviction, to the service of the Lyceum; James Freeman Clarke was a force for popular culture; and Edwin P. Whipple made the history of literature attractive in a long succession of literary courses, as in our time Prof. Winchester has taught willing listeners where to look for the best in literature, and how to find it. The rare spirit of W. E. Channing, the pure mind of Starr King, the interesting recollections of James T. Fields, the finished eloquence of Edward Everett, the rich diction of Dr. R. S. Storrs, gave the highest dignity and greatest range to the discussion of the platform.

In England, Coleridge, Hazlitt, Carlyle, Ruskin, Charles Kingsley, Thackeray, Matthew Arnold, and John Morley have sustained the dignity of letters in public discourse. Thackeray's visits to this country in 1853 and again in 1855 are among the most interesting events in the history of the Lyceum in America. To the remarkable gifts of exposition of Tyndall, Huxley, and other eminent scientists the wide

expansion of popular interest in science has owed much.
Among contemporary men of letters who have been heard on the lecture platform or on special occasions are Mr. Warner, Mr. Howells, Mr. Stedman, Mr. Mitchell, Dr. Hale, Colonel Higginson, Mr. Page, Mr. Matthews, Dr. van Dyke, Mr. John Fiske, Mr. Clemens, Mr. Cable, Mr. Garland, Mr. Bliss Perry, Mr. Crawford, Mr. Burroughs; a list of names which suggests the possible closeness of connection between the lecture and literature. When it is remembered that a large part of the works of Coleridge and Hazlitt, Carlyle's "Heroes," Arnold's discourses, many of Ruskin's most characteristic chapters, Emerson's addresses, Thackeray's "English Humorists" and "The Four Georges," Whipple's "Literature of the Age of Elizabeth," were first given to the world in the form of lectures, it becomes clear that the Lyceum has been from the beginning and still is one of the prime avenues of approach to the general mind of the country open to the thinker and writer.

The Commencement address has a setting of unusual dignity, and in its appeal to the ultimate motives of life and its emphasis on the ethical and intellectual interests of society, has touched the highest levels both of thought and of expression. Emerson, Curtis, and Whipple were heard at many college festivals, as were many of their contemporaries who had secured reputation on the lecture platform. The college anniversary, with its happy combination of scholarly, literary, and personal associations, demanded high thought, sound form and dignity of manner. The requirements of the occasion sifted the orators of the day and selected those who brought to the platform the finer qualities of public speech.

During the deep stirring of the intellectual and spiritual life of New England, of which the Transcendental movement, the anti-slavery agitation, and the rapid production of a native American literature were the chief signs and fruits, the interest in college festivities was deep and serious, and the speaker was sure of an audience worthy of the place, the time, and his best thought. Later, in the older sections of the country, there was a marked decline of general interest in the exercises of Commencement Day. In many institutions the old-time high-school program of addresses by the members of the graduating class was closely followed. Of late, however, there has been a noticeable change; student speakers have been replaced by a speaker of distinction or, at least, of note in some department, the occasion has been invested with greater academic dignity and there has been, in consequence, a marked revival of interests in the exercises of the day.

In the majority of the colleges in this country, however, the Commencement oration has been delivered for many years by a speaker of reputation; and the opportunities are so many that the Commencement address holds a place of its own in the field of oratory. Men of letters, heads of colleges, teachers, lawyers, clergymen, scholars, public men, and scientists of distinction find in college audiences an intelligent open-mindedness which invites the freest and freshest thought. On the college platform the problems of modern life in every field can be discussed in the most serious spirit and with uncompromising freedom. Many notable utterances are heard, and, with much that is formal and academic, there is also much that is significant and prophetic. These addresses set the standards of noble public speech, and their educational value in a democratic society can hardly be overvalued. They keep before the mind of a country rapidly becoming almost incredibly rich the unchangeable scale of spiritual values; restating in the hearing of thousands of young graduates the noble truth which Emerson proclaimed at Dartmouth College two generations ago: "When you shall say, 'As others do, so will I: I renounce, I am sorry for it, my early visions; I must eat the good of the land and let learning and romantic expectations go, until a more convenient season';—then dies the man in you; then once more perish the buds of art, and poetry, and science, as they have died already in a thousand thousand men. The hour of that choice is the crisis of your history, and see that you hold yourself fast by the intellect."

ADDRESSES
LITERARY, EDUCATIONAL, SOCIAL

CHARLES FRANCIS ADAMS

A COLLEGE FETISH

Address by Charles Francis Adams, lawyer, publicist, historical writer (born in Boston, 1835; died 1915, delivered before the Harvard Chapter of the Fraternity of the Phi Beta Kappa in Sanders Theater, Cambridge, Mass., June 8, 1883. This address, here abridged, was in a way epoch-making, for it hastened the abandonment of the study of the classical languages as the basis of our education. An after-dinner speech by Mr. Adams is printed in Volume I.

I AM here to-day for a purpose. After no little hesitation I accepted the invitation to address your Society, simply because I had something which I much wanted to say; and this seemed to me the best possible place, and this the most appropriate occasion, for saying it. My message, if such I may venture to call it, is in nowise sensational. On the contrary, it partakes, I fear, rather of the commonplace. Such being the case, I shall give it the most direct utterance of which I am capable.

It is twenty-seven years since the class of which I was a member graduated from this college. I am glad that I came here, and glad that I took my degree. But as a training-place for youth to enable them to engage to advantage in the struggle of life—to fit them to hold their own in it, and to carry off the prizes—I must in all honesty say, that, in looking back through the years, and recalling the requirements and methods of the ancient institution, I am unable to speak of it with all the respect I could wish. Such training as I got, useful for the struggle, I got after, instead of before graduation, and it came hard; while I never have been able—and now, no matter how long I may live, I never shall be able—to overcome some

Copyright, 1883, by C. F. Adams, Jr.

great disadvantages which the superstitions and wrong theories and worse practices of my *alma mater* inflicted upon me. And not on me alone. The same may be said of my contemporaries as I have observed them in success and failure. What was true in this respect of the college of thirty years ago, is, I apprehend, at least partially true of the college of to-day; and it is true not only of Cambridge, but of other colleges, and of them quite as much as of Cambridge. They fail properly to fit their graduates for the work they have to do in the life that awaits them. This is harsh language to apply to one's nursing mother, and it calls for an explanation. That explanation I shall try to give.

Now as respects the college preparation we received to fit us to take part in this world's debate. As one goes on in life, especially in modern life, a few conclusions are hammered into us by the hard logic of facts. Among these conclusions I think I may, without much fear of contradiction, enumerate such practical common sense and commonplace precepts as that superficiality is dangerous, as well as contemptible, in that it is apt to invite defeat; or, again, that what is worth doing at all is worth doing well; or, third, that when one is given work to do, it is well to prepare one's self for that specific work, and not to occupy's one's time in acquiring information, no matter how innocent or elegant, or generally useful, which has no probable bearing on that work; or, finally—and this I regard as the greatest of all practical precepts—that every man should in life master some one thing, be it great or be it small, so that thereon he may be the highest living authority: that one thing he should know thoroughly.

How did Harvard College prepare me, and my ninety-two classmates of the year 1856, for our work in a life in which we have had these homely precepts brought close to us? In answering the question it is not altogether easy to preserve one's gravity. The college fitted us for this active, bustling, hard-hitting, many-tongued world, caring nothing for authority and little for the past, but full of its living thoughts and living issues, in dealing with which there was no man who did not stand in pressing and constant need of every possible preparation as respects knowledge and exactitude and thoroughness—

the poor old college prepared us to play our parts in this world by compelling us, directly and indirectly, to devote the best part of our school lives to acquiring a confessedly superficial knowledge of two dead languages.

Such is the theory. Now what is the practice? Thirty years ago, as for three centuries before, Greek and Latin were the fundamentals. The grammatical study of two dead languages was the basis of all liberal education. It is still its basis.

But in pursuing Greek and Latin we had ignored our mother tongue. We were no more competent to pass a really searching examination in English literature and English composition than in the languages and literature of Greece and Rome. We were college graduates; and yet how many of us could follow out a line of sustained, close thought, expressing ourselves in clear, concise terms? The faculty of doing this should result from a mastery of well selected fundamentals. The difficulty was that the fundamentals were not well selected, and they had never been mastered. They had become a tradition. They were studied no longer as a means, but as an end—the end being to get into college. Accordingly, thirty years ago there was no real living basis of a Harvard education. Honest, solid foundations were not laid. The superstructure, such as it was, rested upon an empty formula.

And here let me define my position on several points, so that I shall be misunderstood only by such as willfully misunderstand, in order to misrepresent. With such I hold no argument. In the first place I desire to say that I am no believer in that narrow scientific and technological training which now and again we hear extolled. A practical, and too often a mere vulgar, money-making utility seems to be its natural outcome. On the contrary, the whole experience and observation of my life lead me to look with greater admiration, and an envy ever increasing, on the broadened culture which is the true end and aim of the university. On this point I cannot be too explicit; for I should be sorry indeed if anything I might utter were construed into an argument against the most liberal education. There is a considerable period in every man's life when the best thing he can do is to let his mind soak and tan in the vats of literature. The atmosphere of a university is breathed into the student's system—it enters by the very pores. But, just as all roads lead to Rome, so I hold there may be a modern road as well as the classic avenue to the goal of a true liberal education. I object to no man's causing his children to approach that goal by the old, time-honored entrance. But I do ask that the modern entrance should not be closed. Vested interests always look upon a claim for simple recognition as a covert attack on their very existence, and the advocates of an exclusively classic college education are quick to interpret a desire for modern learning, as a covert attack on dead learning. I have no wish to attack it, except in its spirit of selfish exclusiveness. I do challenge the right of the classicist to longer say that by his path, and by his path only, shall the university be approached. I would not narrow the basis of liberal education; I would broaden it. No longer content with classic courses, I would have the university seek fresh inspiration at the fountains of living thought; for Goethe I hold to be the equal of Sophocles, and I prefer the philosophy of Montaigne to what seem to me the platitudes of Cicero.

I was fitted for college in the usual way. I went to the Latin School; I learned the two grammars by heart; at length I could even puzzle out the simpler classic writings with the aid of a lexicon, and apply more or less correctly the rules of construction. This, and the other rudiments of what we are pleased to call a liberal education, took five years of my time. I was fortunately fond of reading, and so learned English myself, and with some thoroughness. I say fortunately, for in our preparatory curriculum no place was found for English; being a modern language, it was thought not worth studying—as our examination papers conclusively showed. We turned English into bad enough Greek, but our thoughts were expressed in even more abominable English. I then went to college—to Harvard. I have already spoken of the standard of instruction, so far as thoroughness was concerned, then prevailing here. Presently I was graduated, and passed some years in the study of the law. Thus far, as you will see, my course was thoroughly correct. It was the course pursued by a large proportion of all graduates then, and the course pursued by more than a third of them now. Then the War of the Rebellion came, and swept me out of a lawyer's office into a cavalry saddle. Let me say, in passing, that I have always felt under deep personal obligation to the War of the Rebellion. Returning presently to civil life, and not taking kindly to my profession, I endeavored to strike out a new path, and fastened myself, not as Mr. Emerson recommends, to a star, but to the locomotive-engine. I made for myself what might perhaps be called a specialty in connection with the development of the railroad system. I do not hesitate to say that I have been incapacitated from properly developing my specialty by the sins of omission and commission incident to my college training. The mischief is done, and so far as I am concerned, is irreparable. I am only one more sacrifice to the fetish. But I do not propose to be a silent sacrifice. I am here to-day to put the responsibility for my failure, so far as I have failed, where I think it belongs—at the door of my preparatory and college education.

Many of you are scientific men; others are literary men; some are professional men. I believe, from your own personal experience you will bear me out when I say that, with a single exception, there is no modern scientific study which can be thoroughly pursued in any one living language, even with the assistance of all the dead languages that ever were spoken. I have admitted there is one exception to this rule. That exception is the law.

The modern languages are thus the avenues to modern life and living thought. Under these circumstances, what was the position of the college towards them thirty years ago? What is its position to-day? It intervened, and practically said then that its graduates should not acquire those languages at that period when only they could be acquired perfectly and with ease. It occupies the same position still. It did and does this none the less effectually because indirectly. The thing came about, as it still comes about, in this way: The college fixes the requirements for admission to its course. The schools and the academies adapt themselves to those requirements. The business of those preparatory schools is to get the boys through their examinations, not as a means, but as an end. They are therefore all organized on one plan. To that plan there is no exception; nor practically can there be any exception. The requirements for admission are such that the labor of preparation occupies fully the boy's study hours. He is not overworked, perhaps, but when his tasks are done he has no more leisure than is good for play; and you cannot take a healthy boy the moment he leaves school and set him down before tutors in German and French. If you do, he will soon cease to be a healthy boy; and he will not learn German or French. Over-education is a crime against youth. But Harvard College says: "We require such and such things for admission to our course." First and most emphasized among them are Latin and Greek. The academies accordingly teach Latin and Greek; and they teach it in the way to secure admission to the college. Hence, because of this action of the college, the schools do not exist in this country in which my children can learn what my experience tells me it is all essential they should know. They cannot both be fitted for college and taught the modern languages. And when I say "taught the modern languages," I mean taught them in the world's sense of the word, and not in the college sense of it, as practiced both in my time and now. And here let me not be misunderstood, and confronted with examination papers. I am talking of really knowing something. I do not want my children to get a smattering knowledge of French and of German, such a knowledge as was and now is given to boys of Latin and Greek; but I do want them to be taught to write and to speak those languages, as well as to read them—in a word, so to master them that they will thereafter be tools always ready to the hand. This requires labor. It is a thing which cannot be picked up by the wayside, except in the countries where the languages are spoken. If academies in America are to instruct in this way, they must devote themselves to it. But the college requires all that they can well undertake to do. The college absolutely insists on Latin and Greek.

I now come to what in plain language I cannot but call the educational cant of this subject. I am told that I ignore the severe intellectual training I got in learning the Greek grammar, and in subsequently applying its rules; that my memory then received an education which, turned since to other matters, has proved invaluable to me; that accumulated experience shows that this training can be got equally well in no other way; that, beyond all this, even my slight contact with the Greek masterpieces has left me with a subtile, but unmistakable residuum, impalpable perhaps, but still there, and very precious; that, in a word, I am what is called an educated man, which, but for my early contact with Greek, I would not be.

It was Dr. Johnson I believe who once said, "Let us free our minds from cant"; and all this, with not undue bluntness be it said, is unadulterated nonsense. The fact that it has been and will be a thousand times repeated cannot make it anything else. In the first place, I very confidently submit, there is no more mental training in learning the Greek grammar by heart than in learning by heart any other equally difficult and, to a boy, unintelligible book. As a mere work of memorizing, Kant's "Critique of Pure Reason" would be at least as good. In the next place, unintelligent memorizing is at best a most questionable educational method. For one, I utterly disbelieve in it. It never did me anything but harm; and learning by heart the Greek grammar, did me harm—a great deal of harm. While I was doing it, the observing and reflective powers lay dormant; indeed, they were systematically suppressed. Their exercise was resented as a sort of impertinence. We boys took up and repeated long rules, and yet longer lists of exceptions to them, and it was drilled into us that we were not there to reason, but to rattle off something written on the blackboards of our minds. The faculties we had in common with the raven were thus cultivated at the expense of that apprehension and reason which, Shakespeare tells us, makes man like the angels and God. I infer this memory-culture is yet in vogue; for only yesterday, as I sat at the Commencement table with one of the younger and more active of the professors of the college, he told me that he had no difficulty with his students in making them commit to memory; they were well trained in that. But when he called on them to observe and infer, then his troubles began. They had never been led in such a path. It was the old, old story—a lamentation and an ancient tale of wrong.

Finally, I come to the great impalpable essence-and-preciousresiduum theory—the theory that a knowledge of Greek grammar, and the having puzzled through the Anabasis and three books of the Iliad, infuses into the boy's nature the imperceptible spirit of Greek literature, which will appear in the results of his subsequent work, just as manure, spread upon a field, appears in the crop which that field bears. But to produce results on a field, manure must be laboriously worked into its soil and made a part of it; and only when it is so worked in, and does become a part of it, will it produce its result. You cannot haul manure up and down and across a field, cutting the ground into deep ruts with the wheels of your cart, while the soil just gets a smell of what is in the cart, and then expect to get a crop. Yet even that is more than we did, and are doing, with Greek. We trundle a single wheelbarrow load of Greek up and down and across the boy's mind; and then we clasp our hands, and cant about a subtile fineness and impalpable but very precious residuum! All we have in fact done is to teach the boy to mistake means for ends, and make a system of superficiality.

On the 9th of July, 1813, the hard political wrangles of their two lives being over, and in the midst of the second war with Great Britain, I find John Adams thus writing to Thomas Jefferson—and I must confess to very much prefer John Adams in his easy letter-writing undress, to John Adams on his dead-learning stilts; he seems a wiser, a more genuine man. He is answering a letter from Jefferson, who had in the shades of Monticello been reviving his Greek:—

Lord! Lord! what can I do with so much Greek? When I was of your age, young man, that is, seven or eight years ago [he was then nearly seventy-nine, and his correspondent a little over seventy], I felt a kind of pang of affection for one of the flames of my youth, and again paid my addresses to Isocrates and Dionysius Halicarnassensis, etc., etc., etc., I collected all my lexicons, and grammars, and sat down to Περὶ συνθέσεως ὀνομάτων. In this way I amused myself for some time, but I found that if I looked a word to-day, in less than a week I had to look it again. It was to little better purpose than writing letters on a pail of water.

This certainly is not much like studying Greek "to any extent with great ease." But I have not done with John Adams yet. A year and one week later I find him again writing to Jefferson. In the interval, Jefferson seems to have read Plato, sending at last to John Adams his final impressions of that philosopher. To this letter, on July 16th, 1814, his correspondent replies as follows:—

I am very glad you have seriously read Plato, and still more rejoiced to find that your reflections upon him so perfectly harmonize with mine. Some thirty years ago I took upon me the severe task of going through all his works. With the help of two Latin translations, and one English and one French translation, and comparing some of the most remarkable passages with the Greek, I labored through the tedious toil. My disappointment was great, my astonishment was greater, and my disgust was shocking. Two things only did I learn from him. First, that Franklin's ideas of exempting husbandmen and mariners, etc., from depredations of war were borrowed from him; and second that sneezing is a cure for the hiccough. Accordingly, I have cured myself and all my friends of that provoking disorder for thirty years, with a pinch of snuff.

So much for what my *alma mater* gave me. In these days of repeating rifles, she sent me and my classmates out into the strife equipped with shields and swords and javelins. We were to grapple with living questions through the medium of dead languages. It seems to me I have heard, somewhere else, of a child's cry for bread being answered with a stone. But on this point I do not like publicly to tell the whole of my own experience. It has been too bitter, too humiliating. Representing American educated men in the world's industrial gatherings, I have occupied a position of confessed inferiority. I have not been the equal of my peers. It was the world's Congress of to-day, and Latin and Greek were not current money there.

Such is the dilemma in which I find myself placed. Such is the common dilemma in which all those are placed who see and feel the world as I have seen and felt it. We are modernists and a majority; but in the eyes of the classicists we are, I fear, a vulgar and contemptible majority. Yet I cannot believe that this singular condition of affairs will last a great while longer. The measure of reform seems very simple and wholly reasonable. The modernist does not have to have German and

French substituted for Greek and Latin as the basis of all college education. We are willing—at least I am willing—to concede a preference, and a great preference, to the dead over the living, to the classic over the modern. All I would ask would be that the preference afforded to the one should no longer, as now, amount to the practical prohibition of the other. If a youth wants to enter college on the least possible basis of solid acquirement, by all means let Greek, as it is, be left open for him. If, however, he takes the modern languages, let him do so with the distinct understanding that he must master those languages. After he enters the examination-room no word should be uttered except in the language in which he is there to be examined.

Consider, now, for a moment, what would be the effect on the educational machinery of the country of this change in the college requirements. The modern, scientific, thorough spirit would at once assert itself. Up to this time it has, by that tradition and authority which are so powerful in things educational, been held in subjection. Remove the absolute protection which hitherto has been and now is accorded to Greek, and many a parent would at once look about for a modern, as opposed to a classical academy. To meet the college requirements, that academy would have to be one in which no English word would be spoken in the higher recitation-rooms. Every school exercise would be conducted by American masters proficient in the foreign tongues. The scholars would have to learn languages by hearing them and talking them. The natural law of supply and demand would then assert itself. The demand is now a purely artificial one, but the supply of Greek and Latin, such as it is, comes in response to it. Once let a thorough knowledge of German and French and Spanish be as good tender at the college-door as a fractional knowledge of either of the two of those languages and of Greek now is, and the academies would supply that thorough knowledge also. If the present academies did not supply it, other and better academies would.

Here I might stop; and here, perhaps, I ought to stop. I am, however, unwilling to do so without a closing word on one other topic. For the sake of my argument, and to avoid making a false issue, I have in everything I have said, as between the classic and modern languages, fully yielded the preference to the former. I have treated a mastery of the living tongues simply as an indispensable tool of trade, or medium of speech and thought. It was a thing which the scholar, the professional man and the scientist of to-day must have, or be unequal to his work. I have made no reference to the accumulated literary wealth of the modern tongues, much less compared their masterpieces with those of Greece or Rome. Yet I would not have it supposed that in taking this view of the matter I express my full belief. On the contrary, I most shrewdly suspect that there is in what are called the educated classes, both in this country and in Europe, a very considerable amount of affectation and credulity in regard to the Greek and Latin masterpieces. That is jealously prized as part of the body of the classics, which if published to-day, in German or French or English, would not excite a passing notice. There are immortal poets, whose immortality, my mature judgment tells me, is wholly due to the fact that they lived two thousand years ago. Even a dead language cannot veil extreme tenuity of thought and fancy; and, as we have seen, John Adams and Thomas Jefferson were in their day at a loss to account for the reputation even of Plato.

In any event, this thing I hold to be indisputable: of those who study the classic languages, not one in a hundred ever acquires that familiarity with them which enables him to judge whether a given literary composition is a masterpiece or not. Take your own case and your own language for instance. For myself, I can freely say that it has required thirty years of incessant and intelligent practice with eye and ear and tongue and pen, to give me that ready mastery of the English language which enables me thoroughly to appreciate the more subtle beauties of the English literature. I fancy that it is in our native tongue alone, or in some tongue in which we have acquired as perfect a facility as we have in our native tongue, that we ever detect those finer shades of meaning, that happier choice of words, that more delicate flavor of style, which alone reveal the master. Many men here, for instance, who cannot speak French or German fluently, can read French and German more readily than any living man can read Greek, or than any, outside of a few college professors, can read Latin; yet they cannot see in the French or German masterpieces what those can see there who are to the language born. The familiarity, therefore, with the classic tongues which would enable a man to appreciate the classic literatures in any real sense of the term is a thing which cannot be generally imparted. Even if the beauties which are claimed to be there are there, they must perforce remain concealed from all, save a very few, outside of the class of professional scholars.

But are those transcendent beauties really there? I greatly doubt. I shall never be able to judge for myself, for a mere lexicon-and-grammar acquaintance with a language I hold to be no acquaintance at all. But we can judge a little of what we do not know by what we do know, and I find it harder and harder to believe that in practical richness the Greek literature equals the German, or the Latin the French. Leaving practical richness aside, are there in the classic masterpieces any bits of literary workmanship which take precedence of what may be picked out of Shakespeare and Milton and Bunyan and Clarendon and Addison and Swift and Goldsmith and Gray and Burke and Gibbon and Shelley and Burns and Macaulay and Carlyle and Hawthorne and Thackeray and Tennyson? If there are any such transcendent bits, I can only say that our finest scholars have failed most lamentably in their attempts at rendering them into English.

For myself, I cannot but think that the species of sanctity which has now, ever since the revival of learning, hedged the classics, is destined soon to disappear. Yet it is still strong; indeed, it is about the only patent of nobility which has survived the leveling tendencies of the age. The man who at some period of his life has studied Latin and Greek is an educated man; he who has not done so is only a self-taught man. Not to have studied Latin, irrespective of any present ability to read it, is accounted a thing to be ashamed of; to be unable to speak French is merely an inconvenience. I submit that it is high time this superstition should come to an end. I do not profess to speak with authority, but I have certainly mixed somewhat with the world, its labors and its literatures, in several countries, through a third of a century; and I am free to say, that, whether viewed as a thing of use, as an accomplishment, as a source of pleasure, or as a mental training, I would rather myself be familiar with the German tongue and its literature than be equally familiar with the Greek. I would unhesitatingly make the same choice for my child. What I have said of German as compared with Greek I will also say of French as compared with Latin. On this last point I have no question. Authority and superstition apart, I am indeed unable to see how an intelligent man, having any considerable acquaintance with the two literatures, can, as respects either richness or beauty, compare the Latin with the French; while as a worldly accomplishment, were it not for fetish-worship, in these days of universal travel the man would be properly regarded as out of his mind who preferred to be able to read the odes of Horace, rather than to feel at home in the accepted neutral language of all refined society. This view of the case is not yet taken by the colleges.

> The slaves of custom and established mode,
> With pack-horse constancy we keep the road,
> Crooked or straight, through quags or thorny dells,
> True to the jingling of our leaders' bells.

And yet I am practical and of this world enough to believe that in a utilitarian and scientific age the living will not forever be sacrificed to the dead. The worship even of the classical fetish draweth to a close; and I shall hold that I was not myself sacrificed wholly in vain, if what I have said here may contribute to so shaping the policy of Harvard that it will not much longer use its prodigious influence towards indirectly closing for its students, as it closed for me, the avenues to modern life and the fountains of living thought.

FELIX ADLER

MARCUS AURELIUS

Address by Professor Felix Adler, lecturer and educator (born in Alzey, Germany, August 13, 1851), delivered before the Society for Ethical Culture of New York, of which Dr. Adler is the lecturer, March 13, 1898.

LADIES AND GENTLEMEN:—Of the five good emperors, as they are called, four had had their day—Nerva, Trajan, Hadrian, and the elder Antonine, when, in the year 161 A.D. Marcus Antoninus, or Marcus Aurelius, as he is commonly styled, ascended the throne. It was a splendid and giddy height to which he was thus raised. The civilized world lay at his feet. The bounds of the empire at that time extended from the Atlantic Ocean in the West to the Euphrates in the East; from the African deserts to the Danube and the Rhine. Italy, Greece, Egypt, Asia Minor, Gaul, Britain and parts of Germany acknowledged the sway of the Roman eagle. And all the vast populations that thronged these lands lived in the sunlight of one's man presence, and their destiny for good or ill depended on his nod.

Rarely has such power been concentrated in the hands of an individual. No wonder that it turned the feeble brain of some who possessed it—of Caligula, for instance, of whom it is related that, at his banquets, he used to chuckle with insane pleasure, at the thought that, by a mere word, he could cause the necks of his guests to be wrung. Yes, the power of life and death, unlimited power, power in all its forms, was at the command of the Roman emperor. The lust of power is said to be one of the mainsprings of human action. The master of the Roman world had the opportunity, if he chose to glut himself with power, to give himself over to the indulgence of it almost

Copyright, 1900, by the Society for Ethical Culture.

without restraint, until the very excess of it might bring with it its natural retribution and unseat his reason, as it did in many an instance.

And all the other forms of enjoyment which mortals ordinarily crave were no less at a Roman emperor's disposal. If power is sweet, so is flattery; and the incense of flattery was constantly burned before him, even by the Senate, which, once the bulwark of republican freedom, had degenerated into a mere simulacrum of its former self. When the emperor spoke, the senators were often ready to applaud his poorest utterances, to go on their knees before him and overwhelm him with their adulation. He was deified while he was still among the living, and the honors of divine worship were exacted for his statues. Could mortal sense and sobriety exist, with such temptations to depart from them? And as for the common pleasures of life —the pleasures of the senses—these, too, were of course at his service: palaces, and feasts and costly robes, the place of highest honor at public gatherings, and the tokens of the willing subordination of others and of his own supereminence wherever he might appear. Such was the place made vacant for Marcus Aurelius in 161. How did he fill it? How did he judge of the things which it put within his reach?

He stood "in that fierce light which beats upon a throne," and yet it is possible to detect but few blemishes in his character, and those of such a nature as do not detract from the general sense of elevation with which he impresses us. He was simple and abstemious in his habits. He combined plain living with high thinking. He set aside, as devoid of intrinsic worth, all those goods which the vulgar regard as the most desirable— wealth, fame, pomp and pleasure—and valued only the things of the soul.

There is a natural delusion which leads the poor to overestimate the satisfactions which wealth and worldly greatness can give. Many a poor lad, passing by the stately mansions of the very rich and catching, perhaps, a glimpse between the silken curtains of the luxury within, says to himself—comparing the mean conditions amid which he himself is compelled to pass his existence;—"Ah! within there it would be possible to live the full, the free, the festal life, to taste the joys that earth is capable of yielding." And if then, perchance, he listens to a preacher who tells him that, if wealth has its undoubted advantages, it has also its serious drawbacks, and that the higher satisfactions of life, fortunately for the human race, are independent of the possession of riches and are accessible to every one; the poor lad listening to such a preacher, may think of the fable of the Fox and the Grapes, and say to himself: "The preacher would sing a different tune if the wealth which he affects to belittle were within his reach. He is seeking to console himself by belittling what he cannot have."

I dare say that, to such a one, the testimony of an emperor might come home with incisive force. For silver and gold and all the joys of the senses were actually his, if he chose to have them. And yet he weighed them in the balance against the higher satisfaction and decided in favor of the latter. His judgment was, at all events, unbiased. It was neither envy nor the bitterness of balked desire that spake from his lips.

But, after all, this argument is an ignoble one fit only for ignoble minds. The testimony of the emperor does not carry conviction with it because he was an emperor, but because quite apart from the imperial station which he filled, his was a great, sane, upright, magnanimous personality. And any person, in whatever rank, who voices the praise of the spiritual treasures with the same first-hand, realizing sense of their value, who is free from malice and the critical, carping disposition, who extols as best the things which he, in his inmost experience, has found to be best, will carry the same conviction to his hearers or his readers.

The proof of this statement is to be found in the fact that there are two men in the ancient world who stand for essentially the same doctrine, and who were nearly, if not quite, contemporaries, the one an emperor, the other a slave; the one having in his veins the purest blood of Roman aristocracy, the other belonging by birth to the dregs of society; the one the type of manly beauty, the other sickly and deformed; the one Marcus Aurelius, the other Epictetus. And the tenets of the Stoical philosophy, which both taught, came as convincingly from the lips of Epictetus as of Marcus. Yes, the emperor to some extent caught his inspiration from the slave, looked up to the latter as a pupil does to a master. Indeed, the whole burden of the teachings of the emperor is that rank and station make no difference; that the principles upon which a man acts, in whatever station, alone count; that it is possible to be a genuine man even in a palace.

Of the salient facts of his career let us give a brief résumé. He was born in the year 121. His father died while he was still in infancy, and he was brought up by his grandfather and his mother. To the latter he was deeply attached. He says of her: "From her I learned to abstain not only from evil deeds, but even from evil thoughts; and, further, I learned from her simplicity in my way of living, far removed from the habits of the rich." And among the things for which he is grateful he mentions that, "though it was my mother's fate to die young, she spent the last years of her life with me."

He had many and excellent teachers, applied himself with severe diligence to the study of jurisprudence and philosophy, and, in a lesser degree, of rhetoric and poetry, while, at the same time, he did not neglect the training of the body, and took delight in manly sports and athletic exercise. He was, from the first, of a healthy turn of mind. Philosophy, with him, did not mean bookishness, nor pedantry, but had about it the breath of the fields and the savor of life. Adopted as son and successor by the reigning emperor, Antoninus Pius, he entered in his nineteenth year into public affairs. He married Faustina, the daughter of his predecessor, and, though there are doubts as to her worthiness, he seems to have been happy with her while she lived and he revered her memory after she was gone.

In 161, as has been said, he ascended the throne. His reign was disturbed from the outset. An inundation of the Tiber destroyed some of the most populous portions of the city; famine followed; earthquakes terrified the inhabitants of Italy; the soldiers returning from the Parthian campaign brought with them a fearful pestilence, the Asiatic plague, which then appeared for the first time in Europe, destroying the majority of the population. Worse than all this, the Germanic tribes—notably the Marcomanni and the Quadi—broke through the defenses of the empire, and for fourteen years the emperor labored—in the end successfully—to drive them back within their own boundaries. From the time when he took the reins of government his life was full of the stir of action; his mind was ceaselessly occupied with the gravest and weightiest affairs of state. The fate of civilization, as it then existed, depended on his efforts. No wonder that he toiled with prodigious industry in the attempt to discharge the duties devolving upon him. He was in the habit of rising betimes in the morning, and often continued his labors till long past midnight.

The tranquillity of his reign was further disturbed by a military insurrection, which broke out in the East, where Avidius Cassius, one of the ablest of the Roman generals, proclaimed himself emperor. The pretender fell by the hand of an assassin and his head was brought to the emperor. The latter neither rewarded nor thanked the doers of the deed, but expressed the wish that the family of the traitor should be pardoned and that no other life should be sacrificed in consequence of this treason. Later on, when he went in person to visit the army of Cassius, the correspondence of the latter was brought to him; but, with singular magnanimity, he caused the papers to be destroyed by fire, so that he might never know who, if any, had been the accomplices of this crime.

Marcus Aurelius died at Vindebona (now Vienna) in the year 180, before the war with the Marcomanni was ended, but after its successful termination was assured. He had commanded in person. He was a general and a statesman, as well as a philosopher, at home in camps as well as in the council chamber.

The "Thoughts," which he has left us as a legacy, were jotted down sometimes on the eve of battles, or amid the press and urgency of public business. They are all the more interesting because it is probable that they were never intended to be seen by the eyes of strangers. The attitude toward life which they reflect is the calm and tranquil one of a mind that remained in complete possession of itself, despite the distractions and anxieties by which it was besieged. Let us examine a little more carefully what that attitude was.

The first striking feature that characterizes his conception of the world is its vastness. There are no confining limits to his thought, as it wanders freely through space. The world is not, for him, a narrow edifice, having the flat earth for its tessellated pavement, and the cope of heaven for its roof, lit by the lamps of the stars. His view of surrounding space implies, like our own, infinite expansion on every hand. The sea, he says, is a drop in the universe; Mt. Athos a clod, Europe and Asia mere nooks. Like his thought of space is that of time. The present time, he says, is a mere point. Before it lies the boundless abyss of the past. Beyond it the equally boundless abyss of the future. The vastness of his notion of space and time is the first point to which I call attention.

Next, his theory of the universe reposes on one main proposition—that reason animates and pervades the world, and permeates every part of it, as the soul does the body. It passes through the world like a torrent ever flowing, like a wind ever blowing. It is to the world what the breath is to the lungs; the world lives by the inhalation and exhalation of it. The stoical philosophy, of which Marcus Aurelius is an interpreter, concentrates its forces on the exaltation of the rational principle in man himself, and in the world outside of him. Assume for a moment, says the emperor, that mere aimless caprice decides the course of events—assume the whole of Nature to be the work of chance, if such an assumption be tolerable; yet, would there exist in Nature one sheltered spot in which chance does not, need not, rule—the soul of man? Man, amid the pathless darkness surrounding him, might still claim the prerogative of bearing the torch of reason. The spot where he dwells would still be a point of light. The path on which he walks would still be a track of light, amid the obscurities. But, in reality, this assumption is perfectly groundless. Can there be a rational principle in you, and not also in the universe of which you are a part, Marcus Aurelius asks. The rational principle is the life in all things, the soul, as has been said, of all things.

But what is this rational principle? It is the principle of unity, and it expresses itself in the order of Nature and in the social order. Order, law, together with that adjustment of means to ends which makes order possible, are its manifestations. It is in the high value which he sets on the social order, and on the political activity designed to maintain it, that Marcus Aurelius differs from other teachers of the same school. He looks upon all civilized mankind as inhabitants of a single city—the city of Reason. He thinks that the rights of every man are to be respected because, in every man, there is contained the rational principle. He says that it is his aim to be the ruler of a state "in which there is the same law for all, which is administered with regard to equal rights and equal freedom of speech, and to carry on a government which respects, most of all, the freedom of the governed." He is a cosmopolitan in the largest sense. He thinks that the word "man" should mean more than "fellow-citizen," in the narrow acceptation of the term; that every man should be regarded as a fellow-citizen in that world-wide city of Reason. And he attaches such importance to the city—or, as we should say, the "commonwealth" —not only because social order and security are the necessary conditions for the exercise of the higher intellectual faculties of man, but because in establishing order we are actively illustrating the rational principle, which is the principle of order. We should establish order, not merely for the happy consequence of it, but just for the sake of order, inasmuch as, in so doing, we are playing a divine part.

And so Marcus Aurelius constantly impresses the duty of performing social acts apart from their benefits, just because they are social; for, "all things exist for the sake of rational beings, but rational beings exist for one another"; and he bids us constantly remember that we are not mere parts, but members of one great organism, which is mankind, and even makes, in one place, the daring assertion that "the intelligence of the world is social,"—by which he means that the rational principle in things, so far as it operates in the sphere of human beings, manifests itself chiefly in the social nexus that unites them. "All things," he says elsewhere, "are implicated in one another, and the bond is holy."

It is true that Marcus Aurelius also declares: "My city and country, so far as I am Antoninus, is Rome; but, so far as I am a man, it is the world. The things, then, which are useful to these cities are alone useful to me." And elsewhere "Always remember to act as becomes a Roman and a man." But he believed that the one city, Rome, existed for the sake of the other; that it was the mission of Rome, and of himself as its ruler, to be the guardian of that larger city, to maintain equal laws for all, equal justice to all—in a word, to maintain civilization as it then existed. And upon this point I must dwell for a moment.

The theory of the Stoics was pantheistical, and Marcus was an interpreter of their theory. Pantheism implies that God is present in the world as the animating spirit in a living organism. He does not dwell in any particular quarter of the world. His throne is not in the heavens, still less does he dwell outside of the world. He is everywhere. Wherever matter is, there he is. The world could not exist without God, says Pantheism; nor could God exist without the world. Among the consequences to which this theory leads is this: that whatever occurs, being directly worked by God's agency, is good; that there can be no real evil in the world; that the apparent evils are "the after products of the good;" "the cuttings and shavings in the shop of the carpenter;" and also, since the whole of God, so to speak, is present in the world, just as it is, there can be no real progress in the world, no increase of the good. Of the two conceptions, Order and Progress, the former, Order, was present in the mind of the Stoics; Progress, the one on which we in modern times lay such stress, was lacking. And this point, more perhaps than any other, marks the difference between our view of life and duty and the Stoic view.

From the Pantheistic standpoint, then, what practically is the attitude prescribed to man? It is to conform his will to the course of events, to consent to what happens of necessity, and to maintain intact the divine content which has been poured into his individual life, and into the life of that society to which he belongs. The *mot d'ordre* of Stoicism is "Hold thine own." There is no thought of new realms to be conquered, new insight to be achieved. To society collectively Stoicism says: "Hold thine own," so far as the rational principle in thee—that is, the principle of order—is concerned. Preserve intact the social order. And to the individual it says: "Hold thine own," rationally speaking; "prevent the rational nature in thee from being submerged by the sense nature."

He who has seized the meaning of this rule of behavior—"Hold thine own"—has discovered, I am persuaded, the keynote of the Stoical philosophy and of the teachings of its great interpreter. Now this command, as has just been said, is capable of two applications: one to society collectively, and one to the individual. And as applied to society collectively, it corresponded exactly with the needs of the world in the days of Marcus Aurelius, and to the policy which was forced upon the emperor. We must remember that the Roman empire at that time represented civilization in general; outside of it, there was no civilization, in our sense of the term. But the empire stood, even at that time, on the defensive, was menaced by those barbarian hordes that hung like a thunder cloud on its northern boundaries, and that eventually destroyed it and plunged Europe into the long night of the Dark Ages in which the culture of antiquity perished. The task devolving upon the emperor—a task to which he devoted himself with unremitting assiduity—was to try to preserve intact the empire entrusted to him—that is to say, to preserve civilization, to preserve social order; in this, the precepts of his philosophy and his duty as a sovereign coincided perfectly.

And in this connection we may briefly consider what is commonly regarded as the gravest blemish in the life and character of Marcus Aurelius. I allude to the persecutions of the Christians that took place under his reign, in which Justin Martyr perished, and the aged Polycarp and Blandina and others at Lyons. How far these harsh measures were undertaken with the direct knowledge of the emperor is uncertain. But they were carried out in his name and under cover of his authority. Marcus Aurelius a persecutor! It seems utterly inexplicable. He has been called the saintliest of the pagans. He was the most benevolent of men. How often did he repeat that we are to regard every human being as our kinsman—akin to us, in spirit and in flesh? His motto was "Bear and forbear." And even of evil-doers, of those who have grievously wronged and injured us, he says, "Teach them, change them, if you can; and, if you cannot, endure them." And such a man was, nevertheless, the author of the severest penalties against an apparently inoffensive sect! It seems to me that his conduct can be explained, if we bear in mind what has just been pointed out, namely, the supreme importance which he attached to the preservation of the social order as rational order, and of the state as the guardian of that order.

Now the Christians not only refused to recognize the religion of the Roman state, and were, on that account, hated as atheists, but they had no true regard or reverence for the state itself. They were in principle individualists, seeking the salvation of the individual soul, little recking the collective interests of the commonwealth. It was at this point, I take it, that Marcus Aurelius felt repelled from them; yes, not only repelled personally, but he must have looked upon them as a disruptive force endangering the state from within, just as the barbarians endangered it from without. But, that he should have gone to such extreme lengths in his dealings with them is, I think, due to a curious fact, of which Marcus Aurelius is by no means the only example. So did Thomas More persecute the Lutherans. So did Plato pronounce the death penalty against atheists, and relegate the souls of the obstinately evil-minded to everlasting perdition. And so do we find in the New Testament, side by side with the sweetest and tenderest precepts the same terrible doctrine of everlasting punishment. There is this paradox, if paradox it be: The highest idealists when touched to the quick, when the things which they hold most precious and essential to the good of mankind are denied, seem capable of passing the harshest judgments on those whom they regarded as the enemies of the human race, and sometimes of following up these judgments with the most relentless acts.

But let us now proceed to give our attention to that side of the teachings of Marcus Aurelius which is best known, which is of the greatest practical interest, and is most characteristic of his view of life. The command "Hold thine own" is addressed to the individual in his rational character. The Stoics have found a way of making man, as they believe, entirely independent of circumstances, assuring him of indestructible tranquillity of mind and surrounding his brow with unwithering wreaths of victory. Is it poverty that pinches? The Stoics make light of poverty. They declare its terrors to be mock terrors—not evils at all. The pains of sickness, too, have somehow the painful quality taken out of them; ignominy, disgrace, loss of reputation, loss of liberty are all, by some strange spell, relieved of their sting. Even the wormwood of bereavement loses its bitterness.

This at least is what the Stoics claim; and, though we may not be able to concede all they claim, there is enough of truth in it to make it eminently worth our while to inquire into their secret. What is their secret? It is simple in statement, difficult of attainment; yet, to some extent, attainable. The secret is this: Accustom thyself to think that the ordinary evils of life are not evils. All the evils that affect thee through thy body are not evil. Thou canst not help feeling pain, but thou canst train thyself to think that the pain affects only thy hand, or thy limb, or thy lung, in short the "kneaded matter" that encompasses thee, but not thee. Thou canst thus localize it in something outside of thee. And what though the pain be going on in the hand, or the limb, or the poor lung, nevertheless, it does not come near to thee.

And the same holds good of the sufferings that come to us through wounded pride, or through the bruising of the affections. All such hurts approach only as far as the periphery of the soul, but do not touch its center. The center is not the part in us that feels but that thinks and wills; and the part that thinks and wills is master over that which feels. It is a brave doctrine and a bracing one, though by the Stoics carried to extremes. It amounts to this—that the evils of existence cease to be evils the moment we cease to think them so. It is our false opinion that makes them evil, and our opinion is based on the delusion of supposing that they affect the citadel of man, whereas they only affect the outworks. Let us conform our opinion to the true facts of the case, and we shall have abolished the evils of life.

Does this doctrine tempt you? Would you like to follow in the footsteps of the Stoics? Remember the price exacted of you, if you would become one of their disciples. If what has been said is true, if nothing is evil which merely hurts the body or the feelings, if only that is evil which hurts the thinking and the willing faculty in us, then it follows, in all consistency, that neither is anything good that is pleasant to the body or joyful to the heart; for, if it were good, the absence of it would be evil. And the Stoics consistently take this ground. They say that there is no good that can come to a man from the outside, not even from his fellow-beings; not the innocent pleasures of the senses, not the delights of companionship, not the endearments of love are to be considered really good. Good can come to a man only from himself, and evil only from himself. The real good is just this sense of his independence, as a thinking and willing being, from the accidents of his corporeal and emotional nature; and the real evil is the want of such independence. Not that the Stoic would have us shrink from or shun what are commonly reckoned among the good things of life, but he would have us regard them as indifferent. Marcus Aurelius bids us behave in life as at a banquet. When the viands are being offered to the guests, do not impatiently wait for your turn to come. When the tempting food is set before you, partake of it moderately. If it happens that you are overlooked, do not show unmannerly irritation. Your true satisfaction is not enhanced by what you enjoy. The serenity of your mind need not be clouded for an instant by what you miss.

It is a proud doctrine, throwing a man back entirely upon his rational self, bidding him erect the structure of his life on reason as on a rock, and to remain unmoved by the gusts of passion, the whirlwinds of affliction, the chances and changes of time. And, if we were merely rational beings, if thinking and willing were all and feeling counted for nothing in the composition of our nature, it would be a wholly true doctrine, as manifestly it is not. But still, there is a mighty element of truth in it, which we can extract from the exaggerations with which it is mingled, and which will then stand us in excellent stead. There is not one of the great systems of philosophy that can be accepted in its entirety, or that should be rejected in its entirety. There is not one of the great philosophical systems—just as there is not one of the great religions—that does not contain some element which we can appropriate and utilize, and that has not made some permanent contribution to the sum of human wisdom and virtue, which we shall be the better for adopting into our own view of life.

Now, the value of Stoicism shines out preëminently at a certain period of life and in certain situations—that period and those situations in which our watchword must really be to "Bear and to forbear." The period of young manhood, or adolescence, I mean, when the blood runs hot and swift in the veins, when the passions are aroused and the craving for the indulgence of natural instincts is intense! Then the Stoic maxim "Forbear" comes home to us with kindly saving influence; then we need to cultivate something of the Stoic attitude which puts us on our mettle as rational, self-directing beings.

The Stoic doctrine tells us that we are not abandoned hopelessly to the impulses of our physical nature or to our feelings; tells us that, from the enjoyment of pleasures which tempt us, but which the mind does not approve, we have it in our power, if we choose, to forbear. For young men, nothing can be better to steel their wills than frequent study of the Stoic writers. They need to have their pride as self-determining natures appealed to; to be told that they can do what is difficult, what to them sometimes seems impossible, because the part that thinks and wills in them can indeed be lord and master over that which feels, if they choose to make it so.

And the situations in which Stoicism helps us are those which call for fortitude. When bodily pain or suffering of any kind becomes so engrossing that we are in danger of becoming wholly occupied with it or with the expectation of it, and find it more and more difficult to hold it at arm's length—then, also, we need to be put upon our mettle and made to realize that there is a fund of mental strength in us which enables us to set our face like flint against the pain, not wincing, not yielding to it; that we can endure unheard-of sufferings, if we bring the force of resistance that is in us into play. Whenever the rational nature is pitted directly against the sense nature, whenever the issue is—Which one of the two shall be overbalanced by the other?—then the Stoic doctrine supplies something of the tonic that we need and helps us to throw our decision in the right scale.

I have still two comments to make. I have spoken of the merits of the Stoic philosophy, and have already indicated some of its defects. There are two practical, palpable defects, which must be brought out in clear relief. The one is the false view which Stoics held with regard to suicide. Plato used the simile that we are like sentinels on guard, and dare not leave our post until we are relieved. The Stoics, on the other hand, held that while it is the supreme duty of man to see to it that the reason in him maintains the upper hand as long as he lives, he may retire from life whenever the operation of the rational faculty in him is impeded. Under such circumstances, Seneca, one of the greatest of the Stoics, says that a man may divest himself of his body as he would take off a threadbare coat which is no longer fit to be worn; that he may leave life as he would leave a house which is filled with smoke and in which it is impossible for him to breathe freely. This view of suicide is the direct consequence of that Pantheism of the Stoics which infects their whole philosophy, and which led them, despite their intensely moral temper, to class life among the things that are indifferent.

The second defect, which has already been emphasized, is the total lack of the idea of progress. The movement of things is circular. Whatever has been, will be. At long intervals—at the end of a "world-year"—the universe is reabsorbed into the divine essence from which it has emanated, and then exactly the same processes that have occurred in the previous "world-year" repeat themselves. There can be no change for the better, there is no movement toward the best. And it is worth while to fix special attention upon this lack of the idea of progress. Our interest in the Stoic philosophy is increased when we remember that it was an attempt to find a substitute for religion, in an age when religion had departed, an age in many respects like our own.

In the second century of our era, while superstition lingered among the masses, faith among the educated had dwindled and seemed on the point of extinction. At that time the Stoic sought to find in man's moral nature a substitute for the belief which had vanished. But Stoicism failed. It founded a school, but it could not take the place of religion. And it failed, because it lacked warmth, because it lacked the element of enthusiasm, because it lacked hope, because it lacked the belief in progress. The religious element in an Ethical Movement must be found precisely in the belief in progress, in devotion to the idea of progress, and it is by this that we are separated from the moral philosophers of the age of the Antonines.

And now, having endeavored to obtain the philosophic key, by the possession of which, in studying the "Thoughts" of Marcus Aurelius, we can arrive at a deeper understanding of them, let me conclude my address by selecting a few of his choicest sayings—that will serve to convey a tincture of his personality and reveal to us something of the lofty, dignified, and yet, withal, sweet and lovable nature of which the sayings are the expression:—

"Be not afraid because some time thou must cease to live, but fear never to have begun truly to live."

"If it is not right, do not do it. If it is not true, do not say it."

"The pride which is proud of its want of pride is the most intolerable pride of all."

Concerning certain particular points of morals, he says:

"I have learned not frequently nor without necessity to say to any one or to write in a letter that I have no leisure, nor continually to excuse neglect of duties by alleging urgent occupation."

"Accustom thyself carefully to attend to what is said by another and as much as possible try to be in the speaker's mind."

"I have learned to receive from friends what are esteemed favors without being humbled or letting them pass unnoticed."

"I have learned that it is possible for a man to live in a palace without wanting either guards or embroidered dresses, and to be content in a palace with a plank bed."

"I have learned to work with my hands."

"Do not speak of thy bodily ailments to those who visit thee when thou art sick."

"The greatest part of what we say and do is really unnecessary. If a man take this to heart he will have more leisure and less uneasiness."

"Do every act in thy life as if it were the last."

"Think of those things only which, if thou shouldst suddenly be asked, 'Pray, what is in thy mind?' thou mightest with perfect frankness lay open as the contents of thy mind."

"A man must stand erect and not be held erect by others."

"Begin the morning by saying to thyself, 'I must rise now from my bed to do the work of a man.' Begin the morning by saying to thyself, 'I shall meet to-day with the busybody, the ungrateful, the arrogant, the deceitful, the envious, the unsocial; but I, who have seen the nature of the good that it is beautiful, and of the bad that it is ugly, and the nature of him that is wrong that it is akin to mine—I cannot be injured by one of them, nor can I be angry since he is my kinsman and I cannot hate him.'"

"We are made for coöperation like feet, hands, like eyelids, like the rows of the upper and lower teeth. Like a hand or foot cut off, such does a man make himself who does anything unsocial."

"What is good for the bee is good for the swarm."

"Reverence that which is best in the universe and in like manner reverence that which is best in thyself, and the one is at the same time as the other."

"Where a man can live, he can also live well; but he may have to live in a palace—well, then he can also live well in a palace."

"Man has sensations and appetites in common with animals. There remains that which is peculiar to man, to be contented with that which is appointed him and not to defy the divinity which is planted within his breast."

"Take me and place me where thou wilt, for there I shall keep my divine part tranquil."

"The pain which is intolerable carries us off, but that which lasts a long time is tolerable."

"The soul of the good is naked and is manifest through the body that surrounds it. There is no veil over a star."

"Be like the promontory against which the waves continually

break; but it stands firm and tames the fury of the water around it."

"Live as on a mountain."

"The soul is a sphere illuminated by light, by which it sees the truth of all things and the truth that is in itself."

"I do my duty; others things trouble me not."

These are a few of the sayings of Marcus Aurelius. There are others like them—apples of gold in baskets of silver.

NATURE AND THE RELIGIOUS MOOD

Prelude to an address delivered at St. Huberts, New York, Sunday, August 28, 1921, by Dr. Felix Adler (born 1851), lecturer, author, founder of the New York Society of Ethical Culture.

It is the high office of religion to influence the feelings, the thoughts, and the behavior of men. It engenders sublime feelings, such as awe, wonder, and the sense of unfathomable mystery. It suggests sublime thoughts, thoughts of a greatness beyond human conception, and it enjoins behavior modeled on a sublime pattern.

As we are living here during these summer months in closer contact with Nature than is permitted us in the cities, I shall briefly touch, by the way of prelude to my address, on certain aspects of Nature that are propitious to the religious feelings, the feelings that go out to the sublime. All natural phenomena that convey a sense of the infinite have this character, and of them the principal ones are the sea, the mountains, the star-sown heavens, and the inexhaustible life of Nature as manifested in the renewal of vegetation in springtime and summer.

But feelings, unless connected with ideas, are apt to be vague, and it may therefore be of interest to analyze a little what we experience, and to discriminate the different ways in which we are affected by the four types of phenomena mentioned.

The sea suggests infinity by its apparently boundless extension. "Thalassa, Thalassa!" exclaimed the Ten Thousand—"The Sea, the Sea!" when they first beheld the main. And we, too, somewhat similarly experience a feeling of exultation and liberation at the first sight of ocean,—for instance, from some bordering bluff or height. For the absence of checks or limitations gives one the sense of freedom; and at sight of the sea we are aware of the possibility of going on and on, as it were, measuring these vast open spaces, unhindered in our imaginary progress. But note that after a time the contrary effect ensues. For we can indeed go on and on, but never seem to come to an end, never seem capable of embracing the whole. And this inability on our part presently neutralizes the sense of ability aroused by the absence of limits,—and this explains the depressing effect of any prolonged intercourse with the ocean. The sobbing of the waves on the shore, the mists that are apt to gather over the waters, tend in their way to deepen this depressing effect.

The mountains uplift us by their height, their grandeur. They suggest, like the sea, progress, but progress upward, directed toward an end. For they taper toward their summits, and their summits point, like cathedral spires, into the infinite blue.

The stars suggest immeasurableness, and therefore once again unhindered progress. But they are unlike the boisterous sea, they are silent, and hence suggest peace, and they are points of splendor in the darkness, and hence produce the glad effect of light.

Finally, the perpetual renewal of vegetation in spring and summer touches us even more closely, since it suggests the continuation of the life of that Nature whereof we are a part, after we shall have disappeared. There is in most men a seemingly ineradicable appetite for perpetuity, a craving to continue to be,—if not in the present form, then in some other form of life; if not in the inconceivable world of spirit, then in the tangible world of physical nature. Nay, the very image of continuity presented to the mind somehow seems to have a tranquillizing effect. As an instance of this, I well remember the last days of a lady, highly esteemed by all her friends, who was slowly dying of a fatal disease. The end came in June. The window of her sick room looked out upon a garden, in which a rose-bush in full bloom was visible. It was strange how she feasted her fading power of sight on those roses, what comfort she seemed to derive from these emblems of beauty and vitality. Strange, I say,—for does it not seem contrary to what might be expected that the greater duration of organisms inferior to our own should be comforting? In fact, length of existence is proportional to inferiority in the scale of existence. The rocks last for thousands on thousands of years. There are trees in these woods whose age already counts by centuries. On my own plot of ground yonder there are beeches, birches, and the tallest hemlocks. At present I am their owner. I vaunt myself the owner of the soil, and of the trees that grow upon it. In a little while, this mortal frame of mine, reduced to dust, will lie somewhere under the soil, while those trees will still tower high into the sky, waving their mighty boughs to the free winds. Who, then, will be owner of the soil, they or I?

I have said all along that certain grand phenomena of Nature suggest to us feelings of the sublime, variously nuanced. Let me put the weight of emphasis on the word *suggest*. The sublimity is not in Nature, but in us. The sea, taken by itself, is just so much briny water. The top of the Giant over there, on which the evening glow lies so solemnly, is just so much cold rock. The stars themselves are neither silent nor peaceful. It is known that they travel at incredible speed through the immensities, and no astronomer has ever succeeded in discovering a plan in their bewildering paths. The morning stars, it is true, still sing together, but their song is discordant. By morning stars I understand stars that are in process of formation. For there are worlds that are coming to the birth, and other dying worlds. The aspects of Nature suggest the sublime, they set in motion in the mind of man certain processes which are colored by the idea of the infinite. But the seat of sublimity is in the mind of man, not in Nature, and it is in the mind of man that the true infinite must be sought.

LORD ALLENBY

OPENING THE HEBREW UNIVERSITY AT JERUSALEM

The following address was delivered by Field Marshal Sir Edmund Allenby, the conqueror of Palestine in the World War and British High Commissioner for Egypt in 1919-1925, at the opening of the Hebrew University in Jerusalem, April 2, 1925.

SEVEN years ago, I had the honor to preside at the celebration of the laying of the foundation stone of the Hebrew University. It is a unique experience to see work begun during the war, finished in time of peace. There are particularly impressed on my memory those moments of the Palestine campaign when our army marched toward Palestine. Every man felt the particular responsibility when he remembered that the goal of the campaign was Jerusalem, and in the hard and bitter fighting our army steadily gained ground until Jerusalem was conquered.

In those days I knew little or nothing about Zionism. I regarded Zionism as a fantastic theory until Dr. Weizmann came. During this visit to our headquarters a revelation of faith came to me. Never in my life have I seen such a man as Dr. Weizmann, who has the ability to convert every one to Zionism by his infectious enthusiasm.

Our military position at the time when the foundation stone for the university was laid was precarious in every way and without an immediate prospect of further advance, but Dr. Weizmann made light of this, and furthering the Zionist plans, he laid the foundation of stone for the university within earshot of the Turkish guns. This extraordinary event and the faith with which he inspired all those who came in contact with him, made us all more confident in the ultimate victory.

Reprinted from the New York *Times*.

STOCKTON AXSON

THE WORLD AND THE NEW GENERATION

Stockton Axson, formerly professor in Princeton and now professor of English in Rice Institute, Houston, Texas, is one of the best known lecturers and speakers in the South. The following is a portion of the Phi Beta Kappa address, delivered at Tulane University, 1922.

THE function of the college, as I see it, is not to tell the student what to think, but to assist him in his own thought-processes, to encourage him to think in terms of ideas, to relate facts to principles, to distinguish between the relevant and irrelevant.

We are conscious that democracy has perilous possibilities, but we are committed to it. Nothing else is thinkable. One of the perils of democracy is the demagogue. The demagogue thrives on ignorance, could not exist amid a thoroughly enlightened constituency, retreats before enlightenment as noisome things of night vanish before the rising sun. An enlightened electorate would distinguish between what is relevant and what is irrelevant in a candidate's recommendations of himself for the office which he seeks—would decline to accept him on the sole ground of his domestic virtues, as filial son, faithful husband, and devoted father,—would inquire into his qualifications of mind and character to assist in shaping the policies and destinies of a nation. Whatever else the new generation will need in meeting the momentous issues bequeathed to them, they will need applied intelligence, ability to think as well as act, and to think in terms somewhat different from the past.

Since the summer of 1914, occurrences have been sudden and on a large scale, by catastrophe rather than by slow and orderly development. In size and character, the war was so different from previous wars, that there seemed to be no analogies in the past on which to calculate future development. It was, in a very real sense, a new and grim adventure. There were quick mechanical adaptations, new protective inventions to resist new forces of destruction: poisonous gases produced gas masks; bombing air-craft produced anti-aircraft guns; submarine attacks produced ingenious devices for detecting and destroying submarines. The great mechanical age developed the most mechanical war in history, and adaptable man, acting on the primal law of self-preservation, made quick adaptations.

But readaptation to changing mental and spiritual conditions progresses more slowly. The elements are numerous and complex, and the primary instinct of self-preservation is not so urgently invoked. Instinct has to be modified by reason, and that is always a slow process. We say the world has changed, but we behave as if it had not. We fight in terms of modern chemistry, but we think in terms of the bow-and-arrow age. We face world-conditions with the instincts of the tribe. Since the war there have been actual regressions. Class feuds have been intensified, and there is even an emergence of religious intolerance, with hints at persecution.

Too complex for facile statement are the psychological laws underlying such reactions. The disease is too deep-seated for easy remedy. The wise distrust panaceas. One thing seems clear: when herded passions are unleashed, they cannot be driven back to kennel as soon as the occasion for their exercise has passed. We grew so accustomed to hating a common enemy that it became easy to hate each other. But no one of us is wise enough or good enough to sit in judgment on the rest of us because of these reactions which follow the finer passions bred by patriotism and war. Neither is any one of us justified in adopting a superior attitude toward the world's political leaders who are perplexed and frustrated by the complicated post-war problems. Burdens grievous to bear have been bound upon their shoulders. Criticism is easier than improvement.

But this is true—and it is part of the difficulty of the situation: world-adjustment has been necessarily committed to people who had formed their mental habits prior to the war and the new situations it developed. So it always is; the young fight,—the elders arrange the settlements. It is unfortunate for themselves and the world that the negotiators of the settlements are called upon to reconstruct their habits of thought after they have passed the age when such reconstructions are easy. In early days of antiseptic surgery, medical students used to smile at a distinguished clinical professor of advanced years who would conscientiously perform all the prescribed ablutions and ceremonies, and then, before beginning to operate, would absent-mindedly turn off a dust-covered steam-cock with the hand he had just carefully sterilized. "It is hard to teach an old dog new tricks." The elder statesmen lay out brave plans for adjusting a new world, but as negotiations progress, they, from sheer force of habit, fall back on the old-style diplomacy of bargain and finesse. Moreover, they know the mental inertia of the compact masses they represent, and hesitate to run even as fast as they might lest they outrun the confidence of their constituencies. Only prophets can live in the present and clearly envision the future, and prophets are seldom trusted by their contemporaries. Meanwhile the problems await solution. The old formulæ do not fit. The new wine is bursting the old bottles. Events have outrun men's thinking.

We of the older generation have failed to grasp with practical understanding the full force of the idea born of the war, the lesson of community interests and their effect upon fundamental relations, such as the relations of classes within the nation, and the relations of nations within the family of nations. We have venerated traditions and rooted prejudices which thwart our full acceptance of the new situation. For instance, we conceive of coöperation only in terms of altruism, and because we believe, and indeed know, that human nature is selfish, we pronounce altruism a futile dream and say that extensive coöperation is therefore impossible.

Yet, all about us, staring us in the face, are examples plain as print, telling us that the most effective coöperations spring up, not out of altruism, but from enlightened self-interest. Not altruism but a recognition of bonds of interest causes progressive business men to affiliate, say in a National Hardware Association, each to improve his own business by all combining to improve the hardware business in general. These intelligent men still compete with each other, but they know that there is a point beyond which competition is suicide. Labor organizations are not formed because of mental and emotional affinities between the men, but for mutual protection of the interests which they have in common. Within the labor union are all sorts of cross divisions. The men belong to different religious groups, different fraternal societies, different political parties, it is a commonplace of American politics that the "labor vote" cannot be "swung" as a unit. Under stress of war-peril, nations found their points of common interest, and gave a brilliant recognition of the idea in the unification of military command under Marshal Foch.

A fundamental problem of the new generation will be to find continually more points of common interest, and to think in larger units than their ancestors, to think across dividing lines of class and group to the common denominator of mutual interests. The accomplishment of this will not mean that they are individually better men than their fathers. It is at least debatable whether the individual develops at all beyond his ancestors. But in different ages, human intelligence is directed into different channels. The predestined channel for the next generation seems to be a higher socialization (which, by the way, has nothing to do with "Socialism") of the race in class relationships and national relationships. Bred to thought in the new age they will presumably approach the problems with more flexible minds than ours.

The Great War thundered the news to all the world that the world has become a neighborhood, bound together, not by choice or brotherly love, but by necessity and the bonds of interest growing out of conditions of modern commerce, modern communication and modern transportation. Just because the millennium is not here, and just because human nature is here, the necessity is great that men control instinct with reason, and coöperate to salvage the world rather than to destroy it in unchecked competition through modern annihilating warfare.

I do not believe that the colleges can give very specific instructions about governing the world in the future. But I do think that the colleges should be places where what we blandly call "thoughtless youth," should be encouraged to become very *thoughtful* youth. Never was there so much need for youth to cultivate habits of high and serious thinking. In education, as in manufactory, the by-products are important. I often think that all that is produced as the result of general courses in literature is a by-product—a little better literary taste than the student would have if he had not studied the authors whose specific works he so promptly forgets. And I take it that even the departments of science produce comparatively few scientific philosophers—but many with widened horizons. So, in general, there is a by-product of seriousness and intellectual activity in the production of which we all have part irrespective of our separating specialties.

There are some fields in which all teachers meet. For instance, speaking from long experience and as one entitled, "Professor of English," I am satisfied that English will never be satisfactorily taught in our schools and colleges until all members of the faculty combine to teach it. In the few hours allotted weekly to the study of English, the student will not become "a well of English undefiled" if he is permitted to be slipshod and ungrammatical in his other courses. Years ago a colleague and a dear friend asked me, "Why can't you people in the English department teach students so to write that they can give me a decent translation of a Greek passage?" The answer was too easy: "Why can't you people in the Department of Classics so teach translation that the students will learn to write English?" The schools and universities of England do not delegate literacy to a single department, and the comparative levels of authorship in the two countries seem to hint that theirs is the more effective method.

Far more important than literary expression, is the cultivation of intelligence in the undergraduate body; and that is no one department's business; it is the the business of the university. It will surely be a grave indictment of the university if it cannot breed and furnish intelligent leadership in the most serious of crises. I crave for the university an influence in quickening the intelligence of the youth of to-day; in deepening their seriousness; in assisting them to define their problems. The troubled world needs not more heat, but more light; not more passion, but more intelligence. The atmosphere is radio-active with proffered solutions, but there is no ready remedy for the disease. The solution must be worked out in toil and patience, little by little and bit by bit. The world needs not more propaganda, but more enlightenment; not more dogma, but more faith in mankind, for man's chief problem is man himself, a new and better behavior in the mass.

He who believes strongly in human nature and its capacities must believe that if mankind will spend a few decades in applying to its human problems the same sort of ingenuity that was expended for a century past in solving mechanical problems, solutions will be found. Great has been the mechanical age; may there follow, and quickly, a great age of socialized endeavor to control what has been invented lest the invention turn upon the inventor and destroy him. The future will test, not man's mechanical ingenuity, but the mind and soul of man himself.

The problem of creating the coöperate mind is not purely an intellectual problem, for the sufficient reason that man is not a purely intellectual animal, but also highly emotional. In its ultimate aspect, the problem is a problem in applied Christianity. And, remembering that world-problems concern not Christendom alone but all nations and races, it is reassuring to remember that other religions and philosophies in their higher reaches and intents sufficiently resemble Christianity to offer a common meeting place for general assembly. Nothing is more desperately needed to-day than that peoples re-discover, re-assimilate, and apply their religions.

But enlightenment is required for that application. There was plenty of personal religion in the Dark Ages, but the Ages were dark because the religious did not see how to apply religion to the things of this world, quite failed to give their religion a social application. Too often they sought to produce conformity with the sword, as we too often seek to produce it through legislation. It is a disheartening fact that quarrel is prompter and more bitter between two pronouncedly religious people than between the religious and the frankly non-religious. The sting in Dean Swift's bitter epigram is the sting of part-truth, "We have just enough religion to make us hate each other." While the individual is seeking the kingdom of heaven by the profession and rule of his own creed, he should be combining with others of other creeds to prepare for the kingdom of heaven on earth.

That we are of one family is palpable fact. It has always been so, but only in recent times have we been made uncomfortably aware of the fact. From the beginning, all mortals have been "in the same boat," which boat, to change the metaphor, is a ball of comparatively diminutive dimensions spinning giddily through space, with the fate of every inhabitant entirely dependent upon its "keeping the track," in which it is held by "laws" which mortals did not decree, cannot alter, and do not understand. This perennial situation has been emphasized during the past hundred years by man's own inventions which have been continually drawing the occupants of the globe closer together until now they are so compactly massed that, as was shown in the Great War, if one makes a motion everybody else is jostled. The question that is pressing for answer is, shall mortals learn to live comfortably in this mass, or, like caged crickets, annihilate each other? In such a congested situation, an ounce of understanding is better than a ton of violence. It is this massing of the terrestrial population which makes increasingly necessary the ability to think in larger units, and makes correspondingly necessary, leaders of enlarged understandings who will rely less on machinery and more on the intelligence of themselves and their constituencies.

Never did the situation of mankind call so loudly for lofty and intelligent leadership—for leaders of widened horizons and enlarged understandings. If leaders come not from the universities, what are the universities for? I crave for my generation and the profession to which I belong a share in the privilege of directing the minds of the new generation toward a land which we ourselves shall not see, except from afar off and with dimming eyes.

ARTHUR J. BALFOUR

ARTHUR JAMES BALFOUR

(SINCE EARL OF BALFOUR)

THE PLEASURES OF READING

Rectorial address given by Arthur James Balfour at the University of St. Andrews, December 10, 1887. This address, here abridged, is in part a criticism of Frederic Harrison's "The Choice of Books," also included in this volume. Other addresses by Lord Balfour are given in Volumes I and XII.

THE question of how to read, and what to read, has of late filled much space in the daily papers, if it cannot, strictly speaking, be said to have profoundly occupied the public mind. But you need be under no alarm. I am not going to supply you with a new list of a hundred books, nor am I about to take the world into my confidence in respect of my favorite passages from the best authors. Nor again do I address myself to the professed student, to the fortunate individual with whom literature or science is the business as well as the pleasure of life. I have not the qualifications which would enable me to undertake such a task with the smallest hope of success. My aim is humble, though the audience to whom I desire to speak is large; for I speak to the ordinary reader with ordinary capacities and ordinary leisure, to whom reading is, or ought to be, not a business but a pleasure; and my theme is the enjoyment—not the improvement, nor the glory, nor the profit, but the *enjoyment*—which may be derived by such a one from books.

It is perhaps due to the controversial habits engendered by my unfortunate profession, that I find no easier method of making my own view clear than by contrasting with it what I regard as an erroneous view held by somebody else; and in the present case the doctrine which I shall choose as a foil to my own is one which has been stated with the utmost force and directness by that brilliant and distinguished writer, Mr. Frederic Harrison. He has given us in a series of excellent essays his opinion on the principles which should guide us in the choice of books. Against that part of his treatise which is occupied with specific recommendations of certain authors I have not a word to say. He has resisted all the temptations to eccentricity which so easily beset the modern critic. Every book which he praises deserves his praise, and has long been praised by the world at large. I do not, indeed, hold that the verdict of the world is necessarily binding on the individual conscience. I admit to the full that there is an enormous quantity of hollow devotion, of withered orthodoxy divorced from living faith, in the eternal chorus of praise which goes up from every literary altar to the memory of the immortal dead. Nevertheless, every critic is bound to recognize, as Mr. Harrison recognizes, that he must put down to individual peculiarity any difference he may have with the general verdict of the ages; he must feel that mankind is not likely to be in a conspiracy of error as to the kind of literary work which conveys to them the highest literary enjoyment, and that in such cases at least *securus judicat orbis terrarum*.

But it is quite possible to hold that any work recommended by Mr. Harrison is worth repeated reading, and yet to reject utterly the theory of study by which these recommendations are prefaced. For Mr. Harrison is a ruthless censor. His *index expurgatorius* includes, so far as I can discover, the whole catalogue of the British Museum, with the exception of a small remnant which might easily be contained in about thirty or forty volumes. The vast remainder he contemplates with feelings apparently not merely of indifference, but of active aversion. He surveys the boundless and ever-increasing waste of books with emotions compounded of disgust and dismay. He is almost tempted to say in his haste that the invention of printing has been an evil one for humanity. In the habits of miscellaneous reading born of a too easy access to libraries, circulating and other, he sees many soul-destroying tendencies; and his ideal reader would appear to be a gentleman who rejects with a lofty scorn all in history that does not pass for being first-rate in importance, and all in literature that is not admitted to be first-rate in quality.

Now, I am far from denying that this theory is plausible. Of all that has been written, it is certain that the professed student can master but an infinitesimal fraction. Of that fraction the ordinary reader can master but a very small part. What advice, then, can be better than to select for study the few masterpieces that have come down to us, and to treat as non-existent the huge but undistinguished remainder? We are like travelers passing hastily through some ancient city filled with memorials of many generations and more than one great civilization. Our time is short. Of what may be seen we can only see at best but a trifling fragment. Let us then take care that we waste none of our precious moments upon that which is less than excellent. So preaches Mr. Frederic Harrison.

Yet I am convinced that, for most persons, the views thus laid down by Mr. Harrison are wrong, and that what he describes, with characteristic vigor, as "an impotent voracity for desultory information," is in reality a most desirable and a not too common form of mental appetite. I have no sympathy whatever for the horror he expresses at the "incessant accumulation of fresh books." I am never tempted to regret that Gutemberg was born in the world. I care not at all though the "cataract of printed stuff," as Mr. Harrison calls it, should flow and still flow on until the catalogues of our libraries should make libraries themselves. I am prepared, indeed, to express sympathy almost amounting to approbation for anyone who would check all writing which was *not* intended for the printer. I pay no tribute of grateful admiration to those who have oppressed mankind with the dubious blessing of the penny post. But the ground of the distinction is plain. We are always obliged to read our letters, and are sometimes obliged to answer them. But who obliges us to wade through the piled-up lumber of an ancient library, or to skim more than we like off the frothy foolishness poured forth in ceaseless stream by our circulating libraries? Dead dunces do not importune us; Grub Street does not ask for a reply by return of post. Even their living successors need hurt no one who possesses the very moderate degree of social courage required to make the admission that he has not read the last new novel or the current number of a fashionable magazine.

But this is not the view of Mr. Harrison. To him the position of anyone having free access to a large library is fraught with issues so tremendous that, in order adequately to describe it, he has to seek for parallels in two of the most highly wrought episodes in fiction—the Ancient Mariner, becalmed and thirsting on the tropic ocean; Bunyan's Christian in the crisis of spiritual conflict. But there is here, surely, some error and some exaggeration. Has miscellaneous reading the dreadful consequences which Mr. Harrison depicts? Has it any of them? His declarations about the intellect being "gorged and enfeebled" by the absorption of too much information, express no doubt with great vigor an analogy, for which there is high authority, between the human mind and the human stomach; but surely it is an analogy, which may be pressed too far.

I have often heard of the individual whose excellent natural gifts have been so overloaded with huge masses of undigested and undigestible learning, that they have had no chance of healthy development. But though I have often heard of this personage, I have never met him, and I believe him to be mythical. It is true, no doubt, that many learned people are dull; but there is no indication whatever that they are dull because they are learned. True dullness is seldom acquired; it is a natural grace, the manifestations of which, however modified by education, remain in substance the same. Fill a man to the brim with knowledge, and he will not become less dull, as the enthusiasts for education vainly imagine; neither will he become duller, as Mr. Harrison appears to suppose. He will remain in essence what he always has been and always must have been. But whereas his dullness would, if left to itself, have been merely vacuous, it may have become, under careful cultivation, pretentious and pedantic.

I would further point out to you, that while there is no ground in experience for supposing that a keen interest in those facts which Mr. Harrison describes as "merely curious" has any stupefying effect upon the mind, or has any tendency to render it insensible to the higher things of literature and art, there is positive evidence that many of those who have most deeply felt the charm of those higher things have been consumed by that omnivorous appetite for knowledge which excites Mr. Harrison's especial indignation. Dr. Johnson, for instance, though deaf to some of the most delicate harmonies of verse, was, without question, a very great critic. Yet, in Dr. Johnson's opinion, literary history, which is for the most part composed of facts which Mr. Harrison would regard as insignificant, about authors whom he would regard as pernicious, was the most delightful of studies. Again, consider the case of Lord Macaulay. Lord Macaulay did everything Mr. Harrison says he ought not to have done. From youth to age he was continuously occupied in "gorging and enfeebling" his intellect by the unlimited consumption of every species of literature, from the masterpieces of the age of Pericles to the latest rubbish from the circulating library. It is not told of him that his intellect suffered by the process; and though it will hardly be claimed for him that he was a great critic, none will deny that he possessed the keenest susceptibilities for literary excellence in many languages and in every form.

If Englishmen and Scotchmen do not satisfy you, I will take a Frenchman. The most accomplished critic whom France has produced is, by general admission, Sainte-Beuve. His capacity for appreciating supreme perfection in literature will be disputed by none; yet the great bulk of his vast literary industry was expended upon the lives and writings of authors whose lives Mr. Harrison would desire us to forget, and whose writings almost wring from him the wish that the art of printing had never been discovered.

I am even bold enough to hazard the conjecture (I trust he will forgive me) that Mr. Harrison's life may be quoted against Mr. Harrison's theory. I entirely decline to believe without further evidence that the writings whose vigor of style and of thought has been the delight of us all, are the product of his own system. I hope I do him no wrong, but I cannot help thinking that, if we knew all, we should find that he followed the practice of those worthy physicians who, after prescribing the most abstemious diet to their patients, may be seen partaking freely, and to all appearances safely, of the most succulent and the most unwholesome of the forbidden dishes.

It has been noted that Mr. Harrison's list of the books which deserve perusal would seem to indicate that, in his opinion, the pleasures to be derived from literature are chiefly pleasures of the imagination. Poets, dramatists, and novelists form the bulk of what is specifically permitted to his disciples. Now, though I have clearly stated that the list is not one of which any person is likely to assert that it contains books which ought to be excluded, yet, even from the point of view of what may be termed æsthetic enjoyment, the field in which we are allowed to take our pleasures seems to me unduly restricted.

Contemporary poetry, for instance, on which Mr. Harrison bestows a good deal of hard language, has, and must have for the generation which produces it, certain qualities not likely to be possessed by any other. Charles Lamb has somewhere declared that a pun loses all its virtue as soon as the momentary quality of the intellectual and social atmosphere in which it was born has changed its character. What is true of this, the humblest effort of verbal art, is true, in a different measure and degree, of all, even of the highest forms of literature.

But I leave this train of thought, which has perhaps already taken me too far, in order to point out a more fundamental error, as I think it, which arises from regarding literature solely from this high æsthetic standpoint. The pleasures of the imagination derived from the best literary models form, without doubt, the most exquisite portion of the enjoyment which we may extract from books; but they do not, in my opinion, form the largest portion, if we take into account mass as well as quality, in our calculation. There is the literature which appeals to the imagination or the fancy, some stray specimens of which Mr. Harrison will permit us to peruse; but is there not also the literature which satisfies the curiosity? Is this vast storehouse of pleasure to be thrown hastily aside because many of the facts which it contains are alleged to be insignificant, because the appetite to which they minister is said to be morbid? Consider a little.

We are here dealing with one of the strongest intellectual impulses of rational beings. Animals, as a rule, trouble themselves but little with anything unless they want either to eat it or to run away from it. Interest in, and wonder at, the works of nature and the doings of man are products of civilization, and excite emotions which do not diminish but increase with increasing knowledge and cultivation. Feed them and they grow; minister to them and they will greatly multiply. We hear much indeed of what is called "idle curiosity," but I am loth to brand any form of curiosity as necessarily idle. Take, for example, one of the most singular, but, in this age, one of the most universal forms in which it is accustomed to manifest itself—I mean that of an exhaustive study of the contents of the morning and evening papers. It is certainly remarkable that any person who has nothing to get by it should destroy his eyesight and confuse his brain by a conscientious attempt to master the dull and doubtful details of the European diary daily transmitted to us by "Our Special Correspondent." But it must be remembered that this is only a somewhat unprofitable exercise of that disinterested love of knowledge which moves men to penetrate the polar snows, to build up systems of philosophy, or to explore the secrets of the remotest heavens. It has in it the rudiments of infinite and varied delights. It *can* be turned, and it should be turned, into a curiosity for which nothing that has been done, or thought, or suffered, or believed—no law which governs the world of matter or the world of mind—can be wholly alien or uninteresting.

Truly it is a subject for astonishment that, instead of expanding to the utmost the employment of this pleasure-giving faculty, so many persons should set themselves to work to limit its exercise by all kinds of arbitrary regulations. Some persons, for example, tell us that the acquisition of knowledge is all very well, but that it must be useful knowledge—meaning usually thereby that it must enable a man to get on in a profession, pass an examination, shine in conversation, or obtain a reputation for learning. But even if they mean something higher than this—even if they mean that knowledge, to be worth anything, must subserve ultimately, if not immediately, the material or spiritual interests of mankind—the doctrine is one which should be energetically repudiated.

I admit, of course, at once, that discoveries the most apparently remote from human concerns have often proved themselves of the utmost commercial or manufacturing value. But they require no such justification for their existence, nor were they striven for with any such object. Navigation is not the final cause of astronomy, nor telegraphy of electrodynamics, nor dye-works of chemistry. And if it be true that the desire of knowledge for the sake of knowledge was the animating motive of the great men who first wrested her secrets from nature, why should it not also be enough for us, to whom it is not given to discover, but only to learn as best we may what has been discovered by others?

Another maxim, more plausible but equally pernicious, is that superficial knowledge is worse than no knowledge at all. That "a little knowledge is a dangerous thing" is a saying which has now got currency as a proverb stamped in the mint of Pope's versification—of Pope who, with the most imperfect knowledge of Greek, translated Homer; with the most imperfect knowledge of the Elizabethan drama, edited Shakespeare; and with the most imperfect knowledge of philosophy, wrote the "Essay on Man." But what is this "little knowledge" which is supposed to be so dangerous? What is it "little" in relation to? If in relation to what there is to know, then all human knowledge is little. If in relation to what actually is known by somebody, then we must condemn as "dangerous" the knowledge which Archimedes possessed of mechanics, or Copernicus of astronomy; for a shilling primer and a few weeks' study will enable any student to outstrip in mere information some of the greatest teachers of the past.

No doubt, that little knowledge which thinks itself to be great, may possibly be a dangerous, as it certainly is a most ridiculous thing. We have all suffered under that eminently absurd individual who, on the strength of one or two volumes, imperfectly apprehended by himself, and long discredited in the estimation of every one else, is prepared to supply you on the shortest notice with a dogmatic solution of every problem suggested by this "unintelligible world"; or the political variety of the same pernicious genus, whose statecraft consists in the ready application to the most complex question of national interest of some high-sounding commonplace which has done weary duty on a thousand platforms, and which even in its palmiest days was never fit for anything better than a peroration. But in our dislike of the individual, do not let us mistake the diagnosis of his disease. He suffers not from ignorance, but from stupidity. Give him learning and you make him not wise, but only more pretentious in his folly.

I say, then, that so far from a little knowledge being undesirable, a little knowledge is all that on most subjects any of us can hope to attain, and that as a source not of worldly profit but of personal pleasure, it may be of incalculable value to its possessor. But it will naturally be asked, "How are we to select from among the infinite number of things which may be known, those which it is best worth while for us to know?" We are constantly being told to concern ourselves with learning what is important, and not to waste our energies upon what is insignificant. But what are the marks by which we shall recognize the important, and how is it to be distinguished from the insignificant? A precise and complete answer to this question which shall be true for all men cannot be given. I am considering knowledge, recollect, as it ministers to enjoyment, and from this point of view each unit of information is obviously of importance in proportion as it increases the general sum of enjoyment which we obtain from knowledge. This, of course, makes it impossible to lay down precise rules which shall be an equally sure guide to all sorts and conditions of men; for in this, as in other matters, tastes must differ, and against real difference of taste there is no appeal.

There is, however, one caution which it may be worth your while to keep in view—Do not be persuaded into applying any general proposition on this subject with a foolish impartiality to every kind of knowledge. There are those who tell you that it is the broad generalities and the far-reaching principles which govern the world, which are alone worthy of your attention. A fact which is not an illustration of law, in the opinion of these persons, appears to lose all its value. Incidents which do not fit into some great generalization, events which are merely picturesque, details which are merely curious—they dismiss as unworthy the interest of a reasoning being.

Though no one can, I think, pretend that science does not concern itself, and properly concern itself, with facts which are not in themselves, to all appearance, illustrations of law, it is undoubtedly true that for those who desire to extract the greatest pleasure from science, a knowledge, however elementary, of the leading principles of investigation and the larger laws of nature, is the acquisition most to be desired. To him who is not a specialist, a comprehension of the broad outlines of the universe as it presents itself to the scientific imagination, is the thing most worth striving to attain. But when we turn from science to what is rather vaguely called history, the same principles of study do not, I think, altogether apply, and mainly for this reason—that while the recognition of the reign of law is the chief amongst the pleasures imparted by science, our inevitable ignorance makes it the least among the pleasures imparted by history.

It is no doubt true that we are surrounded by advisers who tell us that all study of the past is barren except in so far as it enables us to determine the laws by which the evolution of human societies is governed. How far such an investigation has been up to the present time fruitful in results I will not inquire. That it will ever enable us to trace with accuracy the course which states and nations are destined to pursue in the future, I do not indeed believe. We are borne along like travelers on some unexplored stream. We may know enough of the general configuration of the globe to be sure we are making our way towards the ocean. We may know enough by experience or theory of the laws regulating the flow of liquids, to conjecture how the river will behave under the varying influences to which it may be subject. More than this we cannot know. It will depend largely upon causes which, in relation to any laws we are ever likely to discover, may properly be called accidental, whether we are destined sluggishly to drift among fever-stricken swamps, to hurry down perilous rapids, or to glide gently through fair scenes of peaceful cultivation.

But leaving on one side ambitious sociological speculations, and even those more modest but hitherto more successful investigations into the causes which have in particular cases been principally operative in producing great political changes, there are still two modes in which we can derive what I may call "spectacular" enjoyment from the study of history. There is first the pleasure which arises from the contemplation of some great historic drama, or some broad and well-marked phase of social development. The story of the rise, greatness, and decay of a nation is like some vast epic which contains as subsidiary episodes the varied stories of the rise, greatness, and decay of creeds, or parties, and of statesmen. The imagination is moved by the slow unrolling of this great picture of human mutability, as it is moved by the contrasted permanence of the abiding stars. The ceaseless conflict, the strange echoes of long-forgotten controversies, the confusion of purpose, the successes which lay deep the seeds of future evils, the failures that ultimately divert the otherwise inevitable danger, the heroism which struggles to the last for a cause foredoomed to defeat, the wickedness which sides with right, and the wisdom which huzzas at the triumph of folly—fate, meanwhile, through all this turmoil and perplexity, working silently towards the predestined end—all these form together a subject, the contemplation of which need surely never weary.

But there is yet another and very different species of enjoyment to be derived from the records of the past, which requires a somewhat different method of study in order that it may be fully tasted. Instead of contemplating, as it were, from a distance, the larger aspects of the human drama, we may elect to move in familiar fellowship amid the scenes and actors of special periods. We may add to the interest we derive from the contemplation of contemporary politics, a similar interest derived from a not less minute, and probably more accurate, knowledge of some comparatively brief passage in the political history of the past. We may extend the social circle in which we move—a circle perhaps narrowed and restricted through circumstances beyond our control—by making intimate acquaintances, perhaps even close friends, among a society long departed, but which, when we have once learnt the trick of it, it rests with us to revive.

That there is such a thing as trifling information, I do not of course question; but the frame of mind in which the reader is constantly weighing the exact importance to the universe at large of each circumstance which the author presents to his notice, is not one conducive to the true enjoyment of a picture whose effect depends upon a multitude of slight and seemingly insignificant touches, which impress the mind often without remaining in the memory. The best method of guarding against the danger of reading what is useless is to read only what is interesting—a truth which will seem a paradox to a whole class of readers, fitting objects of our commiseration, who may be often recognized by their habit of asking some adviser for a list of books, and then marking out a scheme of study in the course of which all these are to be conscientiously perused.

These unfortunate persons apparently read a book principally with the object of getting to the end of it. They reach the word *"Finis"* with the same sensation of triumph as an Indian feels who strings a fresh scalp to his girdle. They are not happy unless they mark by some definite performance each step in the weary path of self-improvement. To begin a volume and not to finish it would be to deprive themselves of this satisfaction; it would be to lose all the reward of their earlier self-denial by a lapse from virtue at the end. To skip, according to their literary code, is a form of cheating: it is a mode of obtaining credit or erudition on false pretenses; a plan by which the advantages of learning are surreptitiously obtained by those who have not won them by honest toil. But all this is quite wrong. In matters literary, works have no saving efficacy. He has only half learnt the art of reading who has not added to it the even more refined accomplishments of skipping and of skimming; and the first step has hardly been taken in the direction of making literature a pleasure until interest in the subject, and not a desire to spare (so to speak) the author's feelings, or to accomplish an appointed task, is the prevailing motive of the reader.

I have now reached, not indeed the end of my subject, which I have scarcely begun, but the limits inexorably set by the circumstances under which it is treated. Yet I am unwilling to conclude without meeting an objection to my method of dealing with it which has, I am sure, been present to the minds of not a few who have been good enough to listen to me with patience. It will be said that I have ignored the higher functions of literature, that I have degraded it from its rightful place, by discussing only certain ways in which it may minister

THE PLEASURES OF READING

to the entertainment of an idle hour, leaving wholly out of sight its contributions to what Mr. Harrison calls our "spiritual sustenance."

Now this is partly because the first of these topics, and not the second, was the avowed subject of my address; but it is partly because I am deliberately of opinion that it is the pleasures and not the profits, spiritual or temporal, of literature which most require to be preached in the ear of the ordinary reader. I hold, indeed, the faith that all such pleasures minister to the development of much that is best in man, mental and moral; but the charm is broken and the subject lost if the remote consequence is consciously pursued to the exclusion of the immediate end.

How great those pleasures may be, I trust there are many here who can testify. When I compare the position of the reader of to-day with that of his predecessor of the sixteenth century, I am amazed at the ingratitude of those who are tempted even for a moment to regret the invention of printing and the multiplication of books. There is now no mood of mind to which a man may not administer the appropriate nutriment or medicine at the cost of reaching down a volume from his book-shelf. In every department of knowledge infinitely more is known, and what is known is incomparably more accessible than it was to our ancestors. The lighter forms of literature, good, bad, and indifferent, which have added so vastly to the happiness of mankind, have increased beyond powers of computation; nor do I believe that there is any reason to think that they have elbowed out their more serious and important brethren.

It is perfectly possible for a man, not a professed student, and who only gives to reading the leisure hours of a business life, to acquire such a general knowledge of the laws of nature and the facts of history, that every great advance made in either department shall be to him both intelligible and interesting; and he may besides have amongst his familiar friends many a departed worthy whose memory is embalmed in the pages of memoir or biography. All this is ours for the asking. All this we shall ask for, if only it be our happy fortune to love, for its own sake, the beauty and the knowledge to be gathered from books. And if this be our fortune, the world may be kind or unkind—it may seem to us to be hastening on the wings of enlightenment and progress to an imminent millennium, or it may weigh us down with the sense of insoluble difficulty and irremediable wrong; but whatever else it be, so long as we have good health and a good library, it can hardly be dull.

GEORGE BANCROFT

THE PEOPLE IN ART, GOVERNMENT, AND RELIGION

Address of George Bancroft, historian and statesman (born in Worcester, Mass., October 3, 1800; died in Washington, D. C., January 17, 1891), delivered before the Adelphi Society, of Williams College, in August, 1835. This address since the time of its delivery has always been considered one of the most notable of American speeches. It was inserted in the first edition of "Modern Eloquence" and crowded out of the last edition to the regret of the editors. The late William J. Bryan called attention to its omission and at his request it is given place in the present edition.

GENTLEMEN OF THE ADELPHI SOCIETY:—The material world does not change in its masses or in its powers. The stars shine with no more luster than when they first sang together in the glory of their birth. The flowers that gemmed the fields and the forests before America was discovered, now bloom around us in their season. The sun that shone on Homer shines on us in unchanging luster; the bow that beamed on the patriarch still glitters in the clouds. Nature is the same. For her no new forces are generated; no new capacities are discovered. The earth turns on its axis, and perfects its revolutions, and renews its seasons without increase or advancement.

But a like passive destiny does not attach to the inhabitants of the earth. For them expectations of social improvement are no delusion; the hopes of philanthropy are more than a dream. The five senses do not constitute the whole inventory of our source of knowledge. They are the organs by which thought connects itself with the external universe; but the power of thought is not merged in the exercise of its instruments. We have functions which connect us with heaven, as well as organs which set us in relation with earth. We have not merely the senses to open to us the external world, but an internal sense, which places us in connection with the world of intelligence and the decrees of God. There is a spirit in man—not in the privileged few, not in those of us only who, by the favor of Providence, have been nursed in public schools; it is in man: it is the attribute of the race. The spirit, which is the guide to truth, is the gracious gift to each member of the family.

Reason exists within every breast. I mean not that faculty which deduces inferences from the experience of the senses, but that higher faculty which, from the infinite treasures of its own consciousness, originates truth and assents to it by the force of intuitive evidence; that faculty which raises us beyond the control of time and space and gives us faith in things eternal and invisible. There is not the difference between one mind and another which the pride of philosophers might conceive. To them no faculty is conceded which does not belong to the meanest of their countrymen. In them there cannot spring up a truth which does not equally have its germ in every mind. They have not the power of creation; they can but reveal what God has implanted in every breast. The intellectual functions by which relations are perceived are the common endowments of the race. The differences are apparent, not real. The eye in one person may be dull, in another quick; in one distorted and in another tranquil and clear; yet the relation of the eye to light is in all men the same. Just so, judgment may be liable in individual minds to bias and passion, and yet its relation to truth is immutable and universal.

In questions of practical duty conscience is God's umpire whose light illumines every heart; there is nothing in books which had not first, and has not still its life within us. Religion itself is a dead letter wherever its truths are not renewed in the soul. The individual conscience may be corrupted by interest or debauched by pride, yet the rule of morality is distinctly marked; its harmonies are to the mind like music to the ear; and the moral judgment when carefully analyzed and referred to its principles is always founded in right. The Eastern superstition which bids its victims prostrate themselves before the advancing car of their idols springs from a noble root, and is but a melancholy perversion of that self-devotion which enables the Christian to bear the cross and subject his personal passions to the will of God. Immorality of itself never won to its support the inward voice; conscience if questioned never forgets to curse the guilty with memory of sin, to cheer the upright with the meek tranquillity of approval. And this admirable power which is the instinct of Deity is the attribute of every man; it knocks at the palace gate, it dwells in the meanest hovel. Duty like death, enters every abode and delivers its message. Conscience like reason and judgment, is universal.

That the moral affections are planted everywhere needs only to be asserted to be received. The savage mother loves her offspring with all the fondness that a mother can know. Beneath the odorous shade of the boundless forests of Chili the native youth repeats the story of love as sincerely as it was ever chanted in the valley of Vaucluse. The affections of family are not the growth of civilization. The charities of life are scattered everywhere; enameling the vales of human being as the flowers upon the meadows. They are not the fruit of study, nor the privilege of refinement, but a natural instinct.

Our age has seen a revolution in works of imagination. The poet has sought his theme in common life. Never is the genius of Scott more pathetic than when as in the "Antiquary" he delineates the sorrows of a poor fisherman, or as in the "Heart of Midlothian" he takes his heroine from a cottage. And even Wordsworth, the purest and most original poet of the day in spite of the inveterate character of his political predilections, has thrown the light of genius on the walks of commonest life; he finds a lesson in every grave of the village churchyard; he discloses the boundless treasures of feeling in the peasant. The laborer and the artisan, the strolling peddler, becomes through his genius a teacher of the sublimest morality; and the solitary wagoner, the lonely shepherd, even the feeble mother of an idiot boy, furnishes lessons in the reverence for humanity.

If from things relating to truth, justice, and affection, we turn to those relating to the beautiful, we may here still further assert that the sentiment for the beautiful resides in the breast. The lovely forms of the eternal world delight us from their adaptation to our powers.

> Yea, what were mighty Nature's self,
> Her features, could they win us,
> Unhelped by the poetic voice
> That hourly speaks within us?

The Indian mother on the borders of Hudson's Bay decorates her manufactures with ingenious devices and lovely colors prompted by the same instinct which guided the pencil and mixed the colors of Raphael. The inhabitant of Nootka Sound tattooes his body with the method of harmonious arabesques. Every form to which the hands of the artist have ever given birth, sprung first into being as a conception of his mind from a natural faculty which belongs not to the artist exclusively, but to man. Beauty like truth and justice lives within us; like virtue and like moral law it is a companion of the soul. The power which leads to the production of beautiful forms or perception of them in the works which God has made is an attribute of humanity.

But I am asked if I despise learning. Shall one who has been much of his life in schools and universities plead the equality of uneducated nature? Is there no difference between the man of refinement and the uneducated savage?

"I am a man," said Black Hawk nobly to the chief of the first republic of the world; "I am a man," said the barbarous chieftain, "and you are another."

I speak for the universal diffusion of human powers, not of human attainments; for the capacity for progress, not for the perfection of undisciplined instincts. The fellowship which we should cherish with the race receives the Comanche warrior and the Caffre within the pale of equality. Their functions may not have been exercised, but they exist. Immure a person in a dungeon; as he comes to the light of day, his vision seems incapable of performing its office. Does that destroy your conviction in the relation between the eye and light? The rioter over his cups resolves to eat and drink and be merry; he forgets his spiritual nature in his obedience to the senses; but does that destroy the relation between conscience and eternity? "What ransom shall we give," exclaimed the senators of Rome to the savage Attila. "Give," said the barbarian, "all your gold and jewels, your costly furniture and treasures, and set free every slave." "Ah," replied the degenerate Romans, "what then will be left to us?" "I leave you your souls," replied the unlettered invader from the steppes of Asia, who had learnt in the wilderness to value the immortal mind and to despise the servile herd that esteemed only their fortunes, and had no true respect for themselves. You cannot discover a tribe of men but you also find the charities of life, and the proofs of spiritual existence. Behold the ignorant Algonquin deposit a bow and quiver by the side of the departed warrior, and recognize his faith in immortality. See the Comanche chieftain, in the heart of our continent, inflict on himself the severest penance, and reverence his confession of the needed atonement for sin. The barbarian who roams o'er the western prairies has like passions and like endowments with ourselves. He bears with him the instinct of Deity; the consciousness of a spiritual nature; the love of beauty; the rule of morality.

And shall we reverence the dark-skinned Caffre? Shall we respect the brutal Hottentot? You may read the right answer written on every heart. It bids me not despise the sable hunter that gathers a livelihood in the forests of southern Africa. All are men. When we know the Hottentot better we shall despise him less.

If it be true that the gifts of the mind and heart are universally diffused, if the sentiment of truth, justice, love, and beauty exists in every one, then it follows as a necessary consequence that the commonest judgment in taste, politics, and religion is the highest authority on earth, and the nearest possible approach to an infallible decision. From the consideration of individual powers I turn to the action of the human mind in masses.

If reason is a universal faculty, universal decision is the nearest criterion of truth. The common mind winnows opinions; it is the sieve which separates error from certainty. The exercise by many of the same faculty on the same subject would naturally lead to the same conclusions. But if not, the very differences of opinion that arise prove the supreme judgment of the general mind. Truth is one. It never contradicts itself. One truth cannot contradict another truth. Hence truth is the bond of union. But error not only contradicts truth but may contradict itself, so that there may be many errors and each at variance with the rest. Truth is therefore of necessity an element of harmony; error as necessarily an element of discord. Thus there can be no continuing universal judgment but a right one. Men cannot agree in an absurdity; neither can they agree in a falsehood.

If wrong opinions have often been cherished by the masses, the cause always lies in the complexity of the ideas presented. Error finds its way into the soul of a nation only through the channel of truth. It is to a truth that men listen; and if they accept error also it is only because error is for the time so closely interwoven with truth that the one cannot readily be separated from the other.

Unmixed error can have no existence in the public mind. Wherever you see men clustering together to form a party you may be sure that however much error may be there truth is there also. Apply this principle boldly, for it contains a lesson of candor and a voice of encouragement. There never was a school of philosophy nor a clan in the realm of opinion but carried along with it some important truth. And therefore every sect that has ever flourished has benefited humanity; for the errors of a sect pass away and are forgotten; its truths are received into the common inheritance. To know the seminal thought of every prophet and leader of a sect is to gather all the wisdom of mankind.

> By heaven! there should not be a seer who left
> The world one doctrine, but I'd ask his lore,
> And commune with his spirit. All the truth
> Of all the tongues of earth I'd have them all,
> Had I the powerful spell to raise their ghosts.

The sentiment of beauty as it exists in the human mind is the criterion in works of art, inspires the conceptions of genius and exercises a final judgment on its productions. For who are the best judges in matters of taste? Do you think the cultivated individual? Undoubtedly not; but the collective mind. The public is wiser than the wisest critic. In Athens the arts were carried to perfection when the "fierce democracy" was in the ascendant; the temple of Minerva and the works of Phidias were planned and perfected to please the common people. When Greece yielded to tyrants, her genius for excellence in art expired, or rather the purity of taste disappeared, because the artist then endeavored to gratify a patron and therefore humored the caprice, while before he had endeavored to delight the race.

When after a long eclipse the arts again burst into a splendid existence it was equally under the popular influence. During the rough contests and feudal tyrannies of the Middle Ages religion had opened in the church an asylum for the people. There the serf and the beggar could kneel; there the pilgrim and the laborer were shrived, and the children of misfortune not less than the prosperous were welcomed to the house of prayer. The church was consequently at once the guardian of equality and the nurse of the arts; and the souls of Giotto, of Perugino, and Raphael, moved by an infinite sympathy with the crowd, kindled into divine conceptions of beautiful forms. Appealing to the sentiment of devotion in the common mind, they dipped their pencils in living colors to decorate the altars where man adored. By degrees the wealthy nobility desired, in like manner, to adorn their palaces; but at the attempt the quick familiarity of the artists with the beautiful declined. Instead of the brilliant works which spoke to the soul a school arose which appealed to the senses; and in the land which had produced the most moving pictures addressed to religious feeling and instinct with the purest beauty, the banquet halls were covered with grotesque forms such as float before the imagination when excited and bewildered by sensual indulgence. Instead of holy families, the ideal representations of the Virgin and the godlike Child, of the enduring faith of martyrs and the blessed benevolence of evangelic love, there came the motley group of fauns and satyrs, of Diana stooping to Endymion, of voluptuous beauty and the forms of licentiousness. Humanity frowned on the desecration of the arts, and painting no longer vivified by a fellow-feeling with the multitude, lost its greatness in the attempt to adapt itself to personal humors.

If with us arts are destined to a brilliant career the inspiration must spring from the vigor of the people. Genius will not create to flatter patrons or decorate salons. It yearns for larger influences, it feeds on wider sympathies, and its perfect display can never exist except in an appeal to the general sentiment for the beautiful.

Again. Italy is famed for its musical compositions, its inimitable operas. It is a well-known fact that the best critics are often deceived in their judgment of them, while the pit, composed of the throng, does without fail, render a true verdict.

But the taste for music, it may be said, is favored by natural organization. Precisely a statement that sets in a clearer light the natural capacity of the race, for taste is then not an acquisition but in part a gift. But let us pass to the works of literature.

Who are by way of eminence the poets of all mankind? Surely Homer and Shakespeare. Now Homer formed his taste as he wandered from door to door a vagrant minstrel paying for hospitality by song, and Shakespeare wrote for an audience composed in a great measure of the common people.

The little story of Paul and Virginia is a universal favorite. When it was first written the author read it aloud to a circle in Paris, composed of the wife of the Prime Minister and the choicest critics of France. They condemned it as dull and insipid. The author appealed to the public, and the children of all Europe reversed the decree of the Parisians. The judgment of children, that is the judgment of the common mind under its most innocent and least imposing form, was more trustworthy than the criticism of the select refinement of the most polished city in the world.

Demosthenes of old formed himself to the perfection of eloquence by means of addresses to the crowd. The great comic poet of Greece, emphatically the poet of the vulgar mob, is distinguished above all others for the incomparable graces of his diction; and it is related of one of the most skillful writers in the Italian that when inquired of where he had learned the purity and nationality of his style, he replied, from listening to country people as they brought their produce to market.

At the revival of letters a distinguished feature of the rising literature was the employment of the dialect of the vulgar. Dante used the language of the populace and won immortality. Wycliffe, Luther, and at a later day Descartes, each employed

ART, GOVERNMENT, AND RELIGION 63

his mother tongue and carried truth directly to all who were familiar with its accents. Each beneficent revolution in letters has the character of popularity; every great reform among authors has sprung from the power of the people in its influence on the development and activity of mind.

The same influence continues unimpaired. Scott in spite of his reverence for the aristocracy spurned a drawing-room reputation; the secret of Byron's superiority lay in part in the agreement which existed between his muse and the democratic tendency of the age. German literature is almost entirely a popular creation. It was fostered by no monarch; it was dandled by no aristocracy. It was plebeian in its origin and therefore manly in its results.

In like manner the best government rests on the people and not on the few, on persons and not on property, on the free development of public opinion and not on authority; because the munificent Author of our being has conferred the gifts of mind upon every member of the human race without distinction of outward circumstances. Whatever of other possessions may be engrossed the mind asserts its own independence. Lands, estates, the produce of minds, the prolific abundance of the seas may be usurped by a privileged class. Avarice assuming the form of ambitious power may grasp realm after realm, subdue continents, compass the earth in its schemes of aggrandizement, and sigh after worlds, but mind eludes the power of appropriation; it exists only in its own individuality, it is a property which cannot be confiscated and cannot be torn away. It laughs at chance, it bursts from imprisonment, it defies monopoly. A government of equal rights must, therefore, rest upon mind, not wealth, not brute force; some of the moral intelligence of the community should rule the state. Prescription can no more assume to be a valid plea for political injustice; society studies to eradicate established abuses and to bring social institutions and laws into harmony with moral right; not dismayed by the natural and necessary imperfections of all human effort, and not giving way to despair because every hope does not at once ripen into fruit.

The public happiness is the true object of legislation and can be secured only by the masses of mankind, themselves awakened to a knowledge and care of their own interests. Our free institutions have reversed the false and ignoble distinctions between men; and, refusing to gratify the pride of caste, have acknowledged the common mind to be the true material for a commonwealth. Everything has hitherto been done for the happy few. It is not possible to endow an aristocracy with greater benefits than they have already enjoyed; there is no room to hope that individuals will be more highly gifted or more fully developed than the great sages of past times. The world can advance only through the culture of the moral and intellectual power of the people. To accomplish this end by means of the people themselves is the highest purpose of government. If it be the duty of the individual to strive after a perfection like the perfection of God, how much more ought a nation to be the image of duty. The common mind is the true Parian marble fit to be wrought into the likeness to a god. The duty of America is to secure the culture and the happiness of the masses by their reliance on themselves.

The absence of the prejudices of the Old World leaves us here the opportunity of consulting independent truth, and man is left to apply the instinct of freedom to every social relation and public interest. We have approached so near to Nature that we can hear her gentlest whispers; we have made humanity our lawgiver and our oracle; and therefore the nation receives, vivifies and applies principles which in Europe the wisest accept with distrust. Freedom of mind and of conscience, freedom of the seas, freedom and industry, equality of franchise—each great truth is firmly grasped, comprehended and enforced, for the multitude is neither rash nor fickle. In truth it is less fickle than those who profess to be its guides. Its natural dialectics surpass the logic of the schools. Political action has never been so constant and so unwavering as when it results from a feeling or a principle diffused through society. The people is firm and tranquil in its movements and necessarily acts with moderation because it becomes but slowly impregnated with new ideas, and effects no changes except in harmony with the knowledge which it has acquired. Besides where it is permanently possessed of power there exists neither the occasion nor the desire for frequent change. It is not the parent of tumult;

sedition is bred in the lap of luxury, and its chosen emissaries are the beggared spendthrift and the impoverished libertine. The government by the people is in very truth the strongest government in the world. Discarding the implements of terror it dares to rule by moral force and has its citadel in the heart.

Such is the political system which rests on reason, reflection, and the free expression of deliberate choice. There may be those who scoff at the suggestion that the decision of the whole is to be preferred to the judgment of the enlightened few. They say in their hearts that the masses are ignorant; that farmers know nothing of legislation; that mechanics should not quit their workshops to join in forming public opinion. But true political science does indeed venerate the masses. It maintains not as has been perversely asserted that "the people can make right," but that the people can discern right. Individuals are but shadows, too often engrossed by the pursuit of shadows, the race is immortal; individuals are of limited sagacity, the common mind is infinite in its experience; individuals are languid and blind, the many are ever wakeful; individuals are corrupt, the race has been redeemed; individuals are time-serving, the masses are fearless; individuals may be false, the masses are ingenuous and sincere; individuals claim the divine sanction of truth for the deceitful conceptions of their own fancies; the Spirit of God breathes through the combined intelligence of the people. Truth is not to be ascertained by the impulse of an individual, it emerges from the contradictions of present opinions; it raises itself in majestic serenity above the strifes of parties and the conflict of sects; it acknowledges neither the solitary mind nor the separate faction as its oracle, but owns as its only faithful interpreter the dictates of pure reason itself proclaimed by the general voice of mankind. The decrees of the universal conscience are the nearest approach to the presence of God in the soul of man.

Thus the opinion which we respect is indeed not the opinion of one or of a few but the sagacity of the many. It is hard for the pride of cultivated philosophy to put its ear to the ground and listen reverently to the voice of lowly humanity, yet the people collectively are wiser than the most gifted individual for all his wisdom constitutes but a part of others'. When the great sculptor of Greece was endeavoring to fashion the perfect model of beauty he did not passively imitate the form of the loveliest woman of his age, but he gleaned the several lineaments of his faultless work from the many. And so it is that a perfect judgment is the result of comparison where error eliminates error and truth is established by concurring witnesses. The organ of truth is the invisible decision of the unbiased world; she pleads before no tribunal but public opinion; she owns no safe interpreter but the common mind; she knows no court of appeals but the soul of humanity. It is when the multitude give counsel that right purposes find safety; theirs is the fixedness that cannot be shaken; theirs is the understanding which exceeds in wisdom; theirs is the heart of which the largeness is as the sand on the seashore.

It is not by vast armies, by immense natural resources, by accumulations of treasures, that the greatest results in modern civilization have been accomplished. The traces of the career of conquest pass away, hardly leaving a scar on the national intelligence. Famous battle-grounds of victory are most of them comparatively indifferent to the human race; barren fields of blood, the scourges of their times, but affecting the social condition as little as the raging of a pestilence. Not one benevolent institution, not one ameliorating principle in the Roman State was a voluntary concession of the aristocracy; each useful element was borrowed from the democracies of Greece or was a reluctant concession to the demands of the people. The same is true in modern political life. It is the confession of an enemy to democracy that "all the great and noble institutions of the world have come from popular efforts."

It is the uniform tendency of the popular element to elevate and bless humanity. The exact measure of the progress of civilization is the degree in which the intelligence of the common mind has prevailed over wealth and brute force; in other words, the measure of the progress of civilization is the progress of the people. Every great object connected with the benevolent exertions of the day, has reference to the culture of those powers which are alone the common inheritance. For this the envoys of a religion cross seas and visit remotest isles; for this the press in its freedom teems with the productions of maturest thought; for this philanthropists plan new schemes of education; for this halls in every city and village are open to the public instructor. Not that we view with indifference the glorious efforts of material industry, the increase in the facility of internal intercourse, the accumulations of thrifty labor, the varied results of concentrated action. But even there it is mind that achieves the triumph. It is the genius of the architect that gives beauty to the work of human hands and makes the temple, the dwelling, or the public edifice an outward representation of the spirit of propriety and order. It is science that guides the zeal of cupidity to the construction of the vast channels of communication which are fast binding the world into one family. And it is as a method of moral improvement that this swifter means of intercourse derives its greatest value. Mind becomes universal property; the poem that is published on the soil of England finds its response on the shores of Lake Erie and the banks of the Missouri, and is admired near the sources of the Ganges. The defense of public liberty in our own halls of legislation penetrates to the plains of Poland, is echoed along the mountains of Greece, and pierces the darkest night of Eastern despotism.

The universality of the intellectual and moral powers and the necessity of their development for the progress of the race proclaim the great doctrine of the natural right of every human being to moral and intellectual culture. It is the glory of our fathers to have established in their laws the equal claims of every child to the public care of its morals and its mind. From this principle we may deduce the universal right to leisure: that is, to time not appropriated to material purposes but reserved for the culture of the moral affections and the mind. It does not tolerate the exclusive enjoyment of leisure by a privileged class, but defending the rights of labor would suffer none to sacrifice the higher purposes of existence in unceasing toil for that which is not life. Such is the voice of nature, such the conscious claim of the human mind. The universe opens its pages to every eye, the music of creation resounds in every ear, the glorious lessons of immortal truth that are written in the sky and on the earth address themselves to every mind and claim attention from every human being. God has made man upright that he might look before and after, and he calls upon every one not merely to labor but to reflect; not merely to practice the revelations of divine will, but to contemplate the displays of divine power. Nature claims for every man leisure, for she claims every man as a witness to the divine glory manifested in the created world.

> Yet evermore, through years renewed
> In undisturbed vicissitude
> Of seasons balancing their flight
> On the swift wings of day and night,
> Kind nature keeps a heavenly door
> Wide open for the scattered poor,
> Where flower-breathed incense to the skies
> Is wafted in loud harmonies;
> And ground fresh cloven by the plow
> Is fragrant with a humbler vow;
> Where birds and brooks from living dells
> Chime forth unwearied canticles,
> And vapors magnify and spread
> The glory of the sun's bright head;
> Still constant in her worship, still
> Conforming to the Almighty will,
> Whether men sow or reap the fields,
> Her admonitions nature yields;
> That not by bread alone we live,
> Or what a hand of flesh can give;
> That every day should leave some part,
> Free for a Sabbath of the heart;
> So shall the seventh be truly blest,
> From morn to eve with hallowed rest.

The right to universal education being thus acknowledged by our conscience not less than by our laws, it follows that the people is the true recipient of truth. Do not seek to conciliate individuals, do not dread the frowns of a sect, do not yield to the prescription of a party, but pour out truth into the common mind. Let the waters of intelligence like the rains of heaven descend on the whole earth, and be not discouraged by the dread of encountering ignorance. The prejudices of ignorance are more easily removed than the prejudices of interest; the first are blindly adopted, the second willfully preferred. Intelligence must be diffused among the whole people, truth must be scattered among those who have no interest to suppress its growth. The seeds that fall on the exchange or in the hum of business may be choked by the thorns that spring up in the hotbed of avarice; the seeds that are let fall in the salon may be like those dropped by the wayside which take no root. Let the young aspirant after glory scatter seeds of truth broadcast on the wide bosom of humanity, in the deep fertile soil of the public mind. There it will strike deep root and spring up and bear a hundredfold and bloom for ages and ripen fruit through remote generations.

It is alone by infusing great principles into the common mind that revolutions in human society are brought about. They never have been, they never can be effected by superior individual excellence. The age of the Antonines is the age of the greatest glory of the Roman empire. Men distinguished by every accomplishment of culture and science for a century in succession possessed undisputed sway over more than one hundred millions of men, until, at last, in the person of Mark Aurelian, philosophy herself seemed to mount the throne. And did she stay the downward tendencies of the Roman empire? Did she infuse new elements of life into the decaying constitution? Did she commence one great beneficent reform? Not one permanent amelioration was effected. Philosophy was clothed with absolute power; and yet absolute power accomplished nothing for humanity. It could accomplish nothing. Had it been possible, Aurelian would have wrought a change. Society can be regenerated, the human race can be advanced, only by moral principles diffused through the multitude.

And now let us take an opposite instance; let us see if amelioration follows when, in despite of tyranny, truth finds access to the common people. Christianity itself shall furnish me the example.

When Christianity first made its way into Rome the Imperial City was the seat of wealth, philosophy, and luxury. Absolute government was already established; and had the will of Claudius been gained or the conscience of Messalina been roused, or the heart of Narcissus, once a slave, then Prime Minister, been touched by the recollections of his misfortunes, the aid of the sovereign of the civilized world would have been engaged. And the messenger of divine truth making his appeal to them —was his mission to the emperor and his minions? To the empress and her flatterers? To the servile senators? To wealthy favorites? Paul preserves for us the names of the first converts: the Roman Mary and Junia, Julia and Nerea, and the beloved brother, all plebeian names unknown to history. "Greet them," he adds, "that be of the household of Narcissus." Now every Roman household was a community of slaves. Narcissus himself, a freedman, was the chief minister of the Roman empire; his ambition had left him no moments for the envoy from Calvary; the friends of Paul were a freedman's slaves. When God selected a channel by which Christianity should make its way in the city of Rome, and assuredly be carried forward to acknowledged supremacy in the Roman empire, he gave to the apostle of the Gentiles favor in the household of Narcissus; he planted the truth deep in the common soil. Had Christianity been received at court it would have been stifled or corrupted by the prodigal vices of the age; it lived in the hearts of the common people; it sheltered itself against oppression in the catacombs and among tombs; it made misfortune its comfort and sorrow its companion, and labor its state. It rested on a rock, for it rested on the people; it was gifted with immortality, for it struck root in the hearts of the millions.

So completely was this greatest of all reforms carried forward in the vale of life, that the great moral revolution, the great step of God's providence in the education of the human race, was not observed by the Roman historians. Once indeed at this early period the Christians are mentioned; for, in the reign of Nero, their purity being hateful to the corrupt, Nero abandoned them to persecution. In the darkness of midnight they were covered with pitch and set on fire to light the streets of Rome, and this singularity has been recorded. But their system of morals and religion, though it was the new birth of the world, escaped all notice.

Paul, who was a Roman citizen, was beheaded just outside the walls of the Eternal City; and Peter, who was a plebeian and could not claim the distinction of the ax and block, was executed on the cross, with his head downwards to increase the pain of the indignity. Do you think the Roman emperor took notice of the names of these men when he signed their death-warrants? And yet, as they poured truth into the common mind, what series of kings, what lines of emperors, can compare with them in their influence on the destinies of mankind?

Yes, reforms in society are only effected through the masses of the people, and through them have continually taken place. New truths have been successively developed and are becoming the common property of the human family for improving its condition. This progress is advanced by every sect precisely because each sect obtained vitality, itself of necessity embodied a truth, by every political party, for the conflicts of party are the war of ideas; by every nationality, for a nation cannot exist as such until humanity makes it special trustee of some part of its wealth for the ultimate benefit of all.

The irresistible tendency of the human race is therefore to advancement, for absolute power has never succeeded and can never succeed in suppressing a single truth. An idea once revealed may find its admission into every living breast and live there. Like God, it becomes immortal and omnipresent. The movement of the species is upward, irresistibly upward. The individual is often lost; Providence never disowns the race. No principle once promulgated has ever been forgotten. No "timely tramp" of a despot's foot ever trod out one idea. The world cannot retrograde; the dark ages cannot return. Dynasties perish, seeds are buried, nations have been victims to error of martyrs for right; humanity has always been on the advance, gaining maturity, universality and power.

Yes, truth is immortal, it cannot be destroyed; it is invincible, it cannot long be resisted. Not every great principle has yet been generated, but when once proclaimed and diffused it lives without end in the safe custody of the race. States may pass away, every just principle of legislation which has been once established will endure. Philosophy has sometimes forgotten God, a great people never did. The skepticism of the last century could not uproot Christianity because it lived in the hearts of the millions. Do you think that infidelity is spreading? Christianity never lived in the hearts of so many millions as at this moment. The forms under which it is professed may decay, for they, like all that is the work of men's hands, are subject to changes and chances of mortal being, but the spirit of truth is incorruptible; it may be developed, illustrated, and applied; it never can die; it never can decline.

No truth can perish, no truth can pass away; the flame is undying, though generations disappear. Wherever moral truth has struck into being, humanity claims and guards the greatest bequest. Each generation gathers together imperishable children of the past, and increases them by new sons of light alike radiant with immortality.

NICHOLAS MURRAY BUTLER

NICHOLAS MURRAY BUTLER

FIVE EVIDENCES OF AN EDUCATION

Dr. Butler is a great teacher both as a speaker and as a writer, from the platform and from his books, and both on educational and other public affairs. He was born in Elizabeth, N. J., in 1862, and has been president of Columbia University since 1902. This address was delivered before the Phi Beta Kappa Society of Vassar College, June 10, 1901. Other speeches by Dr. Butler are given in Volumes I and VIII.

"If you had had children, sir," said Boswell, "would you have taught them anything?" "I hope," replied Doctor Johnson, "that I should have willingly lived on bread and water to obtain instruction for them; but I would not have set their future friendship to hazard, for the sake of thrusting into their heads knowledge of things for which they might not perhaps have either taste or necessity. You teach your daughters the diameters of the planets, and wonder when you have done that that they do not delight in your company." From which it appears that Doctor Johnson, by a sort of prolepsis, was moved to contribute to the discussion of one of the vexed questions of our time. Who is the educated man? By what signs shall we know him?

"In the first golden age of the world," Erasmus observes, in his "Praise of Folly," "there was no need of these perplexities. There was then no other sort of learning but what was naturally collected from every man's common sense, improved by an easy experience. What use could there have been of grammar, when all men spoke the same mother tongue, and aimed at no higher pitch of oratory than barely to be understood by each other? What need of logic, when they were too wise to enter

Reprinted with permission of author and publisher from "The Meaning of Education." Copyright, 1915, Charles Scribner's Sons.

into any dispute? Or what occasion for rhetoric, where no difference arose to require any laborious decision?" Surely, in contrasting this picture of a far-off golden age with our present-day strenuous age of steel, we must be moved to say, with the preacher: "In much wisdom is much grief; and he that increaseth knowledge increaseth sorrow."

It is only two hundred and fifty years ago that Comenius urged, with ardent zeal, the establishment in London of a college of learned men who should bring together in one book the sum total of human wisdom, so expressed as to meet the needs of both the present and all future generations. This scheme for a Pansophia, or repository of all learning, proved very attractive in the seventeenth century, for it easily adjusted itself to the notions of a period which looked upon learning as a substantial and measurable quantity, to be acquired and possessed. Unfortunately, this quantitative ideal of education, with its resultant processes and standards, is still widely influential, and it tempts us to seek the evidences of an education in the number of languages learned, in the variety of sciences studied, and generally in the quantity of facts held in the memory reserve. But, on the other hand, any serious attempt to apply quantitative standards to the determination of education quickly betrays their inadequacy and their false assumptions. If to be educated means to know nature in systematic fashion and to be able to interpret it, then nearly every man of letters, ancient or modern, must be classed with the uneducated. Or if to be educated means to have sympathetic, almost affectionate, insight into the great masterpieces of art and of literature, then innumerable great men of action, who have fully represented the ideals and the power of their time and who manifested most admirable qualities of mind and of character, were uneducated. The case is even worse to-day. A host of knowledges compass us about on every side and bewilder by their variety and their interest. We must exclude the many to choose the one. The penalty of choice is deprivation; the price of not choosing is shallowness and incapacity. The quantitative method of estimating education breaks down, then, of its own weight. A true standard is to be sought in some other direction.

A full analysis of the facts of life as they confront us today would show, I feel confident, that all knowledges and all influences are not on a single plane of indifference toward the human mind that would be educated. All parts of the spiritual machine are not mutually interchangeable. There are needs to be met and longings to be satisfied that will not accept any vicarious response to their demands. The scientific, the literary, the æsthetic, the institutional, and the religious aspects of life and of civilization, while interdependent, are yet independent of each other, in the sense that no one of them can be reduced to a function of another, or can be stated in terms of another. Therefore, each of these five aspects must, I think, be represented in some degree in every scheme of training which has education for its end. Nevertheless, this training when it arrives at education will not suffer itself to be measured and estimated quantitatively in terms either of science, of letters, of art, of institutions, or of religion. It will have produced certain traits of intellect and of character which find expression in ways open to the observation of all men, and it is toward these traits or habits, not toward external and substantial acquisition or accomplishment, that one must turn to find the true and sure evidences of an education, as education is conceived to-day.

First among the evidences of an education I name correctness and precision in the use of the mother tongue. Important as this power is, and is admitted to be, it is a comparatively new thing in education. The modern European languages took on educational significance only when the decentralization of culture began at the close of the Middle Ages. So late as 1549 Jacques du Bellay supported the study of French with the very mild assertion that it is "not so poor a tongue as many think it." Mulcaster, writing a little later, found it necessary to tell why his book on education was put in English rather than in Latin, and to defend the vernacular when he referred to its educational usefulness. Melanchthon put German in a class with Greek and Hebrew, and contrasted all three unfavorably with Latin. Indeed it was not until the present German Emperor plainly told the Berlin School Conference of 1890 that a national basis was lacking in German education; that the foundation of the gymnasium course of study must be German; that the duty of the schoolmasters was to train the young to become Germans, not Greeks and Romans; and that the German language must be made the center around which all other subjects revolved, that a revision of the official school program was brought about that made place for the really serious study of the German language and literature. And to-day, where the influence of the English universities and of not a few American colleges is potent, the study of English is slight and insignificant indeed. The superstition that the best gate to English is through the Latin is anything but dead.

But for the great mass of the people the vernacular is not only the established medium of instruction, but fortunately also an important subject of study. A chief measure of educational accomplishment is the ease, the correctness, and the precision with which one uses this instrument.

It is no disrespect to the splendid literatures which are embodied in the French and the German tongues, and no lack of appreciation of the services of those great peoples to civilization and to culture, to point out that of modern languages the English is easily the first and the most powerful, for "it is the greatest instrument of communication that is now in use among the men upon the earth." It is the speech of an active people among whom individual liberty and personal initiative are highly prized. It falls short, no doubt, of the philosophical pliability of the Greek and of the scientific ductility of the German; but what is there in the whole field of human passion and human action that it cannot express with freedom and with a power all its own? Turn "Othello" into German, or compare the verse of Shelley or of Keats with the graceful lines of some of their French contemporaries, and learn the peculiar power of the English speech. In simple word or sonorous phrase it is unequaled as a medium to reveal the thoughts, the feelings, and the ideals of humanity.

One's hold upon the English tongue is measured by his choice of words and by his use of idiom. The composite character of modern English offers a wide field for apt and happy choice of expression. The educated man, at home with his mother tongue, moves easily about in its Saxon, Romanic, and Latin elements, and has gained by long experience and wide reading a knowledge of the mental incidence of words as well as of their artistic effect. He is hampered by no set formulas, but manifests in his speech, spoken and written, the characteristic powers and appreciation of his nature. The educated man is of necessity, therefore, a constant reader of the best written English. He reads not for conscious imitation, but for unconscious absorption and reflection. He knows the wide distinction between correct English on the one hand, and pedantic, or, as it is sometimes called, "elegant," English on the other. He is more likely to "go to bed" than to "retire," to "get up" than to "arise," to have "legs" rather than "limbs," to "dress" than to "clothe himself," and to "make a speech" rather than to "deliver an oration." He knows that "if you hear poor English and read poor English, you will pretty surely speak poor English and write poor English," and governs himself accordingly. He realizes the power and place of idiom and its relation to grammar, and shows his skill by preserving a balance between the two in his style. He would follow with intelligent sympathy the scholarly discussions of idiom and of grammar by Professor Earle and would find therein the justification of much of his best practice. In short, in his use of his mother tongue he would give sure evidence of an education.

As a second evidence of an education I name those refined and gentle manners which are the expression of fixed habits of thought and of action. "Manners are behavior and good breeding," as Addison said, but they are more. It is not without significance that the Latin language has but a single word (*mores*) both for usages, habits, manners, and for morals. Real manners, the manners of a truly educated man or woman, are an outward expression of intellectual and moral conviction. Sham manners are a veneer which falls away at the dampening touch of the first selfish suggestion. Manners have a moral significance, and find their basis in that true and deepest self-respect which is built upon respect for others. An infallible test of character is to be found in one's manners toward those whom, for one reason or another, the world may deem his inferiors. A man's manners toward his equals or his superiors are shaped by too many motives to render their interpretation either easy or certain. Manners do not make the man, but manners reveal the man. It is by the amount of respect, deference, and courtesy shown to human personality as such that we judge whether one is on dress parade or whether he is so well-trained, well-educated and so habitually ethical in thought and action that he realizes his proper relation to his fellows and reveals his realization in his manners. As Kant insisted more than a century ago, a man exists as an end in himself, and not merely as a means to be arbitrarily used by this or that will; and in all his actions, whether they concern himself alone or other rational beings, he must always be regarded as an end. True manners are based upon a recognition of this fact, and that is a poor education indeed which fails to inculcate the ethical principle and the manners that embody it.

As a third evidence of an education I name the power and habit of reflection. It is a frequent charge against us moderns, particularly against Americans, that we are losing the habit of reflection, and the high qualities which depend upon it. We are told that this loss is a necessary result of our hurried and busy lives, of our diverse interests, and of the annihilation of space and time by steam and electricity. The whole world and its happenings are brought to our very doors by the daily newspaper. Our attention leaps from Manila to Pekin, from Pekin to the Transvaal, and from the Transvaal to Havana. We are torn by conflicting or unconnected emotions, and our minds are occupied by ideas following each other with such rapidity that we fail to get a firm and deep hold of any of the great facts that come into our lives. This is the charge which even sympathetic critics bring against us.

If it be true—and there are some counts in the indictment which it is difficult to deny—then one of the most precious evidences of an education is slipping from us, and we must redouble our efforts to keep fast hold upon it. For an unexamined life, as Socrates unceasingly insisted, is not worth living. The life which asks no questions of itself, which traces events back to no causes and forward to no purposes, which raises no vital issues of principle, and which seeks no interpretation of what passes within and without, is not a human life at all; it is the life of an animal. The trained and the untrained mind are perhaps in sharpest contrast at this very point. An armory of insights and convictions always ready for applications to new conditions, and invincible save by deeper insights and more rational convictions, is a mark of a trained and educated mind. The educated man has standards of truth, of human experience, and wisdom by which new proposals are judged. These standards can be gained only through reflection. The undisciplined mind is a prey to every passing fancy and the victim of every plausible doctrinaire. He has no permanent forms of judgment which give him character.

Renan was right when he held that the first condition for the development of the mind is that it shall have liberty; and liberty for the mind means freedom from the control of the unreasonable, and freedom to choose the reasonable in accordance with principle. A body of principles is a necessary possession of the educated man. His development is always with reference to his principles, and proceeds by evolution, not revolution.

Philosophy is, of course, the great single study by which the power of reflection is developed until it becomes a habit, but there is a philosophic study of literature, of politics, of natural science, which makes for the same end. The question how, whose answer is science, and the question why, whose answer is philosophy, are the beginnings of reflection. A truly educated man asks both questions continually, and as a result is habituated to reflection.

As a fourth evidence of an education I name the power of growth. There is a type of mind which, when trained to a certain point, crystallizes, as it were, and refuses to move forward thereafter. This type of mind fails to give one of the essential evidences of an education. It has perhaps acquired much and promised much; but somehow or other the promise is not fulfilled. It is not dead, but in a trance. Only such functions are performed as serve to keep it where it is; there is no movement, no development, no new power or accomplishment. The impulse to continuous study, and to that self-education which are the conditions of permanent intellectual growth, is wanting. Education has so far failed of one of its chief purposes.

A human mind continuing to grow and to develop throughout a long life is a splendid and impressive sight. It was that characteristic in Mr. Gladstone which made his personality so attractive to young and ambitious men. They were fired by his zeal and inspired by his limitless intellectual energy. To have passed from being "the rising hope of the stern and unbending Tories" in 1838 to the unchallenged leadership of the anti-Tory party in Great Britain a generation later, and to have continued to grow throughout an exceptionally long life is no mean distinction and it is an example of what, in less conspicuous ways, is the lot of every mind whose training is effective. Broadened views, widened sympathies, deepened insights are the accompaniments of growth.

For this growth a many-sided interest is necessary, and this is why growth and intellectual and moral narrowness are eternally at war. There is much in our modern education which is uneducational because it makes growth difficult, if not impossible. Early specialization, with its attendant limited range both of information and of interest, is an enemy of growth. Turning from the distasteful before it is understood is an enemy of growth. Failure to see the relation of the subject of one's special interest to other subjects is an enemy of growth. The pretense of investigation and discovery before mastering existent knowledge is an enemy of growth. The habit of cynical indifference toward men and things and of aloofness from them, sometimes supposed to be peculiarly academic, is an enemy of growth. These, then, are all to be shunned while formal education is going on, if it is to carry with it the priceless gift of an impulse to continuous growth. "Life," says Bishop Spalding in an eloquent passage, "is the unfolding of a mysterious power, which in man rises to self-consciousness, and through self-consciousness to the knowledge of a world of truth and order and love, where action may no longer be left wholly to the sway of matter or to the impulse of instinct, but may and should be controlled by reason and conscience. To further this process by deliberate and intelligent effort is to educate"—and, I add, to educate so as to sow the seed of continuous growth, intellectual and moral.

And as a fifth evidence of an education I name efficiency

—the power to do. The time has long since gone by, if it ever was, when contemplation pure and simple, withdrawal from the world and its activities, or intelligent incompetence was a defensible ideal of education. To-day the truly educated man must be, in some sense, efficient. With brain, tongue, or hand he must be able to express his knowledge, and so leave the world other than he found it. Mr. James is simply summing up what physiology and psychology both teach when he exclaims: "No reception without reaction, no impression without correlative expression—this is the great maxim which the teacher ought never to forget. An impression which simply flows in at the pupil's eyes or ears, and in no way modifies his active life, is an impression gone to waste. It is physiologically incomplete. It leaves no fruits behind it in the way of capacity acquired. Even as mere impression, it fails to produce its proper effect upon the memory; for, to remain fully among the acquisitions of the latter faculty, it must be wrought into the whole cycle of our operations. Its motor consequences are what clinch it." This is just as true of knowledge in general as of impressions. Indefinite absorption without production is fatal both to character and to the highest intellectual power. Do something and be able to do it well; express what you know in some helpful and substantial form; produce, and do not everlastingly feel only and revel in feelings—these are counsels which make for a real education and against that sham form of it which is easily recognized as well-informed incapacity. Our colleges and universities abound in false notions, notions as unscientific as they are unphilosophical, of the supposed value of knowledge, information, for its own sake. It has none. The date of the discovery of America is in itself as meaningless as the date of the birth of the youngest blade of grass in the neighboring field; it means something because it is part of a larger knowledge-whole, because it has relations, applications, uses; and for the student who sees none of these and knows none of them, America was discovered in 1249 quite as much as it was in 1492.

High efficiency is primarily an intellectual affair, and only *longo intervallo* does it take on anything approaching a mechanical form. Its mechanical form is always wholly subordinate to its springs in the intellect. It is the outgrowth of an established and habitual relationship between intellect and will, by means of which knowledge is constantly made power. For knowledge is not power, Bacon to the contrary notwithstanding, unless it is made so, and it can be made so only by him who possesses the knowledge. The habit of making knowledge power is efficiency. Without it education is incomplete.

These five characteristics, then, I offer as evidences of an education—correctness and precision in the use of the mother tongue; refined and gentle manners, which are the expression of fixed habits of thought and action; the power and habit of reflection; the power of growth; and efficiency, or the power to do. On this plane the physicist may meet with the philologian, and the naturalist with the philosopher, and each recognize the fact his fellow is an educated man, though the range of their information is widely different, and the centers of their highest interests are far apart. They are knit together in a brotherhood by the close tie of those traits which have sprung out of the reaction of their minds and wills upon that which has fed them and brought them strength. Without these traits men are not truly educated and their erudition, however vast, is of no avail; it furnishes a museum, not a developed human being.

It is these habits, of necessity made by ourselves alone, begun in the days of school and college, and strengthened with maturer years and broader experience, that serve to show to ourselves and to others that we have discovered the secret of gaining an education.

THOMAS CARLYLE

INAUGURAL ADDRESS AT EDINBURGH

This address was delivered when Carlyle was installed as Rector of Edinburgh University, April 2, 1866, and was described as a "perfect triumph" by Mrs. Carlyle. It is perhaps the most famous of all rectorial or university addresses. The veteran author was received with the greatest enthusiasm by the students, and he spoke with unwonted geniality. The address is somewhat abridged.

GENTLEMEN:—I have accepted the office you have elected me to and it is now my duty to return thanks for the great honor done me. Your enthusiasm towards me, I must admit, is in itself very beautiful, however undeserved it may be in regard to the object of it. It is a feeling honorable to all men, and one well known to myself when I was of an age like yours, nor is it yet quite gone. I can only hope that, with you too, it may endure to the end,—this noble desire to honor those whom you think worthy of honor; and that you will come to be more and more select and discriminate in the choice of the object of it:—for I can well understand that you will modify your opinions of me and of many things else, as you go on. [Laughter and cheers.] It is now fifty-six years, gone last November, since I first entered your City, a boy of not quite fourteen; to attend the classes here, and gain knowledge of all kinds, I could little guess what, my poor mind full of wonder and awe-struck expectation; and now, after a long course, this is what we have come to. [Cheers.] There is something touching and tragic, and yet at the same time beautiful, to see, as it were, the third generation of my dear old native land rising up and saying, "Well, you are not altogether an unworthy laborer in the vineyard; you have toiled through a great variety of fortunes, and have had many judges: this is our judgment of you!" As the old proverb says, "He that builds by the wayside has many masters." We must expect a variety of judges; but the voice of young Scotland, through you, is really of some value to me; and I return you many thanks for it,—though I cannot go into describing my emotions to you, and perhaps they will be much more perfectly conceivable if expressed in silence. [Cheers.]

. . . .

Meanwhile, the duty I at present have,—which might be very pleasant, but which is not quite so, for reasons you may fancy—is to address some words to you, if possible not quite useless, nor incongruous to the occasion, and on subjects more or less cognate to the pursuits you are engaged in. Accordingly, I mean to offer you some loose observations, loose in point of order, but the truest I have, in such form as they may present themselves; certain of the thoughts that are in me about the business you are here engaged in, what kind of race it is that you young gentlemen have started on, and what sort of arena you are likely to find in this world. I ought, I believe, according to custom, to have written all that down on paper, and had it read out. That would have been much handier for me at the present moment [A laugh];—but on attempting the thing, I found I was not used to writing speeches, and that I didn't get on very well. So I flung that aside; and could only resolve to trust, in all superficial respects, to the suggestion of the moment, as you now see. You will therefore have to accept what is readiest; what comes direct from the heart; and you must just take that in compensation for any good order or arrangement there might have been in it. I will endeavor to say nothing that is not true, so far as I can manage; and that is pretty much all I can engage for. [A laugh.]

Advices, I believe, to young men, as to all men, are very seldom much valued. There is a great deal of advising, and very little faithful performing; and talk that does not end in any kind of action is better suppressed altogether. I would not, therefore, go much into advising; but there is one advice I must give you. In fact, it is the summary of all advices, and doubtless you have heard it a thousand times; but I must nevertheless let you hear it the thousand-and-first time, for it is most intensely true, whether you will believe it at present or not,—namely, that above all things the interest of your whole life depends on your being *diligent,* now while it is called to-day, in this place where you have come to get education! Diligent: that includes in it all virtues that a student can have; I mean it to include all those qualities of conduct that lead on to the acquirement of real instruction and improvement in such a place. If you will believe me, you who are young, yours is the golden season of life. As you have heard it called, so it verily is, the seed-time of life; in which, if you do not sow, or if you sow tares instead of wheat, you cannot expect to reap well afterwards, and you will arrive at little. And in the course of years, when you come to look back, if you have not done what you have heard from your advisers,—and among many counselors there is wisdom,—you will bitterly repent when it is too late. The habits of study acquired at universities are of the highest importance in after-life. At the season when you are young in years, the whole mind is, as it were, fluid, and is capable of forming itself into any shape that the owner of the mind pleases to allow it, or constrain it, to form itself into. The mind is then in plastic or fluid state; but it hardens gradually, to the consistency of rock or of iron, and you cannot alter the habits of an old man: he, as he has begun, so he will proceed and go on to the last.

By diligence I mean, among other things, and very chiefly too, —honesty, in all your inquiries, and in all you are about. Pursue your studies in the way your conscience can name honest. More and more endeavor to do that. Keep, I should say for one thing, accurate separation between what you have really come to know in your minds and what is still unknown. Leave all that latter on the hypothetical side of the barrier, as things afterwards to be acquired, if acquired at all; and be careful not to admit a thing as known when you do not yet know it. Count a thing known only when it is imprinted clearly on your mind, and has become transparent to you, so that you may survey it on all sides with intelligence. There is such a thing as a man endeavoring to persuade himself, and endeavoring to persuade others, that he knows things, when he does not know more than the outside skin of them; and yet he goes flourishing about with them. [Hear, hear, and a laugh.] There is also a process called cramming, in some universities [A laugh],

—that is, getting-up such points of things as the examiner is likely to put questions about. Avoid all that, as entirely unworthy of an honorable mind. Be modest, and humble, and assiduous in your attention to what your teachers tell you, who are profoundly interested in trying to bring you forward in the right way, so far as they have been able to understand it. Try all things they set before you, in order, if possible, to understand them, and to follow and adopt them in proportion to their fitness for you. Gradually see what kind of work you individually can do; it is the first of all problems for a man to find out what kind of work he is to do in this universe. In short, morality as regards study is, as in all other things, the primary consideration, and overrules all others. A dishonest man cannot do anything real; he never will study with real fruit; and perhaps it would be greatly better if he were tied up from trying it. He does nothing but darken counsel by the words he utters. That is a very old doctrine, but a very true one; and you will find it confirmed by all the thinking men that have ever lived in this long series of generations of which we are the latest.

I daresay you know, very many of you, that it is now some seven hundred years since universities were first set-up in this world of ours. Abelard and other thinkers had arisen with doctrines in them which people wished to hear of, and students flocked towards them from all parts of the world. There was no getting the things recorded in books, as you now may. You had to hear the man speaking to you vocally, or else you could not learn at all what it was that he wanted to say. And so they gathered together, these speaking ones,—the various people who had anything to teach;—and formed themselves gradually, under the patronage of kings and other potentates who were anxious about the culture of their populations, and nobly studious of their benefit; and became a body-corporate, with high privileges, high dignities, and really high aims, under the title of a University.

Possibly too you may have heard it said that the course of centuries has changed all this; and that "the true university of our day is a collection of books." And beyond doubt, all this is greatly altered by the invention of printing, which took place about midway between us and the origin of universities. Men have not now to go in person to where a professor is actually speaking; because in most cases you can get his doctrine out of him through a book; and can then read it, and read it again and again, and study it. That is an immense change, that one fact of printed books. And I am not sure that I know of any university in which the whole of that fact has yet been completely taken in, and the studies molded in complete conformity with it. Nevertheless, universities have, and will continue to have, an indispensable value in society;— I think, a very high, and it might be, almost the highest value. They began, as is well known, with their grand aim directed on theology—their eye turned earnestly on heaven. And perhaps, in a sense, it may be still said, the very highest interests of man are virtually intrusted to them. In regard to theology, as you are aware, it has been, and especially was then, the study of the deepest heads that have come into the world,— what is the nature of this stupendous universe, and what are our relations to it, and to all things knowable by man, or known only to the great Author of man and it. Theology was once the name for all this; all this is still alive for man, however dead the name may grow! In fact, the members of the Church keeping theology in a lively condition [Laughter] for the benefit of the whole population, theology was the great object of the universities. I consider it is the same intrinsically now, though very much forgotten, from many causes, and not so successful [A laugh] as might be wished, by any manner of means!

It remains, however, practically a most important truth, what I alluded to above, that the main use of universities in the present age is that, after you have done with all your classes, the next thing is a collection of books, a great library of good books, which you proceed to study and to read. What the universities can mainly do for you,—what I have found the university did for me, is, that it taught me to read, in various languages, in various sciences; so that I could go into the books which treated of these things, and gradually penetrate into any department I wanted to make myself master of, as I found it suit me.

Well, Gentlemen, whatever you may think of these historical

points, the clearest and most imperative duty lies on every one of you to be assiduous in your reading. Learn to be good readers,—which is perhaps a more difficult thing than you imagine. Learn to be discriminative in your reading; to read faithfully, and with your best attention, all kinds of things which you have a real interest in, a real not an imaginary, and which you find to be really fit for what you are engaged in. Of course, at the present time, in a great deal of the reading incumbent on you, you must be guided by the books recommended by your professors for assistance towards the effect of their prelections. And then, when you leave the university, and go into studies of your own, you will find it very important that you have chosen a field, some province specially suited to you, in which you can study and work. The most unhappy of all men is the man who cannot tell what he is going to do, who has got no work cut-out for him in the world, and does not go into it. For work is the grand cure of all the maladies and miseries that ever beset mankind,—honest work, which you intend getting done.

If, in any vacant vague time, you are in a strait as to choice of reading,—a very good indication for you, perhaps the best you could get, is towards some book you have a great curiosity about. You are then in the readiest and best of all possible conditions to improve by that book. It is analogous to what doctors tell us about the physical health and appetites of the patient. You must learn, however, to distinguish between false appetite and true. There is such a thing as a false appetite, which will lead a man into vagaries with regard to diet; will tempt him to eat spicy things, which he should not eat at all, nor would, but that the things are toothsome, and that he is under a momentary baseness of mind. A man ought to examine and find out what he really and truly has an appetite for, what suits his constitution and condition; and that, doctors tell him, is in general the very thing he ought to have. And so with books.

As applicable to all of you, I will say that it is highly expedient to go into history; to inquire into what has passed before you on this earth, and in the family of man.

. . . .

First, however, one remark more about your reading. I do not know whether it has been sufficiently brought home to you that there are two kinds of books. When a man is reading on any kind of subject, in most departments of books,—in all books, if you take it in a wide sense,—he will find that there is a division into good books and bad books. Everywhere a good kind of book and a bad kind of book. I am not to assume that you are unacquainted, or ill acquainted, with this plain fact; but I may remind you that it is becoming a very important consideration in our day. And we have to cast aside altogether the idea people have, that if they are reading any book, that if an ignorant man is reading any book, he is doing rather better than nothing at all. I must entirely call that in question; I even venture to deny that. [Laughter and cheers.] It would be much safer and better for many a reader, that he had no concern with books at all. There is a number, a frightfully increasing number, of books that are decidedly, to the readers of them, not useful. [Hear.] But an ingenuous reader will learn, also, that a certain number of books were written by a supremely noble kind of people,—not a very great number of books, but still a number fit to occupy all your reading industry, do adhere more or less to that side of things. In short, as I have written it down somewhere else, I conceive that books are like men's souls; divided into sheep and goats. [Laughter and cheers.] Some few are going up, and carrying us up, heavenward; calculated, I mean, to be of priceless advantage in teaching,—in forwarding the teaching of all generations. Others, a frightful multitude, are going down, down; doing ever the more and the wider and the wilder mischief. Keep a strict eye on that latter class of books, my young friends!—

And for the rest, in regard to all your studies and readings, here, and to whatever you may learn, you are to remember that the object is not particular knowledges,—not that of getting higher and higher in technical perfections, and all that sort of thing. There is a higher aim lying at the rear of all that, especially among those who are intended for literary or speaking pursuits, or the sacred profession. You are ever to bear in mind that there lies behind that the acquisition of what may be called wisdom;—namely, sound appreciation and just decision as to all the objects that come round you, and the habit of behaving with justice, candor, clear insight, and loyal adherence to fact. Great is wisdom; infinite is the value of wisdom. It cannot be exaggerated; it is the highest achievement of man: "Blessed is he that getteth understanding." And that, I believe, on occasion, may be missed very easily; never more easily than now, I sometimes think. If that is a failure, all is failure!—However, I will not touch further upon the matter.

But I should have said, in regard to book-reading, if it be so very important, how very useful would an excellent library be in every university! I hope that will not be neglected by the gentlemen who have charge of you; and, indeed, I am happy to hear that your library is very much improved since the time I knew it, and I hope it will go on improving more and more. Nay, I have sometimes thought, why should not there be a library in every county town, for benefit of those that could read well, and might if permitted? True, you require money to accomplish that;—and withal, what perhaps is still less attainable at present, you require judgment in the selectors of books; real insight into what is for the advantage of human souls, the exclusion of all kinds of clap-trap books which merely excite the astonishment of foolish people [Laughter], and the choice of wise books, as much as possible of good books. Let us hope the future will be kind to us in this respect.

In this university, as I learn from many sides, there is considerable stir about endowments; an assiduous and praiseworthy industry for getting new funds collected to encourage the ingenuous youth of universities, especially of this our chief university. [Hear, hear.] Well, I entirely participate in everybody's approval of the movement. It is very desirable. It should be responded to, and one surely expects it will. At least, if it is not, it will be shameful to the country of Scotland, which never was so rich in money as at the present moment, and never stood so much in need of getting noble universities, and institutions to counteract many influences that are springing up alongside of money. It should not be slack in coming forward in the way of endowments [A laugh]; at any rate, to the extent of rivaling our rude old barbarous ancestors, as we have been pleased to call them. Such munificence as theirs is beyond all praise; and to them, I am sorry to say, we are not yet by any manner of means equal, or approaching equality. [Laughter.] There is an abundance and over-abundance of money. Sometimes I cannot help thinking that probably never has there been, at any other time, in Scotland, the hundredth part of the money that now is, or even the thousandth part. For wherever I go, there is that same gold-nuggeting [A laugh],—that "unexampled prosperity," and men counting their balances by the million sterling. Money was never so abundant, and nothing that is good to be done with it. [Hear, hear, and a laugh.] No man knows,—or very few men know,—what benefit to get out of his money. In fact, it too often is secretly a curse to him. Much better for him never to have had any. But I do not expect that generally to be believed. [Laughter.] Nevertheless, I should think it would be a beneficent relief to many a rich man who has an honest purpose struggling in him, to bequeath some house of refuge, so to speak, for the gifted poor man who may hereafter be born into the world, to enable him to get on his way a little. To do, in fact, as those old Norman kings whom I have been describing; to raise some noble poor man out of the dirt and mud, where he is getting trampled on unworthily by the unworthy, into some kind of position where he might acquire the power to do a little good in his generation! I hope that as much as possible will be achieved in this direction; and that efforts will not be relaxed till the thing is in a satisfactory state. In regard to the classical department, above all, it surely is to be desired by us that it were properly supported,—that we could allow the fit people to have their scholarships and subventions, and devote more leisure to the cultivation of particular departments. We might have more of this from Scotch universities than we have; and I hope we shall.

I am bound, however, to say that it does not appear as if, of late times, endowment were the real soul of the matter. The English, for example, are the richest people in the world for endowments in their universities; and it is an evident fact that, since the time of Bentley, you cannot name anybody that has gained a European name in scholarship, or constituted a point of revolution in the pursuits of men in that way. The man who does so is a man worthy of being remembered; and he is poor, and not an Englishman. One man that actually did constitute a revolution was the son of a poor weaver in Saxony: who edited his Tibullus, in Dresden, in a poor comrade's garret, with the floor for his bed, and two folios for pillow; and who, while editing his Tibullus, had to gather peasecods on the streets and boil them for his dinner. That was his endowment. [Laughter.] But he was recognized soon to have done a great thing. His name was Heyne. [Cheers.]

I can remember, it was quite a revolution in my mind when I got hold of that man's edition of Virgil. I found that, for the first time, I understood Virgil; that Heyne had introduced me, for the first time, into an insight of Roman life and ways of thought; had pointed out the circumstances in which these works were written, and given me their interpretation. And the process has gone on in all manner of developments, and has spread out into other countries.

On the whole, there is one reason why endowments are not given now as they were in old days, when men founded abbeys, colleges, and all kinds of things of that description, with such success as we know. All that has now changed; a vast decay of zeal in that direction. And truly the reason may in part be, that people have become doubtful whether colleges are now the real sources of what I called wisdom; whether they are anything more, anything much more, than a cultivating of man in the specific arts. In fact, there has been in the world a suspicion of that kind for a long time. [A laugh.] There goes a proverb of old date, "An ounce of mother-wit is worth a pound of clergy." [Laughter.] There is a suspicion that a man is perhaps not nearly so wise as he looks, or because he has poured out speech so copiously. [Laughter.] When "the seven free arts," which the old universities were based on, came to be modified a little, in order to be convenient for the wants of modern society,—though perhaps some of them are obsolete enough even yet for some of us,—there arose a feeling that mere vocality, mere culture of speech, if that is what comes out of a man, is not the synonym of wisdom by any means. That a man may be a "great speaker," as eloquent as you like, and but little real substance in him,—especially, if that is what was required and aimed at by the man himself, and by the community that set him upon becoming a learned man. Maid-servants, I hear people complaining, are getting instructed in the "ologies," and are apparently becoming more and more ignorant of brewing, boiling, and baking [Laughter]; and above all, are not taught what is necessary to be known, from the highest of us to the lowest,—faithful obedience, modesty, humility, and correct moral conduct.

Oh, it is a dismal chapter all that, if one went into it,—what has been done by rushing after fine speeches! I have written down some very fierce things about that, perhaps considerably more emphatic than I could now wish them to be; but they were and are deeply my conviction. [Hear, hear.] There is very great necessity indeed of getting a little more silent than we are. It seems to me as if the finest nations of the earth,—the English and the American, in chief,—were going all off into wind and tongue. [Applause and laughter.] But it will appear sufficiently tragical by and by, long after I am away out of it. There is a time to speak, and a time to be silent. Silence withal is the eternal duty of a man. He won't get to any real understanding of what is complex, and what is more than aught else pertinent to his interests, without keeping silence too. "Watch the tongue," is a very old precept, and a most true one.

I don't want to discourage any of you from your Demosthenes, and your studies of the niceties of language, and all that. Believe me, I value that as much as any one of you. I consider it a very graceful thing, and a most proper, for every human creature to know what the implement which he uses in communicating his thoughts is, and how to make the very utmost of it. I want you to study Demosthenes, and to know all his excellences. At the same time, I must say that speech, in the case even of Demosthenes, does not seem, on the whole, to have turned to almost any good account. He advised next to nothing that proved practicable; much of the reverse. Why tell me that a man is a fine speaker, if it is not the truth that he is speaking? Phocion, who mostly did not speak at all, was a great deal nearer hitting the mark than Demosthenes. [Laughter.] He used to tell the Athenians, "You can't fight Philip. Better if you don't provoke him, as Demosthenes is always urging you to do. You have not the slightest chance with Philip. He is a man who holds his tongue; he has great disciplined armies; a full treasury; can bribe anybody you like in your cities here; he is going on steadily with an unvarying aim towards his object; while you, with your idle clamorings, with your Cleon the Tanner spouting to you what you take for wisdom—! Philip will infallibly beat any set of men such as you, going on raging from shore to shore with all that rampant nonsense." Demosthenes said to him once, "Phocion, you will drive the Athenians mad some day, and they will kill you." "Yes," Phocion answered, "me, when they go mad; and as soon as they get sane again, you!" [Laughter and applause.]

It is also told of him how he went once to Messene, on some deputation which the Athenians wanted him to head, on some kind of matter of an intricate and contentious nature: Phocion went accordingly; and had, as usual, a clear story to have told for himself and his case. He was a man of few words, but all of them true and to the point. And so he had gone on telling his story for a while, when there arose some interruption. One man, interrupting with something, he tried to answer; then another, the like; till finally, too many went in, and all began arguing and bawling in endless debate. Whereupon Phocion struck down his staff; drew back altogether, and would speak no other word to any man. It appears to me there is a kind of eloquence in that rap of Phocion's staff which is equal to anything Demosthenes ever said: "Take your own way, then; I go out of it altogether." [Applause.]

Such considerations, and manifold more connected with them,—innumerable considerations, resulting from observation of the world at this epoch,—have led various people to doubt of the salutary effect of vocal education altogether. I do not mean to say it should be entirely excluded; but I look to something that will take hold of the matter much more closely, and not allow it to slip out of our fingers, and remain worse than it was. For, if a "good speaker," never so eloquent, does not see into the fact, and is not speaking the truth of that, but the untruth and the mistake of that,—is there a more horrid kind of object in creation? Of such speech I hear all manner of people say, "How excellent!" Well really, it is not the speech, but the things spoken, that I am anxious about! I really care very little how the man said it, provided I understand him, and it be true. Excellent speaker? But what if he is telling me things that are contrary to the fact; what if he has formed a wrong judgment about the fact,—if he has in his mind (like Phocion's friend, Cleon the Tanner) no power to form a right judgment in regard to the matter? An excellent speaker of that kind is, as it were, saying, "Ho, every one that wants to be persuaded of the thing that is not true; here is the man for you!" I recommend you to be very chary of that kind of excellent speech.

Well, all that sad stuff being a too well-known product of our method of vocal education,—the teacher merely operating on the tongue of the pupil, and teaching him to wag it in a particular way [Laughter],—it has made various thinking men entertain a distrust of this not very salutary way of procedure; and they have longed for some less theoretic, and more practical and concrete way of working-out the problems of education; —in effect, for an education not vocal at all, but mute except where speaking was strictly needful. There would be room for a great deal of description about this, if I went into it; but I must content myself with saying that the most remarkable piece of writing on it is in a book of Goethe's,—the whole of which you may be recommended to take up, and try if you can study it with understanding. It is one of his last books; written when he was an old man about seventy years of age: I think, one of the most beautiful he ever wrote; full of meek wisdom, of intellect and piety; which is found to be strangely illuminative, and very touching, by those who have eyes to discern and hearts to feel it. This about education is one of the pieces in "Wilhelm Meister's Travels"; or rather, in a fitful way, it forms the whole gist of the book. I first read it many years ago; and, of course, I had to read into the very heart of it while I was translating it [Applause]; and it has ever since dwelt in my mind as perhaps the most remarkable bit of writing which I have known to be executed in these late centuries. I have often said that there are some ten pages of that, which, if ambition had been my only rule, I would rather have written, been able to write, than have written all the books that have appeared since I came into the world. Deep, deep is the meaning of what is said there. Those pages turn on the Christian religion, and the religious phenomena and ancient world: altogether sketched out in the most aërial, graceful, delicately wise kind of way, so as to keep himself out of the common controversies of the street and of the forum, yet to indicate what was the result of things he had been long meditating upon.

. . . .

The highest outcome, and most precious of all the fruits that are to spring from this ideal mode of educating, is what Goethe calls Art:—of which I could at present give no definition that would make it clear to you, unless it were clearer already than is likely. [A laugh.] Goethe calls it music, painting, poetry: but it is in quite a higher sense than the common one; and a sense in which, I am afraid, most of our painters, poets and music-men would not pass muster. [A laugh.] He considers this as the highest pitch to which human culture can go; infinitely valuable and ennobling; and he watches with great industry how it is to be brought about in the men who have a turn for it. Very wise and beautiful his notion of the matter is. It gives one an idea that something far better and higher, something as high as ever, and indubitably true too, is still possible for man in this world.—And that is all I can say to you of Goethe's fine theorem of mute education.

I confess it seems to me there is in it a shadow of what will one day be; will and must, unless the world is to come to a conclusion that is altogether frightful: some kind of scheme of education analogous to that; presided over by the wisest and most sacred men that can be got in the world, and watching from a distance; a training in practicality at every turn; no speech in it except speech that is to be followed by action, for that ought to be the rule as nearly as possible among men. Not very often or much, rather rarely, should a man speak at all, unless it is for the sake of something that is to be done; this spoken, let him go and do his part in it, and say no more about it.

I will only add, that it is possible,—all this fine theorem of Goethe's, or something similar! Consider what we have already; and what "difficulties" we have overcome. I should say there is nothing in the world you can conceive so difficult, *prima facie,* as that of getting a set of men gathered together as soldiers. Rough, rude, ignorant, disobedient people; you gather them together, promise them a shilling a day; rank them up, give them very severe and sharp drill; and by bullying and drilling and compelling (the word *drilling,* if you go to the original, means "beating," "steadily *tormenting*" to the due pitch), they do learn what it is necessary to learn; and there is your man in red coat, a trained soldier; piece of an animated machine incomparably the most potent in this world; a wonder of wonders to look at. He will go where bidden; obeys one man, will walk into the cannon's mouth for him; does punctually whatever is commanded by his general officer. And, I believe, all manner of things of this kind could be accomplished, if there were the same attention bestowed. Very many things could be regimented, organized into this mute system;—and perhaps in some of the mechanical, commercial and manufacturing departments some faint incipiences may be attempted before very long. For the saving of human labor, and the avoidance of human misery, the effects would be incalculable, were it set about and begun even in part.

Alas, it is painful to think how very far away it all is, any real fulfillment of such things! For I need not hide from you, young Gentlemen,—and it is one of the last things I am going to tell you,—that you have got into a very troublous epoch of the world; and I don't think you will find your path in it to be smoother than ours has been, though you have many advantages which we had not. You have careers open to you, by public examinations and so on, which is a thing much to be approved of, and which we hope to see perfected more and more. All that was entirely unknown in my time, and you have many things to recognize as advantages. But you will find the ways of the world, I think, more anarchical than ever. Look where one will, revolution has come upon us. We have got into the age of revolutions. All kinds of things are coming to be subjected to fire, as it were: hotter and hotter blows the element round everything. Curious to see how, in Oxford and other places that used to seem as lying at anchor in the stream of time, regardless of all changes, they are getting into the highest humor of mutation, and all sorts of new ideas are afloat. It is evident that whatever is not inconsumable, made of *asbestos,* will have to be burnt, in this world. Nothing other will stand the heat it is getting exposed to.

And in saying that, I am but saying in other words that we are in an epoch of anarchy. Anarchy *plus* a constable! [Laughter.] There is nobody that picks one's pocket without some policeman being ready to take him up. [Renewed laughter.] But in every other point, man is becoming more and more the son, not of Cosmos, but of Chaos. He is a disobedient, discontented, reckless and altogether waste kind of object (the commonplace man is, in these epochs); and the wiser kind of man,—the select few, of whom I hope you will be part, —has more and more to see to this, to look vigilantly forward; and will require to move with double wisdom. Will find, in short, that the crooked things he has got to pull straight in his own life all round him, wherever he may go, are manifold, and will task all his strength, however great it be.

But why should I complain of that either? For that is the thing a man is born to, in all epochs. He is born to expend every particle of strength that God Almighty has given him, in doing the work he finds he is fit for; to stand up to it to the last breath of life, and do his best. We are called upon to do that; and the reward we all get,—which we are perfectly sure of if we have merited it—is that we have got the work done, or at least that we have tried to do the work. For that is a great blessing in itself; and I should say, there is not very much more reward than that going in this world. If the man gets meat and clothes, what matters it whether he buys those necessaries with seven thousand a year, or with seven million, could that be, or with seventy pounds a year? He can get meat and clothes for that; and he will find intrinsically, if he is a wise man, wonderfully little real difference. [Laughter.]

On the whole, avoid what is called ambition; that is not a fine principle to go upon,—and it has in it all degrees of *vulgarity,* if that is a consideration. "Seekest thou great things, seek them not:" I warmly second that advice of the wisest of men. Don't be ambitious; don't too much need success; be loyal and modest. Cut down the proud towering thoughts that get into you, or see that they be pure as well as high. There is a nobler ambition than the gaining of all California would be, or the getting of all the suffrages that are on the planet now.

Finally, Gentlemen, I have one advice to give you, which is practically of very great importance, though a very humble one. In the midst of your zeal and ardor,—for such, I foresee, will rise high enough, in spite of all the counsels to moderate it that I can give you,—remember the care of health. I have no doubt you have among you young souls ardently bent to consider life cheap, for the purpose of getting forward in what they are aiming at on high; but you are to consider throughout, much more than is done at present, and what it would have been a very great thing for me if I had been able to consider, that health is a thing to be attended to continually; that you are to regard that as the very highest of all temporal things for you. There is no kind of achievement you could make in the world that is equal to perfect health. What to it are nuggets and millions? The French financier said, "Why is there no sleep to be sold!" Sleep was not in the market at any quotation.

It is a curious thing, which I remarked long ago, and have often turned in my head, that the old word for "holy" in the Teutonic languages, *heilig,* also means "healthy." Thus *Heilbronn* means indifferently "holy-well" or "health-well." We have in the Scotch, too, "hale," and its derivatives; and, I suppose, our English word "whole" (with a "w"), all of one piece, without any *hole* in it, is the same word. I find that you could not get any better definition of what "holy" really is than "healthy." Completely healthy; *mens sana in corpore sano.* [Applause.] A man all lucid, and in equilibrium. His intellect a clear mirror geometrically plane, brilliantly sensitive to all objects and impressions made on it, and imaging all things in their correct proportions; not twisted up into convex and concave, and distorting everything, so that he cannot see the truth of the matter without endless grouping and manipulation: healthy, clear and free, and discerning truly all round him. We never can attain that at all. In fact the operations we have got into are destructive of it. You cannot, if you are going to do any decisive intellectual operation that will last a long while; if, for instance, you are going to write a book, —you cannot manage it (at least, I never could) without getting decidedly made ill by it; and really one nevertheless must; if it is your business, you are obliged to follow out what you are at, and to do it, if even at the expense of health. Only remember, at all times, to get back as fast as possible out of it into health; and regard that as the real equilibrium and center of things. You should always look at the *heilig,* which means "holy" as well as "healthy."

And that old etymology,—what a lesson it is against certain gloomy, austere, ascetic people, who have gone about as if this world were all a dismal prison-house! It has indeed got all the ugly things in it which I have been alluding to; but there is an eternal sky over it, and the blessed sunshine, the green of prophetic spring, and rich *harvests* coming,—all this is in it too. Piety does not mean that a man should make a sour face about things, and refuse to enjoy wisely what his Maker has given. Neither do you find it to have been so with the best sort,—with old Knox, in particular. No; if you look into Knox, you will find a beautiful Scotch humor in him, as well as the grimmest and sternest truth when necessary, and a great deal of laughter. We find really some of the sunniest glimpses of things come out of Knox that I have seen in any man; for instance, in his "History of the Reformation,"—which is a book I hope every one of you will read, a glorious old book.

On the whole, I would bid you stand up to your work, whatever it may be, and not be afraid of it; not in sorrows or contradictions to yield, but to push on towards the goal. And don't suppose that people are hostile to you or have you at ill-will, in the world. In general, you will rarely find anybody designedly doing you ill. You may feel often as if the whole world were obstructing you, setting itself against you: but you will find that to mean only, that the world is traveling in a different way from you, and, rushing on in its own path, heedlessly treads on you. That is mostly all: to you no specific ill-will;—only each has an extremely good-will to himself, which he has a right to have, and is rushing on towards his object. Keep out of literature, I should say also, as a general rule [Laughter],—though that is by the bye. If you find many people who are hard and indifferent to you, in a world which you consider to be inhospitable and cruel, as often indeed happens to a tenderhearted, striving young creature, you will also find there are noble hearts who will look kindly on you; and their help will be precious to you beyond price. You will get good and evil as you go on, and have the success that has been appointed you.

I will wind up with a small bit of verse, which is from Goethe also, and has often gone through my mind. To me it has something of a modern psalm in it, in some measure. It is deep as the foundations, deep and high, and it is true and clear:—no clearer man, or nobler and grander intellect has lived in the world, I believe, since Shakespeare left it. This is what the poet sings;—a kind of road-melody or marching music of mankind:

> The Future hides in it
> Gladness and sorrow;
> We press still thorow,
> Nought that abides in it
> Daunting us,—onward.
>
> And solemn before us,
> Veiled, the dark Portal;
> Goal of all mortal:—
> Stars silent rest o'er us,
> Graves under us silent!
>
> While earnest thou gazest,
> Comes boding of terror,
> Comes phantasm and error;
> Perplexes the bravest
> With doubt and misgiving.
>
> But heard are the Voices,
> Heard are the Sages,
> The Worlds and the Ages:
> "Choose well; your choice is
> Brief, and yet endless.
>
> Here eyes do regard you,
> In Eternity's stillness;
> Here is all fullness,
> Ye brave, to reward you;
> Work, and despair not."

Work, and despair not: *Wir heissen euch hoffen,* "We bid you be of hope!"—let that be my last word. Gentlemen, I thank you for your great patience in hearing me; and, with many most kind wishes, say adieu for this time.

JOHN JAY CHAPMAN

THE UNITY OF HUMAN NATURE

Address by John Jay Chapman, lawyer and essayist (born in New York City, March 2, 1862), delivered before the Hobart Chapter of the Phi Beta Kappa Society, at Hobart College, Geneva, N. Y., on Commencement Day, June 20, 1900.

If one could stand on the edge of the moon and look down through a couple of thousand years on human politics, it would be apparent that everything that happened on the earth is directly dependent on everything else that happened there. Whether the Italian peasant shall eat salt with his bread, depends upon Bismarck. Whether the prison system in Russia shall be improved, depends upon the ministry of Great Britain. If Lord Beaconsfield is in power, there is no leisure in Russia for domestic reform. The lash is everywhere lifted in a security furnished by the concurrence of all the influences upon the globe that favor coercion. In like manner, the good things that happen are each the product of all extant conditions. Constitutional government in England qualifies the whole of Western Europe. Our slaves were not set free without the assistance of every liberal mind in Europe; and the thoughts which we think in our closet affect the fate of the Boer in South Africa. That Tolstoi is to-day living unmolested upon his farm instead of serving in a Siberian mine, that Dreyfus is alive and not dead, is due directly to the people of this audience and to others like them scattered over Europe and America.

The effect of enlightenment on tyranny is not merely to make the tyrant afraid to be cruel, it makes him not want to be cruel. It makes him see what cruelty is. And reciprocally the effect of cruelty on enlightenment is to make that enlightenment grow dim. It prevents men from seeing what cruelty is.

THE UNITY OF HUMAN NATURE 103

The subtle influences that modern nations exert over one another illustrate the unity of life on the globe. But if we turn to ancient history we find in its bare outlines staggering proof of the interdependence of nations. The Greeks were wiped out. They could not escape their contemporaries any more than we can escape the existence of the Malays. Israel could not escape Assyria, nor Assyria Persia, nor Persia Macedon, nor Macedon Rome, nor Rome the Goths. Life is not a boarding-school where a bad boy can be dismissed for the benefit of the rest. He remains. He must be dealt with. He is as much here as ourselves. The whole of Europe and Asia and South America and every Malay and every Chinaman, Hindoo, Tartar and Tagal—of such is our civilization.

Let us for the moment put aside every dictate of religion and political philosophy. Let us discard all prejudice and all love. Let us regard nothing except facts. Does not the coldest conclusion of science announce the fact that the world is peopled, and that every individual of that population has an influence upon the conduct of all the rest, an influence as certain and far more discoverable than the influence of the weight of his body upon the solar system?

A Chinaman lands in San Francisco. The Constitution of the United States begins to rock and tremble. What shall we do with him? The deepest minds of the past must be ransacked to the bottom to find an answer. Every one of seventy-million Americans must pass through a throe of thought that leaves him a modified man. The same thing is true when the American lands in China. These creatures have thus begun to think of each other. It is unimaginable that they should not hereafter incessantly and never-endingly continue to think of each other. Out of their thoughts grows the destiny of mankind.

We have an inherited and stupid notion that the East does not change. If Japan goes through a transformation scene under our eyes, we still hold to our prejudice as to the immutability of the Chinese. If our own people and the European nations seem to be meeting and surging and reappearing in unaccustomed rôles every ten years, till modern history looks like a fancy ball, we still go on muttering some old ignorant shibboleth about East and West, Magna Charta, the Indian mutiny, and Mahomet. The chances are that England will be dead-letter, and Russia progressive, before we have done talking. Of a truth, when we consider the rapidity of visible change and the amplitude of time,—for there is plenty of time,—we need not despair of progress.

The true starting-point for the world's progress will never be reached by any nation as a whole. It exists and has been reached in the past as it will in the future by individuals scattered here and there in every nation. It is reached by those minds which insist on seeing conditions as they are, and which cannot confine their thoughts to their own kitchen, or to their own creed, or to their own nation. You will think I have in mind poets and philosophers, for these men take humanity as their subject and deal in the general stuff of human nature. But the narrow spirit in which they often do this cuts down their influence to parish limits. I mean rather those men who in private life act out their thoughts and feelings as to the unity of human life; those same thoughts which the poets and philosophers have expressed in their plays, their sayings, and their visions. There have always been men who in their daily life have fulfilled those intimations and instincts which, if reduced to a statement, receive the names of poetry and religion. These men are the cart-horses of progress, they devote their lives to doing things which can only be justified or explained by the highest philosophy. They proceed as if all men were their brothers. These practical philanthropists go plodding on through each century and leave the bones of their character mingled with the soil of their civilization.

See how large the labors of such men look when seen in historic perspective. They have changed the world's public opinion. They have molded the world's institutions into forms expressive of their will. I ask your attention to one of their achievements. We have one province of conduct in which the visions of the poets have been reduced to practice,—yes erected into a department of government,—through the labors of the philanthropists. They have established the hospital and the reformatory and these visible bastions of philosophy hold now a more unchallenged place in our civilization than the Sermon on the Mount on which they comment.

THE UNITY OF HUMAN NATURE

The truth which the philanthropists of all ages have felt, is that the human family was a unit—and this truth being as deep as human nature, can be expressed in every philosophy—even in the inverted utilitarianism now in vogue. The problem how to treat insane people and criminals has been solved to this extent, that every one agrees that nothing must be done to them which injures the survivors. That is the reason we do not kill them. It is unpleasant to have them about, and this unpleasantness can be cured only by our devotion to them. We must either help the wretched or we ourselves become degenerate. They have thus become a positive means of civilizing the modern world, for the instinct of self-preservation has led men to deal with this problem in the only practical way.

The appeal of physical suffering makes the strongest attack on our common humanity. Even zealots and sectaries are touched. The practice and custom of this kind of mercy have therefore become established, while other kinds of mercy which require more imagination are still in their infancy. But at the bottom of every fight for principle you will find the same sentiment of mercy. If you take a slate and pencil and follow out the precise reasons and consequences of the thing, you will always find that a practical and effective love for mankind is working out a practical betterment of human conditions through a practical self-sacrifice. The average man cannot do the sum, he does not follow the reasoning, but he knows the answer. The deed strikes into his soul with a mathematical impact and he responds like a tuning-fork when its note is struck.

Every one knows that self-sacrifice is a virtue. The child takes his nourishment from the tale of heroism as naturally as he takes milk. He feels that the deed was done for his sake. He adopts it; it is his own. The nations have always stolen their myths from one another and claimed each other's heroes. It has required all the world's heroes to make the world's ear sensitive to new statements, illustrations and applications of the logic of progress. Yet their work has been so well done that all of us respond to the old truths in however new a form. Not France alone but all modern society owes a debt of gratitude to Zola for his rescue of Dreyfus. The whole world would have been degraded and set back, the whole world made less decent and habitable but for those few Frenchmen who took their stand against corruption.

Now the future of civil society upon the earth depends upon the application to international politics of this familiar idea, which we see prefigured in our mythology, and monumentalized in our hospitals—the principle that what is done for one is done for all. When you say a thing is "right," you appeal to mankind. What you mean is that every one is at stake. Your attack upon wrong amounts to saying that some one has been left out in the calculation. Both at home and abroad you are always pleading for mercy, and the plea gains such a wide response that some tyranny begins to totter, and its engines are turned upon you to get you to stop. This outcry against you is the pressure of your effectiveness. If you imitate Zola and attack some nuisance in this town to-morrow you will bring on every symptom and have every experience of the Dreyfus affair. The cost is the same, for cold looks are worse than imprisonment. The emancipation is the same, for if a man can resist the influences of his townsfolk, if he can cut free from the tyranny of neighborhood gossip, the world has no terrors for him; there is no second inquisition. The influence is the same, for every citizen can thereafter look a town officer in the face with more self-respect. But not to townsmen, nor to neighboring towns, nor to Parisians is this force confined. It goes out in all directions, continuously. The man is in communication with the world. This impulse of communication with all men is at the bottom of every ambition. The injustice, cruelty, oppression in the world are all different forms of the same non-conductor, that prevents utterances, that stops messages, that strikes dumb the speaker and deafens the listener. You will find that it makes no difference whether the non-conductor be a selfish oligarchy, a military autocracy, or a commercial ring. The voice of humanity is stifled by corruption: and corruption is only an evil because it stifles men.

Try to raise a voice that shall be heard from here to Albany and watch what it is that comes forward to shut off the sound. It is not a German sergeant, nor a Russian officer of the precinct. It is a note from a friend of your father's offering you

THE UNITY OF HUMAN NATURE

a place in his office. This is your warning from the secret police. Why, if any of you young gentlemen have a mind to get heard a mile off, you must make a bonfire of your reputation, and a close enemy of most men who wish you well.

And what will you get in return? Well, if I must for the benefit of the economists, charge you up with selfish gain, I will say that you get the satisfaction of having been heard, and that this is the whole possible scope of human ambition.

When I was asked to make this address I wondered what I had to say to you boys who are graduating. And I think I have one thing to say. If you wish to be useful, never take a course that will silence you. Refuse to learn anything that you cannot proclaim. Refuse to accept anything that implies collusion, whether it be a clerkship or a curacy, a legal fee or a post in a university. Retain the power of speech, no matter what other power you lose. If you can, take this course, and in so far as you take it, you will bless this country. In so far as you depart from this course you become dampers, mutes, and hooded executioners. As for your own private character it will be preserved by such a course. Crime you cannot commit, for crime gags you. Collusion gags you. As a practical matter a mere failure to speak out upon occasions where no opinion is asked or expected of you, and when the utterance of an uncalled-for suspicion is odious, will often hold you to a concurrence in palpable iniquity. It will bind and gag you and lay you dumb and in shackles like the veriest serf in Russia. I gave you this one rule of conduct. Do what you will, but speak out always. Be shunned, be hated, be ridiculed, be scared, be in doubt, but don't be gagged.

The choice of Hercules was made when Hercules was a lad. It cannot be made late in life. It will perhaps come for each one of you within the next eighteen months. I have seen ten years of young men who rush out into the world with messages and when they find how deaf the world is, they think they must save their strength and get quietly up on some little eminence from which they can make themselves heard. "In a few years," reasons one of them, "I shall have gained a standing, and then I shall use my power for good." Next year comes, and with it a strange discovery. The man has lost his horizon of thought. His ambition has evaporated; he has nothing to say. The great occasion that was to have let him loose on society was some little occasion that nobody saw, some moment in which he decided to obtain a standing. The great battle of a lifetime has been fought and lost over a silent scruple. But for this, the man might, within a few years, have spoken to the nation with the voice of an archangel. What was he waiting for? Did he think that the laws of nature were to be changed for him? Did he think that a "notice of trial" would be served on him? Or that some spirit would stand at his elbow and say, "Now's your time?" The time of trial is always. Now is the appointed time. And the compensation for beginning at once is that your voice carries at once. You do not need a standing. It would not help you. Within less time than you can see it, you will have been heard. The air is filled with sounding-boards and the echoes are flying. It is ten to one that you have but to lift your voice to be heard in California, and that from where you stand. A bold plunge will teach you that the visions of the unity of human nature which the poets have sung were not fictions of their imagination, but a record of what they saw. Deal with the world, and you will discover their reality. Speak to the world, and you will hear their echo.

Social and business prominence look like advantages, and so they are if you want money. But if you want moral influence you may bless God you have not got them. They are the payment with which the world subsidizes men to keep quiet, and there is no subtlety or cunning by which you can get them without paying in silence. This is the great law of humanity, that has existed since history began, and will last while man lasts—evil, selfishness, and silence are one thing.

The world is learning, largely through American experience, that freedom in the form of a government is no guarantee against abuse, tyranny, cruelty, and greed. The old sufferings, the old passions are in full blast among us. What, then, are the advantages of self-government? The chief advantage is that self-government enables a man in his youth, in his own town, within the radius of his first public interests, to fight the important battle of his life while his powers are at their strongest, and the powers of oppression are at their weakest. If a man acquires the power of speech here, if he says what he means now, if he makes his point and dominates his surroundings at once, his voice will, as a matter of fact, be heard instantly in a very wide radius. And so he walks up into a new sphere and begins to accomplish great things. He does this through the very force of his insistence on the importance of small things. The reason for his graduation is not far to seek. A man cannot reach the hearts of his townsfolk, without using the whole apparatus of the world of thought. He cannot tell or act the truth in his own town without enlisting every power for truth, and setting in vibration the cords that knit that town into the world's history. He is forced to find and strike the same note which he would use on some great occasion when speaking for all mankind. A man who has won a town-fight is a veteran, and the country is full of these young men. Tomorrow their force will show in national politics, and in that moment the fate of the Malay, the civilization of South Africa and the future of Japan will be seen to have been in issue. I think it likely that the next thirty years will reveal the recuperative power of American institutions. One of you young men might easily become a reform President, and be carried into office and held in office by the force of that private opinion which is now being sown broadcast throughout the country by just such men as yourselves. You will concede the utility of such a President. Yet it would not be the man but the masses behind him that did his work.

Democracy thus lets character loose upon society and shows us that in the realm of natural law there is nothing either small or great; and this is the chief value of democracy. In America the young man meets the struggle between good and evil in the easiest form in which it was ever laid before men. The cruelties of interest and of custom have with us no artificial assistance from caste, creed, race prejudice. Our frame of government is drawn in close accordance with the laws of nature. By our documents we are dedicated to mankind: and hence it is that we can so easily feel the pulse of the world and lay our hand on the thriving organism of humanity.

EUGENE V. DEBS

ON RECEIVING SENTENCE

The following speech was made by Eugene Debs upon receiving sentence for a term in prison for obstructing the draft. For forty years preceding his conviction he had been active in Socialist agitation and was five times the nominee of the Socialist party for President. His prison sentence was finally commuted by President Harding. Mr. Debs died on October 20, 1926. His speech in court reveals both his emotional power on the platform and the sincerity of his personality.

Your Honor, years ago I recognized my kinship with all living beings, and I made up my mind that I was not one bit better than the meanest of earth. I said then, I say now, that while there is a lower class, I am in it; while there is a criminal element, I am of it; while there is a soul in prison, I am not free. . . .

If the law under which I have been convicted is a good law, then there is no reason why sentence should not be pronounced upon me. I listened to all that was said in this court in support and justification of this law, but my mind remains unchanged. I look upon it as a despotic enactment in flagrant conflict with democratic principles and with the spirit of free institutions.

Your Honor, I have stated in this court that I am opposed to the form of our present Government; that I am opposed to the social system in which we live; that I believed in the change of both—but by perfectly peaceable and orderly means.

Let me call your attention to the fact this morning that in this system five per cent of our people own and control two-thirds of our wealth; sixty-five per cent of the people, embracing the working class who produce all wealth, have but five per cent to show for it.

Standing here this morning, I recall my boyhood. At fourteen, I went to work in the railroad shops; at sixteen, I was firing a freight engine on a railroad. I remember all the hardships, all the privations, of that earlier day, and from that time until now, my heart has been with the working class. I could have been in Congress long ago. I have preferred to go to prison. The choice has been deliberately made. I could not have done otherwise. I have no regret.

In the struggle—the unceasing struggle—between the toilers and producers and their exploiters, I have tried, as best I might, to serve those among whom I was born, with whom I expect to share my lot until the end of my days.

I am thinking this morning of the men in the mills and factories; I am thinking of the women who, for a paltry wage, are compelled to work out their lives; of the little children who, in this system, are robbed of their childhood, and in their early, tender years, are seized in the remorseless grasp of mammon, and forced into the industrial dungeons, there to feed the machines while they themselves are being starved body and soul. I can see them dwarfed, diseased, stunted, their little lives broken, and their hopes blasted, because in this high noon of our twentieth century civilization money is still so much more important than human life. Gold is god and rules in the affairs of men. The little girls, and there are a million of them in this country—this, the most favored land beneath the bending skies, a land in which we have vast areas of rich and fertile soil, material resources in inexhaustible abundance, the most marvelous productive machinery on earth, millions of eager workers ready to apply their labor to that machinery to produce an abundance for every man, woman and child—and if there are still many millions of our people who are the victims of poverty, whose life is a ceaseless struggle all the way from youth to age, until at last death comes to their rescue and stills the aching heart, and lulls the victim to dreamless sleep, it is not the fault of the Almighty, it can't be charged to nature; it is due entirely to an outgrown social system that ought to be abolished, not only in the interest of the working class, but in a higher interest of all humanity.

I think of these little children—the girls that are in the

textile mills of all description in the east, in the cotton factories of the south—I think of them at work in a vitiated atmosphere, I think of them at work when they ought to be at play or at school, I think that when they do grow up, if they live long enough to approach the marriage state, they are unfit for it. Their nerves are worn out, their tissue is exhausted, their vitality is spent. They have been fed to industry. Their lives have been coined into gold. Their offspring are born tired. That is why there are so many failures in our modern life.

Your Honor, the five per cent of the people that I have made reference to constitute that element that absolutely rules our country. They privately own all our public necessities. They wear no crowns; they wield no scepters; they sit upon no thrones; and yet they are our economic masters and our political rulers. They control this Government and all of its institutions. They control the courts.

And, your Honor, if you will permit me, I wish to make just one correction. It was stated here that I had charged that all federal judges are crooks. The charge is absolutely untrue. I did say that all federal judges are appointed through the influence and power of the capitalist class and not the working class. If that statement is not true, I am more than willing to retract it.

The five per cent of our people who own and control all of the sources of wealth, all of the nation's industries, all of the means of our common life—it is they who declare war; it is they who make peace; it is they who control our destiny. And so long as this is true, we can make no just claim to being a democratic Government—a self-governing people.

I believe, Your Honor, in common with all Socialists, that this nation ought to own and control its industries. I believe, as all Socialists do, that all things that are jointly needed and used ought to be jointly owned—that industry, the basis of life, instead of being the private property of the few and operated for their enrichment, ought to be the common property of all, democratically administered in the interest of all.

John D. Rockefeller has to-day an income of sixty million dollars a year, five million dollars a month, two hundred thousand dollars a day. He does not produce a penny of it. I make no attack upon Mr. Rockefeller personally. I do not in the least dislike him. If he were in need, and it were in my power to serve him, I should serve him as gladly as I would any other human being. I have no quarrel with Mr. Rockefeller personally, nor with any other capitalist. I am simply opposing a social order in which it is possible for one man who does absolutely nothing that is useful, to amass a fortune of hundreds of millions of dollars, while millions of men and women who work all of the days of their lives secure barely enough for existence.

This order of things cannot always endure. I have registered my protest against it. I recognize the feebleness of my effort, but fortunately I am not alone. There are multiplied thousands of others who, like myself, have come to realize that before we may truly enjoy the blessings of civilized life, we must reorganize society upon a mutual and coöperative basis; and to this end we have organized a great economic and political movement that is spread over the face of all the earth.

There are to-day upwards of sixty million Socialists, loyal, devoted adherents to this cause, regardless of nationality, race, creed, color or sex. They are all making common cause. They are all spreading the propaganda of the new social order. They are waiting, watching and working through all the weary hours of the day and night. They are still in the minority. They have learned how to be patient and abide their time. They feel—they know, indeed—that the time is coming in spite of all opposition, all persecution, when this emancipating gospel will spread among all the peoples, and when this minority will become the triumphant majority and, sweeping into power, inaugurate the greatest change in history.

In that day we will have the universal commonwealth—not the destruction of the nation, but, on the contrary, the harmonious coöperation of every nation with every other nation on earth. In that day war will curse this earth no more.

I have been accused, your Honor, of being an enemy of the soldier. I hope I am laying no flattering unction to my soul when I say that I don't believe the soldier has a more sympathetic friend than I am. If I had my way there would be no soldiers. But I realize the sacrifice they are making, your

Honor. I can think of them. I can feel for them. I can sympathize with them. That is one of the reasons why I have been doing what little has been in my power to bring about a condition of affairs in this country worthy of the sacrifices they have made and that they are now making in its behalf.

Your Honor, in a local paper yesterday there was some editorial exultation about my prospective imprisonment. I do not resent it in the least. I can understand it perfectly. In the same paper there appears an editorial this morning that has in it a hint of the wrong to which I have been trying to call attention. [Reading] "A Senator of the United States receives a salary of $7,500—$45,000 for the six years for which he is elected. One of the candidates for Senator from a state adjoining Ohio is reported to have spent through his committee $150,000 to secure the nomination. For advertising he spent $35,000; for printing $30,000; for traveling expenses, $10,000, and the rest in ways known to political managers."

The theory is that public office is as open to a poor man as to a rich man. One may easily imagine, however, how slight a chance one of ordinary resources would have in a contest against this man who was willing to spend more than three times his six years' salary merely to secure a nomination. Were these conditions to hold in every state, the Senate would soon become again what it was once held to be—a rich man's club.

Campaign expenditures have been the subject of much restrictive legislation in recent years, but it has not always reached the mark. The authors of primary reform have accomplished some of the things they set out to do, but they have not yet taken the bank roll out of politics.

They never *will* take it out of politics, they never *can* take it out of politics, in this system.

Your Honor, I wish to make acknowledgment of my thanks to the counsel for the defense. They have not only defended me with exceptional legal ability, but with a personal attachment and devotion of which I am deeply sensible, and which I can never forget.

Your Honor, I ask no mercy. I plead for no immunity. I realize that finally the right must prevail. I never more clearly comprehended than now the great struggle between the powers of greed on the one hand and upon the other the rising hosts of freedom.

I can see the dawn of a better day of humanity. The people are awakening. In due course of time they will come to their own.

When the mariner, sailing over tropic seas, looks for relief from his weary watch, he turns his eyes toward the Southern Cross, burning luridly above the tempest-tossed ocean. As the midnight approaches, the Southern Cross begins to bend, and the whirling worlds change their places, and with starry finger-points the Almighty marks the passage of time upon the dial of the universe, and though no bell may beat the glad tidings, the lookout knows that the midnight is passing—that relief and rest are close at hand.

Let the people take heart and hope everywhere, for the cross is bending, the midnight is passing, and joy cometh with the morning. . . .

Your Honor, I thank you, and I thank all of this court for their courtesy, for their kindness, which I shall remember always.

I am prepared to receive your sentence.

HENRY DRUMMOND

"FIRST!"

Address by Henry Drummond, author and clergyman (born in Stirling, Scotland, August 17, 1851; died in Tunbridge Wells, England, March 11, 1897), delivered to the members of the Boys' Brigade, in the City Hall, Glasgow, Scotland, on a Sunday afternoon. It is a good example of Drummond's simplicity and effectiveness, in treating practical subjects, and especially before a juvenile audience. Before beginning the address, he requested the boys to read in unison this passage from the sixth chapter of Matthew: "But seek ye first the kingdom of God and His righteousness, and all these things shall be added unto you."

I HAVE three heads to give you. The first is "Geography," the second is "Arithmetic," and the third is "Grammar."

First. Geography tells us where to find places. Where is the kingdom of God? It is said that often, when a Prussian officer was killed in the Franco-Prussian war, a map of France was found in his pocket. When we wish to occupy a country, we ought to know its geography. Now, where is the kingdom of God? A boy over there says, "It is in heaven." No; it is not in heaven. Another boy says, "It is in the Bible." No; it is not in the Bible. Another boy says, "It must be in the Church." No; it is not in the Church. Heaven is only the *capital* of the kingdom of God; the Bible is the Guide-book to it; the Church is the weekly Parade of those who belong to it. If you would turn to the seventeenth chapter of St. Luke you will find out where the kingdom of God really is. "The kingdom of God is within you"—*within* you. The kingdom of God is *inside people*.

I remember once taking a walk by the river near where the Falls of Niagara are, and I noticed a remarkable figure walking along the river bank. I had been some time in America. I had seen black men, and red men, and yellow men, and white men; black men, the Negroes; red men, the Indians; yellow men, the Chinese; white men, the Americans. But this man looked quite different in his dress from anything I had ever seen. When he came a little closer, I saw he was wearing a kilt; when he came a little nearer still, I saw that he was dressed exactly like a Highland soldier. When he came quite near, I said to him, "What are you doing here?" "Why should I not be here?" he said. "Don't you know this is British soil? When you cross the river you come into Canada." This soldier was thousands of miles from England, and yet he was in the kingdom of England. Wherever there is an English heart beating loyal to the Queen of Britain, there is England. Wherever there is a boy whose heart is loyal to the King of the kingdom of God, the kingdom of God is within him.

What is the kingdom of God? Every kingdom has its exports, its products. Go down to the river here, and you will find ships coming in with cotton; you know they come from America. You will find ships with tea; you know they are from China. Ships with wool; you know they come from Australia. Ships with sugar; you know they come from Java. What comes from the kingdom of God? Again we must refer to our Guide-book. Turn to Romans, and we shall find what the kingdom of God is. I will read it: "The kingdom of God is righteousness, peace, joy"—three things. "The kingdom of God is righteousness, peace, joy." Righteousness, of course, is just doing what is right. Any boy who does what is right has the kingdom of God within him. Any boy who, instead of being quarrelsome, lives at peace with the other boys, has the kingdom of God within him. Any boy whose heart is filled with joy because he does what is right, has the kingdom of God within him. The kingdom of God is not going to religious meetings, and hearing strange religious experiences: the kingdom of God is doing what is right—living at peace with all men, being filled with joy in the Holy Ghost.

Boys, if you are going to be Christians, be Christians as boys, and not as your grandmothers. A grandmother has to be a Christian as a grandmother, and that is the right and the beauful thing for her; but if you cannot read your Bible by the hour as your grandmother can, or delight in meetings as she can, don't think you are necessarily a bad boy. When you are your grandmother's age you will have your grandmother's kind of religion. Meantime, be a Christian as a boy. Live a boy's life. Do the straight thing; seek the kingdom of righteousness and honor and truth. Keep the peace with the boys about you, and be filled with the joy of being a loyal, and simple, and natural, and boy-like servant of Christ.

You can very easily tell a house, or a workshop, or an office where the kingdom of God is *not*. The first thing you see in that place is that the "straight thing" is not always done. Customers do not get fair play. You are in danger of learning to cheat and to lie. Better, a thousand times, to starve than to stay in a place where you cannot do what is right.

Or, when you go into your workshop, you find everybody sulky, touchy, and ill-tempered, everybody at daggers drawn with everybody else: some of the men not on speaking terms with some of the others, and the whole *feel* of the place miserable and unhappy. The kingdom of God is not there, for *it* is peace. It is the kingdom of the Devil that is anger and wrath and malice.

If you want to get the kingdom of God into your workshop, or into your home, let the quarreling be stopped. Live in peace and harmony and brotherliness with every one. For the kingdom of God is a kingdom of brothers. It is a great society, founded by Jesus Christ, of all the people who try to be like Him, and live to make the world better and sweeter and happier. Wherever a boy is trying to do that, in the house or in the street, in the workshop or on the baseball field, there is the kingdom of God. And every boy, however small or obscure or poor, who is seeking that, is a member of it. You see now, I hope, what the kingdom is.

I pass, therefore, to the second head: What was it? "Arithmetic." Are there any arithmetic words in this text? "Added," says one boy. Quite right, *added*. What other arithmetic word? "First." Yes, *first*—"first," "added." Now, don't you think you could not have anything better to seek "first" than the things I have named—to do what is right, to live at peace, and be always making those about you happy? You see at once why Christ tells us to seek these things first—because they are the best worth seeking. Do you know anything better than these three things, anything happier, purer, nobler? If you do, seek them first. But if you do not, seek first the kingdom of God. I am not here this afternoon to tell you to be religious. You know that. I am not here to tell you to seek the kingdom of God. I have come to tell you to seek the kingdom of God *first*. First. Not many people do that. They put a little religion into their life—once a week, perhaps. They might just as well let it alone. It is not worth seeking the kingdom of God unless we seek it *first*. Suppose you take the helm out of a ship and hang it over the bow, and send that ship to sea, will it ever reach the other side? Certainly not. It will drift about anyhow. Keep religion in its place, and it will take you straight through life, and straight to your Father in heaven when life is over. But if you do not put it in its place, you may just as well have nothing to do with it. Religion out of its place in a human life is the most miserable thing in the world. There is nothing that requires so much to be kept in its place as religion, and its place is what? Second? Third? "First." Boys, carry that home with you to-day—*first* the kingdom of God. Make it so that it will be natural to you to think about that the very first thing.

There was a boy in Glasgow apprenticed to a gentleman who made telegraphs. One day this boy was up on the top of a four-story house with a number of men fixing up a telegraph-wire. It was getting late, and the men said they were going away home, and the boy was to nip off the ends of the wire himself. Before going down they told him to be sure to go back to the workshop, when he was finished, with his master's tools. "Do not leave any of them lying about, whatever you do," said the foreman. The boy climbed up the pole and began to nip off the ends of the wire. It was a very cold winter night and the dusk was gathering. He lost his hold and fell upon the slates, slid down, and then over and over to the ground below. A clothes-rope caught him on the chest and broke his fall; but the shock was terrible, and he lay unconscious among some clothes. An old woman came out; seeing her rope broken and the clothes all soiled, thought the boy was drunk, shook him, scolded him, and went for a policeman. And the boy came back to consciousness, rubbed his eyes, and got upon his feet. What do you think he did? He staggered, half blind, away up the stairs. He climbed the ladder. He got up on to the roof of the house. He gathered up his tools, put them into his basket, took them down, and when he got to the ground again, fainted away. Just then the policeman came, saw there was something seriously wrong, and carried him away to the hospital. I am glad to say he got better. What was his first thought at that terrible moment? His duty. He was not thinking of himself; he was thinking about his master. First, the kingdom of God.

But there is another arithmetic word. What is it? "Added." There is not one boy here who does not know the difference between addition and subtraction. Now, that is a very important difference in religion, because—and it is a very strange thing—very few people know the difference when they begin to talk about religion. They often tell boys that if they seek the kingdom of God, everything else is going to be subtracted from them. They tell them that they are going to become gloomy, miserable, and will lose everything that makes a boy's life worth living—that they will have to stop baseball and story-books, and become little old men, and spend all their time in going to meetings and singing hymns. Now, that is not true. Christ never said anything like that. Christ says we are to "seek first the kingdom of God," and everything else worth having is to be added unto us. If there is anything I would like you to take away with you this afternoon, it is these two arithmetic words, "first" and "added." I do not mean by added that if you become religious you are all going to become rich. Here is a boy, who, in sweeping out the shop to-morrow morning, finds sixpence lying among the orange-boxes. Well, nobody has missed it. He puts it in his pocket, and it begins to burn a hole there. By breakfast-time he wishes that sixpence were in his master's pocket. And by and by he goes to his master. He says (to himself, and not to his master), "I was at the Boys' Brigade yesterday, and I was to seek *first* that which was right." Then he says to his master, "Please, sir, here is sixpence that I found upon the floor." The master puts it in the till. What has the boy got in his pocket? Nothing; but he has got the kingdom of God in his heart. He has laid up treasure in heaven, which is of infinitely more worth than sixpence. Now, that boy does not find a shilling on his way home. I have known that happen, but that is not what is meant by "adding." It does not mean that God is going to pay him in his own coin, for He pays in better coin.

Yet I remember once hearing of a boy who was paid in both ways. He was very, very poor. He lived in a foreign country, and his mother said to him one day that he must go into the great city and start in business, and she took his coat and cut it open and sewed between the lining and the coat forty golden dinars, which she had saved up for many years to start him in life. She told him to take care of robbers as he went across the desert; and as he was going out of the door she said: "My boy, I have only two words for you—'Fear God, and never tell a lie.'" The boy started off, and toward evening he saw glittering in the distance the minarets of the great city, but between the city and himself he saw a cloud of dust; it came nearer; presently he saw that it was a band of robbers. One of the robbers left the rest and rode toward him, and said: "Boy, what have you got?" And the boy looked him in the face and said. "I have forty golden dinars sewed up in my coat." And the robber laughed and wheeled round his horse and went away back. He would not believe the boy. Presently another robber came, and he said. "Boy, what have you got?" "Forty golden dinars sewed up in my coat." The robber said: "The boy is a fool," and wheeled his horse and rode away back. By and by the robber captain came, and he said: "Boy, what have you got?" "I have forty golden dinars sewed up in my coat." And the robber dismounted and put his hand over the boy's breast, felt something round, counted one, two, three, four, five, till he counted out the forty golden coins. He looked the boy in the face and said: "Why did you tell me that?" The boy said: "Because of God and my mother." And the robber leaned on his spear and thought, and said: "Wait a moment." He mounted his horse, rode back to the rest of the robbers, and came back in about five minutes with his dress changed. This time he looked not like a robber, but like a merchant. He took the boy up on his horse and said: "My boy, I have long wanted to do something for my God and for my mother, and I have this moment renounced my robber's life. I am also a merchant. I have a large business house in the city. I want you to come and live with me, to teach me about your God; and you will be rich, and your mother some day will come and live with us." And it all happened. By seeking first the kingdom of God, all these things are added unto him.

Boys, banish forever from your minds the idea that religion is *subtraction*. It does not tell us to give things up, but rather gives us something so much better that they give themselves up. When you see a boy on the street whipping a top, you know, perhaps, that you could not make that boy happier than by giving him a top, a whip, and half an hour to whip it. But next birthday, when he looks back, he says, "What a goose I was last year to be delighted with a top; what I want now is a baseball bat." Then when he becomes an old man he does not care in the least for a baseball bat—he wants rest, and a snug fireside, and a newspaper every day. He wonders how he could ever have taken up his thoughts with baseball bats and whipping tops. Now, when a boy becomes a Christian, he grows out of the evil things one by one—that is to say, if they are really evil—which he used to set his heart upon (of course I do not mean baseball bats, for they are not evils); and so instead of telling people to give up things, we are safer to tell them to "seek first the kingdom of God," and then they will get new things and better things, and the old things will drop off of themselves. This is what is meant by the "new heart." It means that God puts into us new thoughts and new wishes, and we become quite different boys.

Lastly, and very shortly. What was the third head? "Grammar." Right: Grammar. Now, I require a clever boy to answer the next question. What is the verb? "Seek." Very good: "Seek." What mood is it in? "Imperative mood." What does that mean? "Command." You boys of the Boys' Brigade know what commands are. What is the soldier's first lesson? "Obedience." Have you obeyed this command? Remember the imperative mood of these words. "Seek first the kingdom of God." This is the command of your King. It *must* be done. I have been trying to show you what a splendid thing it is; what a reasonable thing it is; what a happy thing it is; but beyond all these reasons it is a thing that must be done, because we are commanded to do it by our Captain. It is one of the finest things about the Boys' Brigade that it always appeals to Christ as its highest Officer, and takes its commands from Him. Now, there is His command to seek *first* the kingdom of God. Have you done it? "Well," I know some boys will say, "we are going to have a good time, enjoy life, and then we are going to seek—*last*—the kingdom of God." Now that is mean; it is nothing else than mean for a boy to take all the good gifts that God has given him, and then give him nothing back in return but his wasted life.

God wants boys' lives, not only their souls. It is for active service soldiers are drilled and trained and fed and armed. That is why you and I are in the world at all—to serve God actively in it *now*. It is monstrous and shameful and cowardly to talk of seeking the kingdom last. Every hour a kingdom is coming in your heart, in your home, in the world near you, be it a kingdom of darkness or a kingdom of light. You are placed where you are, in a particular business, in a particular street, to help on there the kingdom of God. You cannot do that when you are old and ready to die.

Very few people have the opportunity to seek the kingdom of God at the end. Christ, knowing all that, knowing that religion was a thing for our life, not merely for our deathbed, has laid this command upon us now: "Seek *first* the kingdom of God." I am going to leave you with this text itself. Every Brigade boy in the world should obey it.

Boys, before you go to work to-morrow, before you go to sleep to-night, before you go to Sunday-school this afternoon, before you go out of the door of the City Hall, resolve that, God helping you, you are going to seek *first* the kingdom of God.

Perhaps some boys here are deserters; they began once before to serve Christ, and they deserted. Come back again, come back again to-day. Others have never enlisted at all. Will you not do it now? You are old enough to decide. And the grandest moment of a boy's life is that moment when he decides to *seek first the kingdom of God.*

EDWARD EGGLESTON

THE NEW HISTORY

Address by Edward Eggleston, editor, author (born in Vevay, Ind., December 10, 1837), delivered at his inauguration as President of the American Historical Association, held in Boston, December, 1900. For the twenty years since this address was given, it has been regarded by many young historians as a sort of creed and gospel, and its influence to-day is probably as great as ever.

MEMBERS OF THE AMERICAN HISTORICAL ASSOCIATION, FELLOW STUDENTS OF HISTORY:—I thank you to-night for your preference in choosing me to the Presidency of the Historical Association. It is one of the honors of my life. I remember hearing Mr. Lowell apologize for reading an address—he had been accustomed to speak off-hand. He said, "I have suffered a loss of the memory of names. It is the first falling of the leaves of memory." I, who have been wont to speak without notes for more than forty years, must come here to-night with Lowell's beautiful apology on my lips. Since a little more than a year ago my memory cannot be depended on for names, and I too am forced to plead "the first falling of the leaves of memory."

Let me begin without further introduction. Let me speak the things of my heart. Let me bring myself along with me, as Wendell Phillips said at Harvard. I propose to speak to you mainly of the New History.

All our learning takes its rise from Greece. No other superstition has held so long as the classic. For five hundred years nearly every historical writer has felt it necessary to touch his cap in a preface to Herodotus and Thucydides. They are certainly models of style, no one contradicting. A man like myself, on whose Greek the rust of thirty-five years has fallen, may be permitted to shelter himself behind so great a Grecian as Professor Jebb. In the following keen words he makes retrenchments on Thucydides: "It is a natural subject of regret, though not a just cause of surprise or complaint, that the history [of Thucydides] tells us nothing of the literature, the art, or the social life under whose influences the author had grown up." ... "Among the illustrious contemporaries," says Jebb, "whose very existence would be unknown to us from his pages were the dramatists Æschylus, Sophocles, Euripides, Aristophanes; the architect Ictinus; the sculptor Phidias; the physician Hippocrates; the philosophers Anaxagoras and Socrates." ... "If Thucydides had mentioned Sophocles," continued he, "as a general in the Samian war, it may be doubted whether he would have noticed the circumstance that Sophocles also wrote dramas, unless it had been for the purpose of distinguishing him from a namesake." Jebb qualifies his statement by urging that Thucydides sought to do only one thing, to write the history of the Peloponnesian war without permitting the intrusion of anything else. But Thucydides must have had the notion that war was the most important thing in the world and that all the art and eloquence of his time were, as he calls them, merely "recreations of the human spirit." Add to this that nearly one-fourth of Thucydides' history is made up of speeches imitated from the epic poets and that most of them were the work of the author. His history is a splendid piece of literature, but it is not a model for a modern writer.

The reductions on Herodotus are essential. His credulity alone is an impairment to his character as a historian. Neither from Herodotus nor from Thucydides can we learn to write history in the modern sense. Their histories will remain, as Thucydides said of his, "a possession forever." But it would be strange if we had not learned anything of the art of writing history in a cycle of nearly twenty-four hundred years. Let us brush aside once for all the domination of the classic tradition.

Let us come to English letters. One of our early examples is one of our best. In English literature Sir Walter Raleigh is in a sense both Herodotus and Thucydides and something more, as became a modern. The title of his fragment, "The History of the World," repels many people, but it were well if his incomparable work were not neglected. What is most admirable in it is its keen modern interest in the little details of life which are a part of what I call the New History. Occasionally it rises into the grandest style. As an instance of felicitous detail, how there lingers in the memory his treatment of the coracle, the little boat made of a bull's hide stretched over a frame! He seizes on a passage of Lucan's and renders it exquisitely and almost literally:—

> The moistened osier of a hoary willow,
>   Is fashioned first into a little boat,
> Then clad in bullock's hide, upon the billow
>   Of a proud river lightly doth it float
> Beneath the waterman.
> So on the waves of overswelling Po
> Rides the Venetian, and the Briton so
> On the outspread ocean.

I have seen in use on the western bays of Ireland the same little boat, there called not the coracle, but a curragh—the original form of the word, no doubt. It was usually occupied by a priest being rowed from island to island to hear confessions. The bull's hide had gone out and a stout canvas had taken its place. But the veritable bull's hide boat of Lucan was in use in our Southern colonies down to the Revolution, and this classic mode of conveyance is yet seen on the Western frontier.

Another instance of Raleigh's delightful particularity is seen in his caution about misunderstanding the speech of savages. All who have seen the ancient maps of North Carolina will remember Win-gin-da-coa as its name. This was the first thing said by a savage to Raleigh's men. In reply to the question, "What is the name of this country?" he answered "Win-gin-da-coa." It was afterward learned that the North Carolina aborigine said in this phrase, "Those are very fine clothes you have on." And so North Carolina carried a fashion-plate label to unsuspecting readers. With such little incidents Raleigh diversifies his history, and with great passages like his apostrophe to Death he carries it to its loftiest climaxes.

Its eloquent by-passages of one kind and another remain to fructify the imagination of later ages.

Never was a falser thing said than that history is dead politics and politics living history. Some things are false and some things are perniciously false. This is one of the latter kind. In this saying Freeman expressed his whole theory of history-writing, and one understands the point of Green's remark to him: "Freeman, you are neither social, literary, nor religious." A worse condemnation of a historian could hardly be made. Politics is the superficial struggle of human ambitions crossed occasionally, but rarely, by a sincere desire to do good. History must take account of politics, as of everything else, but let it remember that politics is in its very nature bold and encroaching, a part of the fierce struggle for existence—a part of the fierce striving for power which is so unlovely. It often sails under false colors and it will deceive the historian unless he is exceedingly vigilant. It likes to call itself patriotism. Lincoln, all ready to carry through a great measure by means that were doubtful—this one an office, that one something else—looked at the work of his hands with disgust. "Hay," he said to his private secretary, "what we call patriotic statesmanship is nothing but a combination of individual meannesses for the general good."

There is doubtless some admixture of real patriotism in politics. But what is patriotism? It is a virtue of the half-developed. Higher than tribal instinct and lower than that great world benevolence that is to be the mark of coming ages. Of all countries in the world we need to be cured of politics. We elect everything from a township trustee to the President of the United States. Every man, if he were an intelligent voter, under our system would be required to canvass every year the merits of whole yards of aspirants for petty office. Why not elect one in a city, a State, and the nation, and leave him to study the yards of aspirants and to appoint?

Buckle's famous and much controverted principle that the origin of all movements is to be sought in the people and not in the leader is as true as it is false. Now and then a movement gets head, it has no apparent leader or it gains one who carries it safely to its goal. Such was the American Revolution. Look for its origin among the people. But many agitations go hither and thither until a leader arises, changes the character of the movement and carries it off another way. Such was the French Revolution. Its beginning gave no hint of its end; it gave no hint of any possible end, indeed. But a Corsican general, of ability unparalleled among military men and an ambition overflowing all bounds, arrested the mob in the streets of Paris and taught it to obey. From the moment that the young Bonaparte had cowed the mob the Revolution was not. Bonaparte dallied with its forms for a while: he would not check it too soon, but he steadily turned it in directions for his own glory. Its original ends were all lost sight of, and that most remarkable movement of modern times, that most aimless and senseless movement, shaking and overturning the thrones of Europe, went where it would without any regulating principle but the will—the capricious will—of a single man. Strangely enough, I may remark in passing, that agitation sowed broadcast over Europe certain actions that have proved and are yet proving fatal to despotism.

History must treat military affairs. War is essentially exciting. Bodies of men are seen in violent movement. Life and death hang upon a hair-trigger, they are in the quick decision and the prompt action. The world looks on and applauds. It is a cock-fight. It is a bull-fight. It is the struggle of the gladiator. It is all of these raised to the hundredth power. But the scene has been so often repeated; the subject has become trite. Man is such a savage that until the lifetime of the present generation he has insisted on settling everything by the gauge of battle. He has strewn the world with a thousand battle-fields. He has strewn these battle-fields with thousands of horses and men, with the hopes and fears of men and women and the fate of little children. What a brute is man! What a hero is man! But the brute age and the age of heroism in the contest with the brute must pass. We cannot always cover our pages with gore. It is the object of history to cultivate this out of man, to teach him the wisdom of diplomacy, the wisdom of avoidance, in short, the fine wisdom of arbitration, that last fruit of human experience.

But how can we treat war so as not to become on the one hand sensational or on the other hand trite? Cannot some philosophy be got out of it? All human progress is interesting, even that of the art of destruction. In all the past the distribution of the arts of living has depended largely upon war. Sometimes there came in a lucky piece of bigotry, like the revocation of the Edict of Nantes, to scatter widely the arts. Oftener war, with its attendant displacements of population, has served this end. In our day emigration and the diffusion of intelligence and a hundred other agencies do the work better, except among barbarians, where every war with a civilized nation brings the good and the evil of civilization to the conquered. Education and greater facilities for intemperance, for example.

The buyer of rare books, whether for historic purposes or other, once in a long time finds a treasure. Such was my lot a few years ago. From the Earl of Westmoreland's library I purchased among other books a little manuscript. It was a complete treatment of the private soldier's duty, written in what is called the secretary's hand. It is not legible except to those trained to read it, withal very beautiful. It was written by some one for Charles I when he was Prince of Wales to make him a competent officer. The date is fixed by an allusion to Charles' romantic trip to Spain. What this little book tells I cannot find anywhere else. Its information was drawn from the Dutch, who were the teachers of the English in so many ways. It is very minute and it almost always quotes Prince Maurice. An army was set forth in that day by solid squares of spearmen surrounded by a few scattering musketeers. The latter were obliged to set on the ground a little forked rest to sustain the weight of the musket—to fire they stooped down and took aim. The musketeers were, according to my manuscript, the poorest soldiers, the main dependence was upon the spearmen. Gunpowder was used thus awkwardly. But, says my writer, Prince Maurice told me that if he had another army to set forth he would reverse the order and put the best soldiers to the musket. It is precisely the point at which gunpowder became the main dependence. The ordinary spear was eighteen feet long, or three times the height of the man, and from one inch to an inch and a half in thickness. The iron jaws of the head were two feet and a half in length.

With such spears the Massachusetts militia was trained for more than forty years, or until the outbreak of Philip's war.

I do not know how long they may have been used in Virginia. Poking Indians armed with muskets out of a swamp with a spear might do for imaginary warfare—for militia warfare—but when it came to real fighting it was very ugly business. The desperate character of the conflicts with Philip and the necessity for the exclusive use of gunpowder became apparent, and the edict went forth that the militia, who were trained to the use of the spear, should take up the musket. With this edict the spear disappeared in this country forever. It went out in England about the same time. Thus do we learn the progress of the human mind in arts of destruction.

In this little book one may learn something of the action of the "forlorn hope." Etymologists have thought that they have tracked this term to the Dutch *verloonen hoop*—lost troop. My little manuscript gives no direct evidence of this, and yet it confirms the theory. For everywhere in it the forlorn hope is called the "perdu"—the lost.

A great deal has been said of late about the use of history in secondary education. A hundred times more history, and what passes for history, is learned in the secondary schools than anywhere else. The celebrated report of the Committee of Ten, a few years ago, was particularly judicious. The errors of the old school-books are repeated from one to another, but they are not usually capital. The great mistake is the misapprehension of the purpose of history. The object of teaching history is narrowly said to be to make good citizens—intelligent voters. In this calculation the girls are left out. The main object of teaching history is to make good men and women, cultivated and broad men and women. A great cry is made by the school-book agents on the importance of having the Constitution in the back of the text-book. Few children of fourteen can understand this legal document. I wonder how many of their elders have ever read the Constitution through attentively. The State of Tennessee will not allow the use of any history that does not include the Constitution. Triumphant politics! The Constitution is there. A schoolboy in Brooklyn was asked: "What is the Constitution of the United States?" He replied: "It is that part in small print in the back of the books that nobody reads."

Some years ago, having an invalid to amuse, I picked up at random a great folio, one of twenty-six that profess to give the history of the world. The volume was a history of Portugal. It was written in an animated style and served my purpose very well. There were weddings, battles, embassies, peace and war, all springing out of the ground with marvelous spontaneity. It reminded me of a fairy story of the olden times in which everything took place without any adequate cause. I read it day after day and forgot it almost as fast as I read it. There was not a word about the people, their manners or customs. Even the manners and customs of the court of Portugal were entirely ignored. It was history hung in the air. It was, indeed, history written after the manner of the early eighteenth century.

According to John Stuart Mill, we owe it to Sir Walter Scott that change in history-writing took place. Scott first related that there were Saxons and Normans living alongside of one another in England—neighbors but most unneighborly—for generations after the Conquest. Why did not the historians tells us so much? Certain French historians—Augustin Thierry and his group—first took the hint from Scott, and in the "Conquest of England" and the "Third Estate" of Thierry and in other writings of the time told the history of the people. Michelet, who labored almost to our time, was one of these. They wrote and men read with delight. The Germans took it up in their heavy way, generally writing one theil on politics and one theil on *cultur-geschichte*. Perhaps of all the peoples those who speak English have been the slowest to introduce the New History.

A few years after the French, and with a French impulse no doubt, Macaulay began to write. His style was brilliant, balanced, antithetical. Shall we say it was too antithetical? Let us remember that he wrote in the first half of the nineteenth century. Macaulay's famous third chapter came to interrupt the course of the history. It had all been brilliant, but if it needed anything to make its fortune Chapter III did it. It begins with taxes and revenues; the customs and revenue lists of the princes are much elaborated and are not very interesting. But by degrees he draws near to manners and he draws near to London. The picture of old London, turned over and over in his mind in those long walks Macaulay is said to have made through every street of the metropolis, is a wonderful piece of history. It is worth the whole history beside. And nobody ever dreamed before that such a subject was in the province of history. I have lately read it over and it excites my wonder again. It is so particular, so minute, so extraordinary. Occasionally he stops to remark on the shortcomings of other histories: "Readers who take an interest in the progress of civilization and of the useful arts will be grateful to the humble topographer who has recorded these facts, and will perhaps wish that historians of far higher pretensions had sometimes spared a few pages from military evolutions and political intrigues for the purpose of letting us know how the parlors and bed-chambers of our ancestors looked." It would be better if he had not done this. But it shows how conscious he was that he was attempting the new. It is the fashion to discredit Macaulay's history—every history goes through a period when its disadvantages of time have come to be appreciated, when it is antiquated without being ancient. But for the faithful use of authority, for the brilliant putting in of particulars, Macaulay remains what a German critic recently called him, the greatest historical writer of the nineteenth century. Time will come when we shall date from Macaulay: English history will never be written just as it was before. He was partisan. It is an unforgivable offense in our time. Macaulay's Puritans, "lank-haired" men who discussed election and reprobation through "their noses," are mere creatures of prejudice and burlesque figures, not, to our generation, funny. But it can be forgiven to one who says so many good things.

Green is not to be omitted. He is not an authority on facts. No man can treat history for a long period, as Green did, without depending on the authority of others. Green put himself into his history. The narrow critic calls it "at least literature." It is literature of a high kind. It is a high and warm nature judging the events of English history. This is why Green's "Shorter History" must remain his great work. Not history in one sense; ten times more history than history itself in another. A philanthropic clergyman, lover of his race to begin with, he gradually outgrew all his doctrinal predilections, until at length there was only the philanthropic impulse left. From this point, and not at all from the theological, he judged all religious life. What is it worth to men and what has it accomplished? He greets the barefoot friar, the Lollard, the Puritan, and the primitive Methodist with the same question. He treats them all as of beneficent origin.

Let us pass by Gardiner, great and in some respects unparalleled historian that he is. He writes with the day of doom in mind, and the crack of doom will be here before the end of his piece. The writings of a more popular, if less able, man must take precedence of Gardiner's. Lecky comes the nearest to realizing the true all-round history. His "History of England in the Eighteenth Century" is in parts exceedingly eloquent and strong. I think I shall find myself on one point at difference with the body of American scholars. Lecky is not satisfactory on the American Revolution. A man cannot embrace two countries. At least no one except De Tocqueville and Bryce has done so. Lecky complains that the Revolution was merely a quarrel about money. What were most of the great struggles of history? About money. What is money? It is bread for women and children. It is liberty. It is power. It is everything that a man wants. Incomparable Burke pointed out that the whole commerce of America had grown up under a system of smuggling and violation of customs laws made abroad. The attempt to suppress this was an attempt to put down trade entirely—to reduce the colonies to gaunt famine.

No man can judge America in the eighteenth century without taking her circumstances into account. Even in little things Lecky fails to understand us—he says Americans invented a new punishment of riding a man on an iron bar. He means riding on a rail, and only a few years before a man had died in the process in London. For the state of America he depends on Washington's letters—letters written always to procure appropriations. But America aside, his "England," and especially his "Ireland," in the eighteenth century, are very great books. Leave the American Revolution to be written by one who understands it and knows what it was.

I remember the enjoyment with which I discovered that Hilliard had inserted here and there a little paragraph on manners. Hilliard used only printed authorities, he was dry, he did not make a lasting history. His touches of folk history are his best work. Bancroft labored long, he labored learnedly. But he has repelled more young people from the study of history than all other influences in America. Nearly twenty years ago I sat at Mr. Parkman's table one Sunday and he remarked with that sweet candor which was characteristic: "I cannot read Bancroft." I replied: "Mr. Parkman, if you had not said it, I should not have dared to say so; but I cannot read Bancroft." A cultivated lady at the table said, "If you gentlemen say that, what is the ground of his great reputation?" We answered simultaneously, "His great knowledge." He knew nearly everything a historian ought to know except culture history. He never conceived of the seventeenth century man as living before science. And one other difficulty he had. He was a politician or, if you please, a statesman. He was a diplomatist. He could not speak candidly. "I hold my hand full," he said, "I open my little finger. The American people cannot stand more." Mr. Bancroft held in his hand a lot of disagreeables. He knew, for instance, that a majority of the pre-Revolutionary ancestors of the post-Revolutionary Americans, Colonial Dames as like as not, came to this country in an unfree condition and were sold off the ship to pay their passage. But he left all that on one side as contemned culture history. This is why his volumes are left in undisturbed repose on those shelves where stand the books which no gentleman's library is complete without.

I must avoid mention of books whose authors are still alive. I must for want of time omit more than complimentary mention of the special studies of our post-graduates on the township community and other institutional history. I am myself greatly indebted to them. See how lame is Macaulay's allusion to enclosures in his third chapter for want of such knowledge.

I must mention with praise the humble historian who writes of town or city the annals that will be greedily sought after in time to come. And I may say that history is the great prophylactic against pessimism. There never was a bad, in the five progressive ages, that was not preceded by a worse. Our working people live from hand to mouth—in the eighteenth century it was from half-empty hand to starving mouth. Never was the race better situated than in this nineteenth century—this twentieth century on the very verge of which we stand.

History will be better written in the ages to come. The soldier will not take the place he has taken. I do not say that the "drum and trumpet history" will have gone out, but when the American Historical Association shall assemble in the closing week a hundred years hence, there will be, do not doubt it, gifted writers of the history of the people. It will not seem so important for impartial Gardiner to weigh the men and motives of the Commonwealth history. We shall have the history of culture, the real history of men and women.

CHARLES WILLIAM ELIOT

DEFECTS IN AMERICAN EDUCATION REVEALED BY THE WAR

This address was delivered before The League for Political Education on November 23, 1918, in Carnegie Hall, New York. It reveals Mr. Eliot in his eighty-fifth year still a leader in educational thought and a master of lucid and incisive expression. Mr. Eliot was born at Boston in 1834, was president of Harvard University for forty years from 1869 to 1909, and continued after his retirement to instruct his countrymen in the paths of wisdom. He died in 1926. Other addresses by Mr. Eliot are given in Volumes II and IV.

THE war has revealed to the American public the unexpected fact that there is a considerable amount of illiteracy in the population, unevenly distributed among the different states, but disappointingly large on the average—7.7 per cent. This illiteracy was conspicuous in the army and navy, which the government undertook to recruit rapidly by draft, and was at once seen to present serious obstacles to the rapid training of effective government forces. The public promptly perceived that the prevention of illiteracy was a national interest, which should never have been left to the states without any supervision by the national government. Although the existing illiteracy and its consequences were brought to the attention of the American people by the war, the whole people at once saw that the public interest in the prevention of illiteracy was not at all confined to war times. They saw that the prevention of illiteracy was even a greater object for the nation as a whole in normal peace times than in abnormal war times; so that the whole people is now prepared to support, and indeed to urge whatever appropriations Congress may think necessary, in order that the national government may bring effective aid to the

CHARLES W. ELIOT

states in extinguishing illiteracy. Here is a defect in American education, revealed by the war, which Congress and the Administration ought to proceed at once to remedy.

The organization and training of the National Army also brought clearly into view the fact that a significant portion of the young men liable to military service were not acquainted with the English language, and that this ignorance made it more difficult to produce promptly an effective army and navy. Private persons and private incorporated societies had already seen that this ignorance of the English language on the part of alien operatives was impairing efficiency and productiveness in various American industries, and had taken some measures to remedy locally this evil. But these efforts were necessarily limited by lack of money, and could only be of the drop-in-the-bucket sort. Here again we discern a national interest, and an urgent need for immediate expenditures on the part of the National Government in aiding all state and municipal efforts to teach English, not only to children of alien birth, but to adults as well. The best form of this aid would be a contribution of money for each pupil that has completed a course of instruction covering a specified number of lessons, and passed an examination prescribed by the national Bureau of Education. It is the attractiveness of the country as a whole to various alien races which has produced this difficulty in the American army and navy and in some important American industries; so that the National Government may fairly take part in abating it. Whether this new function of the Government will become permanent or not will depend on the renewal of immigration from Asia and southern Europe. Possibly the people who have been coming hither in large numbers from those regions will think that under the conditions of the new peace they will be well enough off in their native lands.

The draft also revealed the prevalence of venereal disease among the civil population of the United States, both urban and rural, to a degree which has appalled the entire people. The War Department and the Navy Department at once set to work to treat venereal diseases within the army and navy, and to prevent the spread of these terribly destructive diseases within the military and naval forces. The campaign conducted by both Departments against these diseases in and about the barracks, camps, and cantonments of soldiers and sailors at home and abroad has had a prompt and large success. To maintain and develop this campaign against these highly communicable diseases after the war ceases will require large appropriations from the National Treasury and the maintenance of a considerable corps of public health officers under the direction of the Division of Venereal Disease which has already been created in the Treasury Department.

This public health service will need the coöperation of all American schools, churches, religious associations like the Young Men's and Young Women's Christian Associations, the Knights of Columbus, and the Jewish Welfare Board, hospitals, asylums, dispensaries, charitable organizations and men's and women's clubs all over the United States. Prior to the outbreak of the Great War in Europe this coöperation could not have been secured. Now it can be; because the American public sees that the venereal diseases can be permanently reduced or restricted only through the use of every possible educational influence which the entire community can exert. Among the agencies which the Division already created in the Treasury Department proposes to use are the public libraries of the country, which are to be provided with lists of carefully selected books for parents of children between six and twelve years of age, for boys and girls who have not reached the age of puberty, for young men and women, for engaged and married people, and for teachers and social workers. We shall owe to the war this permanent national organization for the defense of modern society against the gravest dangers to which it is exposed. The American Government is the only one in the world which thus far has undertaken to defend modern society effectively against the scourges which punish with crushing severity lust, prostitution, and alcoholism in combination.

The sporadic inspections of school children and the medical examinations of young men drafted for the National Army have revealed a percentage of defective bodies in the youth of the country very mortifying to thinking Americans. Many of these bodily defects are remediable; but thus far the organization and enforcing of remedial and preventive processes have been

DEFECTS IN AMERICAN EDUCATION 139

by no means adequate for coping with existing evils. Most of the attempts at remedy and prevention have been made in towns or cities; and the national government and the state governments have not yet attacked seriously the general problem. Both the national and the state governments should at once plan and carry into execution a great expansion of the functions of the medical examiner, the school nurse, and the district nurse, and these officials should work all through the year on the detection and treatment of defects and diseases in children, and the instruction of parents and children as to remedial and preventive action in their homes.

These permanent officials should also give public instruction in regard to diet, nutrition, housing, community cleanliness, and the medical means of controlling epidemics. They should be employed at public expense; and access to this instruction should be free to all comers of whatever age, race, or condition. This is the most legitimate kind of public instruction in a democracy, because the kind most directly and immediately useful to the entire community. A strong beginning should be made at once, and the national, state and municipal governments should all take part in the good work. In order that the future fathers and mothers may be able to understand thoroughly the instruction to be given by physicians, nurses, and health officers, all school children should receive at the appropriate time instruction in so much chemistry, physics, and biology as is necessary to the comprehension of what is meant by a complete diet for infant, child, or adult, and to the mastery by both sexes of the processes of cooking and serving food in wholesome ways. That amount of applied science should be learned by every boy and girl in every American school before the age of sixteen years; and no subject, except the English language, should be more carefully provided for in school programs than that amount of applied science.

In Europe the war has increased infant mortality and diminished the birth-rate in most countries, and these grievous happenings have directed the attention of the American people to the high infant mortality at home, especially where the population is congested. The diffusion of the knowledge of the elements of personal and community hygiene through all classes of society is the best means of reducing infant mortality. In the promotion of this reform it is highly desirable that the national government should use the present moment to insist that the public registration of births, deaths, and diseases should be made obligatory all over the United States. In large areas of the country there is at present no registration at all of this sort.

The opening of many industries and occupations to women, which is apparently to be a consequence of the enlistment of women in new employments during the war, emphasizes the need of more attention to the phenomena of delayed marriage, reduced birth-rate, and higher infant mortality which are likely to result from the employment of multitudes of women in the indoor machinery industries. This is an important subject for study by the national and state departments, or bureaus, of labor and public health. Any effective campaign against these threatening evils must be essentially an open educational campaign, conducted at public expense.

Tuberculosis is another widespread evil which cannot be successfully contended against except by educational processes through the combined efforts of the national, state, and municipal governments intelligently directed to overcoming the general ignorance of the common people on this subject. The medical profession and private philanthropy have taught how to reduce sickness and mortality from tuberculosis, and so to put an end to the great impairment of national prosperity and private happiness caused by this disease; but only the public treasuries can pay the cost of carrying on an active and comprehensive campaign against this deep-seated evil.

The National Government has made some successful efforts to abate, during this nineteen months' war, the hideous evils of alcoholism, tuberculosis, and venereal disease, and every effort in this direction should be continued and developed now that the war is over. The states and municipalities should join in this effort; and it is the duty of every educational force in the country—universities, colleges, technical institutes, school boards, medical schools and normal schools—to join in remedying in the rising generation the physical and mental defects from which they are suffering, and in delivering the coming generation from the diseases of vice or ignorance from which their predecessors have suffered so intensely. In so doing they will be striving to eradicate defects in American education which have been emphasized by the war, though antedating it.

The war has brought home to millions of young men and to other millions of their relatives, friends, and acquaintances, that in the new kind of fighting, by means of innumerable applications of chemical and physical science, the soldier or the sailor needs intelligence, personal initiative, well-trained senses, and some skill of eye, ear or hand. All the belligerent governments have learned this lesson. They have learnt that armies and navies need a large proportion of skilled workmen in the field, at the front as well as behind the front. They have learnt that every private soldier or sailor needs to understand orders, to remember them, and to comprehend the plan and objects of a given attack, so that he can carry out the orders even if no officer or non-commissioned officer be left to guide him. If then a nation may be called on to put an effective army into the field at short notice, its schools should give constant attention to the training of the senses and the memory, and to the acquisition of skill. All American schools must, therefore, add to their present programs, which are based chiefly on literature and mathematics, instruction in the sciences of observation, in the arts and crafts, and in the elements of music, drawing, modeling, and architecture; and must give all pupils practice in the use of their own eyes, ears and hands in productive labor, and in the inductive method of reasoning.

The war has also placed in a clear light the need all over the world of a more productive agriculture, and has shown how that need may be satisfied by giving instruction to children and adults in the means of increasing agricultural productiveness through the study of soils, seeds, food plants, domestic animals, and the best means of cultivating and improving the soil. It follows that the teaching of agricultural science and art should be an important feature in the education of every child in both the urban and the rural populations. Fortunately the agricultural arts afford admirable means of training children and adults to accurate seeing and recording, and then to sound reasoning on the records made.

The war has made plain to multitudes of people what was known before to a few, that human testimony is, as a rule, untrustworthy, not because the witnesses intended to deceive but because they were unable to see, hear, or describe correctly what happened in their presence. This inability to see, hear, touch and describe accurately is by no means confined to ignorant or uneducated people. Many highly educated American professional men have never received any scientific training, have never used any instrument of precision, possess no manual skill whatever, and cannot draw, sing, or play upon a musical instrument. Their entire education dwelt in the region of language, literature, philosophy, and history. Their habits of thought permit vagueness, obscurity, and inaccuracy, and their spoken or written statements have these same defects. These facts suggest strongly the urgent need of modifying profoundly the programs of American elementary and secondary schools. They must no longer cling almost exclusively to languages and literature and the elements of mathematics. They must give a considerable part of school time to the sciences and arts, and to the acquisition by every pupil of some skill of eye or hand or both, and at the same time must increase rather than diminish the amount of training they give in memorizing to hold, in discrimination between the true and the false, the wise and the foolish, the good and the bad, in the selection of premises, and in sound reasoning.

In order to introduce the new subjects and the new methods into the existing schools of the United States, it would be necessary to reduce somewhat the number of periods assigned to the memory subjects and to mathematics, and also to utilize more hours in the school day, and reduce the long summer vacation. The new subjects and methods require a good deal of bodily as well as mental exertion; so that they can be added to the school program without risking the health of the children, provided that all school-rooms, including shops and laboratories, be well ventilated. Moreover, much of the instruction in geography and agriculture can be given out of doors, the teachers taking part in the necessary excursions.

It is an essential part of the new methods of instruction that the pupils should be stimulated to hard work in every subject, including the literary ones, by interesting them in doing things themselves rather than in reading about objects or events, or being told about them. To this end all teaching should be as concrete as possible, and every subject, including of course the literary and historical subjects, should be illustrated by the study of personages, places, charts, diagrams and pictures. It is indispensable to success with the new subjects that the pupils should use their own eyes and hands, and themselves describe and coördinate their own observations. In the study of the notes and records they have made out of their own observations, they must apply their own powers of memory, discrimination, and expression.

Every child should be encouraged and induced to acquire the habit of giving an account to the teacher, or the class, or the whole school, of anything he has himself read or seen or done. An excellent way to teach English composition is to provide a daily exercise, oral, or written, or both, for every pupil in this sort of description, the teacher restricting her own performance to showing the pupil where he has failed in simplicity, directness, or accuracy of description. It is important that all subjects whenever possible be taught from actual objects to be accurately observed and described by the pupils themselves. Pictures or drawings of objects will not answer the same purpose. It should also be the incessant effort of the teacher to relate every lesson to something in the life of the child; so that he may see the useful applications of the lesson, and how it concerns him.

Again, much time may be saved in teaching the familiar as well as the new subjects in the revised programs by teaching groups of subjects together in their natural and inevitable relations. For example, arithmetic, algebra, and geometry should be taught together from beginning to end, each subject illustrating and illuminating the other two. A great gain in the time consumed and in the interest of the pupils will be made by teaching the elements of government, economics, and sociology together, and the elements of history, biography, geography, and travel together. So in the later years of the total course it would be advantageous to deal with chemistry, physics, biology, and geology together, because these subjects are generally found intimately associated in most natural processes of growth, decay, creation, or extinction, and may be wisely separated only for advanced pupils who need to see how theories, guesses, and imaginings have proved useful guides in experimentation and research.

The wise maker of school programs will henceforth reduce class work and the size of classes, and increase individual work. He will also discourage uniformity and to the utmost limit of his budget increase variety in the instruction given, and will make as frequent as possible the sortings, shiftings, and promotions among the pupils. The worst thing a teacher can do for a group of pupils committed to her charge is to try to keep them together in their attainments or their progress, holding back the bright pupils and pushing on the dull.

It is obvious that it will cost more to carry into effect the new methods of instruction in the new subjects than the American public has been accustomed heretofore to spend on their schools. The buildings must be more carefully heated and ventilated, because the pupils are to spend more hours a day in them. The equipment of the laboratories and the shops required for the scientific subjects will be costly, both at the first outlay and in the maintenance. The supply of materials for the shops, laboratories, gardens, and greenhouses will be a new and no inconsiderable charge on the annual budget of the schools. And a new sort of teacher will be required—a teacher better trained herself in the arts and sciences, and herself brought up to see, record, remember, and describe accurately. Therefore, the whole people should spend much more money on their free schools.

These reforms in American schools have been introduced in a few private or endowed schools, and some of them have been introduced in part in a few public schools. But they cannot be introduced on a large scale until the normal schools of the country are much improved. On the other hand, the reform cannot have full sweep until the secondary schools prepare a better class of candidates for admission to the normal schools. The first efforts of any community toward the great improvement of their schools, which the war has taught the American public to desire, must be directed simultaneously to the secondary schools and the normal schools. The secondary schools are generally under the management of municipalities—town or city; the normal schools are usually controlled by the state. The budgets of the secondary schools are municipal budgets; the appropriations for normal schools come from state legislatures. The public must therefore urge the desired improvements on municipal governments and state legislatures. The campaign must be a wide one; and the national government should contribute to the improvements with money and expert supervision.

When the results were published of the physical examinations of the men drafted for the army and navy, the whole American public was much disappointed at the large percentage of rejections. Men in large numbers proved to have physical defects which incapacitated them for the work of either a soldier or a sailor. When the accepted men were brought together in camp a large proportion of them seemed deficient in muscular power, and the majority of them seemed never to have been trained to a good carriage of the body or a vigorous and graceful bearing. It tooks weeks and months in the training camps to produce in many of the recruits an adequate muscular development and an erect carriage. These good physical qualities are not only desirable and even necessary in a soldier or a sailor, but they are equally desirable for all industrial workers, and indeed, for the entire people. If every American child, boy or girl, receives an adequate course of physical training while at school, the industrial efficiency of the nation will be greatly increased in the normal times of peace, and if war came again, the necessary military training would be made shorter than it was in 1917 and 1918, because it could be assumed that a good training of the muscles and a thorough setting-up drill had already been accomplished. To secure for every child in the country a complete course of physical training is a great national object for war times and for peace times alike, and such a course should be planned and enforced by national authorities, and part of the expense of the course should be borne by the national government. The Swiss Federal Council prescribes a program of physical training for every school in Switzerland, and appoints and pays the national inspectors who see that this program is carried out. The Federation also makes a small contribution to the cost of this physical training throughout the republic. The Congress of the United States should immediately provide for some national aid to the states and municipalities in putting into force in all schools a course of physical training planned and watched by the national government. When a proper course of physical training has been in operation all over the United States for ten years, the productiveness of the national industries will show a great increase, the number of children in the average family will also increase, and there will not be so many stooping, crooked, stunted, slouching, awkward people in the streets and factories as there are now.

The war has brought to light the fact that American schools and ordinary American life for more than a hundred years have failed to keep alive one sentiment of public duty which was natural to the early American communities on the shores of the Atlantic, because they lived under the constant pressure of public dangers and apprehensions. When the Pilgrim Fathers first planted their settlement at Plymouth they took it for granted that every able-bodied man was to bear arms in defense of the community. The Puritan Colony of Massachusetts Bay made the same assumption; and both these pioneering communities relied for many years on a militia to which every able-bodied man belonged as a matter of course. In the adventurous Puritan settlements on the border, the men carried their guns with them into the fields where they worked and to church on Sundays. Every able-bodied man felt that he might at any time encounter wounds and death in defense of his home and village. Military service from him was the country's due.

In recent American generations this sense of personal individual duty to the country has been lost, and it has taken a great war in defense of human liberty to reëstablish it. Now, it is for the schools and colleges of the country to maintain this sense of obligation in all the generations to come by direct and positive teachings, and by coöperating with the family and church in training boys and girls and young men and women to render gladly free, unpaid service in their homes, to the neighbors and friends whom they can help, and to the stranger within their gates. Every secondary school should give concrete and well-illustrated instruction in all the coöperative enterprises in which young people can take part for the benefit of the community, and in all the protective and helpful services which young citizens can render. The altruistic sentiments and services should be set before the pupils, and should be exemplified in the lives of their teachers, parents, and natural leaders. The influence of all teachers and parents should be steadily exerted to diminish the selfishness and self-reference which often accompany thoughtless childhood, and to develop, as early as possible, good will and serviceableness towards others, and consideration for the needs of others.

It should be made a special object in all schools to develop among the children and youth what is called in sports "team play"; to impress all the pupils with the high value of coöperative discipline, that is, of the discipline imposed with the consent of the subject of discipline in order to increase the efficiency of the group and therefore the satisfaction of every member in his own contribution. This content in a strict discipline which he has a share in planning and imposing is to-day the chief need of all workmen in industries which require punctuality, order, system, and a common purpose to be efficient on the part of all concerned. There should be many opportunities during school life to learn this enjoyable acquiescence in the strict, coöperative discipline necessary when many persons have to combine in the prompt and accurate production of a given effect or result. Some of the familiar means to this end are singing in parts, producing music in a band or orchestra, folk-dancing, combining in groups to perform gymnastic feats, acting plays, and giving descriptions or narratives before a school audience in which many speakers combine to produce one harmonious and consecutive story. In modern warfare a soldier's work in an active army depends for its success chiefly upon the soldier's skill and satisfaction in action, guided and determined by strict, coöperative discipline. The same is true in almost all the large national industries. Success in them involves the general submission of all participants to a strict, coöperative discipline. This discipline does not much resemble the old-fashioned, automatic, unthinking obedience which was long the ideal in military and industrial organization. It requires the voluntary coöperation of intelligent, free individuals whose wills consent to the discipline for an object which seems good to them, in a method which they think reasonable and appropriate. All schools and colleges should systematically provide much practice in this kind of discipline.

Because of the complete detachment of church from state in this country, and of the existence here of a great variety of churches based on different dogmas and creeds, or on different observances, rituals, rites, and symbols, or on different forms of ecclesiastical government, all of which are tolerated and protected by the national and state governments, it has been considered impossible to allow in the free schools which are supported by general taxation any of the teachings or practices ordinarily called religious. A bad result of this condition is that there has been in the public schools no systematic inculcation of duty towards parents, neighbors, teachers, friends, or country, or of reverence towards God; although some practical virtues essential to the conduct of a school have always been inculcated, such as punctuality, order, and respect for the neighbor's rights and for constituted authority. Accordingly, reverence for prophets, saints, and spiritual heroes has been taught only incidentally and with caution, lest the religious sentiments of one church or another be shocked.

It is one of the best lessons of the war that millions of American youth, trained in schools of this negative character as regards things spiritual, many of whom were not connected with any church, have developed in the presence of the hardships, horrors, and risks of war sentiments which may be properly called religious, and might be expressly inculcated in American public schools.

Most of the young men who have filled the National Army and Navy went to the war in a gregarious way, because their comrades did, or because they were drafted, or because their friends and relatives would be proud, though troubled, to have them go; but when they came to face imminent death or wounds, when they realized that at any moment they themselves might be called on to make the supreme sacrifice, many of them began to consider why they were in such a novel and horrible situation, and some of them found a satisfactory answer to that question. Innumerable soldiers from many races, dying, or realizing in hospitals that they were crippled for life, have said that they were dying, or were crippled, for the sake of their country—France, England, Scotland, America—or for their dear home, or for their children, or for the next generation—that they may have a better world to live in than the present generation found prepared for themselves. Multitudes of the American soldiers and sailors in this war have perceived, for the first time, that their own prime motive in life has been the desire to be of service to other people, though they had lived the ordinary life of daily labor and play, of family affection, and careless gaiety, without much reflection on the great issues of life and death, or on the deep things of love and duty. The tremendous emotions of battle and the sense of comradeship which the sharing of great dangers and hardship creates, develop in them feelings and states of mind which may properly be called religious. They learn what self-sacrifice means and practice it contentedly; they learn that a man may gladly risk his life or lay it down for his friends; they learn that service to others is immeasurably happier than thought for self; they hate war and everything about it, but fight on resolutely in the hope so beautifully expressed by Alan Seager,

> That other generations might possess,
> From shame and menace free in years to come,
> A richer heritage of happiness,
> He marched to that heroic martyrdom.

They learn that brotherhood is the very essence of practical religion. A letter written by a young man, who enlisted after having served his term as a convict in Sing Sing prison and then had trying experiences during several months in the French trenches, to the former warden of the prison, who had been a good friend to him, dealt mostly with the ordinary tediums, trials, and hardships of the private soldier's life; but this was one of its broken sentences: "Religion? This battalion is a band of brothers."

Some line officer, who has been intimate with his men when in hospital or in their rest-places, or some chaplain who has shared with the privates their hardships and their dangers and written letters home for them as they lay wounded or dying, ought to prepare a manual of religion of the thinking soldier in this war for the freedom and security of mankind. It would contain no dogma, creed, or ritual, and no church history; but it would set forth the fundamental religious ideas which ought to be conveyed to every American child and adolescent in the schools of the future. Such teaching would counteract materialism, promote reverence for God and human nature, strengthen the foundations of a just and peace-loving democracy, and conform to Micah's definition of religion: "What doth the Lord require of thee but to do justly, to love mercy, and to walk humbly with thy God?"

The manuals of American history for use in the public schools will hereafter tell how, in 1917, the American people, with remarkable unanimity, went into a ferocious war of European origin in the hope and expectation of putting down divine-right government, secret diplomacy, and militarism, of making justice and kindness the governing principles in international relations, and of promoting among the masses of mankind the kind of liberty under law which they had themselves long enjoyed. In contributing to the vigorous and successful prosecution of this war they spent their money like water, upset their industries and their habits of life, laid on their posterity an immense burden of debt, and put at risk the lives of millions of their sons and daughters. At the same time they gave huge sums of money to relieve the miseries and woes which war now entails on combatants and non-combatants alike.

No great church and no single religious organization incited the American people to this disinterested crusade. Nevertheless, the united action of the people for the nineteen months past testifies that they are guided and inspired by certain simple religious teachings of supreme efficacy. They evidently mean to do unto others as they wish others to do to them, to love their neighbors as themselves, to imitate the example of the Good Samaritan in binding up the wounds of mankind, and to love truth, freedom, and righteousness.

That is the religion which ought to be taught hereafter in all American schools.

THE DURABLE SATISFACTIONS OF LIFE

This address was delivered to the new students at Harvard University, on October 3, 1905.

For educated men what are the sources of the solid and durable satisfaction of life? I hope you are all aiming at the solid, durable satisfactions of life, not primarily the gratifications of this moment or of to-morrow, but the satisfactions that are going to last and grow. So far as I have seen, there is one indispensable foundation for the satisfaction of life—health. A young man ought to be a clean, wholesome, vigorous animal. That is the foundation for everything else, and I hope you will all be that, if you are nothing more. We have to build everything in this world of domestic joy and professional success, everything of a useful, honorable career, on bodily wholesomeness and vitality.

This being a clean, wholesome, vigorous animal involves a good deal. It involves not condescending to the ordinary barbaric vices. One must avoid drunkenness, gluttony, licentiousness, and getting into dirt of any kind, in order to be a clean, wholesome, vigorous animal. Still, none of you would be content with this achievement as the total outcome of your lives. It is a happy thing to have in youth what are called animal spirits—a very descriptive phrase; but animal spirits do not last even in animals; they belong to the kitten or puppy stage. It is a wholesome thing to enjoy for a time, or for a time each day all through life, sports and active bodily exercise. These are legitimate enjoyments, but, if made the main object of life, they tire. They cease to be a source of durable satisfaction. Play must be incidental in a satisfactory life.

What is the next thing, then, that we want in order to make sure of durable satisfactions in life? We need a strong mental grip, a wholesome capacity for hard work. It is intellectual power and aims that we need. In all the professions—learned, scientific, or industrial—large mental enjoyments should come to educated men. The great distinction between

Copyright, 1910, Thomas Y. Crowell & Co. Reprinted with the permission of author and publisher.

the privileged class to which you belong, the class that had opportunity for prolonged education, and the much larger class that has not that opportunity, is that the educated class lives mainly by the exercise of intellectual powers and gets therefore much greater enjoyment out of life than the much larger class that earns a livelihood chiefly by the exercise of bodily powers. You ought to obtain here, therefore, the trained capacity for mental labor, rapid, intense, and sustained. That is the great thing to get in college, long before the professional school is entered. Get it now. Get it in the years of college life. It is the main achievement of college life to win this mental force, this capacity for keen observation, just inference, and sustained thought, for everything that we mean by the reasoning power of man. That capacity will be the main source of the intellectual joys and of happiness and content throughout a long and busy life.

But there is something more, something beyond this acquired power of intellectual labor. As Shakespeare puts it, "the purest treasure mortal times afford is spotless reputation." How is that treasure won? It comes by living with honor, on honor. Most of you have begun already to live honorably and honored, for the life of honor begins early. Some things the honorable man cannot do, never does. He never wrongs or degrades a woman. He never oppresses or cheats a person weaker or poorer than himself. He never betrays a trust. He is honest, sincere, candid, and generous. It is not enough to be honest, an honorable man must be generous, and I do not mean generous with money only. I mean generous in his judgments of men and women, and of the nature and prospects of mankind. Such generosity is a beautiful attribute of the man of honor.

How does honor come to a man? What is the evidence of the honorable life? What is the tribunal which declares at last, "This was an honorable man?" You look now for the favorable judgment of your elders,—of parents and teachers and older students; but these elders will not be your final judges, and you had better get ready now in college to appear before the ultimate tribunal, the tribunal of your contemporaries and the younger generations. It is the judgment of your contemporaries that is most important to you; and you will find that the judgment of your contemporaries is made up alarmingly early,—it may be made up this year in a way that sometimes lasts for life and beyond. It is made up in part by persons to whom you have never spoken, by persons who in your view do not know you, and who get only a general impression of you; but always it is contemporaries whose judgment is formidable and unavoidable. Live now in the fear of that tribunal, —not an abject fear, because independence is an indispensable quality in the honorable man. There is an admirable phrase in the Declaration of Independence, a document which it was the good fashion of my time for boys to commit to memory. I doubt if that fashion still obtains. Some of our public action looks as if it did not. "When, in the course of human events, it becomes necessary for one people to dissolve the political bands which have connected them with another, and to assume among the powers of the earth the separate and equal station to which the laws of nature and of nature's God entitle them, a decent respect to the opinions of mankind requires that they should declare the causes which impel them to the separation." That phrase "a decent respect," is a very happy one. Cherish "a decent respect to the opinions of mankind," but never let that interfere with your personal declaration of independence. Begin now to prepare for the judgment of the ultimate human tribunal.

Look forward to the important crises of your life. They are nearer than you are apt to imagine. It is a very safe protective rule to live to-day as if you were going to marry a pure woman within a month. That rule you will find a safeguard for worthy living. It is a good rule to endeavor hour by hour and week after week to learn to work hard. It is not well to take four minutes to do what you can accomplish in three. It is not well to take four years to do what you can perfectly accomplish in three. It is well to learn to work intensely. You will hear a good deal of advice about letting your soul grow and breathing in without effort the atmosphere of a learned society or place of learning. Well, you cannot help breathing and you cannot help growing; those processes will take care of themselves. The question for you from day to day is how to learn to work to advantage, and college is the place and now is the time to win mental power. And, lastly, live to-day and every day like a man of honor.

ON HIS NINETIETH BIRTHDAY

It is not often that a man has occasion to speak to a large audience on his ninetieth birthday. The following address was made by President Eliot on the occasion of the celebration of his ninetieth birthday on March 20, 1924, at Harvard University, over which he presided for many years. The celebration was under the leadership of an honorary committee of which the Honorable Calvin Coolidge was a chairman and the then living ex-presidents the Honorable William Howard Taft and the Honorable Woodrow Wilson were vice-chairmen. At a meeting held in Sanders Theater congratulations and messages were delivered by President Lowell and others. President Lowell's speech is printed in this volume. Other addresses by President Eliot are to be found in Volumes II and IV.

DEAR FRIENDS: The affectionate note of these tributes goes straight to my heart. It fills me with wonder; but it touches me deeply. This day is going to be one of the happiest and most delightful of my memories. I have received the encomiums of the speakers with a certain sense that I have not been fully understood. One of them said that I had an unusual amount of courage. That has never entered my mind. I confess to recognizing another quality to which President Lowell referred—a readiness for combat. I look back upon my life as a boy, sometimes engaged in the rough-and-tumble fights which we boys used to have on Boston Common, and I recognize that at a tender age I did display considerable enjoyment of fighting. But when it comes to maturer life, I find that the course of this quality described as courage is simply this—that I never stopped in any attempts of mine because I encountered opposition. I was just regardless of risks and opposition. I was eager to do something in the future. It was that part of my nature which enabled me to look forward and not back, to look out and not in.

Now at the close of my life, or near the close, I do not know any better advice to give to the graduates of Harvard College,

ON HIS NINETIETH BIRTHDAY

or to the undergraduates, than that contained in those two phrases of Edward Everett Hale's: "Look forward and not backward—Look out and not in."

I confess I received with great delight what the President of the University said about the spreading influence of Harvard in the present day; but we of the household do not say much about that.

I recognize that I have been unusually strong and have had unusually good health, and that a great deal of the influence I have exerted—what has been described as my personality—is derived from those two facts, strength and health; and with those two advantages went a great joy in work,—just in work. I do not stop to consider why I had joy in work. I never looked in enough to think of that. But joy in work has been the source of a large part of the satisfactions of my life. Now, that is just a gift of nature—from grandparents as well as from parents. Those inheritances determined my life in many respects. They determined my natural disposition towards work, towards research, towards persistent inquiry. This liking for research was developed in me in Harvard College through the personal kindness of my teacher in chemistry, Professor Josiah P. Cooke, who took me into his private laboratory. He gave me (from 1850 to 1853) the opportunity to learn what the process of scientific experimentation and search for truth was. My friends, I was the only undergraduate between 1849 and 1853 who had any such blessing. It was a sense of this privilege that first enlisted me, when I became a teacher of Harvard College, in the advocacy of choice among studies; it first induced me to call for volunteers from my class in prescribed mathematics to do a hard piece of surveying work—the first call for extra work in the field that was ever made on a college class.

To go back to the description given by another of the speakers of my conduct as President, I may say that I recognize the accuracy of his description, particularly when he said that in listening to debates in the Faculty and in inviting my opponents to speak, I was probably pursuing with a good deal of perspicacity a study of those men—that I was making up my mind whether these zealous opponents were of the right stuff to be made professors in Harvard University. That is just what I was doing.

Consider now the sources of my career as a teacher. Those sources were in the times, in that wonderful period of human history, in which my whole educational career lay. Think of it! When I was coming on as a teacher in Harvard, the great prophets and exponents of experimental science in Europe and America were taking possession of that great field. Think how the philosophers of the world were preaching attention to the individual and proclaiming the immense variety in human nature. Think how James Russell Lowell told us in 1886 that democracy must not only raise the average mass, but must give a free field to all the finest qualities of human nature; for that is the only salvation for democracy. Think how Emerson came into power in the days of my youth. Think how Oliver Wendell Holmes, as a teacher of anatomy, physiology, and the carrying of contagion, enlarged the conception of human sagacity, penetration, and discrimination, and combined with that instruction great power of expression in both prose and poetry. Think how Asa Gray, Joseph Henry, Jeffries Wyman, Benjamin Peirce, and Louis Agassiz were the leaders in American science and in methods of teaching science. All that came out of the times when I was a young teacher in Harvard; out of that extraordinary period have come the ideals and the lessons which I have followed all through my active career. Then, as the years went by and the period of combat and persistent effort against opposition passed, and the new structure of Harvard University began to take effect, think how the Divisions and the Faculties gave me the opportunity to see where modern education was going, and where it ought to go. Now and then I could help their labors, especially in the Medical Faculty; but it was the strength of the Harvard Faculties themselves which filled me with strength and what is called leadership. I gave expression and opportunity to their hopes, aspirations, and devotions; and great was the privilege of so doing. You must therefore attribute the successes which I have been privileged to win to the very fortunate circumstances of my life, to the leadership of the extraordinary philosophers and scientists of my time.

And now I want to say a word to the graduates of Harvard here assembled. I cannot find better words than those I used in my inaugural address in October, 1869. They apply to-day.

"There have been doubts, in times yet recent, whether culture were not selfish; whether men of refined tastes and manners could really love Liberty, and be ready to endure hardness for her sake. . . . In yonder old playground, fit spot whereon to commemorate the manliness which there was nurtured, shall soon rise a noble monument which for generations will give convincing answer to such shallow doubts; for over its gates will be written: 'In memory of the sons of Harvard who died for their country.' The future of the University will not be unworthy of its past."

How the young Harvard men have demonstrated in the World War that that last line is true—"The future of the University will not be unworthy of its past." But let me, finally, emphasize the duty of Harvard men, of all educated men, to serve their country in peace as well as in war. I call upon the younger Harvard graduates, and by and by I shall call on the undergraduates, to serve their country with devotion and at sacrifice in peace as well as in war.

GLENN FRANK

A WELCOME TO THE FRESHMEN

Glenn Frank became president of the University of Wisconsin in 1925 after a notable career as author and editor. He was born in Queen City, Missouri, in 1887, graduated from Northwestern University in 1912, was assistant to the president at Northwestern 1912-1916, was associated with Edward A. Filene of Boston 1916-1919, became associate editor of the *Century Magazine* in 1919 and editor-in-chief in 1921. He is the author of various books and is well known throughout the country as a lecturer. The following address of welcome to the freshman class was given in September, 1925, at the opening of President Frank's administration.

As administrative head of the University of Wisconsin, I welcome you to its halls and to its opportunities.

In a sense there is just a trace of impropriety in my presuming to welcome you to this University in view of the fact that I arrived on its campus only three short weeks in advance of your coming. But in a deeper sense I shall never again be as well fitted to welcome an incoming class as I am this morning, because, for the second time in my life, I know exactly how a freshman feels. I speak as a freshman to freshmen.

I know the ancient and anesthetic ritual of presidential welcomes. I think I know most of the stock advice that has been given to freshmen from the days of Abelard to the epoch-making entrance of the class of '29 to the University of Wisconsin. But I shall indulge in none of that advice this morning. I want only to share with you my feelings about this University, which is to you and to me alike a new world of allurement and challenge.

From slightly different angles, you and I are together setting out on a great adventure this morning. Together we are going to find out whether it is possible for young men and young

GLENN FRANK

women to make themselves really at home in the modern world, able to work in harmony with the creative forces of their time instead of at cross-purposes to them. This is the research magnificent which you are about to undertake. And unless I completely misread the genius of this institution, you could not find a better setting for your experiment.

You will find the University of Wisconsin a very human place. The distinguished scholars of the several faculties with whom it will be your privilege to associate are not scowling taskmasters but sympathetic friends.

You cannot be long on this campus without discovering the kind of teacher who represents the authentic Wisconsin tradition. The University of Wisconsin is not interested in teachers who are mere merchants of dead yesterdays; it covets and captures men who are guides into unborn to-morrows, men who have objects as well as subjects, men who refuse to put conformity to old customs above curiosity about new ideas, men who are not content to be peddlers of petty accuracies when they are called to be priests and prophets of abundant living. You will find among the scholars of these faculties men who know how to be great specialists without becoming specialized men, men who have reverence for their materials, men who have mastered the facts in their respective fields, but men who see that all facts are dead until they are related to the rest of knowledge and to the rest of life. In short you are to have the high privilege of associating with distinguished scholars who know how to "relate the coal scuttle to the universe," men who are shepherds of the spirit as well as masters of the mind.

But you will not expect too much of these teachers. In the deepest sense of the word, they cannot teach you anything; they can only help you to learn for yourselves.

In the social associations of this University you will acquire a poise and polish that you might not otherwise acquire, but this is not the primary end and aim of this institution. The University of Wisconsin is not built around a ballroom. It would be a sorry sort of young man who had to spend four expensive years in order to pick up a valet's knowledge of dress and demeanor.

In the pomp and pageantry of great games you will come to know the thrill of athletic victories as you throw your bodies into play or merge yourselves with the cheering thousands in the stadium. But the primary end and aim of this institution is not athletics. At the University of Wisconsin athletics will be no mere interloper in our academic life but a fine and fundamental part of our whole educational process. At the University of Wisconsin athletics will be a vivid symbol of the fact that here we recognize that the truly educated man must have not only a sound mind but a sound body. And you will find that under such policies a university will produce more winning teams than could possibly be produced by an institution that regarded athletics as a mere adjunct to the educational process, very much as it might play impresario to a bullfight in an arena.

In the classrooms of this University you will hear many doctrines discussed, but in the deepest sense of the word it is not the business of this University to fill your minds with doctrines. As I have said many times and in many places, it is not the business of a university to teach its students what to think but to teach them how to think, and then to trust them to decide what to think as year by year they face the changing facts of a changing world.

The University of Wisconsin does not exist to furnish your minds as an interior decorator might furnish your house; the University of Wisconsin exists to free your minds.

The University of Wisconsin does not exist merely to train you to be clever competitors in the world as it is; it exists to help you to become creative coöperators in the making of the world as it ought to be.

The University of Wisconsin wants you to know the past in order that you may live wisely in the present.

I hope that you may find in the University of Wisconsin a temporary retreat from the world in which you may become emancipated from the dead dogmas, the obsolete opinions, the irrational inhibitions, the silly superstitions, the foolish fears, and the cowardly cautions that crush and kill the uneducated mind.

One would have to be very old and very cold not to respond

A WELCOME TO THE FRESHMEN 161

to the prospect of life in a university the very air of which is electric with the thrill of intellectual and spiritual adventure.

It is the determined purpose of all of us who have anything to do with the purpose and procedure of this institution to see to it that the University of Wisconsin be and remain such a place.

As the administrative head of the University of Wisconsin, I welcome you to its halls and to its opportunities.

ZONA GALE

THE NOVEL AND THE SPIRIT

Zona Gale, born at Portage, Wisconsin, 1874, achieved in her "Miss Lulu Bett" one of the most remarkable of American novels. The address which follows was delivered at Columbia University before an audience of graduate students in literature in July, 1921.

A FEW years ago it was the habit of the New York newspapers to instruct their reporters that, whatever the nature of the story which they brought to the city room, one rule must be regarded: the story must be reduced to the briefest possible statement and this statement would constitute the first paragraph of the newspaper account.

Thus: Clarence Thorne, eight-year-old son of Mr. and Mrs. C. E. Thorne, living at 500 West 500th Street, was run over by a sprinkling cart yesterday afternoon at four o'clock as he was playing before his parents' door, and was instantly killed.

Recently I read in *The New York Times* an account of a similar accident and the account ran like this:

The children living in West 500th Street wish that yesterday had not been a holiday because, if it had not been so, little Clarence Thorne, eight-year-old son of Mr. and Mrs. Clarence Thorne living at No. 500, would have been busy at school with his books instead of playing hopscotch in the street before his parents' door where yesterday afternoon at four o'clock he met his death.

This opening paragraph tells the story, to be sure, briefly and yet in so different a tone from its first statement that the paragraph may be said to regard a new ruling. Very few years have crept between the two fashions but the whole feeling of the treatment has changed.

Reprinted from *The Yale Review*, October, 1922, with Miss Gale's permission.

Certain habits of the novel vary quite as nimbly. As in "Père Goriot," when the misfortunes of the Pension Vauquer have gathered and multiplied, one guest after another has dropped away, even that admirable Vautrin of whom they made a convict, and to Madame Vauquer, receiving blow after blow, the final one is administered by Sophie the maid who enters and cries out that the cat is missing: "Madame, I have not seen Mistigris all day." "Ah, this, . . ." cries Madame. The poor creature lifted her hands to her head. . . .

Imagine Mr. Sinclair Lewis seeking to heighten a situation by a device like that. In such an hour Mr. Lewis would be far more likely to introduce Sophie saying that the green grocer had come for his order and would madame have beans.

But however the mode of expression of a news story may vary, the character of the news itself remains unaltered. News is news. All the news is the news. News may be colored or suppressed but to the city room and the public it is none the less news and has remained essentially the same since newswriting has attained a professional status. It is only recently that the novel has attained to this honest estate. For though the novel has been slowly extending its technical frontiers, changing its style even as the newspapers, yet it is only of late that the novel has, so to say, begun to try to include all the news.

It is a great moment in any art when the artist transfers his attention from the extension of his methods to the extension of his material. From a preoccupation with technical areas and rebellion at their limitations, the novelist seems now to have come to the unique delight of the artist, namely, such strong excitement in the presence of life that he must express that excitement. And if it is said that he has always been doing this, yes, he has done this for crises, for moments of extreme action, for acute situations, for the comedy, the tragedy, the zeniths, and the nadirs; but never before has he done this for life's sheer deadly death-dealing routine. As a gatherer of materials he now rivals the newspapers and is saying: *"All* the news for the novel, whether the public knows it as news or not." He is on his way from the old artificial selectiveness to a new selectiveness of still unknown standards.

Consider these three family groups and their comparative value to the fiction writers of to-day and yesterday:

The setting for the first is a little house where lives alone a man in the eighties, alert, humorous, tolerant, well, who refuses to give up his home of a lifetime to go to live with children and grandchildren in the same town. "Here I stay," he says decisively, "I will go back and forth but here I stay." And among all the many members of that family there is a relationship so tender that it would not be welcome material for any modern novelist.—Over the hill are three or four houses tenanted by members of a second family and these continually at war. They do not admire one another's in-laws and a pending property distribution darkens the sky. Winds of bitterness and clamor rock those houses and the town hears the impact. Rich material this, for any novelist of any period.—But now in the "residence part," as the townfolk say, there is a third group of whom the town has a stock observation: "Aren't the Blanks a lovely family?" In this family are the father, a business and church pillar of hackneyed composition; the mother who does her best as a matter of course and never questions either; the three adult daughters, potentially charming women, without the initiative or the independence to accept life; and the one adult son Gracchus—a model. "Gracchus Blank is such a nice man," says the town. In that home thoughts of 1895 are household words. A patriarchal family, with money. And the town says: "Aren't the Blanks a lovely family?"

Now of these three families the first, the tender family, and the second, the bitter family, have often furnished legitimate news for the novelist. So has the third, the patriarchal family, *as viewed by the townspeople*. But the novelist of to-day has discovered the breakfast table and the luncheon table and the evening lamp of that third family, not in crises, but day by day. And he has discovered what goes on within the pillar and the painstaking mother and the three daughters and Gracchus the model, judged, not by the standards of the town, but to some extent by the standards of the new knowledge concerning renunciation and repression and hypocrisy and business and the church: And the transvaluation of that patriarchal family thus requires a new geometry and all but requires another space.

THE NOVEL AND THE SPIRIT

Not, observe, that family in crisis so much as that family at breakfast, living its routine life much as you and I live ours.

Of course the novelist has always handled such a family if he could satirize it, blur it, trick it, caricature it. But to record it has not interested him. Indeed under the old theology, the old sociology, the old psychology, he could not record it because he did not see it. So he was content to cover circumstance with something like the bright veil which we throw about the late doings of the dead.

Especially has he been content to use those bright veils in the ceremonies incident to his two most ancient incantations. Two valid incantations the novel has always known, the novel of every land which knows the novel: namely, romantic love, in an exhaustless number of colorful arrangements; and moral aspiration. On these virtually all novels have depended for their breath. Love and honor.

And among us these two enchantments have been pronounced in but one tongue and according to one tradition, the Anglo-Saxon. Not only has the American novel clung steadfastly to these two interests but for years it never departed from the Anglo-Saxon interpretation of these two interests. Now of late the American novelist has made two discoveries.

The first discovery is that the American novel may treat of romantic love and moral aspiration not according to the Anglo-Saxon tradition but according to the Anglo-Saxon habit of life—quite another matter.

The second discovery is that love and idealism are after all only two of the factors of existence; and that a large part of even the Anglo-Saxon life is occupied with neither the one nor the other.

Here are thus opened to the novelist masses of fresh material in whose treatment, so far as the Anglo-Saxon habit of life is concerned, it is impossible for him to be imitative. It is the opening up of a new country. His country, his own people as they are and not as they think they are. His native sources of supply.

These native sources of supply are not identical with 1776 and 1849 and 1865 and 1917. Nor, in spite of the sins of many, do they depend upon the use of bad English. Gradually in New England, in Virginia, in Indiana, in Kansas, in California, in New York, mine after mine of these native supplies has begun to yield its peculiar ore, an ore not so much dependent upon the dynamite of plot as upon a mere surface shovel to reveal its shining. For it is merely the immemorial richness of human relationship as touched specifically by two influences. One, and that one of lesser importance, is regional color. The second and inestimably the more vital is the national genius. Regional color has often been far too thickly overlaid, has become the "local discoloration" into which Wilde saw local color degenerating. To the national genius the novel of any nation will always be delivered.

The distinctive fashion in which the desire for growth and change expresses itself is the manifestation of the genius of a nation. In the American national genius we have a spirit now considerably crippled but still recognizably at one with the spirit of the colonies and therefore now definitely at variance with many traditions, both native and world traditions, crystallized in unforeseen forms. For it seems that the right of the individual to life, liberty, and the pursuit of happiness is not limited, as we had earlier supposed, by his politics and his religion. And with this emphasis the national novel is now concerned, in common with the novels of the rest of the world. The novelist who is creative is bound to extend the principles of the national genius and is found applying it to all else which affords the growth of the individual: Marriage, the great American home, relatives, institutions, conventions, traditions, and the accepted virtues in the routine of his civilization. But if crude aspects of this routine are presented by him, or crude characters questioning this routine at any point, somebody is going to say: "I don't like that book. It isn't about pleasant people. I shouldn't care to know them. Why write about them?" Conceivably it may not be about pleasant people. What are we going to do about it? Change the novel or change the people?

Recently in an evening of discussion on the English novel I heard a distinguished professor of science declare that all that he wanted of a novel was help in forgetting himself. That seems a crass confession akin to one which might be made by

THE NOVEL AND THE SPIRIT 167

a devotee of the motion picture. Developed drama or a symphony does not help one to forget oneself—they deepen one's sensibilities. It is this which one may ask of any art. It is this which one may ask of the novel. In that case the man of science was right, though not in the way that he meant. For to deepen one's sensibilities is of course to take one out of one's lesser self into one's wider incarnations.

It is precisely this process which, by a method known to the most elementary logic, the modern English novelists including the American novelists have more or less unconsciously begun to attempt. See, they say, not your greater incarnation but its opposite, for so long not considered news for the novel at all. Read of the complacent deaths which you live; if you like, count them—if you can. And thus drop deeper into your pit where you may better see the star of our potential life. Of course as a matter of fact they say nothing of the sort. They merely let us enter the dark and they leave us there to dream of the light if we have it in us.

The following is quoted from a recent American novel.

"The butcher had a hooked nose and when he smiled his nose seemed to press down his thick brown moustache that framed his even teeth so beautifully. He settled his apron over his stomach and gazed at her hungrily above the glass top of the counter as though he were trying to hypnotize her into buying some of the coral pink sausages which reposed beside a block of ice in the transparent case. . . . The meat shop was as white as death. It smelled of blood and sawdust. . . . 'I want a—can you give me a nice rib roast to-day? What do you ask for those hens?' Mrs. Farley, as always, hesitated when she spoke. Her vague squinting eyes travelled undecidedly over the big pieces of meat, the shoulders, the forelegs, the haunches, . . . the fowls dangling in a row a little before the meat. 'I will take two of the hens,' said Mrs. Farley. 'Be sure you give me fat ones,' she added frowning. She fumbled . . . for the money. She made her way through the bitter-smelling gloom." And so on.

Intolerable, certainly. But the novel did not manufacture the butcher-shop. It merely confessed it. Or this:

"Dr. Beach had gone but the nurse was still in the room. She had her back turned towards the door and was folding up some clothes. The gas flame had been extinguished. The window curtains were open. Objects in the room were plainly visible throwing no anchorage of shadow. Lawrence went towards the bed. He set his feet down carefully as if he were afraid of being heard. When he reached her he saw that she had not moved. She would never move. A sob of agony and relief shook him. He kneeled by the bed. She had not moved. Stillness revolved about him in eternal motion."

Obviously "The Narrow House" did not manufacture that terrible sob of agony and relief. Or the terrible commonplace of the story which lead up to it. Our novels have been accustomed for long to the good taste of hypocrisy. We have never been willing to admit life in art any more than in life.

However, there is now no hypocrisy, there are no veils, there is not even good taste in the novels intent on leading us into the dark and leaving us there to listen to its terrible breathing. All the news about living goes into these novels. And it is with this wholesale process that the use of the commonplace is concerned. In a majority of the realistic American novels of today we have a voice not of evil but of the commonplace. It is as if all the banalities of our lives—brushes, combs, coat-hangers, the defiling and scouring of dishes, the idiotic recreations, the stodgy generalizations, the sad commercialism, the tragic nothings which collect about us were suddenly to cry out in a single voice in these books. And you hear the naïve antiphonal chorus: "I don't like those books. . . . I wouldn't care to know those people." It is wholly unimportant whether or not we like the people. In some of our moments all of us are those people. Such novels are merely saying: "Look at us." And why should not the realistic novel say that which is being said by a laboring music, a four dimensional art, and an ambiguous social order: "Look at us. Us gods, fallen into more kinds of pits than seem possible." These are no trumpet voices, no pulses of propaganda. They are mere recording voices, conversational, table-talking voices saying: "My dear gods, not only in your crises but at your very breakfasts you are in a pit of your digging."

THE NOVEL AND THE SPIRIT

We have then in the American novel of to-day the facing of the Anglo-Saxon habit of life, the admission that it concerns itself with other things than love and aspiration, a tardy turning to our native sources of supply, the recognition of the value of the commonplace, and at last an honest expression of the national genius. But is there anything which the American novel signally lacks? What other material, in what way conditioned, might the novel require in its business of imaginatively recording us? Are there any sources of material which we here in America are neglecting? Is there any omission by which we are flawing our fiction as hypocrisy once flawed it? Has the American novel a malady?

The malady of our novels is an immemorial malady, namely, their lack of power to express beauty. Beauty as a force. Inhering beauty. Almost, one adds, incommunicable beauty.

"Beauty old yet ever new, eternal voice and inward word." The momentary lift and urge which comes from the reading of that line carved on the New York library façade, what novel can ever capture and sustain that? Perhaps it cannot yet be sustained in a novel, cannot even be borne by us, as it could not be borne to see a god. And yet it is a part of life, operative in beings. And there is that other line carved on the same façade: "But above all things truth beareth away the victory." Without beauty a record of truth is like the Borglum gargoyle at Princeton—the ill-equipped things, having one arm and one wing. The novel which has not beauty has but one aspect of truth. And where in the American novel have we beauty?

We have it occurring here and there in volumes which will present themselves at once—well-remembered bits from Mrs. Wharton, from Howells, from James; from a half dozen of the moderns. Something of beauty lurks in the work of many whom we moment by moment recall. But not enough beauty. Beauty has never yet been captured even approximately by any of them. Not captured, one may say, so nearly in the novel as Henry Adams captured it in "The Hall of the Dynamos" —and there at the last it eluded him too. In the novel as America has developed it, there is offered as yet no veiled wonder.

As between that which we called beauty in the novel fifty years ago and phases of that which we call merely realism now, you and I may prefer the merely realistic, phases of which indeed may have become our idea of beauty. Beauty changes its form. Consider one worn instance of beauty, an instance to which we were long accustomed to refer as the loveliest chapter in the Victorian novel—the meeting of Richard Feverel and Lucy by the weir. We still love it but do we not love it indulgently, as we love Cruikshank? Lift beside it a page of Conrad, a mere hurrying wing of a sail in the dark and brooding figures black against a red moon, intent in talk which is half eloquent elision—and we know that beauty, such as we have, has changed its form. Or in "The Rescue," the meeting of the two women, the catching up of the reality behind the racial difference, the reaching up to an evolutionary meaning, the dramatization of the cleft cut by centuries of breeding, the delicate shadowing forth of all that is to come, the fascination of the fragile yet firm effects won by every flawless sentence; and from restraint that always rhythmic slip back to the gorgeous tapestry of the tropics, all this sustained with other and yet other strands interwoven—the unconscious genius of love in Linyard, the genius of his friend of the one great passion; the whole forever pointing, pointing to the inevitable imperious—but how melodramatic!—conclusion: "Steer north!" This is beauty as we know it now in the novel; and incidentally it is of the essence of Conrad. By it we mean infinitely more than the beauty of a mosaic. We mean the beauty of an organism.

But even organic beauty such as is fundamental to "The Rescue" is to be transcended. There is beauty already actually incarnate in life but in novels seldom operative and never treated as casually existent, like flowers. For refinements of human conduct have run far ahead of their reflection in the novel—the novel is still intent on crude aspects of behavior already by at least a measurable proportion of the race left behind.

To be sure, the use of the Ten Commandments as direct fictional motives has been outgrown. Characters in fiction who ordered their lives under the conscious stimulus of the Ten

Commandments would be ridiculous. The Ten Commandments as immediate dictators of action obviously have no literary value. It is only in that area which lies beyond precept, in the shadowy caves of cross current and counter current that the novel can employ them at all.

But among these derivatives the novel seems usually to seize upon crass examples. Witness that highest moment in "The Rescue"—Linyard's resolute "Steer north!" The moment when the yacht has left the island and has taken away all that Linyard cared for in the world:

". . . Carter approached him and spoke quietly: 'The tide has turned and the night is coming on. Hadn't we better get away from these shoals, sir?' . . .

"Linyard came out of his absorption with a deep tremor of his powerful frame like the shudder of an uprooted tree.

"'How was the yacht heading when you lost sight of her?' he asked.

"'South, as near as possible,' answered Carter. 'Will you give me a course to steer for the night, sir?'

"Linyard's lips trembled before he spoke but his voice was calm. 'Steer north,' he said."

Here is one of the exalted moral beauties of the novel—renunciation. And yet in "The Rescue"—and how much more patently in the novels of any other—what a grandiose gesture it is. "Steer north" is clear melodrama. Renunciation represents a stage in human conduct but it may be a crude stage. We have James and Conrad as apostles of renunciation and on their heels comes a psychology isolating and defining repression so that already there dawns for us the gospel of transmutation: not to deny or to renounce but to transcend; not to waste force but to transform it; not to thwart but to exceed; to turn passion into power. Here are fields for the fortitude and the delicacy of the novelist beside which undiscriminating renunciation is as crude as blind obedience. Here fall nuances of creative conduct beside which "Steer north" bears an odor of bad taste, insisting too much—as does the Golden Rule, on that precept for the child in process of becoming so sensitized that he will do unto others the right for its own sake. But these and their like are favorite nobilities of the novel—the glorified detective story with a man himself as both culprit and keeper; or of late as pleased fugitive from the whole case.

Now there are in the world countless persons of humor and variety for whom certain crude moral struggles no longer exist. There are those in whose conduct money questionably touched could enter no more than murder; by whom the truth is spoken quite as simply and naturally as good English; in whom good faith is not an accomplishment like harp-playing but a function like sight; those in whom the social consciousness is a passion beside which any personal profit can live not even as an impulse; those who do not brawl in their families or shout "me first" in any of its tongues. Those whose reactions are in the main socialized, spiritualized, humanized. And who—the point is here—are conscious of but a quite ordinary functioning. No grandiose gestures from them! Merely records of reaction, rich in humor and misadventure and delight and deep waters: the old, dreaming beyond dreams; youth, with its new æsthetic; the middle generation, understanding neither; folk of pressing preoccupations, inarticulacies, flashes of insight; of heart-breaking misapprehension, memories, inevitabilities, who go rekindling old fires, what have these tragedies to do with raw "right" and "wrong"? Great areas of living involve for such folk as these no crude moral choices at all. But they are rarely admitted to the pages of the modern novel, at least without a fanfare. Their moral matter-of-course becomes in the novel heavily featured. Good faith and the social passion, for example, are there employed in isolated self-conscious moments, not called casual but made crucial; or else are challenged, re-valued, abandoned.

Eventually we shall have, we must believe, occasional novels taking for granted a certain degree of moral health and going about a brighter business. Indeed this may be the only way in which we shall succeed in getting rid of self-conscious idealism as a root motif of the novel, an idealism to which the Anglo-Saxon novel-reader clings as tenderly as the Anglo-Saxon in his daily life likes to believe that he himself clings. We shall be rid of this motif not by challenging order or by stopping in the welter on this side, but by writing of these who have transcended chaos.

"Do you not see," offers the devotee of the "red-blooded" novel, "with the use of such material you'd have no novel? Because you'd have no struggle."

But we hear the unimaginative say that if the economic struggle were removed, life would not be worth living. The novel in which a crude moral struggle, either lost or won, is the highest motif is as primitive in art as is the economic struggle in life.

Also the reader of the red-blooded novel holds that such serene folk are too rare to become suitable fiction material. Even if they are rare they should have in the novel a place as secure as the pathologic and the drunken who seem always to be welcome. The sophisticated reader ventures that by such novels we should be dangerously approaching, in the usual spiral of experience, an apotheosis of the condition through which the novel earlier took its way; the perfect family relationship, the perfect lover, perfection *ad nauseam*. Even if this were true it would not matter. The novel must deliver itself to material which bears no relation to self-conscious perfection. It is precisely the weakness of Anglo-Saxon morality and novel-making alike that they can imagine no such occasions.

Yet in experience it is not until "temptations" are left behind that really beautiful living can begin. Previous to that time everything is crude and experimental. All the loveliest nuances of relationship lie in the region beyond such voices. Human experiences reveal new faces in this clear air. Whole planes of experience are to be treated for which only the reasonably evolved can possibly furnish material. And always there is the free spirit within in fleeting union with an exquisite and inexorable spirit without—the great inner history, useless, or no more than incidental to the novel so long as the shackles of a crude idealism have not fallen away. Nor need these adventures by any means be confined to the sophisticated, the formally choice. Homely hearts and hearths furnish their high proportion of unconscious fineness—the unconscious, which always matters most. Theirs are the choice to some extent already bred into the race.

The chief concern of the American novel of to-morrow will be to uncover the beauty of our essential commonplace living as the novel of to-day has triumphantly uncovered its ugliness. To uncover beauty not by denying ugliness—the novel of to-day has made that forever impossible—but first by accepting all of life, something which we in America have never been willing to do either in art or in life; and then by a new selectiveness. It is only after a broadly affirmative art arises that a really selective art become possible. The modern realistic novel performs the inestimable service of extending our admissions, our affirmations. It has chosen to affirm the commonplace, the sordid, the ugly because that is most obvious; also it is far easier to record; is, in fine, the natural gesture away from sentimentality and hypocrisy and smugness. Of course the gesture has been too violent. As Conrad says in his "Notes on Life and Letters":

It seems as if the discovery made by many men at various times that there is much evil in the world were a source of unholy joy unto some of the modern writers. It gives an author—goodness only knows why—an elated sense of his new superiority. And there is nothing more dangerous than such an elation to that absolute loyalty towards his feelings and sensations an author should keep hold of in his most exalted moments of creation.

And it is true that the novel here in America, having at last eaten of the tree of good and evil and of the commonplace—doubtless unknown in Eden—has learned to admit not only that life is not all apples, but has occasionally led us to suppose that orchards bear exclusively cores—or even worms.

There is, however, nothing ultimately pessimistic about our present records of the commonplace. Nothing inexorable is expected by these modern novels to crush us. There is in them no sense of fate—that is not the way of the national genius. Even Mr. Hergesheimer in his records of a debased society though he is ironic is still rather wistful. All these novels are merely saying: "Look at us, gods in the pit—but a pit of our own digging. And we are worth digging out. If we were not so we wouldn't have mentioned it."

This so far is the sum of their affirmations; a broad enough extension if one considers the inhibitions of the 'nineties when our novels were either formed for vigilance committees or else were "light."

THE NOVEL AND THE SPIRIT

So in the revealing of life to which every generation of novelists succeeds, their entire work has as yet hardly touched at life's inner magic. And the greatest of this magic, it is predictable, will be the magic of love. It may be against love that the sins of our modern novels are greatest. For it may appear that love is only one aspect of that heightening of faculty and perception towards which the race seems to be tending. Or what if it is true that the extensions of faculty of the race are to be developed by those in the heightened perception known as "being in love"? Consider what may lie in store for us when novels shall reflect these courts. Picture that sort of love story and compare it with our love stories of now, with the hackneyed lure of the Third-at-the-threshold, the use of the pathologic, the drunken. To these the novel is still serving its brief bondage.

Poetry, pictorial and plastic art, and music, all so much more highly developed than fiction or than the society which fiction now depicts, have always risen to that medium of expression which now we seek for the novel—expression which does not merely record beauty but rises to the actual planes of beauty itself.

It is upon these lovely areas that fiction must adventure. It must know beauty, it must be beauty. Not the beauty of the flesh but the beauty of the cell and of its unknown urge. Inhering beauty. The utter beauty of our essential living.

SIR AUCKLAND CAMPBELL GEDDES

COMMENCEMENT ADDRESS

Address by the British Ambassador to the United States before George Washington University, at Washington, May 31, 1920. Another speech by Sir Auckland Geddes is printed in Volume II. President Collier of the University in conferring upon Sir Auckland Geddes the degree of Doctor of Laws, said:

"Auckland Campbell Geddes, educator, soldier, administrator, diplomat; for many years a Professor of Anatomy in the University of Edinburgh and in the Royal College of Surgeons at Dublin; later Minister of Reconstruction of Great Britain; displaying in the first position profound knowledge of the human body and in the second, consummate skill in putting together the shattered body-politic; to-day as British Ambassador to the United States demonstrating that he understands human nature as well as the human frame. This degree of Doctor of Laws is conferred upon him as a recognition of his own preëminent talents and achievements and his invaluable services to his country and to humanity; also as a compliment to the great sister institution of learning, McGill University, of which he was principal-elect when accredited to the United States; and also a tribute of our admiration and gratitude to the mighty Empire which he so worthily represents and whose laws and customs and institutions have so profoundly influenced those of our own land and have served as an inspiration to freemen everywhere."

Mr. Chairman, Ladies and Gentlemen:—To-night many of you pass a milestone on the road of life—birth, school, college, graduation, are the common landmarks in the pre-professional life of the university man. Of these the graduation stone is in many cases the most memorable, for just beyond it comes the point at which all must leave the highway they have trodden with the carefree crowd of their contemporaries to pass into the jungle of life and cut their own trail. For most the bush is thick and thorny; the ground rough and rocky. He is rare who never casts regretful longings backward to the road that ended for him just beyond the graduation mile.

One peculiarity of that jungle is that none who has gone before can tell the new recruit what difficulties he will meet or what clearings he may hope to find. Still an elder member of the brotherhood of university graduates may be able to peer a little farther through the bush or perhaps his acquired knowledge of life-woodcraft may make it not too unwise for him to give advice that may save some bleeding feet.

Let us take a general view, if possible a world view, for a few moments.

I doubt if ever before was the future for so many nations, as many individuals, so closely shrouded in dark clouds pregnant with storm. As one looks ahead there is little light save when dazzling flash on flash writes a great interrogation on the murky background.

In Europe we know that an age is dying. Here it would be easy to miss the signs of coming change, but I have little doubt that it will come.

A realization of the aimlessness of life lived to labor and to die, having achieved nothing but avoidance of starvation and the birth of children also doomed to the weary treadmill, has seized the minds of millions. The lightnings as they flash the great interrogation sear their eyes. They ask Why? They say to one another Why? They look and see others who picnic by flowery paths while life slips by, themselves and their like grimy with toil and spent with labor. For them evening and morning, night and day, storm and shine pose the same problem—Why?

You and we and all our allies have fought together the greatest war that was ever fought—we have suffered and inflicted untold misery. Millions of young men have gone to their death serene in the faith that they died for a cause worthy of sacrifice. Millions more have died angry and protesting and asking—Why? Why was life and happiness and love not for them? Why were they doomed to suffer incredible hells on earth?

Questioning everything, accepting nothing, humanity moves once more. So far, only the swell of the storm centered in Europe laps your coasts; yet your daily press is already filled with news of strikes of what is vaguely called industrial unrest.

We all know that it was your tradition to keep clear of European entanglements—here is a European disentanglement that is already piling the waters on your social beaches, a disentanglement of the complicated interweaving of man and man in the social fabric.

Into a storm-racked world you new graduates have to pass and press forward in a struggle demanding your every effort. To press forward, yes; but whither?

I have asked myself that question all my conscious years. In search of an answer I have read many books, some that men would call sacred, some the reverse. I have tried to understand anatomy and embryology in the widest meanings of those terms. I have studied comparative religion and have trodden slowly and laboriously in the footsteps of Sir James Frazer in his mazy dance around "The Golden Bough." I have searched the poets. I have spent years about the business and still ask myself—Whither?

I cannot tell you. I do not know. But some things have become clear to me.

First, I believe that there is a great purpose running through all our strivings which is not of us, but from above us. The end to which that purpose moves is impenetrably hidden from mortal eyes, but the direction in which the end lies, the direction in which we should move, is not hidden, but clear.

We are not as beasts. We have power to choose and to decide. We are not physically great and powerful creatures. We have not horns and hoofs and scales. But though our bodies are weak and soft, our brains are things of marvel, and through those brains there come to each of us many different thoughts and promptings, but to all of us come three that are not animal in origin, are not concerned with the life of the body, but are, I believe, beams from spiritual lighthouses for the guidance of our earthly voyage.

I used to be a teacher and was happier teaching than I have ever been before or since, but as I look back I see that my pupils taught me nearly all that really matters which I know. They taught me that in my years of study, in my delvings into books, in my work in the research laboratory, I had been looking in the wrong place for the answer I sought. They taught me that the book which contained the truth was the human heart.

In that warm palpitating book I read and learned that each of us had a desire inborn, an instinct, if you will, for beauty; a desire to serve his fellows; a desire to know the truth.

I do not mean that each sees beauty as each other sees it. But within the range of his understanding, within the limits of his vision, each desires beauty in his surroundings, beauty of form, beauty of color, beauty of sound.

Again, I do not mean that each sees service to his fellows in the same light, but the impulse to serve, the instinct of altruism, is in the heart of each.

Again, I do not mean that each is interested in the same branch of knowledge, but the desire to know the truth is there.

What I do mean is that each young soul, still tender from its earthly birth and not hardened by the hammer of the world, has these three longings. It is true that the first, the desire for beauty, links with the impulse of sex; that the second, the desire for service, links with the most wonderful of the animal instincts, mother love, yet each is so different from its linked animal instinct as to be separate from it. The third, the desire for truth, links with nothing that I know of, unless it be the instinct of curiosity.

In many adults these spiritual desires are atrophied and have ceased to trouble or to guide the man or woman, but in simple people they are apt to remain alive in a way and to an extent that astonishes the sophisticated. To retain the eyes of the child, to see the world anew every morning, is a privilege shared by few of the learned and fewer still of what men call the successful.

In some the desire for knowledge is atrophied, though the other two remain. In more the desires for knowledge and for service are atrophied, though the desire for beauty remains, but these are maimed beings who have lost something more wonderful and more precious than any wealth or any position can buy.

The great danger which attaches to university education is

that it kills the thirst for beauty and service and limits the desire for knowledge to the field of a microscope—sometimes to the field of a high-power oil immersion objective and replaces the glad free roaming after truth by a seeking for all knowledge in the slime of the cart rut. That is the danger of specialization.

One of the reasons for the present mental turmoil of the peoples is that their leaders have lost the spiritual instincts, while they in some measures have retained theirs. The simple know less and feel more, and despise those who know more and feel less.

That is the danger. Knowing nothing or at best, little of the civilization which knowledge has made possible through the application of steam and steel and credit to the affairs of men, many of the common people are seeking to give free rein to feeling uncontrolled by understanding. That way lies disaster. Without continuous application of knowledge the edifice of civilization will fall down, but without continuous application of the three spiritual instincts to the ordering of society it will blow up. The fact that civilization is in danger in parts of Europe is proof that the leaders and rulers of the past either never knew or forgot that merely to apply specialized technical knowledge is to give a stone to humanity clamoring for bread.

You are to be leaders or you will be nothing. If after your university training you are not in the way to qualify for leadership you had better plow the land or grow food for the peoples, for a university man or woman who is not at least a subordinate leader is a parasite, or at best a seton in the body politic. And to you leaders of the future I hand all the knowledge that remains to me from years of striving to find the answer to the question, Whither?

It is simply this: Humanity moves to a haven which we cannot see, but though the sea is dark there are three lighthouses to help each pilot, and the first of these is beauty, the second, service, the third, truth. Keeping those three ever in view, civilization will sail safely. Let one be occulted and civilization is in danger. Let two be occulted and peril is nigh. Let three be occulted and civilization falls.

Thus Babylon fell, thus Egypt, thus Rome, in many ways the

greatest and proudest civilization that has been. So I doubt not fell all the civilizations of the past. So to-day civilization totters.

To you and to those like you the civilization of the world is committed. Be faithful to your trust. Before almost you have realized that you are no longer boys and girls you will find yourselves the men and women of the new generation.

If any one had spoken to me the day I obtained my first degree as I have spoken to you to-night I should have written him down a consummate ass. I was sure then where I am uncertain now, or am now certain in an opposite sense to my earlier surety. If the effect of education has been in the case of any one to turn him or her into an atheist or an agnostic or a materialist or any other brand of non-religious thinker I beg him not to imagine that he is the first or will be the last. Let him not commit himself for ten years to any expression of opinion in that direction. Let him wait for the revelations and miracles that are to come, for the days of revelations and of miracles are not yet ended.

No man could have had a much more romantic or interesting life than I, and yet I almost find it in my heart to envy you. Why? Because the next fifty or sixty years are going to be the most glorious or the most disastrous in the history of the world. My generation cannot hope to see a successful end to the world revolution which is now in progress, though yours may. You have still a few years in which to grow strong in the battle of life before the full burden of responsibility descends upon you. You must prepare. Let me tell you how. Keep ever before you the sense of your responsibility. Seek without ceasing an answer to the question, Whither away? And, though you will never know the end to which the great purpose moves, there will be continually revealed to you the general direction in which to press. Keep the three lights of life steadily in your own view. Help your fellow-men, not to lose them from your sight. Bend all your knowledge and all your power to the day's work. Thus you will live greatly.

To-day is the day on which you recall the names and glorify the memory of those who died for America. They gave their all for you. It was hard for them to leave their cheerful and happy world even for a great cause, and you do well to hold them in pious memory, but for some it is harder to live for the same great cause, the cause of freedom and right and humanity. I hope that the call will come to you to live and not to die, but whichever is your lot you will find it difficult. Believe me, to live rightly requires much more understanding, much more vigilance than to die nobly. I urge you to dig deep into the hidden meanings and implications of the spiritual longings for beauty, service and truth, and if my wishes can benefit you now or hereafter I wish you, novitiates in the brotherhood of university men and women, health and strength to serve and happiness in serving the nation to which you owe allegiance and through which, if you so will, you can serve mankind.

JAMES, CARDINAL GIBBONS

JAMES, CARDINAL GIBBONS

SUPREMACY OF THE CATHOLIC RELIGION

Address by Cardinal Gibbons of the Roman Catholic Church (born in Baltimore, Md., July 23, 1834; died, 1921), delivered before the Parliament of Religions, held during the Columbian Exposition, at Chicago, September 14, 1893.

WE live and move and have our being in the midst of a civilization which is the legitimate offspring of the Catholic religion. The blessings resulting from our Christian civilization are poured out so regularly and so abundantly on the intellectual, moral, and social world, like the sunlight and the air of heaven and the fruits of the earth, that they have ceased to excite any surprise except in those who visit lands where the religion of Christ is little known. In order to realize adequately our favored situation, we should transport ourselves in spirit to ante-Christian times, and contrast the condition of the pagan world with our own.

Before the advent of Christ, the whole world, with the exception of the secluded Roman province of Palestine, was buried in idolatry. Every striking object in nature had its tutelary divinities. Men worshiped the sun and moon and stars of heaven. They worshiped their very passions. They worshiped everything except God, to whom alone divine homage is due. In the words of the Apostle of the Gentiles: "They changed the glory of the incorruptible God into the likeness of the corruptible man, and of birds and beasts and creeping things. They worshiped and served the creature rather than the Creator who is blessed forever."

But, at last, the great light for which the prophets had sighed and prayed, and toward which the pagan sages had stretched forth their hands with eager longing, arose and shone unto them "that sat in the darkness and the shadow of death." The truth concerning our Creator, which had hitherto been hidden in Judea, that there it might be sheltered from the world-wide idolatry, was now proclaimed, and in far greater clearness and fullness unto the whole world. Jesus Christ taught all mankind to know one true God—a God existing from eternity to eternity, a God who created all things by His power, who governs all things by His wisdom, and whose superintending Providence watches over the affairs of nations as well as of men, "without whom not even a sparrow falls to the ground." He proclaimed a God infinitely holy, just, and merciful. This idea of the Deity so consonant to our rational conceptions was in striking contrast with the low and sensual notions which the pagan world has formed of its divinities.

The religion of Christ imparts to us not only a sublime conception of God, but also a rational idea of man and of his relations to his Creator. Before the coming of Christ, man was a riddle and a mystery to himself. He knew not whence he came, nor whither he was going. He was groping in the dark. All he knew for certain was that he was passing through a brief phase of existence. The past and future were enveloped in a mist which the light of philosophy was unable to penetrate. Our Redeemer has dispelled the cloud and enlightened us regarding our origin and destiny and the means of attaining it. He has rescued man from the frightful labyrinth of error in which Paganism had involved him.

The Gospel of Christ as propounded by the Catholic Church has brought, not only light to the intellect, but comfort also to the heart. It has given us "that peace of God which surpasseth all understanding," the peace which springs from the conscious possession of truth. It has taught us to enjoy that triple peace which constitutes true happiness, as far as it is attainable in this life—peace with God by the observance of His commandments, peace with our neighbor by the exercise of charity and justice toward him, and peace with ourselves by repressing our inordinate appetites, and keeping our passions subject to the law of reason, and our reason illumined and controlled by the law of God.

All other religious systems prior to the advent of Christ were national, like Judaism, or State religions, like Paganism. The

SUPREMACY OF THE CATHOLIC RELIGION 185

Catholic religion alone is world-wide and cosmopolitan, embracing all races and nations and peoples and tongues. Christ alone, of all religious founders, had the courage to say to His disciples: "Go, teach all nations. Preach the Gospel to every creature. You shall be witness to me in Judea and Samaria, and even to the uttermost bounds of the earth. Be not restrained in your mission by national or state lines. Let my gospel be as free and universal as the air of heaven. The earth is the Lord's and the fullness thereof. All mankind are the children of my father and my brethren. I have died for all, and embrace all in my charity. Let the whole human race be your audience, and the world be the theater of your labors!"

It is this recognition of the fatherhood of God and the brotherhood of Christ that has inspired the Catholic Church in her mission of love and benevolence. This is the secret of her all-pervading charity. This idea has been her impelling motive in her work for the social regeneration of mankind. "I behold," she says, "in every human creature a child of God and a brother or sister of Christ, and therefore I will protect helpless infancy and decrepit old age. I will feed the orphan and nurse the sick. I will strike the shackles from the feet of the slave, and will rescue degraded woman from the moral bondage and degradation to which her own frailty and the passions of the stronger sex had consigned her."

Montesquieu has well said that the religion of Christ, which was instituted to lead men to eternal life, has contributed more than any other institution to promote the temporal and social happiness of mankind. The object of this Parliament of Religions is to present to the thoughtful, earnest, and inquiring minds the respective claims of the various religions, with the view that they would "prove all things, and hold that which is good," by embracing that religion which above all others commends itself to their judgment and conscience. I am not engaged in this search for the truth, for, by the grace of God, I am conscious that I have found it, and instead of hiding this treasure in my own breast, I long to share it with others, especially as I am none the poorer in making others the richer. But, for my part, were I occupied in this investigation, much as I would be drawn toward the Catholic Church by her admirable unity of faith which binds together in common worship two hundred and fifty million souls, much as I would be attracted toward her by her sublime moral code, by her world-wide catholicity and by that unbroken claim of apostolic succession which connects her indissolubly with apostolic times, I could be drawn still more forcibly toward her by that wonderful system of organized benevolence which she has established for the alleviation and comfort of suffering humanity.

Let us briefly review what the Catholic Church has done for the elevation and betterment of humanity:—

I. The Catholic Church has purified society in its very fountain, which is the marriage bond. She has invariably proclaimed the unity and sanctity and indissolubility of the marriage tie by saying with her founder that: "What God hath joined together, let no man put asunder." Wives and mothers, never forget that the inviolability of the marriage contract is the palladium of your womanly dignity and of your Christian religion. And if you are no longer the slaves of man and the toy of his caprice, like the wives of Asiatic countries, but the peers and partners of your husbands; if you are no longer tenants at will, like the wives of pagan Greece and Rome, but the mistresses of your households; if you are no longer confronted by uprising rivals, like Mohammedan and Mormon wives, but are the queens of domestic kingdoms, you are indebted for this priceless boon to the ancient Church, and particularly to the Roman pontiffs who inflexibly upheld the sacredness of the nuptial bond against the arbitrary power of kings, the lust of nobles, and the lax and pernicious legislation of city governments.

II. The Catholic religion has proclaimed the sanctity of human life as soon as the body is animated with the vital spark. Infanticide was a dark stain on pagan civilization. It was universal in Greece with the exception of Thebes. It was sanctified and even sometimes enjoined by such eminent Greeks as Plato and Aristotle, Solon, and Lycurgus. The destruction of infants was also very common among the Romans. Nor was there any legal check to this inhuman crime, except at rare intervals. The father had the power of life and death over his child. And as an evidence that human nature does not improve with time and is everywhere the same, unless it is permeated with the leaven of Christianity, the wanton sacrifice of infant life is probably as general to-day in China and other heathen countries as it was in ancient Greece and Rome. The Catholic Church has sternly set her face against this exposure and murder of innocent babes. She has denounced it as a crime more revolting than that of Herod, because committed against one's own flesh and blood. She has condemned with equal energy the atrocious doctrine of Malthus, who suggested unnatural methods for diminishing the population of the human family. Were I not restrained by the fear of offending modesty and of imparting knowledge where "ignorance is bliss," I would dwell more at length on the social plague of antenatal infanticide, which is insidiously and systematically spreading among us, in defiance of civil penalties and of the Divine law which says: "Thou shalt not kill."

III. There is no phase of human misery for which the Church does not provide some remedy or alleviation. She has established infant asylums for the shelter of helpless babes who have been cruelly abandoned by their own parents, or bereft of them in the mysterious dispensations of Providence before they could know and feel a mother's love. These little waifs, like the infant Moses drifting in the turbid Nile, are rescued from an untimely death and are tenderly raised by the daughters of the Great King, those consecrated virgins who become nursing mothers to them. And I have known more than one such motherless babe, who, like Israel's law-giver in after years, became a leader among his people.

IV. As the Church provides homes for those yet on the threshold of life, so, too, does she secure retreats for those on the threshold of death. She has asylums in which aged men and women find at one and the same time a refuge in their old age from the storms of life and a novitiate to prepare them for eternity. Thus, from the cradle to the grave, she is a nursing mother. She rocks her children in the cradle of infancy, and she soothes them to rest on the couch of death. Louis XIV erected in France the famous Hotel des Invalides for the veterans of France who had fought in the service of their country. And so has the Catholic religion provided for those who have been disabled in the battle of life, a home in which they are tenderly nursed in their declining years by devoted sisters. The Little Sisters of the Poor, whose congregation was founded in 1840, have now charge of over two hundred and fifty establishments in different parts of the globe, the aged inmates of those houses numbering thirty thousand, upward of seventy thousand having died under their care up to 1889. To these asylums are welcomed, not only the members of the Catholic religion, but those also of every form of Christian faith, and even those without any faith at all. The Sisters make no distinction of person, or nationality, or color, or creed—for true charity embraces all. The only question proposed by the Sisters to the applicant for shelter is this: Are you oppressed by age and penury? If so, come to us and we will provide for you.

V. She has orphan asylums where children of both sexes are reared and taught to become useful and worthy members of society.

VI. Hospitals were unknown to the pagan world before the coming of Christ. The copious vocabularies of Greece and Rome had no word even to express the term. The Catholic Church has hospitals for the treatment and cure of every form of disease. She sends her daughters of charity and mercy to the battle-field and to the plague-stricken city. During the Crimean War I remember to have read of a Sister who was struck dead by a ball while she was in the act of stooping down and bandaging the wound of a fallen soldier. Much praise was then deservedly bestowed on Florence Nightingale for her devotion to the sick and wounded soldiers. Her name resounded in both hemispheres. But in every Sister you have a Florence Nightingale, with this difference—that, like ministering angels, they move without noise along the path of duty, and like the angel Raphael, who concealed his name from Tobias, the Sister hides her name from the world.

Several years ago I accompanied to New Orleans eight Sisters of Charity who were sent from Baltimore to reënforce the ranks of their heroic companions, or to supply the places of their devoted associates who had fallen at the post of duty in the fever-stricken cities of the South. Their departure for the scene of their labors was neither announced by the press nor heralded by public applause. They went calmly into the jaws of death, not bent on deeds of destruction, like the famous Six Hundred, but on deeds of mercy. They had no Tennyson to sound their praises. Their only ambition was,—and how lofty is that ambition—that the recording angel might be their biographer, that their names might be inscribed in the Book of Life, and that they might receive the recompense from Him who has said: "I was sick and ye visited me; for as often as ye did it to one of the least of my brethren, ye did it to me." Within a few months after their arrival, six of the eight Sisters died victims to the epidemic. These are a few of many instances of heroic charity that have fallen under my own observation. Here are examples of sublime heroism not culled from the musty pages of ancient martyrologies, or books of chivalry, but happening in our day and under our own eyes. Here is a heroism not aroused by the emulation of brave comrades on the battlefield, or by the clash of arms, or the strains of martial hymns, or by the love of earthly fame, but inspired only by a sense of Christian duty and by the love of God and her fellow-beings.

VII. The Catholic religion labors not only to assuage the physical distempers of humanity, but also to reclaim the victims of moral disease. The redemption of fallen women from a life of infamy was never included in the scope of heathen philanthropy and man's unregenerate nature is the same now as before the birth of Christ. He worships woman as long as she has charms to fascinate, but she is spurned and trampled upon as soon as she has ceased to please. It was reserved for him who knew no sin to throw the mantle of protection over sinning woman. There is no page in the Gospel more touching than that which records our Savior's merciful judgment on the adulterous woman. The Scribes and Pharisees, who had, perhaps, participated in her guilt, asked our Lord to pronounce sentence of death upon her, in accordance with the Mosaic law. "Hath no one condemned thee?" asked our Savior. "No one, Lord," she answered. "Then," said he, "neither will I condemn thee. Go, and sin no more." Inspired by this divine example, the Catholic Church shelters erring females in homes not inappropriately called Magdalene Asylums and Houses of the Good Shepherd. Not to speak of other institutions established for the moral reformation of women, the congregation of the Good Shepherd at Angers, founded in 1836, has charge to-day of one hundred and fifty houses, in which upward of four thousand Sisters devote themselves to the care of over twenty thousand females, who had yielded to temptation or were rescued from impending danger.

VIII. The Christian religion has been the unvarying friend and advocate of the bondman. Before the dawn of Christianity, slavery was universal in civilized, as well as in barbarous nations. The Apostles were everywhere confronted by the children of oppression. Their first task was to mitigate the horrors and alleviate the miseries of human bondage. They cheered the slave by holding up to him the example of Christ, who voluntarily became a slave that we might enjoy the glorious liberty of children of God. The bondman had an equal participation with his master in the sacraments of the Church, and in the priceless consolation which religion affords. Slave-owners were admonished to be kind and humane to their slaves, by being reminded with apostolic freedom that they and their servants had the same master in heaven, who had no respect of persons. The ministers of the Catholic religion down the ages sought to lighten the burden and improve the condition of the slave, as far as social prejudices would permit, till, at length, the chains fell from his feet. Human slavery has, at last, thank God, melted away before the noon-tide sun of the Gospel. No Christian country contains to-day a solitary slave. To paraphrase the words of a distinguished Irish jurist—as soon as a bondman puts his foot in a Christian land, he stands redeemed, regenerated, and disenthralled, on the sacred soil of Christendom.

IX. The Savior never conferred a greater temporal boon on mankind than by ennobling and sanctifying manual labor, and by rescuing it from the stigma of degradation which had been branded upon it. Before Christ appeared among men, manual and even mechanical work was regarded as servile and degrading to the freeman of pagan Rome, and was consequently relegated to slaves. Christ is ushered into the world, not amid the pomp and splendor of imperial majesty, but amid the environments of a humble child of toil. He is the reputed son of an artisan, and his early manhood is spent in a mechanic's shop. "Is not this the carpenter, the son of Mary?" The primeval curse attached to labor is obliterated by the toilsome life of Jesus Christ. Ever since he pursued his trade as a carpenter, he has lightened the mechanic's tools, and shed a halo around the workshop. If the profession of a general, a jurist, and a statesman is adorned by the example of a Washington, a Taney, and a Burke, how much more is the character of a workman ennobled by the example of Christ. What De Tocqueville said of the United States sixty years ago is true to-day—that with us every honest labor is laudable, thanks to the example of Christ.

To sum up: The Catholic Church has taught man the knowledge of God and of himself; she has brought comfort to his heart by instructing him to bear the ills of life with Christian philosophy; she has sanctified the marriage bond; she has proclaimed the sanctity and inviolability of human life from the moment that the body is animated by the spark of life, till it is extinguished; she has founded asylums for the training of children of both sexes and for the support of the aged poor; she has established hospitals for the sick and homes for the redemption of fallen women; she has exerted her influence toward the mitigation and abolition of human slavery; she has been the unwavering friend of the sons of toil. These are some of the blessings which the Catholic Church has conferred on society.

I will not deny—on the contrary, I am happy to avow—that the various Christian bodies outside the Catholic Church have been, and are to-day, zealous promoters of most of these works of Christian benevolence which I have enumerated. Not to speak of the innumerable humanitarian houses established by our non-Catholic brethren throughout the land, I bear cheerful testimony to the philanthropic institutions founded by Wilson, by Shepherd, by Johns Hopkins, Enoch Pratt, and George Peabody, in the city of Baltimore. But will not our separated brethren have the candor to acknowledge that we had first possession of the field, that these beneficent movements have been inaugurated by us, and that the other Christian communities in their noble efforts for the moral and social regeneration of mankind, have, in no small measure, been stimulated by the example and emulation of the ancient Church?

Let us do all we can in our day and generation in the cause of humanity. Every man has a mission from God to help his fellow-beings. Though we differ in faith, thank God there is one platform on which we stand united, and that is the platform of charity and benevolence. We cannot, indeed, like our Divine Master, give sight to the blind, hearing to the deaf, speech to the dumb, and strength to the paralyzed limb, but we can work miracles of grace and mercy by relieving the distress of our suffering brethren. And never do we approach nearer to our Heavenly Father than when we alleviate the sorrows of others. Never do we perform an act more Godlike than when we bring sunshine to hearts that are dark and desolate. Never are we more like to God than when we cause the flowers of joy and gladness to bloom in souls that were dry and barren before. "Religion," says the apostle, "pure and undefiled before God and the Father, is this: To visit the fatherless and widows in their tribulation, and to keep oneself unspotted from the world." Or to borrow the words of pagan Cicero, *"Homines ad deos nulla re propius accedunt quam salutem hominibus dando."* (There is no way by which men can approach nearer to the gods than by contributing to the welfare of their fellow-creatures.)

DANIEL COIT GILMAN

THE CHARACTERISTICS OF A UNIVERSITY

Address by Daniel Coit Gilman, first president of Johns Hopkins University, inaugurated in 1875 (born in Norwich, Conn., 1831; died 1908), delivered at the commemoration of the two hundred and fiftieth anniversary of Harvard University, in Cambridge, Mass., July 1, 1886. The introduction which is omitted here, deals with the historical side of the subject. As president of Johns Hopkins, Dr. Gilman did much to realize the vision of a university which he here describes.

SURELY it is time for the scholars of the country to take their bearings. In Cambridge, the anniversary so soon to be celebrated will not be allowed to pass without munificent contributions for most noble ends; the president of Yale College, who this day assumes his high office with the unanimous plaudits of Yalensians, is the representative of the university idea based upon academic traditions; the voice of Princeton, like a herald, has proclaimed its purposes; Cornell has succeeded in a litigation which establishes its right to a large endowment; the Secretary of the Interior has commended to Congress the importance of a national university, and a bill has been introduced looking toward such an establishment; the Roman Catholic Church, at its recent council in Baltimore, initiated measures for a university in the capital of the nation; while on the remotest borders of the land the gift of many millions is assured for promoting a new foundation. Already in the Mississippi Valley men are laboriously unfolding their lofty ideals. It is therefore a critical time. Wise plans will be like good seed; they will spring up and bear fruit a hundredfold. Bad plans

Copyright, by The Century Company. Published by permission.

will be like tares growing up with the wheat, impossible to eradicate.

It is obvious that the modes of organization will vary, so that we shall have many different types of universities. Four types have already appeared: those which proceed from the original historic colleges; those established in the name of the State; those avowedly ecclesiastical; and those which are founded by private benefactions. Each mode of organization has advantages which may be defended, each its limitations. If the older colleges suffer from traditions, the younger lack experience and historic growth. The State universities are liable to political mismanagement; ecclesiastical foundations are in danger of being narrow.

Under these circumstances, I ask you to consider the characteristics of a university, the marks by which it should be distinguished. It is needless before this audience to repeat the numerous definitions which have been framed, or to rehearse the brilliant projects which have been formed by learned, gifted men; but it will not be amiss to recall some of the noble aims which have always inspired endeavors to establish the highest institutions of learning.

Among the brightest signs of a vigorous university is zeal for the advancement of learning. Another phrase has been lately used, the "endowment of research." I prefer the other term, for it takes us back to the dawn of modern science, and connects our efforts with those of three hundred years ago, when Francis Bacon gave an impulse to all subsequent thought, and published what his recent biographer has called the first great book in English prose of secular interest—"the first of a long line of books which have attempted to teach English readers how to think of knowledge, to make it really and intelligently the interest, not of the school or the study or the laboratory only, but of society at large. It was a book with a purpose, new then, but of which we have seen the fulfillment."

The processes by which we gain acquaintance with the world are very slow. The detection of another asteroid, the calculation of a new orbit, the measurement of a lofty peak, the discovery of a bird, a fish, an insect, a flower, hitherto "unknown to science," would be but trifles if each new fact remained

CHARACTERISTICS OF A UNIVERSITY 195

apart from other facts; but when among learned men discoveries are brought into relations with familiar truths, the group suggests a law; the law an inference; the inference an experiment; the experiment a conclusion; and so from fact to law, and from law to fact, with rhythmic movement, knowledge marches on, while eager hosts of practical men stand ready to apply to human life each fresh discovery.

Investigation, coördination, and promulgation are not performed exclusively by universities; but these processes, so fruitful in good, are most efficient where large numbers of the erudite and the acute, of strong reasoners and faithful critics, are associated for mutual assistance, correction, and encouragement. It is an impressive passage with which the lamented Jevons closed his "Principles of Science." After reminding the reader of the infinite domain of mathematical inquiry, compared with which the whole accomplishments of a Laplace or a Lagrange are as the little corner of the multiplication table, which has really an indefinite extent, he goes on to say that inconceivable advances will be made by the human intellect unless there is an unforeseen catastrophe to the species of the globe. "Since the time of Newton and Leibnitz, whole worlds of problems have been solved, which before were hardly conceived as matters of inquiry. In our own day, extended methods of mathematical reasoning, such as the system of quarternions, have been brought into existence. What intelligent man will doubt that the recondite speculations of a Cayley or a Sylvester may possibly lead to some new methods, at the simplicity and power of which a future age will wonder, and yet wonder more that to us they were so dark and difficult?"

Let me draw an illustration from another science which will be acknowledged as of transcendent importance even by those, if such skeptics there be, who have no confidence in transcendental mathematics. Cohnheim, the great pathologist of Germany, whose death occurred in 1884, declares, in the introduction to his "General Pathology," that the study of the causes of disease is absolutely without limits, for it touches upon the most heterogeneous branches of science. Cosmical physics, meteorology, and geology, not less than the social sciences, chemistry, as well as botany and zoölogy, all bring their contributions to that branch of pathology. So with all his knowledge and ability this leader in pathology restricted his own work to the study of disordered physiological functions. But what prevention of suffering, what sanitary alleviations, what prolongation of life, may we not anticipate in future generations, when man thoroughly understands his complex environment and adapts himself to it?

In the accumulation of knowledge, as of other forms of wealth, saving must follow earning. So among the offices of a university we find the conservation of experience. Ignorant as the nineteenth century appears when we survey the long category of inquiries now held in abeyance by mathematicians, astronomers, physicists, chemists, and biologists, by ethnologists, philologers, historians, and publicists, remember how much man has advanced since the ages of stone, of iron, and of brass. Such books as Tylor's and Morgan's, such observations as those of Livingstone and Stanley, show us what man is without a history; what society is where no storage is provided for the lessons learned by successive generations, and where the wisest and best are content to pass away, leaving no sign. It is the business of universities not only to perpetuate the records of culture, but to bring them out in modern, timely, and intelligible interpretations, so that all may know the laws of human progress, the dangers which imperil society, the conditions of advancing civilization. Experiments upon fundamental laws, such as the establishment of home rule, or the adjustment of the discord between industry and capital, may destroy or may promote the happiness of many generations. That mistakes may not be made, historical politics must be studied, and what is this but the study of the experience of mankind in endeavors to promote the social welfare?

As there have been great lawgivers in the past, whose codes have been put to secular tests, so momentous experiments have run through centuries and involved the welfare of nations—experiments which have been recorded and interpreted, but which call for still closer study, by the wisest intellects, before their lessons are exhausted. Can such researches be made in a moment? Can they be undertaken by a knight of labor? Are the facts to be gathered in a circulating library? Or must we depend upon scholars trained to handle the apparatus of learning? Gladstone and Bryce and Morley may or may not be right in all the subordinate features of the measures which they are advocating; but their influence at this very moment is resting on the fulcrum of historic knowledge, the value of local self-government. Hamilton, Jefferson, Madison, and Marshall were far from being "inspired" when they initiated the constitutional measures by which the United States is governed, and there is abundant evidence to show that they were students of the past experience of mankind in confederated politics. The compact of the *Mayflower* was reduced to writing within the sheltering arm of Cape Cod, but its ideas are those of men who knew the laws of Moses and Solomon, and who had seen in Holland, as well as in England, what favors and what hinders the development of civil and religious liberty. Within the shadow of the University of Leyden a stone marks the spot where John Robinson lived, taught, and died; and the name of Elder Brewster of the *Mayflower* has been recently discovered among the matriculates of Peterhouse, Cambridge, the oldest of the colleges on the Cam.

The universities are the natural conservators of educational experience, and should be recognized as the guides of public education. In a better state of society means will be found to make the men of learning in a given generation responsible for the systems of primary teaching, giving potency to their counsel not only at the end but in every stage of scholastic life. Upon text-books, courses of study, methods of discipline, the qualifications of teachers, the value of rewards, honors, and examinations, the voice of the universities should be heard. The confusion and uncertainty which now prevail are indications that, in schools of the lowest as of the highest grades, readjustments are needed which can only be wisely directed by those whose learning embraces the experience of many generations. The wisest are none too wise in pedagogics, but they are better counselors than the ignorant.

Dr. Lieber, in a letter to Secretary Seward, at the close of the Civil War, presented a strong plea for the reference of international disputes to universities. Reminding the secretary that their authority had been invoked upon internal controversies in France and Germany, he asked, why not refer to them in international affairs? The law faculty of a renowned university in a minor State would seem, he says, "almost made for this high function, and its selection as a court of international arbitration would be a measure worthy of England and the United States"; and he risks the prophecy that "the cis-Caucasian race will rise at no very distant day to the selection of such umpires, far more dignified than a crowned arbitrator can be."

Among the offices of a university there is one too often undervalued or perhaps forgotten—the discovery and development of unusual talent. I do not speak of genius, which takes care of itself. Nobody can tell how it comes to pass that men of extraordinary minds are born of commonplace parentage and bred in schools of adversity away from books and masters. Institutions are not essential to their education. But every one who observes in a series of years the advancement of men of talents, as distinguished from men of genius, must believe that the fostering diet of a university—its "plain living and high thinking"—favors the growth of scholars, investigators, reasoners, orators, statesmen of enduring reputation, poets, and discoverers. Such men are rarely produced in the freedom of the wilderness, in the publicity of travel and of trade, or in the seclusion of private life; they are not the natural product of libraries and museums, when these stand apart from universities; they are rarely produced by schools of a lower grade. Exceptions are familiar, but the history of civilization declares that promising youth should have the most favorable opportunities for intercourse with other minds, living as well as dead, comrades as well as teachers, governors as well as friends. It declares that in most cases talents will seize opportunity, and opportunity will help talents. Just now, in our own country, there is special reason for affirming that talents should be encouraged without respect to property. Indeed, it is quite probable that the rich need the stimulus of academic honors more than the poor; certainly the good of society requires that intellectual power, wherever detected, should be encouraged to exercise its highest functions.

Cardinal Newman (in a page which refers to Sir Isaac Newton's perception of truths, mathematical and physical, though proof was absent, and to Professor Sylvester's discovery, a century and half later, of the proof of Newton's rule for ascertaining the imaginary roots of equations) says that a parallel gift is the intuitive perception of character possessed by certain men, as there are physicians who excel in diagnosis, and lawyers in the detection of crime.

Maurice, the great theologian of our day, was so strong an advocate of university education that he suggests a sort of *quo warranto* forcing "those who are destined by their birth or property to anything above the middle station in society, and intended to live in England, . . . to show cause why they do not put themselves in the best position for becoming what Coleridge calls the *clerisy* of the land."

Devotion to literature will always distinguish a complete university. Within the academic walls you may always find the lover of humanities; here, in perpetual residence, those who know the Athenian dramatists, the Augustan poets, the mediæval epic writers, Chaucer and Shakespeare, and the leaders in literature of every name and tongue. In the classrooms of the university, successive generations of youth should be presented to these illustrious men. The secrets of their excellence should be pointed out, the delights of literary enjoyment should be set forth, the possibilities of production in our day should be indicated, and withal the principles of criticism should be inculcated, as remote from sarcasm and fault-finding, on the one hand, as from prostrate adoration and overwrought sympathy, on the other.

It is common in these days to lament that the taste of the public, as indicated by the remorseless self-recording apparatus of the public libraries and the glaring advertisements of the book-stalls, is depraved; but it is well to remember that many counteracting influences are vigorous. Never was Shakespeare read and studied as he is to-day; never was Chaucer so familiar to the youth at school; never was the Bible so widely read; never were such translations accessible as are now within reach of all. In all this the power of the universities is felt; give them the credit. But in the future let more attention than ever before be given to the study of literature and art. Fortunate would it be if in every seat of learning such a living teacher could be found as a Wordsworth, a Tennyson, a Browning, an Arnold, or a Lowell.

Among the characteristics of a university I name the defense of ideality, the maintenance of spirituality. There are those in every generation who fear that inquiry is hostile to religion. Although universities are the children of the Christian church, although for a long period the papal sanction was desirable, if not essential, to their establishment, although the earliest colleges in this country were strictly religious, and although almost every denomination in the land desires its own university, there is an undercurrent of talk which shows that the influence of the higher education is now regarded in certain circles as adverse to spiritual and religious life. If this were so, many would prefer to see the academic walls fall down in a night, and the treasures of the ages reduced to smoke and ashes. But, fortunately indeed, there is no such danger. Alarmists are cowards. That piety is infantile which apprehends that knowledge is fatal to reverence, devotion, righteousness, and faith.

As the most recent utterances of science point more and more steadily to the plan of a great designer, as the studies of psychology and of history confirm the doctrine, at least as old as Solomon, that righteousness exalteth a nation, so we may affirm that the two essentials of Christianity, on which hang all the law and the prophets,—the love of God and the love of our neighbor,—are enforced and not weakened by the influence of universities. We may also rest assured that institutions devoted to the ascertainment of truth as the ultimate object of intellectual exertion, and to the promulgation of truth as an imperative moral obligation, are not the harbingers of harm. Individuals will err; generations will labor under false ideas; domineering intellects will dazzle for a time the ordinary mind; error, like disease, must be clearly understood before the mode of correction can be formulated; but there is no better way known to man for securing intellectual and moral integrity than to encourage those habits, those methods, and those pursuits which tend to establish truth.

Near the close of his address before the University of Munich, at the celebration of its jubilee in 1872, a great theologian, Dr.

Döllinger, referred to the perils of the times in words which were received with prolonged applause. "Who knows," said he, "but that for a time Germany may remain confined in that strait prison, without air and light, which we call materialism? This would be a forerunner of approaching national ruin. But this can only happen in case the universities of Germany, forgetting their traditions and yielding to a shameful lethargy, should waste their best treasures. But no; our universities will form the impregnable wall ready to stop the devastating flood."

The maintenance of a high standard of professional learning may also be named among the requisites of a university. So it is on the continent of Europe, so partially in Great Britain, so it should be everywhere. The slender means of our fathers compelled them to restrict their outlays to that which was regarded as fundamental or general education, and so it came to pass (as we have already been reminded) that professional schools were established in this country as independent foundations. Even where they are placed under the university ægis, they have been regarded as only children by adoption, ready enough for the funds which have been provided for academic training, but without any claims to inherit the birthright. The injury to the country from this state of things is obvious. The professional schools are everywhere in danger of being—nay, in many places they actually are—places of technical instead of liberal education. Their scholars are not encouraged to show a proficiency in those fundamental studies which the experience of the world has demanded for the first degree in arts. It is well known that many a medical school graduates young men who could not get admission to a college of repute; ought we then to wonder that quackery is popular, and that it is better to own a patent medicine than a gold mine? It was a wise and good man who said that there is no greater curse to a country than an uneducated ministry; and yet how common it is for the schools of theology in this country to be isolated from the best affiliations! Lawyers are too often trained with reference to getting on at the bar, and find themselves unprepared for the higher walks of jurisprudence and statesmanship; and members of Congress and of the State legislatures frequently exhibit to the world poverty of preparation for the critical duties which devolve upon them.

I am far from believing that university schools of law, medicine, and theology will settle the perplexing questions of the day, either in science, religion, or politics; but if the experience of the world is worth anything, it can nowhere be so effectively and easily acquired as in the faculties of a well-organized university, where each particular study is defined and illuminated by the steady light which comes from collateral pursuits and from the bright suggestions of learned and gifted teachers. Moreover, science has developed in modern society scores of professions each of which requires preparation as liberal as law, medicine, or theology. The schools in which modern sciences are studied may indeed grow up apart from the fostering care of universities, and there is some advantage doubtless, while they are in their early years, in being free from academic traditions; but schools of science are legitimate branches of a modern university, and are gradually assuming their proper relations.

Finally, among the merits of a university is the cultivation of a spirit of repose. As the distractions of modern civilization multiply, as newspaper enterprise brings to our daily vision the conflicts and transactions of mankind, as books become superabundant, and periodicals more and more indispensable, and more and more technical, some corrective must exist, or there will be no more enjoyment in an intellectual life than there is in making money in the turmoil of the bourse. The whirl of the nineteenth century has already affected the colleges, with detriment to that seclusion which best promotes the acquisition of knowledge. A man of varied experience in public affairs has said that a great university should be at once "the best place of education, the greatest machine for research, and the most delicious retreat for learned leisure." This is doubtless the truth, but it is only a half-truth. Universities with ample resources for the support of investigators, scholars, thinkers, and philosophers, numerous enough, learned enough, and wise enough to be felt among the powers of the age, will prove the safeguards of repose, not only for those who live within their learned cloisters, but for all who come under their influence. A society of the choicest minds produced in any country, engaged in receiving and imparting knowledge, devoted to the study of nature, the noblest monuments of literature, the marvelous abstractions of mathematical reasoning, the results of historical evidence, the progress of human civilization, and the foundations of religious faith, will be at once an example of productive quietude and an incitement to the philosophic view of life, so important to our countrymen in this day, when the miserable cry of pessimism, on the one hand, and the delightful but deceitful illusions of optimism, on the other hand, are in danger of leading them from the middle path, and from that reasonableness of mind which first recognizes that which is, and then has the hope and courage to strive for the better.

In what has now been said, it has been made apparent that our fathers brought with them to the western world the idea of a university as an institution superior to, though not exclusive of, college, and that this idea, sometimes obscured by mist, has never lost its radiance. I have also called your attention to some of the functions which are embodied in the conception of a university: the advancement of learning, the conservation of knowledge, the development of talent, the promotion of spirituality, the cultivation of literature, the elevation of professional standards, and the maintenance of repose.

I add a few suggestions of a practical character which I hope will be approved in this seat of learning. We should look for the liberal endowment of universities to the generosity of wealthy individuals. It is doubtful whether the national government, or the government of any State, will ever provide funds which will be adequate for the highest education. There is a growing disposition, in the Eastern States, to restrict all provision for public instruction to schools of primary and secondary rank. Were any legislative body to appropriate a sufficient financial support, there is nothing in the tendencies of modern politics to show that the representatives of the people, as they are in these days elected, would have the wisdom to mark out the pathway of a great university. Ecclesiastical zeal is more likely to be successfully invoked. The conception of a university pervaded by a spirit of enlightened Christianity is inspiring to the mind of every believer. It seems to associate religion and science as co-workers for the good of man. It is more than probable, under this consideration, that a Catholic university will ere long be initiated; and if it succeeds, the example may lead to a union of Protestants for a kindred object.

But it would be a misfortune and an injury, as I believe, to the religious progress of the country, if each of the denominations into which the evangelical world is divided were to aim at the maintenance of a university under its own sectarian name. The endowments which are called for are too large to be made up by petty contributions. Great gifts are essential, and consequently those who, in the favorable conditions of this fruitful and prosperous land, have acquired large fortunes, should be urged by all the considerations of far-sighted philanthropy to make generous contributions for the development of the highest institutions of learning. There is now in the golden book of our republic a noble list of such benefactors. Experience has shown no safer investments than those which have been given to learning—none which are more permanent, none which yield a better return.

It is a common error in this country to suppose that we need many universities. Just the reverse is true—we need but few, but we need them strong. There is a great danger that funds will be scattered, teachers isolated, and scholars kept away from their proper fields, by attempts, of which we have seen too many, to establish post-graduate courses with very inadequate means. Even professional schools have been initiated where the fees of the pupils have been the only criteria of success. We should lend our influence as scholars to enlarge the resources of the universities which are strong, and to discourage new foundations unless there is a positive guaranty that they are also to be strong. There are half a dozen or more places which could be named where a million dollars would be more fruitful than thrice that sum in any new establishment. No greater service could be rendered at this time than a rigid enforcement of the scriptural rule, "For whosoever hath, to him shall be given, and he shall have more abundance: but whosoever hath not, from him shall be taken away even that he hath."

There is another danger to which I will call attention—the danger of an incorrect conception of the purposes which should influence young men in pursuing university courses beyond the college curriculum. Those who have watched the tendencies of graduated students must have observed with a good deal of alarm the disposition which they sometimes show to concentrate attention upon very special subjects. Unfortunately, many of these persons are entirely dependent for their support on the salaries which they may earn. Now, instead of bringing to the educational exchange qualities which are always in demand and which always receive remuneration, they come forward as Doctors of Philosophy, with special attainments in some limited field, and are saddened to find that there is no demand for the acquisitions which they offer. I do not hesitate to say that, if the drift of university work in this country is toward premature and excessive specialization, many a mariner is doomed to shipwreck on that rock. Even in Germany, where specialization has been favored, the cry is heard, too many specialists, too many university candidates. It would be a misfortune to this country if we should find, in the course of a few years, a superabundance of men with rare acquisitions of a kind for which there is no demand. It would then be rightly said that our universities did not produce the fruit which had been expected. On the other hand, if residence in a university, beyond the college course, is found to widen the student's capacities as it increases his knowledge; if he learns the art of imparting what he knows, if he acquires the sense of proportion and sees the subjects which he studies with the right perspective, if he strengthens the foundations as he carries upward the obelisk, then he will gain and not lose by prolonged preparation for the duties of life.

For every individual who may with wisdom be encouraged to devote himself to a very limited domain, there are scores who may be bidden to widen their culture. I do not now refer to those upon whom fortune has smiled, and who have the means to do as they please in preparing for life; but I have in mind many a struggling aspirant for the scholar's fame who would be a happier and a more useful man if he had not set his face so resolutely against those studies which adorn the intellectual character and give grace, dignity, and acceptability to their possessor. The first business of every man is to win his bread; if he is sure of that, he may wander at his own sweet will through meadows and woods.

In all the difficulties which are encountered by those who are endeavoring to advance the institutions of this country to their highest usefulness, great encouragement may be derived from the study of the results secured in other countries and in other ages. It is only by the review of long periods of time that the most instructive lessons can be learned. The history of European universities is yet to be written by one who has the requisite vision, and who can estimate with an accurate judgment the various forces by which they have been molded, and the various services they have rendered to humanity. But there are many histories of famous foundations, many biographies of illustrious teachers, many surveys of literature, science, and education, many elaborate schemes of organization, and many proposals of reform. The mind of a master is indeed needed to coördinate what is thus recorded, to be the Interpreter of the House called Beautiful. But the American scholar need not wait for such a comprehensive work; the American philanthropist need not delay his benefactions until more experience is secured. The centuries speak with many voices, but they are all harmonious. From the revival of letters until now, from the days of Gerson, the great chancellor of the University of Paris, five hundred years ago, every advance in civilization has been dependent upon the influences which have proceeded from the seats of learning. Their light has illuminated the foremost nations of Christendom. In days to come, more than in days that are past, their power for good will be felt upon the interests of mankind. Let us hope and believe, let us labor and pray, that the American universities when they are fully organized may be worthy allies of the strongest and best foundations—steady promoters of knowledge, virtue, and faith.

ARTHUR TWINING HADLEY

MODERN CHANGES IN EDUCATIONAL IDEALS

Address by Arthur T. Hadley, President of Yale University from 1899 to 1921 (born in New Haven, Conn., April 23, 1836), delivered at the fourth celebration of Founders' Day at the Carnegie Institute, Pittsburgh, Pa., November 2, 1899. Assistant W. N. Frew, President of the Institute, occupied the chair. Another address by Mr. Hadley is printed in Volume XII.

MR. PRESIDENT, LADIES AND GENTLEMEN:—Many names have been applied to the nineteenth century by those who have striven to anticipate the verdict of posterity. It has been called an age of steam, and an age of steel; an age of newspapers, and an age of societies. What will be its final title in the light of the calmer judgment of the twentieth century, I shall not undertake to prophesy. But, whatever that name may be, I feel sure that it will be connected with the inward rather than the outward character of our age; with the fundamental ideas which have pervaded the life of the century, rather than with manifestations which are but incidents in its development.

If we seek for some underlying quality by which to characterize the years which have just passed, we find nothing more marked than the tendency toward expansion of things which were once narrow, and consolidation of things which were once separated. We may fairly call the nineteenth century an age of synthesis—an age of putting together what previous centuries had tended to keep apart. In science and in art, in business and in religion, there is everywhere manifest this widening and consolidating activity, which does not rest satisfied with looking at some detail by itself, but makes it a part of some large and harmonious whole.

We see this exemplified on the material side in the progress of industrial consolidation. The wagon has given place to the railroad, the retail storekeeper to the department store. Separate workshops have been supplanted by large factories, and these factories have in turn consolidated their business operations in trusts which regulate the industry of the whole country. These facts are so familiar that they have become a commonplace theme of everyday discussion.

If we turn from the sphere of commerce to that of science, a similar change is no less apparent. At the beginning of the century we had many separate branches of human knowledge, each studied by its own rules and its own methods. To-day the different physical sciences have been consolidated into one. The law of the conservation of energy makes the phenomena of motion and sound and heat and light appear, not as separate isolated things, but as transmutations of a single force which is never lost and never destroyed. And in like manner, as we pass from physical to biological science, the application of the doctrine of natural selection has brought into one large and well-ordered whole those detached parts on which the naturalists of a century ago were compelled to concentrate their attention. No longer do we believe in the separate creation of thousands of species, each living for itself and by itself. We have attained to a broader conception of the phenomena of organic life as a whole.

But these transformations of business and of science are perhaps not the most important exemplifications of our principle which the nineteenth century has witnessed. There is a transformation in our way of regarding human life which touches us all more closely—an expansion of our ideas of educations; a consolidation into one connected whole of parts of our life and our duty which were once conceived as separated and even antagonistic. No longer do we make the sharp distinction which was once made between the period of training and of performance. No longer do we find the antagonism which was once thought to exist between work and play.

In the old-fashioned view of life, each human being went through a period of preparation, which was followed by a distinct and separate period of life-work. When such a person left school or college he was thought to have finished his education and to have begun serious business. I think we have all come to see how artificial was this distinction and how evil were many of the results which followed from it. We now understand that well-developed men and women should allow their education to cease only when their life ceases. We no longer attempt to separate our years into two periods, one of training and the other of work. We hold rather that work should begin in the period of training and that training should continue throughout the period of active work.

What this idea has done for the schools we can see in the new interest which has everywhere been awakened, from kindergarten to university, through the introduction of exercises which teach people to do things instead of simply to learn things. What it has done for after life an institution like this can best bear witness. The education which the grown man or woman receives in the library is more independent and more self-directed than that which the boy has received in school, but it is none the less a training, a means of mental and moral growth, without which human life tends constantly toward stagnation. The modern library or museum supplements and carries to its logical conclusion the education which is furnished by the modern school.

In the first place, it furnishes a means of technical instruction. Each one of us in our life's business, whether in the office or in the store, in the factory or the household, cannot help feeling a certain narrowing effect from his daily routine. That same experience which makes him more skillful in what he does may render his vision of the possibilities of his business less broad. But the habit of reading books that deal with the subject which he pursues counteracts this tendency. Such books give him command of data a hundred times wider than his own. Science clearly developed and presented is but a summary of the world's experience in its several lines of observation. He who deals with the world's experience instead of his own broadens his work and his capacity for observation instead of narrowing it. [Applause.]

But applied science is far from constituting the whole theme of a library; nor is the study of such science the highest object which it stimulates. We are citizens as well as wage-earners, sharing in the making of our institutions, in the government of ourselves and our fellow men. If we look only at the immediate political condition by which we are surrounded we tend to narrow our political ideas, as surely as the man who looks simply at his own business narrows his business ideas. To fit ourselves to be citizens of a growing commonwealth we must read history; we must familiarize ourselves with the record of the deeds of great men in other times and in other nations. The new problems which come before us in our territorial expansion only increase the necessity of knowing what others have done. The larger the world in which we live, the greater the demands it places upon us.

But neither business success, nor even political achievement, constitutes the whole of a nation's life. The development of personal character is more important than either; and the study of literature, be it poetry or prose, drama or fiction, furnishes the needed stimulus for such development. There are, of course, some people who seem to be born great, whose character stands out grander amid unfavorable surroundings; but these are rare exceptions. In general, people who live only in the narrow world of the day will be narrow in their ideals and aims; while those who have felt the inspiration of great works of fiction and poetry, though they may not always be better men and women, will yet have far higher ideals.

There is yet another distinction, and perhaps a more fundamental one, which the nineteenth century is gradually obliterating, and in whose obliteration an institute like this furnishes all-powerful aid—the distinction between work and play.

In old times it was the fashion to divide our actions more or less consciously into two groups: on the one hand, those that we did because necessity or duty compelled us to do them, which we characterized as work; and on the other hand, those that we did because we liked them, which we characterized as play. Actions of the former class were praised; those of the latter class were distrusted. They were looked upon with suspicion as being trifling things, unworthy of the attention of a serious-minded man, and presumptively guilty unless proved to be innocent. It is one of the glories of the nineteenth century that it has discovered the falseness of this antithesis. That we like doing a thing and desire to do it is no bar to its good results, but rather a help. Whether in school life or in after life, work is better done when it becomes play; play most interesting when it has an element of work. The combination instead of the separation of the two things makes the fulfillment of our own desires helpful to others, and gives the work which we do for others additional vigor and efficiency because it is a pleasure no less than a duty.

We see this combination of play and work in the life of our schoolboys where, to cite but one instance among many, the development of modern athletics has made the playground an unrivaled field for training in honorable self-denial. We see it at a little later stage in the daily experience of colleges and universities, where the old-time drudgery of student duties, unwillingly rendered, is, with our improved methods, giving place to an active interest in preparation for life which the student himself scarcely knows whether to call a labor or a pleasure. We see it exemplified still later and still more completely in the privileges and enjoyments furnished by a library or museum or concert hall. The education which these places give is play, in the sense that it contributes to the enjoyment of those who use them; it is work, and the very best sort of work, in that it makes those persons better fitted to serve their fellow men in every department of life. Of all the combinations and syntheses of the nineteenth century, we have here the profoundest—that combination which does away with the distinction of worktime and playtime, and which makes of all life a harmony rather than a conflict between pleasure and duty.

Nor is this its most wide-reaching consequence. Its effect on the life of the body politic is even more marked than its effect on the life of the individual. It establishes the foundations of true democracy more firmly than they have ever stood in the past. It makes it possible to maintain an equality of political rights and obligations in the midst of advancing civilization. This equality is always a precarious thing in any community where work is regarded solely as a task or a burden to be shifted as far as possible on to other shoulders. In such a community the strongest will always seek to impose this burden upon the weakest; and this effort, so far as it is successful, will cause a separation into social classes. The obligation to work becomes a badge of inferiority; the right to play becomes an exclusive privilege of the few. This separation into classes, so fatal to real democracy, has in the past been avoided only in those cases where nature was so niggardly as to deprive all men of the chance to play and render the existence of leisure impossible, or where religious Puritanism was so rigid as to lead all members of the community voluntarily to renounce the chance for such leisure and the opportunities for improvement which come with it.

Under an advancing civilization the former alternative is done away with and the latter becomes increasingly difficult to maintain. Improvement in the arts of life, at Athens or Rome or Florence, meant loss of democratic spirit to the community as a whole, because people had not learned to combine work and play, and therefore separated themselves into working classes and leisure classes as soon as leisure came into existence at all. But if we have learned aright this greatest lesson of the nineteenth century, democracy in America can escape this danger. If work and play are mingled one with another; if service becomes in the popular mind not a badge of inferiority, but a means of self-development, then it lies in our power to realize, as the world has never realized before, the possibilities of government by the people.

Our thanks are due to those who have brought this combination within the reach of their fellow men, not alone for the pleasure which they have directly given, nor for the work which they have made possible, but for the stimulus which they have given to a new conception of the relations between work and play, which will make the twentieth century greater and better than the nineteenth. Whether they have identified themselves with better methods of education in school and college, which help to give work the vigor and spontaneity of play or with better methods of recreation in after life, which give play the unselfishness and permanent value of work, they have in either case contributed to an expansion of our conceptions and a consolidation of our ideas greater far in historic importance than all other movements of expansion and consolidation, whether in the world of science, business, or politics.

FREDERIC HARRISON

THE CHOICE OF BOOKS

Address by Frederic Harrison, lawyer and critic (born in London, England, 1831, died 1923), delivered before the London Institution for the Diffusion of Knowledge, in 1878.

IT is the fashion for those who have any connection with letters to expatiate on the infinite blessings of literature, and the miraculous achievements of the press: to extol, as a gift above price, the taste for study and the love of reading. Far be it from me to gainsay the inestimable value of good books, or to discourage any man from reading the best; but I often think that we forget that other side to this glorious view of literature —the misuse of books, the debilitating waste of brain in aimless, promiscuous, vapid reading, or even, it may be, in the poisonous inhalation of mere literary garbage and bad men's worst thoughts.

For what can a book be more than the man who wrote it? The brightest genius seldom puts the best of his own soul into his printed page; and some famous men have certainly put the worst of theirs. Yet are all men desirable companions, much less teachers, able to give us advice, even of those who get reputation and command a hearing? To put out of the question that writing which is positively bad, are we not, amidst the multiplicity of books and writers, in continual danger of being drawn off by what is stimulating rather than solid, by curiosity after something accidentally notorious, by what has no intelligible thing to recommend it, except that it is new? Now, to stuff our minds with what is simply trivial, simply curious, or that which at best has but a low nutritive power, this is to close our minds to what is solid and enlarging and spiritually sustaining.

Whether our neglect of the great books comes from our not reading at all, or from an incorrigible habit of reading the little books, it ends in just the same thing. And that thing is ignorance of all the greater literature of the world. To neglect all the abiding parts of knowledge for the sake of the evanescent parts is really to know nothing worth knowing. It is in the end the same, whether we do not use our minds for serious study at all, or whether we exhaust them by an impotent voracity for desultory "information"—a thing as fruitful as whistling. Of the two evils I prefer the former. At least, in that case, the mind is healthy and open. It is not gorged and enfeebled by excess in that which cannot nourish, much less enlarge and beautify our nature.

But there is much more than this. Even to those who resolutely avoid the idleness of reading what is trivial, a difficulty is presented—a difficulty every day increasing by virtue even of our abundance of books. What are the subjects, what are the class of books we are to read, in what order, with what connection, to what ultimate use or object?

Even those who are resolved to read the better books are embarrassed by a field of choice practically boundless. The longest life, the greatest industry, joined to the most powerful memory, would not suffice to make us profit from a hundredth part of the world of books before us. If the great Newton said that he seemed to have been all his life gathering a few shells on the shore, whilst a boundless ocean of truth still lay beyond and unknown to him, how much more to each of us must the sea of literature be a pathless immensity beyond our powers of vision or of reach—an immensity in which industry itself is useless without judgment, method, discipline; where it is of infinite importance what we can learn and remember, and of utterly no importance what we may have once looked at or heard of. Alas! the most of our reading leaves as little mark even in our own education as the foam that gathers round the keel of a passing boat.

For myself, I am inclined to think the most useful help to reading is to know what we should not read, what we can keep out from that small cleared spot in the overgrown jungle of "information," the corner of which we can call our ordered patch of fruit-bearing knowledge. The incessant accumulation of fresh books must hinder any real knowledge of the old; for the multiplicity of volumes becomes a bar upon our use of any. In literature especially does it hold—that we cannot see the wood for the trees.

How shall we choose our books? Which are the best, the eternal, indispensable books? To all to whom reading is something more than a refined idleness these questions recur, bringing with them the sense of bewilderment; and a still, small voice within us is forever crying out for some guide across the Slough of Despond of an illimitable and ever-swelling literature. How many a man stands beside it, as uncertain of his pathway as the Pilgrim, when he who dreamed the immortal dream heard him "break out with a lamentable cry; saying, what shall I do?" And this, which comes home to all of us at times, presses hardest upon those who have lost the opportunity of systematic education, who have to educate themselves, or who seek to guide the education of their young people.

Systematic reading is but little in favor even amongst studious men; in a true sense it is hardly possible for women. A comprehensive course of home study, and a guide to books, fit for the highest education of women, is yet a blank page remaining to be filled. Generations of men of culture have labored to organize a system of reading and materials appropriate for the methodical education of men in academic lines. Teaching equal in mental caliber to any that is open to men in universities, yet modified for the needs of those who must study at home, remains in the dim pages of that melancholy volume entitled *"Libri valde desiderati."*

I do not aspire to fill one of those blank pages; but I long to speak a word or two, as the Pilgrim did to Neighbor Pliable, upon the glories that await those who will pass through the narrow wicket-gate. On this, if one can find anything useful to say, it may be chiefly from the memory of the waste labor and pitiful stumbling in the dark which fill up so much of the travail that one is fain to call one's own education. We who have wandered in the wastes so long, and lost so much of our lives in our wandering, may at least offer warnings to younger wayfarers, as men who in thorny paths have borne the heat and burden of the day might give a clue to their journey to those who have yet a morning and a noon. As I look back and think of those cataracts of printed stuff which honest compositors set up, meaning, let us trust, no harm, and which at least found them in daily bread,—printed stuff which I and the rest of us to our infinitely small profit, have consumed with our eyes, not even making an honest living of it, but much impairing our substance,—I could almost reckon the printing press as amongst the scourges of mankind. I am grown a wiser and sadder man, importunate, like that Ancient Mariner, to tell each blithe wedding guest the tale of his shipwreck on the infinite sea of printers' ink, as one escaped by mercy and grace from the region where there is water, water, everywhere, and not a drop to drink.

A man of power, who has got more from books than most of his contemporaries, once said: "From a habit of reading, do not mind what you read; the reading of better books will come when you have a habit of reading the inferior." We need not accept this *obiter dictum* of Lord Sherbrooke. A habit of reading idly debilitates and corrupts the mind for all wholesome reading; the habit of reading wisely is one of the most difficult habits to acquire, needing strong resolution and infinite pains; and reading for mere reading's sake, instead of for the sake of the good we gain from reading, is one of the worst and commonest and most unwholesome habits we have.

And so our inimitable humorist has made delightful fun of the solid books,—which no gentleman's library should be without,—the Humes, Gibbons, Adam Smiths, which, he says, are not books at all, and prefers some "kind-hearted play-book," or at times the *Town and Country* magazine.

Poor Lamb has not a little to answer for, in the revived relish for garbage unearthed from old theatrical dung-heaps. Be it jest or earnest, I have little patience with the Elia-tic philosophy of the frivolous. Why do we still suffer the traditional hypocrisy about the dignity of literature—literature, I mean, in the gross, which includes about equal parts of what is useful and what is useless? Why are books as books, writers as writers, readers as readers, meritorious, apart from any good in them, or anything that we can get from them? Why do we pride ourselves on our powers of absorbing print, as our grandfathers did on their gifts of imbibing port, when we know that there is a mode of absorbing print, which makes it impossible that we can ever learn anything good out of books?

Our stately Milton said in a passage which is one of the watchwords of the English race, "as good almost kill a Man as kill a good Book." But has he not also said that he would "have a vigilant eye how Bookes demeane themselves, as well as men; and do sharpest justice on them as malefactors"? ... Yes! they do kill the good book who deliver up their few and precious hours of reading to the trivial book; they make it dead for them; they do what lies in them to destroy "the precious lifeblood of a master-spirit, imbalm'd and treasured upon purpose to a life beyond life"; they "spill that season's life of man preserv'd and stor'd up in Bookes." For in the wilderness of books most men, certainly all busy men, must strictly choose. If they saturate their minds with the idler books, the "good book," which Milton calls "an immortality rather than a lie" is dead to them: it is a book sealed up and buried.

It is most right that in the great republic of letters there should be freedom of intercourse and a spirit of equality. Every reader who holds a book in his hand is free of the inmost minds of men past and present; their lives both within and without the pale of their uttered thoughts are unveiled to him; he needs no introduction to the greatest; he stands on no ceremony with them; he may, if he be so minded, scribble "doggerel" on his Shelley, or he may kick Lord Byron, if he please, into a corner. He hears Burke perorate, and Johnson dogmatize, and Scott tell his border tales, and Wordsworth muse on the hillside, without the leave of any man, or the payment of any toll. In the republic of letters there are no privileged orders or places reserved. Every man who has written a book, even the diligent Mr. Whittaker, is in one sense an author; "a book's a book although there's nothing in't"; and every man who can decipher a penny journal is in one sense a reader. And your "general reader," like the grave-digger in "Hamlet," is hail-fellow with all the mighty dead; he pats the skull of the jester; batters the cheek of lord, lady or courtier; and uses "imperious Cæsar" to teach boys the Latin declensions.

But this noble equality of all writers—of all writers and of all readers—has a perilous side to it. It is apt to make us indiscriminate in the books we read, and somewhat contemptuous of the mighty men of the past. Men who are most observant as to the friends they make, or the conversation they share, are carelessness itself as to the books to whom they intrust themselves, and the printed language with which they saturate their minds. Yet can any friendship or society be more important to us than that of the books which form so large a part of our minds and even of our characters? Do we in real life take any pleasant fellow to our homes and chat with some agreeable rascal by our firesides, we who will take up any pleasant fellow's printed memoirs, we who delight in the agreeable rascal when he is cut up into pages and bound in calf? If any person given to reading were honestly to keep a register of all the printed stuff that he or she consumes in a year—all the idle tales of which the very names and the story are forgotten in a week, the book-maker's prattle about nothing at so much a sheet, the fugitive trifling about silly things and empty people, the memoirs of the unmemorable, and lives of those who never really lived at all—of what a mountain of rubbish would it be the catalogue! Exercises for the eye and the memory, as mechanical as if we set ourselves to learn the names, ages, and family histories of every one who lives in our own street, the flirtations of their maiden aunts, and the circumstances surrounding the birth of their grandmother's first baby.

It is impossible to give any method to our reading till we get nerve enough to reject. The most exclusive and careful amongst us will (in literature) take boon companions out of the street, as easily as an idler in a tavern. "I came across such and such a book that I never heard mentioned," says one, "and found it curious, though entirely worthless." "I strayed on a volume by I know not whom, on a subject for which I never cared." And so on. There are curious and worthless creatures enough in any pot-house all day long; and there is incessant talk in omnibus, train, or street by we know not whom, about we care not what. Yet if a printer and a bookseller can be induced to make this gabble as immortal as print and publication can make it, then it straightway is literature, and in due time it becomes "curious."

I have no intention to moralize or to indulge in a homily against the reading of what is deliberately evil. There is not so much need for this now, and I am not discoursing on the whole duty of man. I take that part of our reading which by itself is no doubt harmless, entertaining, and even gently instructive. But of this enormous mass of literature how much deserves to be chosen out, to be preferred to all the great books of the world, to be set apart for those precious hours which are all that the most of us can give to solid reading? The vast proportion of books are books that we shall never be able to read. A serious percentage of books are not worth reading at all. The really vital books for us we also know to be a very trifling portion of the whole. And yet we act as if every book were as good as any other, as if it were merely a question of order which we take up first, as if any book were good enough for us, and as if all were alike honorable, precious, and satisfying. Alas! books cannot be more than the men who write them; and as a fair proportion of the human race now write books, with motives and objects as various as human activity, books, as books, are entitled *a priori*, until their value is proved, to the same attention and respect as houses, steam-engines, pictures, fiddles, bonnets, and other products of human industry.

In the shelves of those libraries which are our pride, libraries public or private, circulating or very stationary, are to be found those great books of the world *rari nantes in gurgite vasto*, those books which are truly "the precious life-blood of a master-spirit." But the very familiarity which their mighty fame has bred in us makes us indifferent; we grow weary of what every one is supposed to have read; and we take down something which looks a little eccentric, some worthless book, on the mere ground that we never heard of it before. Thus the difficulties of literature are in their way as great as those of the world, the obstacles to finding the right friends are as great, the peril is as great of being lost in a Babel of voices and an ever-changing mass of beings.

Books are not wiser than men, the true books are not easier to find than the true men, the bad books or the vulgar books are not less obtrusive and not less ubiquitous than the bad or vulgar men are everywhere; the art of right reading is as long and difficult to learn as the art of right living. Those who are on good terms with the first author they meet, run as much risk as men who surrender their time to the first passer in the street; for to be open to every book is for the most part to gain as little as possible from any. A man aimlessly wandering about in a crowded city is of all men the most lonely; so he who takes up only the books that he "comes across" is pretty certain to meet but few that are worth knowing.

Now this danger is one to which we are specially exposed in this age. Our high-pressure life of emergencies, our whirling industrial organization or disorganization have brought us in this (as in most things) their peculiar difficulties and drawbacks. In almost everything vast opportunities and gigantic means of multiplying our products bring with them new perils and troubles which are often at first neglected. Our huge cities, where wealth is piled up and the requirements and appliances of life extended beyond the dreams of our forefathers, seem to breed in themselves new forms of squalor, disease, blights, or risks to life such as we are yet unable to master. So the enormous multiplicity of modern books is not altogether favorable to the knowing of the best. I listen with mixed satisfaction to the pæans that they chant over the works which issue from the press each day; how the books poured forth from Paternoster Row might in a few years be built into a pyramid that would fill the dome of St. Paul's. How in this mountain of literature am I to find the really useful book? How, when I have found it, and found its value, am I to get others to read it? How am I to keep my head clear in the torrent and din of works, all of which distract my attention, most of which promise me something, whilst so few fulfill that promise? The Nile is the source of the Egyptian's bread, and without it he perishes of hunger. But the Nile may be rather too liberal in his flood, and then the Egyptian runs imminent risk of drowning.

And thus there never was a time, at least during the last

two hundred years, when the difficulties in the way of making an efficient use of books were greater than they are to-day, when the obstacles were more real between readers and the right books to read, when it was practically so troublesome to find out that which it is of vital importance to know; and that not by the dearth, but by the plethora of printed matter. For it comes to nearly the same thing whether we are actually debarred by physical impossibility from getting the right book into our hand, or whether we are choked off from the right book by the obtrusive crowd of the wrong books; so that it needs a strong character and a resolute system of reading to keep the head cool in the storm of literature around us. We read nowadays in the market-place—I would rather say in some large steam factory of letter-press, where damp sheets of news print whirl round us perpetually—if it be not rather some noisy book-fair where literary showmen tempt us with performing dolls, and the gongs of rival booths are stunning our ears from morn till night.

Contrast with this pandemonium of Leipsic and Paternoster Row the sublime picture of our Milton in his early retirement at Horton, when, musing over his coming flight to the epic heaven, practicing his pinions, as he tells Diodati, he consumed five years of solitude in reading the ancient writers—

<blockquote>Et totum rapiunt me, mea vita, libri.</blockquote>

Who now reads the ancient writers? Who systematically reads the great writers, be they ancient or modern, whom the consent of ages has marked out as classics: typical, immortal, peculiar teachers of our race? Alas! the "Paradise Lost" is lost again to us beneath an inundation of graceful academic verse, sugary stanzas of ladylike prettiness, and ceaseless explanations in more or less readable prose of what John Milton meant or did not mean, or what he saw or did not see, who married his great-aunt, and why Adam or Satan is like that, or unlike the other. We read a perfect library about the "Paradise Lost," but the "Paradise Lost" itself we do not read.

I am not presumptuous enough to assert that the larger part of modern literature is not worth reading in itself, that the prose is not readable, entertaining, one may say highly instructive. Nor do I pretend that the verses which we read so zealously in place of Milton's are not good verses. On the contrary, I think them sweetly conceived, as musical and as graceful as the verse of any age in our history. A great deal of our modern literature is such that it is exceedingly difficult to resist it, and it is undeniable that it gives us real information. It seems perhaps unreasonable to many to assert that a decent readable book which gives us actual instruction can be otherwise than a useful companion and a solid gain. Possibly many people are ready to cry out upon me as an obscurantist for venturing to doubt a genial confidence in all literature simply as such. But the question which weighs upon me with such really crushing urgency is this: What are the books that in our little remnant of reading time it is most vital for us to know? For the true use of books is of such sacred value to us that to be simply entertained is to cease to be taught, elevated, inspired by books; merely to gather information of a chance kind is to close the mind to knowledge of the urgent kind.

Every book that we take up without a purpose is an opportunity lost of taking up a book with a purpose—every bit of stray information which we cram into our heads without any sense of its importance, is for the most part a bit of the most useful information driven out of our heads and choked off from our minds.

It is so certain that information, i. e., the knowledge, the stored thoughts and observations of mankind, is now grown to proportions so utterly incalculable and prodigious, that even the learned whose lives are given to study can but pick up some crumbs that fall from the table of truth. They delve and tend but a plot in that vast and teeming kingdom, whilst those whom active life leaves with but a few cramped hours of study can hardly come to know the very vastness of the field before them, or how infinitesimally small is the corner they can traverse at the best. We know all is not of equal value. We know that books differ in value as much as diamonds differ from the sand on the seashore, as much as our living friend differs from a dead rat. We know that much in the myriad-peopled world of books—very much in all kinds—is trivial, enervating, inane, even noxious. And thus, where we have infinite opportunities of wasting our efforts to no end, of fatiguing our minds without enriching them, of clogging the spirit without satisfying it, there, I cannot but think, the very infinity of opportunities is robbing us of the actual power of using them. And thus I come often, in my less hopeful moods, to watch the remorseless cataract of daily literature which thunders over the remnants of the past, as if it were a fresh impediment to the men of our day in the way of systematic knowledge and consistent powers of thought, as if it were destined one day to overwhelm the great inheritance of mankind in prose and verse.

I remember, when I was a very young man at college, that a youth, in no spirit of paradox, but out of plenary conviction, undertook to maintain before a body of serious students, the astounding proposition that the invention of printing had been one of the greatest misfortunes that had ever befallen mankind. He argued that exclusive reliance on printed matter had destroyed the higher method of oral teaching, the dissemination of thought by the spoken word to the attentive ear. He insisted that the formation of a vast literary class looking to the making of books as a means of making money rather than as a social duty, had multiplied books for the sake of the writers rather than for the sake of the readers; that the reliance on books as a cheap and common resource had done much to weaken the powers of memory; that it destroyed the craving for a general culture of taste, and the need of artistic expression in all the surroundings of life. And he argued lastly that the sudden multiplication of all kinds of printed matter had been fatal to the orderly arrangement of thought, and had hindered a system of knowledge and a scheme of education.

I am far from sharing this immature view. Of course I hold the invention of printing to have been one of the most momentous facts in the whole history of man. Without it universal social progress, true democratic enlightenment, and the education of the people would have been impossible, or very slow, even if the cultured few, as is likely, could have advanced the knowledge of mankind without it. We place Gutenberg amongst the small list of the unique and special benefactors of mankind, in the sacred choir of those whose work transformed the conditions of life, whose work, once done, could never be repeated. And no doubt the things which our ardent friend regarded as so fatal a disturbance of society were all inevitable and necessary, part of the great revolution of mind through which men grew out of the mediæval incompleteness to a richer conception of life and of the world.

Yet there is a sense in which this boyish anathema against printing may become true to us by our own fault. We may create for ourselves these very evils. For the art of printing has not been a gift wholly unmixed with evils; it must be used wisely if it is to be a boon to man at all; it entails on us heavy responsibilities, resolution to use it with judgment and self-control, and the will to resist its temptations and its perils. Indeed, we may easily so act that we may make it a clog on the progress of the human mind, a real curse and not a boon. The power of flying at will through space would probably extinguish civilization and society, for it would release us from the wholesome bondage of place and rest. The power of hearing every word that had ever been uttered on this planet would annihilate thought, as the power of knowing all recorded facts by the process of turning a handle would annihilate true science. Our human faculties and our mental forces are not enlarged simply by multiplying our materials of knowledge and our facilities for communication. Telephones, microphones, pantoscopes, steam-presses, and ubiquity-engines in general may, after all, leave the poor human brain panting and throbbing under the strain of its appliances, no bigger and no stronger than the brains of the men who heard Moses speak, and saw Aristotle and Archimedes pondering over a few worn rolls of crabbed manuscript. Until some new Gutenberg or Watt can invent a machine for magnifying the human mind, every fresh apparatus for multiplying its work is a fresh strain on the mind, a new realm for it to order and to rule.

And so, I say it most confidently, the first intellectual task of our age is rightly to order and make serviceable the vast realm of printed material which four centuries have swept across our path. To organize our knowledge, to systematize our reading, to save, out of the relentless cataract of ink, the immortal thoughts of the greatest—this is a necessity, unless

THE CHOICE OF BOOKS

the productive ingenuity of man is to lead us at last to a measureless and pathless chaos. To know anything that turns up is, in the infinity of knowledge, to know nothing. To read the first book we come across, in the wilderness of books, is to learn nothing. To turn over the pages of ten thousand volumes is to be practically indifferent to all that is good.

But this warns me that I am entering on a subject which is far too big and solemn. It is plain that to organize our knowledge, even to systematize our reading, to make a working selection of books for general study, really implies a complete scheme of education. A scheme of education ultimately implies a system of philosophy, a view of man's duty and powers as a moral and social being—a religion. Before a problem so great as this, on which readers have such different ideas and wants, and differ so profoundly on the very premises from which we start, before such a problem as a general theory of education, I prefer to pause. I will keep silence even from good words. I have chosen my own part, and adopted my own teacher. But to ask men to adopt the education of Auguste Comte, is almost to ask them to adopt Positivism itself. Nor will I enlarge on the matter for thought, for foreboding, almost for despair, that is presented to us by the fact of our familiar literary ways and our recognized literary profession. That things infinitely trifling in themselves: men, events, societies, phenomena, in no way otherwise more valuable than the myriad other things which flit around us like the sparrows on the housetop, should be glorified, magnified, and perpetuated, set under a literary microscope and focused in the blaze of a literary magic-lantern—not for what they are in themselves, but solely to amuse and excite the world by showing how it can be done—all this is to me so amazing, so heart-breaking, that I forbear now to treat it, as I cannot say all that I would.

The choice of books is really the choice of our education, of a moral and intellectual ideal, of the whole duty of man. But though I shrink from any so high a theme, a few words are needed to indicate my general point of view in the matter.

In the first place, when we speak about books, let us avoid the extravagance of expecting too much from books, the pedant's habit of extolling books as synonymous with education. Books are no more education than laws are virtue; and just as profligacy is easy within the strict limits of law, a boundless knowledge of books may be found with a narrow education. A man may be, as the poet saith, "deep vers'd in books, and shallow in himself." We need to know in order that we may feel rightly and act wisely. The thirst after truth itself may be pushed to a degree where indulgence enfeebles our sympathies and unnerves us in action. Of all men perhaps the book-lover needs most to be reminded that man's business here is to know for the sake of living; not to live for the sake of knowing. A healthy mode of reading would follow the lines of a sound education. And the first canon of a sound education is to make it the instrument to perfect the whole nature and character. Its aims are comprehensive, not special; they regard life as a whole, with mental curiosity; they have to give us, not so much materials, as capacities. So that, however moderate and limited the opportunity for education, in its way it should be always more or less symmetrical and balanced, appealing equally in turn to the three grand intellectual elements —imagination, memory, reflection: and so having something to give us in poetry, in history, in science, and in philosophy.

And thus our reading will be sadly one-sided, however voluminous it be, if it entirely close to us any of the great types and ideals which the creative instinct of man has produced, if it shut out from us either the ancient world, or other European poetry, as important almost as our own. When our reading, however deep, runs wholly into "pockets," and exhausts itself in the literature of one age, one country, one type, then we may be sure that it is tending to narrow or deform our minds. And the more it leads us into curious byways and nurtures us into indifference for the beaten highways of the world, the sooner we shall end, if we be not specialists and students by profession, in ceasing to treat our books as the companions and solace of our lifetime, and in using them as the instruments of a refined sort of self-indulgence.

A wise education, and so judicious reading, should leave no great type of thought, no dominant phase of human nature, wholly a blank. Whether our reading be great or small, so far as it goes, it should be general. If our lives admit of but a short space for reading, all the more reason that, so far as may be, it should remind us of the vast expanse of human thought, and the wonderful variety of human nature.

To read, and yet so to read that we see nothing but a corner of literature, the loose fringe, or flats and wastes of letters, and by reading only deepen our natural belief that this island is the hub of the universe, and the nineteenth century the only age worth notice, all this is really to call in the aid of books to thicken and harden our untaught prejudices. Be it imagination, memory, or reflection that we address—that is, in poetry, history, science or philosophy—our first duty is to aim at knowing something at least of the best, at getting some definite idea of the mighty realm whose outer rim we are permitted to approach.

But how are we to know the best; how are we to gain this definite idea of the vast world of letters? There are some who appear to suppose that the "best" are known only to experts in an esoteric way, who may reveal to inquirers what schoolboys and the betting-men describe as "tips." There are no "tips" in literature; the "best" authors are never dark horses; we need no "crammers" and "coaches" to thrust us into the presence of the great writers of all time. "Crammers" will only lead us wrong. It is a thing far easier and more common than many imagine, to discover the best. It needs no research, no learning, and is only misguided by recondite information. The world has long ago closed the great assize of letters, and judged the first places everywhere. In such a matter the judgment of the world, guided and informed by a long succession of accomplished critics, is almost unerring. When some Zoilus finds blemishes in Homer, and prefers, it may be, the work of some Apollonius of his own discovering, we only laugh. There may be doubts about the third and fourth rank; but the first and the second are hardly open to discussion.

The gates which lead to the Elysian fields may slowly wheel back on their adamantine hinges to admit now and then some new and chosen modern. But the company of the masters of those who know, and in especial degree of the great poets, is a roll long closed and complete, and they who are of it hold ever peaceful converse together. Hence we may find it a useful maxim that, if our reading be utterly closed to the great poems of the world, there is something amiss with our reading. If you find Milton, Dante, Calderon, Goethe, so much "Hebrew-Greek" to you; if your Homer and Virgil, your Molière and Scott, rest year after year undisturbed on their shelves beside your school trigonometry and your old college text-books; if you have never opened the "Cid," the "Nibelungen," "Crusoe," and "Don Quixote," since you were a boy, and are wont to leave the Bible and the Imitation for some wet Sunday afternoon—know, friend, that your reading can do you little real good. Your mental digestion is ruined or sadly out of order.

No doubt, to thousands of intelligent educated men who call themselves readers, the reading through a Canto of "The Purgatorio," or a Book of the "Paradise Lost," is a task as irksome as it would be to decipher an ill-written manuscript in a language that is almost forgotten. But, although we are not to be always reading epics, and are chiefly in the mood for slighter things, to be absolutely unable to read Milton or Dante with enjoyment, is to be in a very bad way. Aristophanes, Theocritus, Boccaccio, Cervantes, Molière are often as light as the driven foam; but they are not light enough for the general reader. Their humor is too bright and lovely for the groundlings. They are, alas! "classics," somewhat apart from our everyday ways; they are not banal enough for us; and so for us they slumber "unknown in a long night," just because they are immortal poets, and are not scribblers of to-day.

When will men understand that the reading of great books is a faculty to be acquired, not a natural gift, at least not to those who are spoiled by our current education and habits of life? *Ceci tuera cela,* the last great poet might have said of the first circulating library. An insatiable appetite for new novels makes it as hard to read a masterpiece as it seems to a Parisian boulevardier to live in a quiet country. Until a man can truly enjoy a draft of clear water bubbling from a mountain side, his taste is in an unwholesome state.

And so he who finds the Heliconian spring insipid should look to the state of his nerves. Putting aside the iced air of the difficult mountain tops of epic, tragedy, or psalm, there are some simple pieces which may serve as an unerring test of a healthy or a vicious taste for imaginative work. If the "Cid," the "Vita Nuova," the "Canterbury Tales," Shakespeare's "Sonnets," and "Lycidas" pall on a man; if he care not for Malory's "Morte d'Arthur" and the "Red Cross Knight"; if he thinks "Crusoe" and the "Vicar" books for the young; if he thrill not with "The Ode to the West Wind," and "The Ode to a Grecian Urn"; if he have no stomach for "Christabel" or the lines written on "The Wye above Tintern Abbey," he should fall on his knees and pray for a cleanlier and quieter spirit.

The intellectual system of most of us in these days needs "to purge and to live cleanly." Only by a course of treatment shall we bring our minds to feel at peace with the grand pure works of the world. Something we ought all to know of the masterpieces of antiquity, and of the other nations of Europe. To understand a great national poet, such as Dante, Calderon, Corneille, or Goethe, is to know other types of human civilization in ways which a library of histories does not sufficiently teach. The great masterpieces of the world are thus, quite apart from the charm and solace they give us, the master instruments of a solid education.

RUSH LA MOTTE HOLLAND

THE ORDER OF THE ELKS

The following address was delivered at the dedication of the Elks' National Memorial Headquarters Building in Chicago on the afternoon of July 14, 1926. This was the high event of the Grand Lodge Convention and one of the most significant occasions in the history of the Order. We print only the opening and closing portions of the eloquent address which covered thoroughly the history and purposes of the Order.

The Honorable Rush La Motte Holland was born in 1867, admitted to the Bar in 1895, was Assistant Attorney-General of the United States, 1921-1925 and is an Odd Fellow, a Shriner, a Mason, 32d degree, as well as Past Grand Exalted Ruler B. P. O. E.

THE Benevolent and Protective Order of Elks had its inception sixty years ago. It must in candor be admitted that it was of humble, almost obscure, origin. Many a place of humble birth has become a shrine where teeming millions have bent the knee and bowed the head in thanksgiving to God for His gift to mankind of men and women of such vision as to become leaders in movements which have made for a better world. By this same token we give thanks, and are justified in the past, the present, and the promise of our Order.

The first years were formative and marked by little progress. The Order had but one Lodge, if, indeed, the mere handful of members could be said to constitute a Lodge, much less an Order. It had no written constitution, no laws, no ritual, but it did have an indefinable something which appealed, fascinated and held, until to-day its lodges number over one thousand five hundred and its membership is well-nigh a million.

It could not thus have attracted men of character and standing in all walks of life had it been without merit and had it lacked genuine appeal to the higher, better and nobler promptings of sterling manhood and womanhood. I say womanhood, for, while it is a man's organization, it would not long have endured had it failed of woman's approval and support. To have thus grown and waxed strong, it must not only have been founded on sound and enduring principles, but it also must have been an aggressive organization, not content with mere preachment but distinguished by actual accomplishment. It is not unbecoming in the individual modestly to take inventory of his life. It often serves a useful purpose, inspiring to greater activity, to higher aims and more noble purposes. Therefore, may we not to-day, in this inspiring presence and standing at the portal of this, our most recent accomplishment, modestly take inventory and gain inspiration to greater achievement in the years to come.

The Order of Elks has no enemies. Sixty years of history, sixty years of activity, and no enemies! Thus have we measurably, at least, demonstrated our right to use the words "Benevolent" and "Protective." "Benevolent" is derived from two Latin words meaning "we wish well." Benevolence is goodwill, kindness, charitableness, liberality, love of mankind, and the promotion of prosperity and happiness. "Protective" also is derived from two Latin words meaning to shield from danger, to guard against injury, to defend, to preserve in safety. With us its application extends to home and fireside, to country and to all mankind. Because we are Benevolent and because we are Protective in thought, word and deed—we have no enemies. We can have none so long as we live up to our name and practice the principles upon which our Order is founded.

The Order had its inception in good-fellowship, in comradeship. The development of these natural and impelling influences in life resulted in adopting as the supporting pillars of the fraternal edifice in the hearts of our members four basic or cardinal virtues—Charity, Justice, Brotherly Love, and Fidelity.

Charity: Not a mere giving of alms; a broad charity of thought; inspiring a charity of word and of deed. It is a charity that "vaunteth not itself, is not puffed up, and doth not behave itself unseemly." It is a spark struck by the hand of Deity, kindling a flame of sympathy, forbearance, tolerance and helpfulness in the hearts of men. It is the kind of charity Paul had in mind when he said, "Though I bestow all my goods to feed the poor, and though I give my body to be burned, and have not charity, it profiteth me nothing." True charity is distinguished from material assistance to the needy. We boast not of the giving of alms but welcome the opportunity thus to serve. We hold such giving secret, for otherwise it loses its sweetness to the giver and brings humiliation to the receiver. Elk charity is typified by a winged figure in flowing robes of white, scattering along Life's stony pathway the flowers of hope, courage and good cheer.

Justice: Ours is not the stern justice of retribution, exacting the extreme penalty for each erring step, but a justice which seeks to judge men by that which is within their hearts. Punishment must come to all who violate the laws of God and man. The most severe punishment, however, is that inflicted by an outraged conscience. If conscience be gone, then is reason dethroned, and man is descended to a mere brute, to whom justice is without meaning. Disraeli once said, "Justice is truth in action." Such is the justice which we acclaim—a justice reckoning with the frailties of human nature, with proneness to err notwithstanding the better promptings of the heart, and with the universal desire of normal man to do right and live right, sometimes measured by different yet always by honest standards. Elk justice is typified not by a blind goddess with stern visage standing stiffly erect, with scales exactly poised and with the sword of execution sharpened to keen edge; but rather by a benign goddess with kindly visage, with clear vision to see the very truth of things, holding in one hand the mirror of introspection and in the other the Book of Divine Law, that those who come before her may search their own hearts and seek their own salvation in God's appointed way as they are given to see that way.

Brotherly Love: That which we acclaim is not effeminate, weak, feeble, fawning or spiritless. It is masculine, strong, virile, sturdy, helpful and vigorous—a manly love of man for man and for things manly. It is bold and daring, valorous and courageous, undaunted, hardy, dignified but responsive. It seeks out character and glorifies it. It recognizes ability and lauds it. It nurtures, sustains and protects. It extends the hand in greeting, in sympathy, in helpfulness, and in the spirit of true friendship. It is an affirmative answer to Cain's inquiry, "Am I my brother's keeper?"

Fidelity: This, indeed, embraces all. What a wealth of meaning in the word fidelity!—adherence to right; steadfastness in the discharge of duty; faithfulness to all obligations; honesty; integrity; faith; fealty; loyalty. Indeed, what a wealth of meaning!

President Harding, himself a member of the Order, in a letter written from the White House shortly before his untimely death, among other things said, "The Order of Elks has grown and will continue to grow because it teaches tolerant idealism." We inveigh against all intolerance. We recognize no religion, or, to speak more accurately, we recognize all religions founded on belief in a Supreme Being. Protestant, Catholic and Jew alike find asylum within our Lodge rooms, with no obligation suggested, with no act performed, with no word spoken conflicting in any way with their religious beliefs. Our teachings constitute an everyday religion as broad as the scheme of the soul's salvation embraced within all such creeds.

. . . .

We had long professed a real patriotism of devotion and of sacrifice if necessary. The war gave us our first opportunity to demonstrate that we were sincere in this profession. We had carried on during the war; we had carried on after the war; but we had not finished the faith. We had followed our boys to railroad stations and with shouts of good cheer, all but smothered in sobs, had seen them off for training camps; we had sent them messages and small remembrances from home; we had with pride watched them develop almost by magic from clerks, laborers, bankers, business men, lawyers, doctors, and farmers into the best and bravest soldiers the world has ever seen; we had bid them bon voyage and safe return when they sailed across the seas to fight an inhuman monster which had laid bloody hands at the throat of civilization and arrested the peace of the world; we had followed them on the long marches through rain and mud; we had gone into the trenches with them and over the top at Château Thierry, in the Argonne, in

Flanders, on the Marne and on scores of other fields of battle; we had wept with them when their comrades were laid to rest in a foreign land; we had helped care for the sick and wounded; we had taken messages from the lips of the dying for loved ones back in the homeland; we had camped with them on the field of victory; we had joined in their hosannas when peace came to a grief-stricken and anxious, waiting world; we had joined in the patriotic demonstrations when they were welcomed back home as real conquering heroes with Old Glory smiling down on them and bands playing the national anthem and "My Country, 'tis of Thee"; we had helped in rehabilitation work; we had extended the hand of assistance to thousands of our boys who found it difficult to recover from the excitement of war and again take up the pursuits of peace; in the doing of all this we had shared, but we had not finished the faith.

Something yet remained for us to do, something which throughout succeeding generations would stand as a testimonial of our unfaltering loyalty to country, and of our ever-increasing gratitude to those who served and suffered, as well as to those who gave life itself that liberty and freedom might not be banished from the world. This sentiment finds physical expression in this memorial which to-day is dedicated in patriotism to patriotism. It will stand until its solid rock, marble and bronze are buried in the dust of ages, e'en then silently proclaiming our love of liberty and our devotion to those who gave us the heritage and those who have made whatever sacrifice was necessary that it might not perish.

On this spot now made sacred to all that we hold dear, where the blue of the great inland seas blends with the azure of western sky, stands this imposing dome, rigid and immovable by day, but in the stilly night, when the stars sing together, it bows as it is faced toward the grave at Arlington and the poppy fields of France.

ERNEST MARTIN HOPKINS

AN ARISTOCRACY OF BRAINS

Ernest Martin Hopkins was born in 1877 and became President of Dartmouth College in 1916. The address which follows attracted very wide attention throughout the United States. It was delivered at the opening of Dartmouth College, September 21, 1922.

THE opening of the college year, with its attendant assembling of upper class men for the continuation of their courses and the incoming of hundreds of men, new to the college environment and to college work, is fitting time for recapitulation and reiteration of the college purpose.

For the individual undergraduate the question of self-determination begins at this period to assume greatly increased importance, both because of the stage of his advance towards maturity and because of the particular conditions of college life, wherein the responsibility is constantly thrust upon him for making decisions. Many of these decisions, under superficial guise of merely temporary consequence, as a matter of fact are destined to be significant to all subsequent phases of his life.

It is at this point, perhaps, that the college fails most definitely. It has not found any sufficient way to make evident to its men the enduring influences upon later career of even minor details of daily life through their influence in forming habit. It does not carry conviction to undergraduates in emphasizing the importance of cultivating those qualities which make for self-directed lives of purpose and strength, rather than of allowing those habits of inertia and indifference to become fastened upon us, which merely in being tolerated become more fixed each day.

It is at this point, likewise, that the undergraduate remains most oblivious of his own best interests. The processes helpful to acquiring mental strength and moral fortitude are at least as important and as rigorous as those required for gaining muscular strength and physical resistance. Nevertheless, it is to be doubted if the coaches and trainers of our athletic teams would be willing to trust solely to suddenly acquired desire to compete or to a sudden burst of enthusiasm on the part of individual men as justification for relying upon them for intercollegiate contests. And yet, the intelligence, the endurance, the consciousness of power, and the will to do, required in even the greatest of athletic contests do not exceed what is daily and hourly required of the man who goes forth from the college to compete with adverse circumstances in the struggle to make his life of consequence, useful to society, and satisfying to his own aspirations.

Shall we not then keep in mind the reason for our undertaking the course upon which to-day we set out and shall we not preserve or cultivate respect for the proved canons of training!

The great question in college life is at what point we are going to apply ourselves and the degree of devotion with which we are willing to commit ourselves to the different interests which will attract our attention. There is on the boards in London at the present time a play written by Mr. Galsworthy entitled, "Loyalties," which, night after night, draws capacity houses. It presents for consideration, in form of the drama, the confusion worked in the human mind by the cross purposes of conflicting loyalties of various sorts, respectively stimulated or repressed by such factors as instinct, desire, racial prejudice, class feeling, professional caste, family ties or interest, abstract justice.

There is no greater problem in life than that of the authenticity of the ideas which we hold or of those which we are disposed to accept as our own. There is no greater necessity upon the college than that it shall proclaim the existence of this problem to the individual man within its walls, that he may be impelled to seek knowledge and command of mental processes wherewith to define for himself the desirable loyalties and that he may be influenced to cultivate the will to pledge himself and all his works wholeheartedly to these.

The college cannot do this for him. All that the college can do is to maintain an atmosphere or to create an influence which will be helpful to such ends for those men who seek to establish contact with the real purpose of the college. It can neither be emphasized too strongly nor too frequently that a college course does not of itself necessarily do away with ignorance, eliminate bigotry, or diminish partisanship, even in the case of many a man who seemingly fulfills all the requirements of the college. The most that can justifiably be claimed is that the college processes, rightly accepted and properly utilized, make it somewhat more feasible for the individual man to do these things intelligently for himself than would be the case otherwise.

Incidentally, it may be observed that within the college life itself, here and now, there are the calls of conflicting loyalties, none unworthy in themselves, but each susceptible to appraisal as to its relative worth in relation to the others. To men genuinely bewildered among these, this assurance can be held out, —that the self-discipline of serious effort to decide intelligently which of the loyalties are of major importance and which are of minor will probably be as helpful to their own development as any work undertaken within the college course.

For the fullest possible common understanding, and the earliest, a few principles applying to our mutual relationship may well be stated at this juncture. These principles are involved particularly at Dartmouth in such policies as the restriction of enrollment, the selective process of admission, and the permanent elimination from the college membership of men incompetent or unwilling to qualify according to the standards which the college seeks to maintain.

Too many men are going to college! The opportunities for securing an education by way of the college course are definitely a privilege and not at all a universal right. The funds available for appropriation to the uses of institutions of higher learning are not limitless and cannot be made so, whether their origin be sought in the resources of public taxation or in the securable benefactions for the enhancing of private endowments. It consequently becomes essential that a working theory be sought that will operate with some degree of accuracy to define the individuals who shall make up the group to whom, in justice to the public good, the privilege shall be extended, and to specify those from whom the privilege should be withheld!

This is a two-fold necessity: on the one hand that men incapable of profiting by the advantages which the college offers, or indisposed, shall not be withdrawn from useful work to spend their time profitlessly, in idleness acquiring false standards of living; and on the other hand that the contribution which the college is capable of making to the lives of competent men and through them to society shall not be too largely lessened by the slackening of pace due to the presence of men indifferent or wanting in capacity.

We hear much of men seeking an education but too often they are only seeking membership in a social organization which has reputation for affording an education, from which reputation they expect to benefit, if they can avoid being detached from the association. The assumption would be humorous if it were not so serious, that enrollment with a college requires that the college shall either force education upon the individual man or surreptitiously bait him to it, rather than that he should crave and at the cost of any effort possess himself of the utmost which the college can give.

It would be incompatible with all of the conceptions of democracy to assume that the privilege of higher education should be restricted to any class defined by the accident of birth or by the fortuitous circumstance of possession of wealth, but there is such a thing as an aristocracy of brains, made up of men intellectually alert and intellectually eager, to whom increasingly the opportunities of higher education ought to be restricted, if democracy is to become a quality product rather than simply a quantity one, and if excellence and effectiveness are to displace the mediocrity towards which democracy has such a tendency to skid.

I wish carefully to safeguard these statements, however, by iteration and reiteration that it behooves all of us to avoid confusing the symbols and the facts of intellectuality and I should hope that under any circumstances we might avoid confusing mental gymnastics and facility in appropriating the ideas of others with genuine thinking. Unfortunately intellectual

AN ARISTOCRACY OF BRAINS

hypocrisy and its complement, intellectual smugness, are not sufficiently infrequent even within college halls, while at the same time I believe that on the whole they are as much to be avoided and that they are as detrimental to the spirit of true scholarship as is ignorance.

In the last analysis, the stimulation in the individual man of his ability to think and the willingness to follow the logic of his carefully considered thought through to conviction is the desirable ambition for the college. This presupposes the acquisition of certain fundamental knowledge, the mastery of the technique of finding new knowledge when needed, acquaintanceship with the method of gaining access to original sources, a disposition to seek all facts and to sort these according to relative importance before accepting conclusions, and finally an open-minded tolerance for new facts if they shall appear and be proved valid, even though they attack conclusions already formed.

This all is simply another way of saying that the college ambition is that its men may be consecrated to the spirit of truth. Such is the essential loyalty. It is, moreover, at this time especially necessary to repeat the statement, for there never was a harder time to know where truth may be found than now, and we have nothing to designate the approach to it except the finely attuned and rigidly disciplined processes of human mind.

The two great conflicting forces of the world at the present time are the spirit of truth and the spirit of propaganda, the former of which leads towards the light and to ultimate peace and happiness for mankind and the latter of which is not only the father of lies but a whole ancestral tree, ultimately making for confusion and distress. Many of us thought we were to have been done with any necessity for thinking of or discussing propaganda, once the war should have been ended, but instead we find ourselves confronted with the definite possibility that what was reluctantly accepted as a war necessity will be imposed upon us in larger dimensions and with greater thoroughness than ever before as a working procedure of daily life, despite its tendency to shrink minds and to soil souls in the muddied waters of things that are not so. Given the necessity for accepting the evils of war to avoid other evils even greater, I do not feel qualified to state the extent to which squeamishness can be expected to affect its conduct, but I assume that in the minds of thinking men there is agreement that in a world seeking a basis of coöperation rather than of conflict, the prevalent war-time practice of distorting truth and of clothing plausible falsehood with respectability should not prevail,—and yet it does prevail!

As a tangible and practical objective, college men could commit themselves to no purpose more in accord with the spirit of foundation from which they seek to benefit than the early and utter elimination of the spirit of propaganda in the affairs of this world, and in the discussion of those of the next. There could be no more genuine consecration to the principle of the search for truth than in militant opposition to and repudiation of this spirit, whether it emanate from the manufacturer's association, the offices of organized labor, the editor's column, the preacher's pulpit, or the college officer's desk. The principle and the method are invariably wrong, however worthy be the motive.

In course of time I hope that some thinker will write a serious dissertation on the subject of labels as related to truth and propaganda. Unfortunately labels do not always accurately designate the goods. The buyer returning from Paris with a few Parisian hats but with a quantity of Parisian labels to be affixed to creations of domestic manufacture may do no great injury to the purchasers of his goods but he certainly will never advance the science of honest merchandising. The duty-dodger who sits on the edge of his berth industriously tearing out from his clothes the firm name of his English tailors and replacing them with labels forehandedly provided, bearing the name of his home town suitmaker, may not greatly damage society but he definitely damages his own capacity to be useful to society when he perjures himself to the government inspector. When we, however, somewhat less consciously disregard the true labels to be affixed to men or causes and, without care in ascertaining the facts, tag them with labels which designate them to be what we wish them to be thought to be, we destroy the essential evidence in regard to their true characteristics and make accurate designation impossible, and thus make unobtainable all thought or action dependent upon accurate knowledge.

We have all seen the effects of this on individuals. To the latent unpopularity of a clubmate, or it may be a popularity so great as to arouse envy, there is attached, through irresponsibility or malice, the whispered implication of some disapproved action. It is immediately assumed that he is not of our kind. It begins to seem that he might be of the kind that he is accused of being, and of a sudden all which has been suggested becomes accepted as fact. The label is affixed and the man is outlawed.

Or again, to the lurking fear that some new movement will disturb the existing order and thus create personal complications for us, is added the suggestion that certain individual crimes of violence, increasingly prevalent, had their origin and instigation within the disliked movement. Immediately there is almost inevitable disposition to assume these things to be fact. We detest and fear the type of crime and we dislike and distrust people who think thus unorthodoxly. What more reasonable than that the two are associated! And immediately, without mental effort and almost without consciousness there is affixed to a group the label which signifies a condition which may or may not be true,—but the group is damned with the crimes ascribed to it by the suggestion of a label.

There would be less point to bringing any such comment as this before an undergraduate audience if judgments of men and policies in undergraduate life were not so frequently derived and held by responsible men on the basis of like labels affixed by other men irresponsible and for reasons insufficient. I am not going into this at length. You men of the college know the facts and can discuss the question as intelligently as can any one. I would simply inquire, as bearing upon any argument, to what extent among us merited and desirable confidence can be destroyed and real worth can be obscured by malevolence, irresponsibility, or carelessness in such cases as affixing the label "yellow" to an athlete, "weir" to a scholar, or "high-brow" to a policy.

If, among a carefully selected group of men, living in a presumably intellectual environment and with unusual freedom of contact with advantageous opportunities, we cannot free ourselves from the curse of judgment by label, then the hope is slim indeed that truth shall be sought and real values shall be conceded to men and policies in the world at large.

I advert once more to the statement which I have made heretofore that a standardized group is a mediocre group and that a conventionalized civilization is a dying civilization. The principles behind these statements are operative in college life as definitely as anywhere else.

The only standardization that I would willingly tolerate for the men of this college would be an imprint that marked them as men craving the mental abilities and the qualities of the soul to know the truth, and as possessing the stamina and constructive force to do it. Even then, with men's attributes as different as they are and with the realization of purpose as distant as it will always be, liberty must be conceded to the individual to choose his own path of approach to the far-off goal.

It is undoubtedly a fact that the hopes of the world are centered now as never before so strongly in the youth of the world. Men trained in old schools of thought and worn by the mental and spiritual struggle of adapting these to new conditions seek relief from further responsibility. Men discouraged either by the inertia in their own ranks or by what seems to them lack of stability in the oncoming generation seek a basis of assurance in regard to the future. Men to whom the past is a sacred thing and to whom its experiences are precious treasure to be transmitted in trust to successors who will cherish and protect these, jostle elbows in our crowded world with those who believe tradition and precedent to be a ball and chain hindering progress, and each seeks a generation which will do its respective will.

It is at such a time, while the forces at the front in anxiety await the men of your generation, that you enter the training camp behind the lines to equip yourselves to take their places. Or, as understudies you stand in the wings while the tired principals play their parts. Are there, within your ranks, the qualities of earnestness, intelligence, goodness and forcefulness to justify the confidence which the world wishes to repose in you?

The answer cannot now be made, but in distant years when judgment is entered may it not only be found that the generation of which you are a part understood and met its responsibilities but also that specifically the promise of this fine group here gathered and the aspiration of this north country college were realized and that herein essential virtue was found and carried forth to dwell among men.

DAVID STARR JORDAN

HIGHER EDUCATION OF WOMEN

Address of David Starr Jordan, President of Leland Stanford Junior University 1891-1913 (born in Gainesville, N. Y., January 19, 1851), delivered in 1895, at Pasadena, Cal.

THE subject of the higher training of young women may resolve itself into three questions:—
1. Shall a girl receive a college education?
2. Shall she receive the same kind of a college education as a boy?
3. Shall she be educated in the same college?

As to the first question: It must depend on the character of the girl. Precisely so with the boy. What we should do with either depends on his or her possibilities. No parents should let either boy or girl enter life with any less preparation than the best they can give. It is true that many college graduates, boys and girls alike, do not amount to much after the schools have done the best they can. It is true, as I have elsewhere insisted, that "you cannot fasten a two-thousand-dollar education to a fifty-cent boy"—or girl either. It is also true that higher education is not alone a question of preparing great men for great things. It must prepare even little men for greater things than they would otherwise have found possible. And so it is with the education of women. The needs of the times are imperative. The highest product of social evolution is the growth of the civilized home—the home that only a wise, cultivated, and high-minded woman can make. To furnish such women is one of the worthiest functions of higher education. No young woman capable of becoming such should be condemned to anything lower. Even with those who are in ap-

Copyright, by David Starr Jordan. Published by permission.

pearance too dull or too vacillating to reach any high ideal of wisdom, this may be said—it does no harm to try. A few hundred dollars is not much to spend on an experiment of such moment. Four of the best years of one's life spent in the company of noble thoughts and high ideals cannot fail to leave their impress. To be wise, and at the same time womanly, is to wield a tremendous influence, which may be felt for good in the lives of generations to come. It is not forms of government by which men are made or unmade. It is the character and influence of their mothers and their wives. The higher education of women means more for the future than all conceivable legislative reforms. And its influence does not stop with the home. It means higher standards of manhood, greater thoroughness of training, and the coming of better men. Therefore, let us educate our girls as well as our boys. A generous education should be the birthright of every daughter of the Republic as well as of every son.

2. Shall we give our girls the same education as our boys? Yes, and no. If we mean by the *same* an equal degree of breadth and thoroughness, and equal fitness for high thinking and wise acting, yes, let it be the same. If we mean this: Shall we reach this end by exactly the *same* course of studies? then my answer must be, No. For the same course of study will not yield the same results with different persons. The ordinary "college course" which has been handed down from generation to generation is purely conventional. It is a result of a series of compromises in trying to fit the traditional education of clergymen and gentlemen to the needs of men of a different social era. The old college course met the needs of nobody, and therefore was adapted to all alike. The great educational awakening of the last twenty years in America has lain in breaking the bonds of this old system. The essence of the new education is individualism. Its purpose is to give to each young man that training which will make a man of *him*. Not the training which a century or two ago helped to civilize the mass of boys of that time, but that which will civilize this particular boy. One reason why the college students of 1895 are ten to one in number as compared with those of 1875, is that the college training now given is valuable to ten times as many

men as could be reached or helped by the narrow courses of twenty years ago.

In the university of to-day the largest liberty of choice in study is given to the student. The professor advises, the student chooses, and the flexibility of the courses makes it possible for every form of talent to receive proper culture. Because the college of to-day helps ten times as many men as that of yesterday could hope to reach, it is ten times as valuable. This difference lies in the development of special lines of work and in the growth of the elective power. The power of choice carries the duty of choosing rightly. The ability to choose has made a man out of the college boy and transferred college work from an alternation of tasks and play to its proper relation to the business of life. Meanwhile the old ideals have not risen in value. If our colleges were to go back to the cutstraw of mediævalism, to their work of twenty years ago their professors would speak to empty benches. In those colleges which still cling to these traditions the benches are empty to-day—or filled with idlers, which to a college is a fate worse than death.

The best education for a young woman is surely not that which has proved unfit for the young man. She is an individual as well as he, and her work gains as much as his by relating it to her life. But an institution which meets the varied needs of varied men can also meet the varied needs of the varied women. The intellectual needs of the two classes are not very different in many important respects. The special or professional needs, so far as they are different, will bring their own satisfaction. Those who have had to do with the higher training of women know that the severest demands can be met by them as well as by men. There is no demand for easy or "goody-goody" courses of study for women except as this demand has been encouraged by men. In this matter the supply has always preceded the demand.

There are, of course, certain average differences between men and women as students. Women have often greater sympathy or greater readiness of memory or apprehension, greater fondness for technique. In the languages and literature, often in mathematics and history, they are found to excel. They lack, on the whole, originality. They are not attracted by unsolved problems, and in the inductive or "inexact" sciences, they seldom take the lead. The "motor" side of their minds and nature is not strongly developed. They do not work for results as much as for the pleasure of study. In the traditional courses of study—traditional for men—they are often very successful. Not that these courses have a fitness for women, but that women are more docile and less critical as to the purposes of education. And to all these statements there are many exceptions. In this, however, those who have taught both men and women must agree; the training of women is just as serious and just as important as the training of men, and no training is adequate for either which falls short of the best.

3. Shall women be taught in the same classes as men? This is partly a matter of taste. It does no harm whatever to either men or women to meet those of the other sex in the same classrooms. But if they prefer not to do so, let them do otherwise. Considerable has been said for and against the union in one institution of technical schools and schools of liberal arts. The technical quality is emphasized by its separation from general culture. But I believe better men are made where the two are not separated. The culture studies and their students gain from the feeling of reality and utility cultivated by technical work. The technical students gain from association with men and influences of which the aggregate tendency is toward greater breadth of sympathy and a higher point of view.

A woman's college is more or less distinctly a technical school. In most cases, its purpose is distinctly stated to be such. It is a school of training for the profession of womanhood. It encourages womanliness of thought as more or less different from the plain thinking which is called manly. The brightest work in women's colleges is often accompanied by a nervous strain, as though its doer were fearful of falling short of some outside standard. The best work of men is natural, is unconscious, the normal result of the contact of the mind with the problem in question.

In this direction, I think, lies the strongest argument for coeducation. This argument is especially cogent in institutions in which the individuality of the student is recognized and respected. In such schools each man, by his relation to action and realities, becomes a teacher of women in these regards, as in other ways, each cultivated woman is a teacher of men.

In woman's education, as planned for women alone, the tendency is toward the study of beauty and order. Literature and language takes precedence over science. Expression is valued more highly than action. In carrying this to an extreme, the scholarship developed is ineffective, because it is not related to success. The educated woman is likely to master technique, rather than art; method, rather than substance. She may know a good deal, but she can do nothing. Often her views of life must undergo painful changes before she can find her place in the world.

In schools for men alone, the reverse often obtains. The sense of reality obscures the elements of beauty and fitness. It is of great advantage to both men and women to meet on a plane of equality in education. Women are brought into contact with men who can do things—men in whom the sense of reality is strong, and who have definite views in life. This influence affects them for good. It turns them away from sentimentalism. It is opposed to the unwholesome state of mind called "monogamic marriage." It gives tone to their religious thoughts and impulses. Above all, it tends to encourage action as governed by ideals, as opposed to that resting on caprice. It gives them better standards of what is possible and impossible when the responsibility for action is thrown upon them.

In like manner, the association with wise, sane, and healthy women has its value for young men. This value has never been fully realized, even by the strongest advocates of coeducation. It raises their ideal of womanhood, and the highest manhood must be associated with such an ideal. This fact shows itself in many ways; but to point out its existence must suffice for the present paper.

At the present time, the demand for the higher education of woman is met in three different ways:—

1. In separate colleges for women, with courses of study more or less parallel with those given in colleges for men. In some of these the teachers are all women, in some mostly men, and in others a more or less equal division obtains. In nearly all of

these institutions those old traditions of education and discipline are more prevalent than in colleges for men, and nearly all retain some trace of religious or denominational control. In all, the *Zeitgeist* is producing more or less commotion, and the changes in their evolution are running parallel with those in colleges for men.

2. In annexes for women to colleges for men. In these, part of the instruction given to the men is repeated for the women, though in different classes or rooms, and there is more or less opportunity to use the same libraries and museums. In some other institutions, the relations are closer, the privileges of study being similar, the difference being mainly in the rules of conduct by which the young women are hedged in, the young men making their own.

It seems to me that the annex system cannot be a permanent one. The annex student does not get the best of the institution, and the best is none too good for her. Sooner or later she will demand it, or go where the best can be found. The best students will cease to go to the annex. The institution must then admit women on equal terms, or not admit them at all. There is certainly no educational reason why a woman should prefer the annex of one institution when another equally good throws its doors wide open for her.

3. The third system is that of coeducation. In this system young men and young women are admitted to the same classes, subjected to the same requirements, and governed by the same rules. This system is now fully established in the State institutions of the North and West, and in most other colleges in the same region. Its effectiveness has long since passed beyond question among those familiar with its operation. Other things being equal, the young men are more earnest, better in manners and morals, and in all ways more civilized than under monastic conditions. The women do more work in a more natural way, with better perspective and with saner incentives than when isolated from the influence and society of men. There is less of silliness and folly where a man is not a novelty. In coeducational institutions of high standards, frivolous conduct or scandals of any form are unknown. The responsibility for decorum is thrown from the school to the woman, and the

woman rises to the responsibility. Many professors have entered Western colleges with strong prejudices against coeducation. These prejudices have never endured the test of experience. What is well done has a tonic effect on the mind and character. The college girl has long since ceased to expect any particular leniency because she is a girl. She stands or falls with the character of her work.

It is not true that the character of college work has been in any way lowered by coeducation. The reverse is decidedly the case. It is true that untimely zeal of one sort or another has filled the West with a host of so-called colleges. It is true that most of these are weak and doing poor work in poor ways. It is true that most of these are coeducational. It is also true that the great majority of their students are not of college grade at all. In such schools, low standards rule, both as to scholarship and as to manners. The student fresh from the country, with no preparatory training, will bring the manners of his home. These are not always good manners, as manners are judged. But none of these defects are derived from coeducation; nor are any of these conditions in any way made worse by it.

A final question: Does not coeducation lead to marriage? Most certainly it does; and this fact need not be and cannot be denied. But such marriages are not usually premature. It is certainly true that no better marriages can be made than those founded on common interests and intellectual friendships.

A college man who has known college women is not drawn to those of lower ideals and inferior training. His choice is likely to be led toward the best he has known. A college woman is not led by propinquity to accept the attentions of inferior men.

I have before me the statistics of the faculty of a university open to both sexes alike. Of the eighty professors and instructors, twenty-seven men and women are still unmarried. Of the remaining fifty-three, twenty-one have taken the Bachelor's degree in coeducational institutions, and have married college associates; twelve, mostly from colleges not coeducational, have married women from other colleges, and in twenty cases the wives are not college graduates.

It will be seen, then, that nearly all those who are graduates of coeducational colleges have married college friends. In most cases college men have chosen college women; and in all cases both men and women are thoroughly satisfied with the outcome of coeducation. It is part of the legitimate function of higher education to prepare women, as well as men, for happy and successful lives.

An Eastern professor, lately visiting a Western State university, asked one of the seniors what he thought of the question of coeducation.

"I beg your pardon," said the student; "what question do you mean?"

"Why coeducation," said the professor; "the education of women in colleges for men."

"Oh," said the student, "coeducation is not a question here."

And he was right. Coeducation is never a question where it has been fairly tried.

ROBERT MARION LA FOLLETTE

WHICH SHALL RULE, MANHOOD OR MONEY?

Robert Marion La Follette was born at Primrose, Wis., in 1855; died in 1925. He graduated from the University of Wisconsin, in 1879, was admitted to the bar in 1880, was made district attorney of Dane County, and was elected as a Republican member of Congress from his native state in 1887. He took a prominent part in framing the McKinley Bill. He was governor of Wisconsin from 1901 to 1905, and then became United States Senator from that state. The following speech was delivered at Milwaukee in the West Side Turner Hall on September 30, 1902.

UNDER our form of government the citizen should determine all the issues, and you will exercise your right of suffrage in this election upon national and upon state questions as well. I would in no wise disparage the importance of national issues in this campaign. But within the limits of a single address I should be unwilling to attempt a thorough discussion of both. I should not feel, however, that I had discharged my duty as a Republican on this occasion if I passed by national issues in silence.

Though there may appear to be differences among Republicans on the tariff issue, it would seem to arise from misunderstanding rather than disagreement. From Hamilton to Clay, and from Clay to McKinley, the principle upon which a protective tariff rested for support has not changed. The true measure of a protective duty when Hamilton wrote his great report on manufactures in 1791 and the true measure of a protective duty to-day is the difference between the cost of production in this country and the competing country. A tariff that is either higher or lower than that should not be called a protective tariff. If it is higher, it is prohibitory; if it is lower, it is not protective.

It is charged that the tariff is responsible for trusts. This charge is most strongly pressed by those who opposed protection before trusts were known. They ignore the fact that the organizations of trusts and combinations began but a few years ago and are fast gaining control of business everywhere. They are not confined to any country, or the offspring of any tariff policy. They rule the market in free trade products in this country, and in whatever products they choose in free trade countries. But the fact remains that the organization of combinations of capital great enough to master the production and fix the price of articles embraced within protective tariff schedules brings upon that system the popular disapproval which the public entertains toward trusts generally.

In these days of marvelous financial and commercial evolution, of colossal combinations of capital, such as the world has never before known, it is well to recall first principles. Every writer on protection, every tariff leader in Congress and before the country, placed free competition between protected industries as a necessary complement to a protective tariff.

When competition was free between protected industries of the country, the fact that a duty was above the level necessary for protection to American labor was not so important, because competition could never be depended upon to reduce the price for the consumer upon any protected product to the lowest point to which it could be produced in this country, and pay American wages to American labor. The natural law of competition was the same protection to the consumer that the tariff was to the producer.

But a new law, an artificial law, is supplanting the natural law of competition. By secret agreement the producers of like articles limit the number or quantity produced and fix prices. Combination is destroying competition.

I believe that the hour has come when tariff revision must stand close guard over tariff schedules. But this revision should be on the true protective principle of guarding American labor from free competition with cheaper foreign labor, and yet take the place of suppressed competition.

I believe the people of Wisconsin indorse the policy outlined by President Roosevelt in his Logansport speech, which should, but for the unfortunate accident we all deplore, have been delivered in Milwaukee. In that address he said:

"It is on every account most earnestly to be hoped that this problem can be solved in some manner into which partisanship shall enter as a purely secondary consideration if at all; that is, in some manner which shall provide for an earnest effort by non-partisan inquiry and action to secure any change, the need of which is indicated by the effect found to proceed from a given rate of duty on a given article; its effect, if any, as regards the creation of a substantial monopoly; its effect upon domestic prices, upon the revenue of the government, upon importations abroad, upon home production, and upon consumption."

I believe that not only all Republicans, but all citizens, independent of political consideration, would concede that tariff revision cannot effectively grapple with, indeed, would be but a feeble, inadequate, and uncertain remedy for the trust evils which confront us to-day. Their gigantic power, their mastery of the industrial world, cannot be exaggerated.

Anthracite coal is not protected by the tariff. But glance at the situation, the problem it presents.

The second most important product of the earth is coal. The supply is severely limited. There is absolutely nothing to take its place for the purpose of fuel and power in the world. The entire wood supply would last but a very short time. The anthracite or hard coal of the United States lies in three different fields, covering in the aggregate not to exceed eight miles by sixty miles. Ninety-five per cent of the entire coal fields is owned and controlled by eight railway companies. The lines of these eight railways furnish the sole available means of transportation of anthracite coal to market. In pursuit of a settled policy these railway companies have forced private owners to sell their coal mines and coal lands at half value, first, by increasing the freight rates, and second, by refusing to carry the coal for private owners at any price whenever such owners could not be brought to terms by the establishment of exorbitant transportation rates. Owning the coal and owning the railroads over which the coal is transported to market, they fixed the freight rates at an exorbitant figure in order to make consumers pay dividends on the over-capitalization of the railroads and coal mines. While rates for other and like products have fallen, anthracite coal rates have been advanced by the railways until they are nearly twice as great as those for cotton or wheat. They limit the supply in order to force a strong demand and high market price. As shown by sworn testimony upon trials and investigation, more than $200,000,000 in excess of a fair market price has been exacted from consumers.

This coal trust bears harder upon the unfortunate, helpless labor that mines the product at the wage level of a generation ago, than upon the consumer who in these days must purchase, hat in hand. Its attitude of indifference to the appeal of press and pulpit suggests utter contempt for public opinion. This is typical of the oppression which awaits the people of this country unless the *Federal government is empowered to strip these combinations of their unlawful power.*

The plan developed and consummated in building up the anthracite coal trust is indicative of the power of the railroads in combination. As the magnitude of the question presented is understood it becomes manifest that no power outside the supreme power of the land can control the situation. These great combinations of wealth, owning most of the material products of the earth, controlling what they do not own, and combining with the railways, forget in their greedy strife for more, that all men are born free and equal and with certain inalienable rights. These trusts, clothed with corporate power, availing themselves of every advantage of the law, yet living and growing in greatness and power in violation of it, constitute a national and interstate problem that must be dealt with fearlessly and effectively.

We believe with the President, as recognized by him in daily speech, that these great monopolies constitute the foremost of national questions. We uphold his hands in his effort to curb these trusts by the enforcement of laws now upon the Statute books. There is probably not an important trust in the United States which does not have the assistance of railroads in destroying its competitors in business. The limitation and control of these public-service corporations in the legitimate field, as common carriers, is an important element in the practical solution of the problem with which we have to deal.

Republicans will support the recommendations made in his message as to the interstate commerce law in which he says:

"The act should be amended. The railway is a public servant. Its rates should be just to and open to all shippers alike. The government should see to it that this is so, and should provide a speedy, inexpensive, and effective remedy to that end."

In accepting renomination for the office of governor at the hands of the Republican party, I said:

"The greatest danger menacing public institutions to-day is the overbalancing control of city, state, and national legislatures by the wealth and power of public service corporations."

I made this statement advisedly then. I repeat it now. Not in a spirit of hostility to any interest, but deeply impressed with its profound significance to republican institutions and its ultimate influence upon all citizens and all citizenship.

The idea is not new. It is not peculiar to Wisconsin.

The responsibility it brings cannot be shirked or pushed aside or postponed. The national government, every state government—particularly that of every rich and prosperous state— every city government—particularly that of every large city —has this problem to solve; not at some other time, but now.

Philadelphia giving away franchises—not supposedly, not guessed at, or estimated to be worth two and a half million dollars, but for which she had been offered two and a half million dollars; Milwaukee giving away her eight-million-dollar street car franchise against the protest and indifferent to the public indignation of her citizens; Chicago discovering that she is robbed in tax payments by corporate owners of property of immense value through fraud and forgery on a gigantic scale; aldermen of St. Louis organized to boodle the city with their criminal compact for secrecy that would chill the blood of common cut-throats—are all a part of the testimony that to-day's daily papers bring of the great proportions and grave seriousness of the problems which control of legislation by aggregate wealth and corporate power presents for solution to this day and generation.

The question of primary elections is one of government for the people and by the people. Under our system of government by political parties, two elements, equal in importance, are involved in the exercise of suffrage; one, the making of the ballot; the other, the casting of the ballot. The right to cast the ballot is regarded as sacred. The right to make the ballot is equally sacred. No man would be willing to delegate his power to vote the ballot at general elections. No man shall be compelled to delegate his power to make his ballot. Boss Tweed said: "You may elect whichever candidates you please to office, if you will allow me to select the candidates." The boss can always afford to say, "You may vote any ticket you please so long as I make all the tickets." The character of the men nominated and the influences to which they owe their nomination determines the character of government.

The result and the only result sought by a primary election is to give to every man an equal voice in the selection of all candidates; to lodge in the people the absolute right to say who their candidates for office shall be; to root out forever the power of the political boss to control the selection of officials through the manipulation of caucuses and conventions. A primary election should provide the same safeguards for nominating candidates as for electing them. It should fix the day, name the hour, use the same polling places, have the same election officers, provide the Australian ballot, containing the names of all the candidates to be voted upon at the election. It should be an election, possessing all the legal sanctions of an election.

It is needless to trace the evolution of the political machine, its combination with aggregate wealth and corporate power, making the interests of the citizen and the state subservient to their selfish ends. The names of the great bosses to-day are better known than the great statesmen. The tendency to monopolization of political control by a few men in each party, county, city, state, and community has operated, except in cases of profound interest, excitement, and tremendous effort, to disfranchise the great majority of citizens in so far as participating in the caucus and convention is concerned.

The day that Chief Justice Ryan prophesied would come is here. The issue he said would arise is pending.

"Which shall rule—wealth or man; which shall lead—money or intellect; who shall fill public stations—educated and patriotic freemen, or the feudal servants of corporate power?"

In this contest the Republican party of Wisconsin to-day stands undeniably, unequivocally, emphatically the organized instrument of the people of the state.

Though it failed to accomplish that which was promised two years ago, it has taken no backward step, yielded no principle, sounded no retreat; it better understands the nature of the conflict; it is better equipped to meet it, more determined in resolution to win a lasting victory and write its platform pledges into statutory law.

These plain truths will triumph. Unless I mistake the temper of Wisconsin citizenship, they will triumph now. Every man of every party who places patriotism above party will bring the support of his convictions, will bring all that is best in him, to this progressive movement for good government, which means so much not alone to Wisconsin, but to all states struggling with the same forces, contending for the same principles. The good citizens of this state will unite to redeem representative government in this commonwealth and make Wisconsin a model state. The way is open and the power is in your hands. Demand of every candidate for the Senate and Assembly that he shall publicly declare how he will vote upon questions in which you are most deeply interested. If he talks about exercising his independent judgment on these issues, have him plainly understand that this is a representative government, and that he has no right to interpose his independent judgment or aught else against the known will of his constituents.

If the chosen representative does not represent the citizen, his voice is stifled; is denied any part in government. If majority decision as determined by the law of the land is ignored and reversed, if the expressed will of the people is scorned and scorned again—then the popular government fails, then government of the people, by the people, and for the people is at an end. Its forms may be observed—you may have the mockery of "elections," and the force of "representation," but a government based upon the will of the people has perished from the earth.

ABBOTT LAWRENCE LOWELL

SCHOLARSHIP

Abbott Lawrence Lowell was born in Boston in 1856, graduated at Harvard in 1877, practiced law in Boston 1880-1897, was professor of the science of government at Harvard 1900-1909 and was elected President of Harvard May 19, 1909. Mr. Lowell's distinction as a scholar and educator has received recognition in honorary degrees from many Universities in Europe as well as in America and of election to learned and honorary societies. The following speech, a model of brevity and effectiveness, was delivered at a luncheon at the installation of James Lukens McConaughy as president of Wesleyan University, June 5, 1925.

WE meet to-day to celebrate the advent of a new leader in an institution that in six years will have fulfilled a century of earnest work; nearly one hundred years of fruitful teaching; almost a century of common aspiration and endeavor by a band of scholars; and we may well ponder on the tie that holds such men together and binds them to a single end. Their pursuits are often far apart, far as the various realms of human thought, and yet their aim is one.

Around King Arthur's hall sat many knights, and when they planned to seek the Holy Grail each to his comrades seemed fairer than before. The cup was seen by some of them, but none could bring it back. Men do not come together now to seek the Grail, but with an object not less sacred, to seek for truth. It lies not here or there but everywhere, nor can it anywhere be found entire. The scholar threading his hidden path finds of it traces and fragments from time to time; and hears with joy the far-off hail of colleagues who in other roads unknown to him have also found a grain of everlasting truth. With patient haste he presses on his never-ending search; conscious that if all truth should be revealed the sacred quest would cease. New truth lies all about him to cheer his labors, but only at infinity is it complete. Seeking and imparting truth provides the link that binds the scholars in their work, and eternally will hold them. Sacred it is, for if the mysteries of nature and the human mind are works of God, exploring them is searching for the Holy Grail.

THE NINETIETH BIRTHDAY OF CHARLES WILLIAM ELIOT

This address was made by President Lowell on the occasion of the celebration of the ninetieth birthday of Charles William Eliot, for many years President of Harvard, on March 20, 1924. President Eliot's response is printed elsewhere in this volume.

ON behalf of the Corporation of the University, whose counsels you directed for forty years, I have the honor to express to you, Sir, their congratulations and their gratefulness.

In the four minutes allotted to each of us it would be futile to try to speak of all the claims to the esteem of his fellow graduates and citizens, of the man we meet to reverence here to-day. Nor would even a brief summary be possible of the work done in his life that now reaches ninety years—a life of unceasing and tireless energy devoted without stint to education and to public interests. Much has been said, and will be said here, of the many achievements in that long career of service. One may, however, dwell for a moment upon some single pervasive quality which, throughout the trials, the obstacles, and the struggles of these years, he has possessed in unfailing and triumphant strength. That quality, unfortunately rare, is courage.

From first to last Mr. Eliot has been an educational warrior. Elected President at thirty-five, dealing with colleagues in Faculties and Governing Boards much older than himself, many of them clinging tenaciously to the traditions of the past, he grappled fearlessly with the problems of the time. Undismayed by the opposition of men of weight among the graduates, by the frowns of almost all rival institutions, and by sharp public criticism, he pursued without flinching the end he had in view. Nor did he ever shun reform in a department of the University because it involved for years a serious falling off in the number of students, but persisted calmly until public confidence should approve the change.

Never in education or in public questions did he shrink from taking the unpopular side, but trusted to his faith in the rectitude of his own convictions. More, perhaps, than ever before is such a quality needed in our leading citizens, and above all is it essential in those who are charged with the training of youth. Like most strong characters he has, no doubt, rated his own courage lightly, for it is an integral part of his vigorous nature; but we who bring him to-day our tribute of respect may well marvel at its force and its resistless potency.

THE ART OF EXAMINATION

Speech delivered by the President of Harvard University at a dinner held in Ann Arbor on the occasion of the inauguration of Marion L. Burton as President of the University of Michigan, October 14, 1920.

WE have met here not only to participate in the inauguration of Mr. Burton as the new President of the University of Michigan, and to express our hope and confidence in the future of that great institution; but also to take an account of stock in the educational progress of the nation. Everyone will admit that the present condition of education in this country has its merits and its defects. The product of our schools and colleges shows a remarkable degree of resourcefulness and adaptability. This may not be wholly due to our educational system, but in part to the environment, which tends to develop these qualities in our people; for they are shown also by men whose systematic education has been exceedingly limited. Nevertheless, it is easy to underrate the effects of schooling. Men often attribute far too little to their instruction, and too much to their inherent qualities. It is certain not only that our education has not tended to diminish natural resourcefulness and adaptability, but that these very traits have been shown most markedly among college-bred men, as was seen among our college graduates in the late war. The two qualities of resourcefulness and adaptability have been, indeed, those that we have most needed in the past. They have been absolutely essential for the great American achievement, unparalleled in so short a period, of bringing under cultivation a vast wilderness, of developing the mines and other natural resources of a continent, and of developing various industries for a hundred millions of people. But all this has now been in large part done; the cream has been skimmed; and the great need of the hour is a better conservation, a more complete and scientific use, of our resources. In short, the time for superficial treatment on a large scale has largely passed, and the time has come for the greater thoroughness of an older civilization.

Wisdom consists, not in glorying in one's merits, but in curing one's defects; and the great defect in American education has been the lack of thoroughness. The European professional man is apt to have a wider knowledge and a broader foundation than the American. Professor Maurice Caullery, in his recent book on the universities and scientific life in the United States, in speaking of engineering education says, "The conditions of the training of the American engineer and his French colleague are very different. The latter has certainly a very marked superiority in theoretical scientific instruction. I am told, indeed, that since the war has brought into the American industries a rather large number of our engineers, this fact is well recognized. There is in the United States nothing to compare with the preparation for our competitive examinations for the *Ecole Polytechnique* and the *Ecole Centrale*. The first-year students —the freshmen—in the engineering schools are very feebly equipped." On the other hand, he says, "It is not less true that the American engineer gives abundant proof of the combination of qualities which he needs." He then goes on to give an example from Mann's "Bulletin on Engineering Education" to show that of the freshmen in twenty-two engineering schools only about one-third could solve a simple algebraic equation. We are told also that the English physiologists have a great

THE ART OF EXAMINATION

advantage over ours in a more comprehensive knowledge of physics and chemistry; and probably anyone familiar with learned professions in the two countries could give other examples.

As usual, a number of causes no doubt contribute to the lack of thoroughness in American education. One obviously is the briefness of time spent in study from birth through graduation from college. This is especially true in the younger years. Our children begin late and go slowly, apparently on the theory that the less conscious effort a boy puts into the process of education the more rapidly will he proceed. Another cause is the constant insertion of new subjects which are either not of a very severe nature or ought to be extra curriculum activities, subjects which are inserted to the displacement of more serious ones. If someone suggests that rural walks and the observation of nature are good, the school, instead of providing for them outside of school hours, inserts them in the school time in the place of language, history, or mathematics.

A third cause is the absence of rigorous standards which, until a few years ago, pervaded most college work more than it does to-day, and which I fear is still too largely present in the schools. Last year a boy from a good high school not far from the central part of the country offered himself for the College Entrance Board examinations. He was the valedictorian of his class, and yet in five subjects—in all of which he had obtained a double A at school—his marks were as follows: English Literature 50; Latin 41; American History 37; Ancient History 30; Plane Geometry 33. In Physics, in which he had a B at school—which is, I suppose, an honor mark—his mark was only 28. The papers of the College Entrance Examination Board are not made out, nor are the books marked, by any one college, but by a body representing the colleges and schools. A difference in preparation might very well affect to some extent an examination in literature and history, possibly even in Latin; but surely a boy who obtains an unusually high mark at school in plane geometry ought not to fail any entrance examination with so low a grade as 33 per cent.

The failure to maintain rigorous standards may well be connected with the American system of measurement by credits instead of by attainment. Courses, whether in school, in college or in any kind of education, instead of being treated as an end, should be regarded as a means; and a test in them should be, not a final reward, but a mere measure of progress. At present the credit for a course is treated like a deposit in a savings bank, without a suspicion that the deposit is not of gold that can be drawn upon at its face value, but of a perishable article. To change the metaphor, we treat it like wheat poured into a grain elevator, whereas it is often more like the contents of a cold storage plant without the means of refrigeration. Indeed, it is sometimes more like the contents of an incinerator.

There is an old saying in England that an educated man should have forgotten Greek. If the adage is true, it is not because the man had forgotten Greek, but because he retained something worth while from having learned it. Even if the material put into the mind be not perishable, we ought to distinguish between information and education. Storing in the mind is not enough; we must also train the student to use the store; and accumulating credits for things done is not the way to attain the result. When a man's life ends, we ask what he has done; but a diploma from a school or a degree from a college or university is not an obituary, and when a student's education ends we should ask, not what he has done, but what he is or has become.

Can we measure what the boy or man is or has become; can we measure him as he stands? It does not seem impossible. Yet most of our examinations are adapted to ascertain little except knowledge, which tends to promote mere cramming; whereas the tests in the great school of active life depend rather upon the ability to use information. Surely examinations can be framed to measure not only knowledge but the ability to comprehend and correlate what is known. In short, to test the grasp of a subject as a whole. Such a grasp requires a more rigorous training in fundamentals than we are in the habit of exacting. An examination of this kind would be not only a measure of that which we desire to ascertain, but it would tend also to direct attention to a field of thought instead of to small isolated fragments of it. In short, it must not be forgotten that examinations essentially control the content of education. If examinations demand a thorough knowledge of fundamental principles, the teachers will provide it and the students will attempt to acquire it. If they require merely a certain amount of miscellaneous knowledge, that will be the aim of instruction; and if, as in many schools, there is no examination at all, there is naturally less inducement to attain a very high standard of any kind.

The mechanical practice of credit for courses is, I believe, the gravest defect in the American educational system, and we ought to strive for some method of general examinations testing the real grasp of a subject as a whole. But if such examinations are possible, it is nevertheless certain that they demand skill which can be acquired only by practice. The art of examination is a difficult one, and in America it is still in its infancy, particularly in the matter of measuring the ability to use one's knowledge. The new psychological tests are interesting as an attempt to do this, to measure the capacity of the boy or man as he stands. They are crude, and for our purpose they suffer under the defect of assuming only the most elementary information. We need tests that will measure ability to use scholarly and specific knowledge. Anyone who attempts to introduce examinations of this kind will be disappointed at first, because the art has not yet been sufficiently developed. To use them effectively, we need to learn that the conduct of examinations is as important and worthy a part of the educational process as giving lectures, and quite as stimulating to the teacher. Ascertaining what the pupil knows, measuring his progress and deficiencies, is, indeed, a part of teaching, and quite as essential a portion of it as the imparting of information. The true teacher should be constantly both developing the mind of his pupil, and ascertaining how rapidly and beneficially the process is going on. One of the defects of much of our teaching—and especially of the lecture system—is that this second part of the function of education is to a great degree lost from sight. An improvement in our examination system which will measure the grasp of a whole subject is, I believe, the most serious advance that can be made in American education to-day.

HENRY EDWARD, CARDINAL MANNING

PERSECUTION OF THE JEWS

Address by Cardinal Manning, English Roman Catholic prelate and religious writer (born in Totteridge, Hertfordshire, July 15, 1808; died in London, January 14, 1892), delivered February 1, 1882, in the Egyptian Hall of the Mansion House, London, at a meeting convened by the Lord Mayor to give expression to the feeling excited in England by the then recently perpetrated atrocities upon the Jews in Russia.

My Lord Mayor, Ladies and Gentlemen:—It has often fallen to my lot to move a resolution in meetings such as this, but never in my memory have I moved one with more perfect conviction of my reason or more entire concurrence of my heart. Before I use any further words, it will, perhaps, be better that I should read what that resolution is. It is, "That this meeting, while disclaiming any right or desire to interfere in the internal affairs of another country, and desiring that the most amicable relations between England and Russia should be preserved, feels it a duty to express its opinion that the laws of Russia relating to the Jews tend to degrade them in the eyes of the Christian population, and to expose Russian Jewish subjects to the outbreaks of fanatical ignorance."

I need not disclaim, for I accept the eloquent disclaimer of the noble lord, that we are not met here for a political purpose. If there were a suspicion of any party politics, I should not be standing here. It is because I believe that we are highly above all the tumults of party politics, that we are in the serene region of human sympathy and human justice, that I am here to-day. I can also declare that nothing can be further from my intention, as I am confident nothing can be further from yours, than to do that which would be a violation of the laws of mutual peace and order, and the respect which binds nations together, or to attempt to interfere or dictate in the domestic legislation of Russia. I am also bound to say that I share heartily in the words of veneration used by the noble earl towards his Imperial Majesty of Russia. No man can have watched the last year of the Imperial family, no man can know the condition in which the Emperor stands now without a profound sympathy which would at once bind every disposition to use a single expression which would convey a wound to the mind of the Czar. Therefore, I disclaim absolutely and altogether that anything that passes from my lips—and I believe I can speak for all—should assume a character inconsistent with veneration for a person charged with a responsibility so great. Further, I may say that while we do not pretend to touch upon any question in the internal legislation of Russia, there are laws larger than any Russian legislation—the laws of humanity and of God, which are the foundation of all other laws, and if in any legislation they be violated, all the nations of Christian Europe, the whole commonwealth of civilized and Christian men would instantly acquire a right to speak out aloud.

And now I must touch upon one point, which I acknowledge has been very painful to me. We have all watched for the last twelve months the anti-Semitic movement in Germany. I look upon it with a twofold feeling—in the first place with horror as tending to disintegrate the foundations of social life, and, secondly, with great fear lest it may light up an animosity, which has already taken flame in Russia and may spread elsewhere. I have read with great regret an elaborate article, full, no doubt, of minute observations, written from Prussia and published in the *Nineteenth Century,* giving a description of the class animosities, jealousies, and rivalries which are at present so rife in that country. When I read that article, my first feeling was one of infinite sorrow that the power and energy of the Old Testament should be so much greater in Brandenburg than those of the New. I am sorry to see that a society penetrated with rationalism has not so much Christian knowledge, Christian power, Christian character, and Christian virtue as to render it impossible that, cultivated, refined, industrious, and energetic as they are, they should endanger the

Christian society of that great kingdom. I have also read with pain accounts of the condition of the Russian Jews, bringing against them accusations which, if I touch upon them, I must ask my Jewish friends near me to believe I reject with incredulity and horror. Nevertheless, I have read that the cause of what has happened in Russia is that the Jews have been pliers of infamous trades—usurers, immoral, demoralizing, and I know not what. When I read these accusations, I ask, Will they be cured by crime, murder, outrage, abominations of every sort? Are they not learning the lesson from those who ought to teach a higher?

Again, if it be true, which I do not believe, that they are in the condition described are they not under penal laws? Is there anything that can degrade men more than to close against intelligence, energy, and industry all the honorable careers of public life? Is there anything that can debase and irritate the soul of man more than to be told, "You must not pass beyond that boundary; you must not go within eighteen miles of that frontier; you must not dwell in that town; you must live only in that province"? I do not know how anyone can believe that the whole population can fail to be affected in its inmost soul by such laws; and if it be possible to make it worse, this is the mode and the discipline to make it so.

They bring these accusations against the Russian Jews; why do they not bring them against the Jews of Germany? By the acknowledgment of the anti-Semitic movement, the Jews in Germany rise head and shoulders above their fellows. Why do they not bring these accusations against the Jews of France? Is there any career of public utility, any path of honor, civil or military, in which the Jews have not stood side by side with their countrymen? If the charge is brought against the Jews of Russia, who will bring it against the Jews of England? For uprightness, for refinement, for generosity, for charity, for all the graces and virtues that adorn humanity, where will be found examples brighter or more true of human excellence than in this Hebrew race? And when we are told that the accounts of those atrocities are not to be trusted, I ask if there were to appear in the newspapers long and minute narratives of murder, rapine, and other atrocities round about the Egyptian

PERSECUTION OF THE JEWS

hall, in Old Jewry, in Houndsditch, in Shoreditch, if it were alleged that the Lord Mayor was looking on, that the metropolitan police did nothing, that the guards at the Tower were seen mingled with the mob, I believe you would thank any man who gave you an opportunity of exposing and contradicting the statement.

Well, then, I say we are rendering a public service to the public departments and Ministry of Russia by what we are doing now, and I believe it will carry consolation to the heart of the great prince who reigns over that vast empire. But let me suppose for a moment that these things are true—I do not found my belief in their truth from what has appeared either in the *Times* newspaper or in the *Pall Mall Gazette*, which has confirmed the statements. I hold the proofs in my own hand. And from whom do they come? From official documents, from the Minister of the Interior, General Ignatieff. The resolution speaks of the laws of Russia as regards its Jewish subjects. I do not assume to be an old jurist in English law, much less to say what the laws of Russia are in this respect. I should not know what to say on the resolution if I did not hold in my hand a rescript of much importance. I hope I shall not be told that, like the ukase, it is a forgery. These horrible atrocities had continued throughout May, June, and July, and in the month of August this document was issued. The first point in it is that it laments and deplores—what? The atrocities on the Jewish subjects of the Czar? By no means, but the sad condition of the Christian inhabitants of the southern provinces. The next point is that the main cause of these "movements and riots," as they are called, to which the Russian nation had been a stranger, is but a commercial one. The third point is that this conduct of the Jews has called forth "protests" on the part of the people, as manifested by acts—of what do you think? Of violence and robbery. Fourthly, we are told by the Minister of the Interior that the country is subject to malpractices, which were, it is known, the cause of the agitation.

My Lord Mayor, if the logic of this document be calm, the rhetoric and insinuation of it are most inflammatory, and I can hardly conceive how, with that rescript in their hands, the Russian population could not have felt that they were encouraged to go on. The document then goes on to say, "We have appointed a Commission to inquire"—into what? "First, what are the trades of the Jews which are injurious to the inhabitants of the place; and, secondly, what makes it impracticable to put into force the already existing laws limiting the rights of the Jews in the matter of buying and farming land and trading in intoxicants and usury. Thirdly, how shall these laws be altered so that the Jews can no longer evade them, and what new laws may be passed to prevent their evasion."

Besides answering the foregoing questions, the following additional information was sought—first, on usury; secondly, on the number of public houses; thirdly, on the number of persons in the service of the Jews; fourthly, on the extent and acreage of the land; and, lastly, on the number of Jewish agriculturists. We have in our hands the Russian laws affecting the Jewish subjects of the Empire. I would ask what is the remedy for a population in this state? Is it more penal laws? Is it to disqualify them from holding land? Is it to forbid them to send their children to higher places of education? No, my Lord Mayor; I believe that the remedy for this state of things is twofold—first, the vital supremacy of Christian law in all its amplitude. It was not by laws like these that the Christians won the world and won the Imperial power to execute justice among men. It will not be by laws other than these that the great Imperial power of Russia will blend with the population of the Empire their Jewish subjects.

The other remedy I believe to be this: a stern and merciful execution of justice upon evil-doers, coupled with a stern and rigorous concession of all that is right in the law of nature and of God to every man. All that is necessary for the protection of life and limb, and liberty and property—all that constitutes human freedom—this, and nothing less than this, will be the remedy for the evil of which the Minister of the Interior complains.

I look very hopefully to what may be the effect of this meeting. Do not let us overrate it. If we believe that this meeting will have done the work, and that we may cease to speak, its effect will not be what we desire. Let us not underrate it either. I believe that all through the United Kingdom there will be a response to this meeting. Manchester and Birmingham have begun; and wheresoever the English tongue is spoken throughout the world, that which your lordship has said so eloquently and so powerfully will be known. I believe at the very moment we are assembled here, a meeting of the same kind is assembled in New York; and what passes here will be translated into every language of Europe, and will pass even the frontiers of Russia. Like the light and the air, it cannot be excluded, and wheresoever there is human sympathy the declarations that are made here and elsewhere will meet with a response that will tend to put an end to these horrible atrocities.

There is a book, my lord, which is common to the race of Israel and to us Christians. That book is a bond between us, and in that book I read that the people of Israel are the eldest people upon the earth. Russia, and Austria, and England of yesterday compared with the imperishable people which, with an inextinguishable life and immutable traditions, and faith in God and in the laws of God, scattered as it is all over the world, passing through the fires unscathed, trampled into the dust, and yet never combining with the dust into which it is trampled, lives still a witness and a warning to us. We are in the bonds of brotherhood with it. The New Testament rests upon the Old. They believe in half of that for which we would give our lives. Let us then acknowledge that we unite in a common sympathy. I read in that book these words, "I am angry with a great anger with the wealthy nations that are at ease, because I was a little angry with Israel, and they helped forward the affliction." That is, my people were scattered; they suffered unknown and unimaginable sufferings, and the nations of the world that dwell at ease and were wealthy, and had power in their hands, helped forward a very weighty affliction which was upon them all.

My lord, I only hope this—that not one man in England who calls himself a civilized or Christian man will have it in his heart to add by a single word to that which this great and ancient and noble people suffer; but that we shall do all we can by labor, by speech, and by prayer to lessen if it be possible, or at least to keep ourselves from sharing in sympathy with these atrocious deeds.

ROBERT ANDREWS MILLIKAN

THE ATOM

Robert Andrews Millikan is one of the most eminent scientists in the world and received the Nobel Prize in Physics in 1923 for isolating and measuring the ultimate electric unit, the electron. He was born in Morrison, Illinois, in 1868, received an A.B. at Oberlin in 1891 and a Ph.D. at Columbia in 1895. He was professor of physics at the University of Chicago until 1921 when he became director of the Norman Bridge Laboratory of Physics in Pasadena, California. The following address was delivered before the sixty-seventh convention of the American Chemical Society, Washington, D. C., April 22, 1924.

ALL scientists agree upon an atom which has a very minute positively charged nucleus surrounded in its outer regions by a number of negative electrons just sufficient to neutralize the free positive charge upon the nucleus.

We all agree that the number of these positive charges upon the nucleus varies from one, in the case of hydrogen, by unit steps up to 92 in the case of uranium, and hence that the number of negatives held in the outer regions also varies from one to 92.

We all agree that the chemical properties of all atoms, and most of the physical properties, too, mass being the chief exception, are determined simply by the number of these electrons; primarily by the number of them which are found in the outermost shell and which we call the valence electrons.

We all agree, too, that the nucleus is extraordinarily minute, so that if all the dimensions of an atom were magnified ten billion times—a magnification which would make a bird shot swell to the size of the earth and would make the diameter of the atom about a meter—the nucleus, on this huge scale of magnification, would not be more than a tenth of a millimeter in diameter—that is, not larger than a mere pin point.

We all agree, too, that in the case of uranium there are packed into that infinitesimal nucleus 238 positive and 146 negative electrons, the exact number of positives being determined simply by the atomic weight, while the number of negatives which bind the positives is the atomic weight minus the atomic number. This obviously means that both positive and negative electrons are so infinitesimally small that for practical purposes we may ignore their dimensions altogether and think of them as mere point charges.

We all agree that so far as physical science has now gone there have appeared but these two fundamental entities, namely, positive and negative electrons[1] which seem to be the building stones of the universe; that these two entities are electrical charges of exactly the same magnitude, but of opposite sign, and that the *mass* or *inertia* associated with the former is 1,845 times that associated with the latter, so that practically the whole mass of the atom is concentrated in the positive electrons within its nucleus.

We all agree that when any of the electrons in the outer regions of the atom are stimulated to radiate, they do so by virtue of falling from a level of higher potential energy to one of lower, i.e., from a level more remote from the nucleus to one nearer to it.

And we all agree that the frequency of the emitted radiations is proportional to the energy loss in the process of changing from the one level to the other. Indeed, one of the most stimulating advances which physicists have made in the past five years consists in the complete demonstration of this Planck-Einstein-Bohr law of radiation. Very recent experiments go even so far

---

[1] It is highly to be desired that this historically correct, etymologically most suitable, and authoritatively recognized nomenclature (see Rutherford's B.A. address, 1923, Nernst's Physical Chemistry, last edition etc., etc.) be retained. When used without a prefix, or qualifying adjective, the word electron may signify both the generic thing, the unit electrical charge (this it does, in fact, signify both historically and derivatively) and at the same time the negative member of the species, in precisely the way in which the word man is used without a prefix to designate both the genus homo and also the male of the species. There is no gain in convenience by the use of the word proton and a distinct loss logically, etymologically and historically.

as to indicate that this law holds not only for the radiations emitted by the changes in energy levels of the electrons *outside* the nucleus, but also for the radiations which originate in the nucleus itself—the so-called gamma-rays which accompany changes within the nuclei of radioactive atoms.

These results upon which we all agree are proof enough of the amazing advances which have taken place, mostly within the past ten years, in our ability to peer inside the atom and to see what kind of entities exist there and what they are doing when they are in the act of radiating.

The only place where we have differences of opinion, or better, in which there are uncertainties, is in the matter of how the electrons spend their leisure time—the portions of their lives in which they are not radiating.

The chemist has in general been content with what I will call the "loafer" electron theory. He has imagined these electrons sitting around on dry goods boxes at every corner ready to shake hands with, or hold on to, similar electrons in other atoms. The physicist, on the other hand, has preferred to think of them as leading more active lives, playing ring-around-the-rosy, crack-the-whip and other interesting games. In other words, he has pictured them as rotating with enormous speeds *in orbits*, and as occasionally flying out of these orbits for one reason or another.

Now the arguments for the "loafer electron" theory, as I have called it, are two in number. The first is that such activity as the physicist postulates would soon wear away all the energy possessed by the electrons—that is, they would tire themselves out and quit their play.

There is no answer to this argument. They would indeed tire themselves out, provided the classical *electro-magnetic laws are universally applicable*—even in the hearts of atoms. And the physicist's only answer to this argument is, "God did not make electrons that way. Why assume that the electro-magnetic laws are universally valid when this is the first chance we have had to test them out in the region of the infinitely small?"

The second argument which has been advanced for the "loafer electron" theory is the existence of localized valences in chemistry. Now, that these localized valences exist is admitted on all hands; but it is simply due to a misunderstanding that this argument was ever used against the orbit theory. *For no physicist—and I wish to emphasize this fact—has ever advanced the theory that the electrons all rotate in coplanar orbits.* Localized valences are just as compatible with the orbit theory when the orbits are properly distributed in space as with the stationary electron conception. All this I pointed out in 1916,[1] trying thereby to clear the misconception which existed in the minds of chemists as to the way in which physicists were thinking.

Let me pass now to the arguments in favor of the orbit theory. They are all of them definite *quantitative* arguments in which purely theoretical considerations lead to exact numerical predictions which can be subjected to the test of experiment.

The first was the exact prediction with the aid of orbit equations of the so-called Rydberg spectroscopic constant which is in agreement, with an accuracy of one part in five hundred, with the directly measured value.

The second quantitative argument comes from the prediction of a difference between the positions in two spectral lines, one due to helium, the other to hydrogen, which two lines should theoretically be one and the same line, if it were not for the fact that the helium nucleus is four times as massive as the hydrogen nucleus.

To make clear the difference which this causes let me ask you to reflect that when an electron revolves around the nucleus of an atom of hydrogen, the real thing that happens is that the two bodies revolve about their common center of gravity, but, since the nucleus is 2,000 times heavier than the electron, this center is exceedingly close to the hydrogen nucleus. If now the hydrogen nucleus is replaced by the nucleus of the helium atom, which is four times as heavy as that of hydrogen, the common center of gravity is still closer to the nucleus so that the helium nucleus describes a much smaller circle than

---

[1] *Phys. Rev.*, May, 1917; presented before the American Physical Society, December 1, 1916.

does the hydrogen nucleus. This situation is responsible for a certain slight but accurately predictable difference in the energies of the two orbits which should cause the lines produced by electron jumps to these two different orbits to be slightly displaced from one another. This displacement is actually found between the corresponding hydrogen and helium lines, and the ratio of the mass of the electron to the mass of the hydrogen atom computed from this displacement agrees with other determinations of this ratio to within a small fraction of a per cent.

The third amazing quantitative success of the orbit theory came when Sommerfeld showed that the Bohr orbit-theory ought to demand two different hydrogen orbits corresponding to the second quantum state, one a circle and one an ellipse. And by applying the relativity theory to the change in mass of the electron with its change in speed, as it moves through the different portions of its orbit, he showed that these two orbits should have slightly different energies, and consequently that both the hydrogen and the helium lines should be doublets.

Now not only is this found to be the fact, but *the measured separation of these two doublet lines agrees precisely with the predicted value,* so that this again constitutes an extraordinary bit of quantitative evidence for the validity of the orbit conceptions underlying the computation.

The fourth quantitative argument was introduced by Epstein when he applied his amazing grasp of orbit theory to the exceedingly difficult problem of computing the perturbations in electron orbits and hence the change in energy of each due to exciting hydrogen and helium atoms to radiate in an electrostatic field. He thus predicted the whole complex character of what we call the Stark effect, showing just how many new lines were to be expected and where each one should fall, and then the spectroscope yielded, in practically every detail, precisely the result which the Epstein theory had foretold.

The fifth quantitative success of the orbit theory is one which Mr. I. S. Bowen and myself at the California Institute have just brought to light. Through creating what we call "hot sparks" in extreme vacuum, we have succeeded in stripping in succession, one, two, three, four, five and six of the valence, or outer, electrons from the atoms studied. In going from lithium through beryllium, boron, and carbon to nitrogen, we have thus been able to play with stripped atoms constituting structures which are all exactly alike, save that the fields in which the single electron which is left is describing its orbit increase in the ratios, one, two, three, four, five, as we go from stripped lithium to stripped nitrogen. *Now we have applied the relativity doublet formula which, as indicated above, Sommerfeld had developed for the simple nucleus-electron system found in hydrogen and ionized helium, and have found that it not only predicts everywhere the observed doublet separation of the spectra produced by all these stripped atoms, but that it enables us to compute the effect which the two electrons close to the nucleus of all these atoms have in screening the outer rotating electron from this nucleus.*

At a sufficient distance from the nucleus these two electrons ought to neutralize exactly two of the free positive charges on the nucleus, *provided, and only provided, the forces emanating from these electrons fall off with the inverse square of the distance.* Our relativity doublet formula, with this assumption and without the introduction of any arbitrary constants whatsoever, enabled us to predict what the screening effect due to those two electrons ought to be. *And now our experiments on doublet-separation reveal that* that screening is exactly two, which checks with what we knew beforehand, from radioactive and chemical data, that it must be. In other words, we have another method, based definitely upon the theory of the change of the mass of the electron with speed in the different portions of its orbit, which enables us with certainty to look inside the atom and find how many electrons are in the inmost shell, and the answer comes out two.

Again, when we examine the spectrum due to the stripped atoms of the group of atoms from sodium to sulfur—one electron having been knocked off from sodium, two from magnesium, three from aluminium, four from silicon, five from phosphorus, and six from sulfur—we should find in every case that the number of screening electrons in the two inmost shells, when tested for sufficiently remote orbits, comes out two plus eight, i.e., ten. *And it does come out in every case precisely as predicted. This constitutes un-ambiguous proof that the electrons themselves do possess Coulomb fields (fields falling off with the inverse square of the distance),* a result entirely incompatible with the loafer-electron theory. The physicist has thus piled Ossa on Pelion in his *quantitative* proof of the existence of these electron orbits.

The new results are, however, incompatible with the precise shapes of orbits with which the physicists have been working in the field of optics during the last five years. They necessitate either the abandonment of the relativity cause for the separation of our measured spectroscopic-doublets or else they require us to cease to play with a nucleus about which the electron orbits are largely symmetrical. In other words, if we retain the relativity explanation of the spectroscopic-doublet formula, we are obliged to suppose that two orbits which have the same shape but different orientations with respect to the nucleus may exhibit widely different screening constants—which is only another way of saying that these orbits may possess widely different energies.

To this extent, then, I am able to help out the chemist in his attack upon the electronic orbits of the physicists. I am able to enable him to say with a good deal of certainty that these orbits can not be of precisely the type which we physicists have been playing with so assiduously for the past five years. If we retain the explanation which has heretofore been given to the relativity doublet formula, an explanation which requires entirely different shapes for the two orbits corresponding to these doublets, then we must begin to work with an atom which is very much less symmetrical with respect to the differently oriented orbits than we have hitherto been imagining.

WILLIAM MORRIS

ART AND THE BEAUTY OF THE EARTH

Address by William Morris, poet, artist, and writer on Socialism (born at Walthamstow, Essex, near London, March 24, 1834: died in Hammersmith, October 3, 1896), delivered at Burslem Town-Hall, October 13, 1881. The opening portion of the address praises the art of the Middle Ages as art of the people, and declares that true art is lacking in the modern industrial era. Only the latter half of the address is given here.

ART will not grow and flourish, nay, it will not long exist, unless it be shared by all people; and for my part I don't wish that it should.

Therefore it is that I stand before you to say that the world has in these days to choose whether she will have art or leave it, and that we also, each one of us, have to make up our minds which camp we will or can join, those that honestly accept art or those that honestly reject it.

Once more let me try to put into words what these two alternatives mean. If you accept it, it must be part of your daily lives, and the daily life of every man. It will be with us wherever we go, in the ancient city full of traditions of past time, in the newly-cleared farm in America or the colonies, where no man has dwelt for traditions to gather round him; in the quiet countryside as in the busy town, no place, shall be without it. You will have it with you in your sorrow as in your joy, in your workaday hours as in your leisure. It shall be no respecter of persons, but be shared by gentle and simple, learned and unlearned, and be as a language that all can understand. It will not hinder any work that is necessary to the life of man at the best, but it will destroy all degrading toil, all enervating luxury, all foppish frivolity. It will be the deadly foe of ignorance, dishonesty, and tyranny, and will foster good-will, fair dealing, and confidence between man and man. It will teach you to respect the highest intellect with a manly reverence, but not to despise any man who does not pretend to be what he is not; and that which will be the instrument that it shall work with and the food that shall nourish it shall be man's pleasure in his daily labor, the kindest and best gift that the world has ever had.

Again I say, I am sure that this is what art means, no less; that if we attempt to keep art alive on other terms we are but bolstering up a sham, and that it would be far better for us to accept the other alternative, the frank rejection of art, as many people, and they not the worst of us, have already done. To these and not to me you must go if you want to have any clear idea of what is hoped for the future of the world when art is laid within her tomb. Yet I think I can in a measure judge from the present tendency of matters what is likely to happen to those things which we handicraftsmen have to deal with.

When men have given up the idea that the work of men's hands can ever be pleasurable to them they must, as good men and true, do their utmost to reduce the work of the world to a minimum; like us artists they must do all they can to simplify the life of man, to reduce his wants as much as possible; and doubtless in theory they will be able to reduce them more than we shall, for it is clear that the waste of tissue caused by a search after beauty will be forbidden: all ornament will cease from the work of men's hands, though still, wherever nature works there will be beauty. The garment shall be unadorned, though the moth that frets it is painted with silver and pearl. London shall be a desert of hideousness, though the blossom of the "London pride" be more daintily flecked than the minutest missal that ever monk painted. And when all is done there will yet be too much work, that is to say, too much pain in the world.

What then? Machines then. Truly we shall have a good stock to start with, but not near enough. Some men must press on to martyrdom, and toil to invent new ones, till at last pretty nearly everything that is necessary to men will be made by machines. I don't see why it should not be done. I myself have boundless faith in their capacity. I believe machines can do everything, except make works of art.

And yet again, what next? Supposing we shall be able to get martyrs enough (or say slaves) to make all the machines that will still be needed, and to work them, shall we still be able to get rid of all labor, of all that which we have found out is an unmitigated curse? And what will our consciences be like (since I started by supposing us all to be conscientious people), when we think we have done all that we can do, and must still be waited upon by groaning, discontented wretches? What shall we do, I say?

Well, I must say that my imagination will stretch no further than to suggest rebellion in general as a remedy, the end of which rebellion, if successful, must needs be to set up some form of art again as a necessary solace of mankind.

But to say the truth, this leads me to making another suggestion, a practical one I consider it. Suppose we start by rebelling at once; because when I spoke of the world having to choose between accepting and rejecting art, I did not suppose that its choice could be final if it chose to reject it. No, the rebellion will have to come and will be victorious, don't doubt that; only if we wait till the tyranny is firmly established our rebellion will have to be a Nihilistic one; every help would be gone save deadly anger and the hope that comes of despair; whereas if we begin now, the change and the counter-change will work together, and the new art will come upon us gradually, and we shall one day see it marching on steadily and victoriously, though its battle has raised no clamor, we, or our sons, or our sons' sons.

How shall our rebellion begin then? What is the remedy for the lack of due pleasure in their work which has befallen all craftsmen, and for the consequent sickness of art and degradation of civilization?

I am afraid whatever answer I may make to that question will disappoint you. I myself suffer so sorely from the lack above mentioned that I have little remedy in myself save that of fostering discontent. I have no infallible nostrum to cure an evil whose growth is centuries old. Any remedies I can think of are commonplace enough. In those old days of popular art, the world in spite of all the ills that beset life, was struggling towards civilization and liberty, and it is in that way which we must also struggle, unless you think that we are civilized enough already, as I must confess I do not. Education on all sides is what we must look to. We may expect, if we do not learn much, to learn this at least, that we know but little, and that knowledge means aspiration or discontent, call it which you will.

I do not doubt that, as far as our schools of art go, education is bringing us to that point. I do not think any reasonable man can consider them a failure when the condition of the ornamental part of the individual arts is considered at the time of their foundation. True it is that those who established them were partly influenced by a delusive expectation that they would presently be able to supply directly a demand which was felt for trained and skillful designers of goods; but, though this hope failed them, they have no doubt influenced both that side of art and others also; among all that they have done not the least is that public recognition of the value of art in general which their very existence implies: or, to speak more correctly, their existence and the interest that is felt in them, is a token of people's uneasiness at the present disorganized state of the arts.

Perhaps you who study here and represent such a large body of people who must needs have some aspirations towards the progress of the arts, will excuse a word or two from me a little less general than the rest I have been saying. I think I have a right to look upon you as enrolled soldiers of that rebellion against blank ugliness that I have been preaching this evening. You, therefore, above all people are bound to be careful not to give cause to the enemy to blaspheme. You are bound to be especially careful to do solid, genuine work, and eschew all pretense and flashiness.

Be careful to eschew all vagueness. It is better to be caught out in going wrong when you have had a definite purpose than to shuffle and slur so that people can't blame you because they don't know what you are at. Hold fast to distinct form in art. Don't think too much of style, but set yourself to get out of you what you think beautiful, and express it, as cautiously as you please, but, I repeat, quite distinctly and without vagueness. Always think your design out in your head before you begin to get it on the paper. Don't begin by slobbering and messing about in the hope that something may come out of it. You must see it before you can draw it, whether the design be of your own invention or nature's. Remember always, form before color, and outline, silhouette, before modeling; not because these latter are of less importance, but because they can't be right if the first are wrong. Now, upon all these points you may be as severe with yourselves as you will, and are not likely to be too severe.

Furthermore, those of you especially who are designing for goods, try to get the most out of your material, but always in such a way as honors it most. Not only should it be obvious what your material is, but something should be done with it which is specially natural to it, something that could not be done with any other. This is the very *raison d'être* of decorative art: to make stone look like ironwork, or wood like silk, or pottery like stone is the last resource of the decrepitude of art. Set yourselves as much as possible against all machine work (this to all men). But if you have to design for machine work, at least let your design show clearly what it is. Make it mechanical with a vengeance, at the same time as simple as possible. Don't try, for instance, to make a printed plate look like a hand-painted one: make it something which no one would try to do if he were painting by hand, if your market drives you into printed plates: I don't see the use of them myself. To sum up, don't let yourselves be made machines, or it is all up with you as artists. Though I don't much love the iron and brass machines, the flesh and blood ones are more terrible and hopeless to me; no man is so clumsy or base a workman that he is not fit for something better than that.

Well, I have said that education is the first remedy for the barbarism which has been bred by the hurry of civilization and competitive commerce. To know that men lived and worked mightily before you is an incentive for you to work faithfully now, that you may leave something to those who come after you.

What next is to be thought of after education? I must here

admit that if you accept art and join the ranks of those who are to rise in rebellion against the Philistines, you will have a roughish time of it. "Nothing for nothing and not much for a dollar," says a Yankee somewhere, and I am sorry to say it is the rule of nature also. Those of us who have money will have to give of it to the cause, and all of us will have to give time, and thought, and trouble to it; and I must now consider a matter of the utmost importance to art and to the lives of all of us, which we can, if we please, deal with at once, but which emphatically claims of us time, thought, and money. Of all the things that are likely to give us back popular art in England, the cleaning of England is the first and the most necessary. Those who are to make beautiful things must live in a beautiful place. Some people may be inclined to say, and I have heard the argument put forward, that the very opposition between the serenity and purity of art and the turmoil and squalor of a great modern city stimulates the invention of artists, and produces special life in the art of to-day. I cannot believe it. It seems to me that at the best it but stimulates the feverish and dreamy qualities that throw some artists out of the general sympathy. But apart from that, these are men who are stuffed with memories of more romantic days and pleasanter lands, and it is on these memories they live, to my mind not altogether happily for their art; and you see it is only a very few men who could have even these doubtful advantages.

I abide by my statement that those who are to make beautiful things must live in beautiful places, but you must understand I do not mean to claim for all craftsmen a share of those gardens of the world, or of those sublime and awe-inspiring mountains and wastes that men make pilgrimages to see; that is to say, not a personal share. Most of us must be content with the tales of the poets and painters about these places, and learn to love the narrow spot that surrounds our daily life for what of beauty and sympathy there is in it.

For surely there is no square mile of earth's inhabitable surface that is not beautiful in its own way, if we men will only abstain from willfully destroying that beauty; and it is this reasonable share in the beauty of the earth that I claim as the right of every man who will earn it by due labor; a decent house with decent surroundings for every honest and industrious family; that is the claim which I make of you in the name of art. Is it such an exorbitant claim to make of civilization? of a civilization that is too apt to boast in after-dinner speeches; too apt to thrust her blessings on far-off peoples at the cannon's mouth before she has improved the quality of those blessings so far that they are worth having at any price, even the smallest.

Well, I am afraid that claim is exorbitant. Both you as representatives of the manufacturing districts, and I as representing the metropolis, seem hitherto to have assumed that, at any rate; nor is there one family in a thousand that has established its claim to the right aforesaid. It is a pity though; for if the claim is to be considered inadmissible, then is it most certain that we have been simply filling windbags and weaving sand-ropes by all the trouble we have taken in founding schools of art, National Galleries, South Kensington Museums, and all the rest of it.

I have said education is good, is necessary, to all people; neither can you if you would withhold it; and yet to educate people with no hope, what do you expect to come of that? Perhaps you might learn what to expect in Russia.

Look you, as I sit at my work at home, which is at Hammersmith, close to the river, I often hear go past the window some of that ruffianism of which a good deal has been said in the papers of late, and has been said before at recurring periods. As I hear the yells and shrieks and all the degradation cast on the glorious tongue of Shakespeare and Milton, as I see the brutal reckless faces and figures go past me, it rouses the recklessness and brutality in me also, and fierce wrath takes possession of me, till I remember, as I hope I mostly do, that it was my good luck only of being born respectable and rich that has put me on this side of the window among delightful books and lovely works of art, and not on the other side, in the empty street, the drink-steeped liquor-shops, the foul and degraded lodgings. What words can say what all that means? Do not think, I beg of you, that I am speaking rhetorically in saying that when I think of all this, I feel that the one great thing I desire is that this great country should shake off from her all foreign and colonial entanglements, and turn that mighty force of her respectable people, the greatest power the world has ever seen, to giving the children of these poor folk the pleasures and the hopes of men. Is that really impossible? is there no hope of it? If so, I can only say that civilization is a delusion and a lie; there is no such thing and no hope of such a thing.

But since I wish to live, and even to be happy, I cannot believe it impossible. I know by my own feelings and desires what these men want, what would have saved them from this lowest depth of savagery: employment which would foster their self-respect and win the praise and sympathy of their fellows, and dwellings which they could come to with pleasure, surroundings which would soothe and elevate them; reasonable labor, reasonable rest. There is only one thing that can give them this, and that is art.

I have no doubt that you think this statement a ridiculous exaggeration, but it is my firm conviction nevertheless, and I can only ask you to remember that in my mind it means the properly organized labor of all men who make anything; that must at least be a mighty instrument in the raising of men's self-respect, in the adding of dignity to their lives. Once more, "Nothing for nothing and very little for a dollar." You can no more have art without paying for it than you can have anything else, and if you care about art, as you must when you come to know it, you will not shrink from the necessary sacrifice. After all, we are the descendants and countrymen of those who have well known how to give the lesser for the greater. What you have to sacrifice is chiefly money, that is, force, and dirt; a serious sacrifice I know; but perhaps, as I have said, we have made greater in England aforetime; nay, I am far from sure that dirt will not in the long run cost us more in hard cash even than art will.

So which shall we have, art or dirt?

What is to be done, then, if we make the better choice? The land we live in is not very big either in actual acreage or in scale of fashion, but I think it is not our natural love for it only that makes us think it as fit as any land for the peaceful dwellings of serious men. Our fathers have shown us that, if it could otherwise be doubted. I say, without fear of contradiction, that no dwelling of men has ever been sweeter or pleasanter than an ancient English house; but our fathers treated our lovely land well, and we have treated it ill. Time was when it was beautiful from end to end, and now you have to pick your way carefully to avoid coming across blotches of hideousness which are a disgrace, I will not say to civilization, but to human nature. I have seen no statistics of the size of these blotches in relation to the unspoiled, or partially spoiled, country, but in some places they run together so as to cover a whole county, or even several counties, while they increase at a fearful rate, fearful in good earnest and literally. Now, while this goes on unchecked, nay, unlamented, it is really idle to talk about art. While we are doing this or letting it be done, we are really covertly rejecting art, and it would be honester and better for us if we did so openly. If we accept art we must atone for what we have done and pay the cost of it. We must turn this land from the grimy back-yard of a workshop into a garden. If that seems difficult, or rather impossible, to some of you, I cannot help it; I only know that it is necessary.

As to its being impossible, I do not believe it. The men of this generation even have accomplished matters that but a very little while ago would have been thought impossible. They conquered their difficulties because their faces were set in that direction; and what was done once can be done again. Why even the money and the science that we expend in devices for killing and maiming our enemies present and future would make a good nest-egg towards the promotion of decency of life if we could make up our minds to that tremendous sacrifice.

However, I am far from saying that mere money can do much or indeed anything: it is our will that must do it. Nor need I attempt to try to show how that will should express itself in action. True I have, in common with some others, ideas as to what steps would best help us on our way, but those ideas would not be accepted by you, and I feel sure that when you are thoroughly intent on the goal you will find the means to reach it, and it is of infinitesimal importance what those means may be. When you have accepted the maxim that the external aspect of the country belongs to the whole public, and that whoever willfully injures that property is a public enemy, the cause will be on its way to victory.

Meantime it is encouraging to me to think there is one thing that makes it possible for me to stand here, in a district that makes as much smoke as pottery, and to say what I have been saying on the subject of dirt, and that is that quite lately there has been visible expression given to a feeling on this subject, which has doubtless been long growing. If I am a crazy dreamer, as well may be, yet there are many members and supporters of such societies as the Kyrle and the Commons Preservation Societies, who have not time to dream, and whose craziness, if that befell them, would be speedily felt throughout the country.

I pray your pardon for having tried your patience so long. A very few words more, and I have done. Those words are words of hope. Indeed, if I have said anything that seemed to you hopeless, it has been, I think, owing to that bitterness which will sometimes overtake an impatient man when he feels how little his own hands can do towards helping the cause that he has at heart. I know that cause will conquer in the end, for it is an article of faith with me that the world cannot drop back into savagery, and that art must be its fellow on the forward march. I know well it is not for me to prescribe the road which that progress must take. I know that many things that seem to me to-day clinging hindrances, nay, poisons to that progress, may be furtherers of it, medicines to it, though they be fated to bring terrible things to pass before the visible good comes of them. But that very faith impels me to speak according to my knowledge, feeble as it may be and rash as the words may sound; for every man who has a cause at heart is bound to act as if it depended on him alone, however well he may know his own unworthiness; and thus is action brought to birth from mere opinion.

And in all I have been saying I have had steadily in mind that you have asked me to speak to you as a friend, and that I could do no less than be quite open and fearless before my friends and fellow-craftsmen.

JOHN R. MOTT

MEDITATION

John R. Mott was born at Livingston Manor, N. Y., in 1865, and graduated from Cornell University in 1888. Since then he has been constantly connected with the Y. M. C. A. organization and has been general secretary of the International Committee Y. M. C. Ass'ns. since 1915. During the War he was general secretary of the National War Work Council of Y. M. C. A. He is the author of many articles and books and has received various honorary degrees and foreign decorations. He is well known throughout this country and abroad as an effective and inspiring speaker.

IN these days the practice of withdrawing from the presence of men and from the ordinary activities that so much absorb us in our everyday work, for the purpose of going alone with God and with His truth, is absolutely necessary. It is necessary because of the marked materialistic tendency of our time. Increasingly have we become busy with the countless applications of science. Long ago Matthew Arnold pointed out the danger of our becoming absorbed with the worship of machinery. Very great, therefore, is the need of the daily practice which will hold in prominence the spiritual meaning of life, and make spiritual things real to us, even more real than the visible and material things.

It has become in these days increasingly difficult to get alone for this central purpose. The greatly improved means of communication have made the world very small. We are constantly in the presence of people. We are all the while hearing voices. We are being reminded every waking hour of the needs of men and of their claims upon us.

Then, there are so many organizations just now: athletic, social, fraternal, commercial, political, scientific, literary and

Reprinted from *The Sphere,* October, 1922, Geneva, Switzerland.

religious. This means conferences, conventions and committees to drive all the machinery. There is great danger that in conducting all these ceaseless activities with highest efficiency men's souls may be starved, and things spiritual may recede and not command us as they should.

Is it not true that life is unprecedentedly busy in these days? Constantly we hear those about us say: "That man does things. He brings things to pass. He puts it across." I would not call a halt on good works, but I would with deep conviction enter a plea for a better balance between the life of activity with men and in the presence of men on the one hand and on the other, the practice of going apart statedly, unhurriedly, for communion with God and for deep meditation upon His truth, in order that we may be most largely helpful to others.

Our danger is not lack of activity: it is that of superficiality in life and in work. One of the great ecclesiastics of the Church of England said: "We have high-churchmen, we have low-churchmen, we have broad-churchmen but even more we need *deep* churchmen." This might be said with like aptness of all other religious bodies or denominations. We need more men and women who have sunk a shaft down deep into the great thoughts of God, have uncovered hidden streams, and have set gushing great vital fountains.

Some say: If we live a life of unbroken communion with God is it necessary that we withdraw at stated times from the presence of men to meditate on His truth and to commune with Him? Have you ever known a person who preserved a life of unbroken communion with God who did not find it necessary to have regular periods for solitary prayer and reflection on spiritual truth? Jesus Christ preserved a life of unbroken communion with the Heavenly Father. No one doubts that. And surely He lived a life of great activity in the presence of men. But notice, as I open up a few windows from the Gospel records. In one place we are told: "He departed into the desert place, there to pray." In another it says: "Rising in the morning while it was still dark [that is quite early] He went apart to pray." In yet another: "He went up into the mountain when evening had come and continued all night in prayer to God." You recall we are told that: "He was alone

MEDITATION

praying," and then again, that He departed a stone's cast [that is, quite a distance] beyond the disciples and knelt down and prayed. A still more illuminating verse is the one that says: "He went, as His custom was, to the Mount of Olives." These are little glimpses into a life of great depth and volume. If Jesus Christ found it necessary—or let me change the language—if Jesus Christ found it desirable to break away from the presence of others, even His most intimate disciples, and go apart for quiet communion with the Heavenly Father, what presumption and folly it is for you and me to assume that in these busy days and in this noisy world we can do without this practice!

There are some reasons in favor of this practice that have ever obtained, not simply to-day, but always, and in every nation.

We need this practice, in the first place, in order to make highly efficient the voice of conscience. It is conscience that says, "This is right and that is wrong." What makes the voice of conscience very efficient? It must be progressively educated. In this respect no one should count himself as having attained. Possibly nobody is so much in danger as the man who assumes that his conscience now is fully educated and that this is not a process. Christ reveals sins; the more He sheds His light, the more things that before had not seemed to men to be sinful became very sinful. With increasing holiness grows the sense of sin. We must keep the light of God turned on by the meditative study of the Bible if those consciences of ours are to be progressively educated and are therefore to speak the loud, the clear, the prompt word.

An efficient conscience is not only progressively educated; but it is also very sensitive. When I was at one of the Lake Geneva student conferences in America, a professor in astronomy in the great Yerkes Observatory took me into the observatory and showed me an instrument which measures the heat of the stars. Imagine the delicacy of mechanism and adjustment! Some Christians have such sensitive consciences that they are able to detect the oncoming of temptation far, far in the distance. Other Christians wait until their temptations sweep in on them like a flood, when it is too late to resist successfully.

An efficient conscience must not only be progressively educated and highly sensitive, but likewise it must be kept unburdened. There is only one thing that can burden a man's conscience, and that is sin; and it does not take a very great sin to weigh a man's conscience down and prevent its doing efficient work.

Now, there is a second reason that has always obtained in every nation in favor of men breaking away from the presence of others, seeking His face and digging deep down into His truth and applying it; and that is in order to take that step which every man of us has to take several times each day, the step between knowing our duty and doing our duty.

We are not atheists. We believe in the living God. We say: "I believe in God, the Father Almighty." Do we? Is there almighty power working in our lives? Have we the practice which makes His power operative in our lives? Remember that word from Isaiah: "They that *wait* upon the Lord shall renew their strength," or better rendered in one of the versions: "They that wait upon the Lord shall change their strength." Change what? Shall change that which they call their strength for the omnipotence of God. But observe it takes time to effect that transfer. It is not those that rush into His presence and rush away, not the men with the watch in hand. But they who wait in His presence, who spend enough time there to have a realizing sense of their limitations, of their shortcomings, of their sins and stains, of their inability to do in their own strength what they know they ought to do. Yes, a good deal more time than that: time to remind themselves of Who He is, what His character is, what His resources are, where He is, why He is there. These men put off their weakness, they take on a power not their own; they take the step between knowing and doing, they mount up on wings as eagles (that is, have real power of vision), they run and are not weary, they walk and are not faint. They are the present-day evidences of Christianity.

There is a third reason why in every nation men must break away from the activities of the ordinary life and from the sight of men to go alone with God, to spread His truth out before them, and to seek its inner meanings; that is in order that they may preserve the power of growth. Was it not George Eliot who said: "Early in life I perceived that the object of life is to grow"? We are not made much wiser or stronger simply by the number of conferences we attend, or by the number of good books we read, or by good sermons or addresses to which we listen. No, we are made stronger and better and richer and more vital by the extent and thoroughness of our meditation upon what we have heard and have read. There are some men so busy attending meetings and reading books and seeking advice and getting good advice that they are starving; they do not take enough time to apply what they hear and incorporate it into life. That is what meditation is. "Thy words were found and I did eat them." I took them into my life; I made them a part of myself.

There is a fourth reason which has always been true in favor of this practice of going alone with God and letting His truth lay powerful hold on us, letting it find us, letting it search us, letting it penetrate us, letting it energize us, letting it vitalize us, and that is that we preserve the power of vision. Possibly this power is more needed now than it has been in any other day—the ability to see things that others do not see, and the ability to see further than others see. Solitude is as necessary for the imagination as society is wholesome for character.

> If chosen men had never been alone
> In deep mid-silence open-doored to God,
> No greatness had been dreamed or done.

It was said of Bushnell, that great mind of New England, that he had this power of vision in a rare degree. Austin Phelps said of him that he seemed to have a realizing sense of Christ all the time. I have read of Bushnell that he had the practice of spending hours night after night in meditation upon God and His truth. It was after one of those nights that he rose and said, "I found the Gospel *last night*." Found it *last night*. He had been preaching it for years with such power that he moved every audience. He meant that he had got a great new load of such wealth and superabundance that it seemed to him like a new Gospel.

We need prophets to-day, men who will speak courageous

and true words, but I despair of their being found unless more men among us say, "Wherever else we fail, we are not going to fail in becoming intimately acquainted with God in the only way that men have ever become intimately acquainted with Him, that is, by taking time for association with Him and time for meditation."

If I were to mention another reason which has always obtained in favor of this practice, it would be that, in order to be most largely helpful to others, we must spend more time alone with God and His life-giving truth. We may not speak so many words to others, but our word will find them. We may not perform so many actions, but we shall not have so much lost motion. Our work will stand. It will not be hay and stubble, but gold and precious stones. Back of all enduring work must lie reflection, deep purpose, pure motive and a sense of dependence on God. We must have reserves. And you do not accumulate reserves in the rush of the crowd. You do not store up conviction, conviction of the kind that deeply moves other people, under pressure; it takes time to get that kind of conviction.

Paul went away into Arabia, and when he came back was able to use this language: "*My* Gospel." He had got hold of Christ and His meaning in such a way that he claimed it as his own, and it came with tremendous power to the brain and the heart of his time and of the subsequent centuries.

I am reminded of words of Henry Drummond when he said to those students who went out from the universities to work in the villages and cities of Scotland. "Say absolutely nothing that you do not believe. Say absolutely nothing that you have not experienced." If every speaker would adopt those two rules, we should not have so many sermons or so many talks, but they would have transforming power. To be most largely helpful to others, I repeat, we must spend much time alone. If we are to feed others, we must store the granary. The most pathetic sight I ever see—and I see it almost every day of my life—is that of men handing out the bread of life with emaciated hands, busy trying to help others but starving themselves.

Now, how are we to form this habit? In the first place, it

will take time; it will take *regular* time. I notice that what is irregular soon slips out of a man's life. Let us have a regular time, a Medean and Persian hour, that is, an unchangeable hour.

Let it also be a *daily* time. You have to feed your body every day to keep it efficient. If you want your mind to be at its best in college, you must hold it to daily tasks. And so it is with the spiritual nature; it requires daily food. Temptations attack us every day; therefore we must daily fortify our lives.

I would urge that it be at the beginning of the day. Let us have a time of meditation at night also if we can, but I have watched the men that say, "We will do it at night." Many a time they are tired out at night, other things crowd in, and they are cheated out of this necessary period. The man who puts this first in the day cannot be cheated out of it. Moreover he is prepared for the day's fight with self and sin and Satan. He does not wait until temptation sweeps in on him like a flood; he enters the day prepared. We cannot afford to have any untaken forts in our rear.

And I would enter a plea that it be unhurried time. You say, "How much time is unhurried time?" I do not know how much is unhurried time for you. It means time enough to forget the watch, the clock and the bell. It means time enough to forget time. It means time enough to meet God and to hear His voice and to be sure that you have heard it; not for you to be able to say, "I spent thirty minutes this morning with my Bible," but for you to be able to say with conscientiousness, "I met God; I had fellowship with Him." It is a reality we are pleading for here.

It will take not only time but also resolution. In the diary of Henry Martyn we read, "The resolution with which I went to bed last night, that I would spend time unhurriedly with God to-day, I have been able to perform." The secret of his spending time unhurriedly with God that morning was that the night before he made a resolution to do so.

A third thing it costs is sacrifice. The more you pay for this life-expanding practice, the more you will receive. I congratulate especially the men and women to whom it is going to be most difficult. Our difficulties have a tremendous advantage: they test our genuineness.

Some men find God best in the presence of His works. Away back in my college days, those gorges near Ithaca were the places where I found it easier to get into touch with the living God. And how many men in God's still places, on a mountain-top, on a hill slope, or on a lake shore, or gazing at night into the starry heavens, have found it easier to see His face!

Others have been greatly helped not only by His works, but by His workers. Was it not Newman that said: "I owe my soul to Thomas Scott"? In my last holiday vacation my soul was greatly refreshed as I read for the first time George Adam Smith's "Minor Prophets." God's workers help us to find Him.

But infinitely more important than His works and His workers is His Word. The men who have helped us most received their inspiration from these writings. Why take our inspiration second hand? Why not go to the fountain head? The cause of all our evils is in our not knowing the Scriptures. It is these that make us acquainted with who God is and what man may become. Whatever else we leave undone, shall we not center our attention here?

My last word is that the practice I am speaking about is one of going alone *with God*. It is solitude, but it is a solitude that is not solitary with His presence. Let us at all costs seek to form this habit which will help to maintain a zone of silence in these days of so much turmoil around these necessarily busy lives of ours.

JOHN HENRY, CARDINAL NEWMAN

KNOWLEDGE VIEWED IN RELATION TO LEARNING

Address by Cardinal Newman, theologian, poet, Cardinal of the Catholic Church from 1879 (born in London, February 21, 1801; died in Birmingham, August 11, 1890), delivered to the Catholics of Dublin in 1852 and published with other discourses under the general title, "The Idea of a University." In these addresses Dr. Newman endeavored to win the sympathy of prelates and gentry to a plan for the higher education of Catholics, at the same time to lay down the lines of organization for the new institution and to define its aims and policy. Only a portion of the address is given here.

Nor indeed am I supposing that there is any great danger, at least in this day, of over-education; the danger is on the other side. I will tell you, gentlemen, what has been the practical error of the last twenty years,—not to load the memory of the student with a mass of undigested knowledge, but to force upon him so much that he has rejected all. It has been the error of distracting and enfeebling the mind by an unmeaning profusion of subjects; of implying that a smattering in a dozen branches of study is not shallowness, which it really is, but enlargement, which it is not; of considering an acquaintance with the learned names of things and persons, and the possession of clever duodecimos, and attendance on eloquent lecturers, and membership with scientific institutions, and the sight of the experiments of a platform and the specimens of a museum, that all this was not dissipation of mind, but progress. All things now are to be learned at once, not first one thing, then another, not one well, but many badly. Learning is to be without exertion, without attention, without toil;

without grounding, without advance, without finishing. There is to be nothing individual in it; and this, forsooth, is the wonder of the age. What the steam engine does with matter, the printing-press is to do with mind; it is to act mechanically, and the population is to be passively, almost unconsciously enlightened, by the mere multiplication and dissemination of volumes. Whether it be the schoolboy, or the schoolgirl, or the youth at college, or the mechanic in the town, or the politician in the senate, all have been the victims in one way or other of this most preposterous and pernicious of delusions. Wise men have lifted up their voices in vain; and at length, lest their own institutions should be outshone and should disappear in the folly of the hour, they have been obliged, as far as they could with a good conscience, to humor a spirit which they could not withstand, and make temporizing concessions at which they could not but inwardly smile.

It must not be supposed that, because I so speak, therefore I have some sort of fear of the education of the people: on the contrary, the more education they have, the better, so that it is really education. Nor am I an enemy to the cheap publication of scientific and literary works, which is now in vogue; on the contrary, I consider it a great advantage, convenience, and gain; that is, to those to whom education has given a capacity for using them. Further, I consider such innocent recreations as science and literature are able to furnish will be a very fit occupation of the thoughts and the leisure of young persons, and may be made the means of keeping them from bad employments and bad companions. Moreover, as to that superficial acquaintance with chemistry, and geology, and astronomy and political economy, and modern history, and biography, and other branches of knowledge, which periodical literature and occasional lectures and scientific institutions diffuse through the community,—I think it is a graceful accomplishment, and a suitable, nay, in this day, a necessary accomplishment, in the case of educated men. Nor, lastly, am I disparaging or discouraging the thorough acquisition of any one of these studies, or denying that, as far as it goes, such thorough acquisition is a real education of the mind. All I say is, call things by their right names, and do not confuse together ideas which are essentially different. A thorough knowledge of one science and a superficial acquaintance with many, are not the same thing; a smattering of a hundred things or a memory for detail, is not a philosophical or comprehensive view. Recreations are not education; accomplishments are not education. Do not say, the people must be educated, when, after all, you only mean amused, refreshed, soothed, put into good spirits and good humor, or kept from vicious excesses. I do not say that such amusements, such occupations of mind are not a great gain; but they are not education. You may as well call drawing and fencing education, as a general knowledge of botany or conchology. Stuffing birds or playing stringed instruments is an elegant pastime, and a resource to the idle, but it is not education, it does not form or cultivate the intellect.

Education is a high word; it is the preparation for knowledge, and it is the imparting of knowledge in proportion to that preparation. We require intellectual eyes to know withal, as bodily eyes for sight. We need both objects and organs intellectual; we cannot gain them, without setting about it; we cannot gain them in our sleep, or by haphazard. The best telescope does not dispense with eyes; the printing-press or the lecture-room will assist us greatly, but we must be true to ourselves, we must be parties in the work. A university is, according to the usual designation, an *alma mater*, knowing her children one by one, not a foundry, or a mint, or a treadmill.

I protest to you, gentlemen, that if I had to choose between a so-called university which dispensed with residence and tutorial superintendence, and gave its degrees to any person who passed an examination in a wide range of subjects, and a university which had no professors or examinations at all, but merely brought a number of young men together for three or four years, and then sent them away as the University of Oxford is said to have done some sixty years since, if I were asked which of these two methods was the better discipline of the intellect,—mind, I do not say which is morally the better, for it is plain that compulsory study must be a good and idleness an intolerable mischief,—but if I must determine which of the two courses was the more successful in training, molding, enlarging the mind, which sent out men the more fitted for their secular duties, which produced better public men, men of the world, men whose names would descend to posterity, I have no hesitation in giving the preference to that university which did nothing, over that which exacted of its members an acquaintance with every science under the sun. And, paradox as this may seem, still if results be the test of systems, the influence of the public schools and colleges of England, in the course of the last century, at least will bear out one side of the contrast as I have drawn it. What would come, on the other hand, of the ideal systems of education which have fascinated the imagination of this age, could they ever take effect, and whether they would not produce a generation frivolous, narrow-minded, and resourceless, intellectually considered, is a fair subject for debate; but so far is certain, that the universities and scholastic establishments to which I refer, and which did little more than bring together first boys and then youths in large numbers, these institutions, with miserable deformities on the side of morals, with a hollow confession of Christianity, and a heathen code of ethics,—I say, at least they can boast of a succession of heroes and statesmen, of literary men and philosophers, of men conspicuous for great natural virtues, for habits of business, for knowledge of life, for practical judgment, for cultivated tastes, for accomplishments, who have made England what it is,—able to subdue the earth, able to domineer over Catholics.

How is this to be explained? I suppose as follows: When a multitude of young men, keen, open-hearted, sympathetic, and observant, as young men are, come together and freely mix with each other, they are sure to learn one from another, even if there be no one to teach them; the conversation of all is a series of lectures to each, and they gain for themselves new ideas and views, fresh matter of thought, and distinct principles for judging and acting, day by day. An infant has to learn the meaning of the information which its senses convey to it, and this seems to be its employment. It fancies all that the eye presents to it to be close to it, till it actually learns the contrary, and thus by practice does it ascertain the relations and uses of those first elements of knowledge which are neces-

JOSEPH FORT NEWTON

sary for its animal existence. A parallel teaching is necessary for our social being, and it is secured by a large school or a college; and this effect may be fairly called in its own department an enlargement of mind. It is seeing the world on a small field with little trouble; for the pupils or students come from very different places, and with widely different notions, and there is much to generalize, much to adjust, much to eliminate, there are interrelations to be defined, and conventional rules to be established, in the process, by which the whole assemblage is molded together, and gains one tone and one character.

Let it be clearly understood, I repeat it, that I am not taking into account moral or religious considerations; I am but saying that that youthful community will constitute a whole, it will embody a specific idea, it will represent a doctrine, it will administer a code of conduct, and it will furnish principles of thought and action. It will give birth to a living teaching, which in course of time will take the shape of a self-perpetuating tradition, or a *genius loci*, as it is sometimes called; which haunts the home where it has been born, and which imbues and forms, more or less, and one by one, every individual who is successively brought under its shadow. Thus it is that, independent of direct instruction on the part of superiors, there is a sort of self-education in the academic institutions of Protestant England; a characteristic tone of thought, a recognized standard of judgment is found in them, which as developed in the individual who is submitted to it, becomes a twofold source of strength to him, both from the distinct stamp it impresses on his mind, and from the bond of union which it creates between him and others,—effects which are shared by the authorities of the place, for they themselves have been educated in it, and at all times are exposed to the influence of its ethical atmosphere. Here then is a real teaching, whatever be its standards and principles, true or false; and it at least tends towards cultivation of the intellect; it at least recognizes that knowledge is something more than a sort of passive reception of scraps and details; it is a something, and it does a something, which never will issue from the most strenuous efforts of a set of teachers, with no mutual sympathies and no intercommunion, of a set of examiners with no opinions which they dare profess, and with no common principles, who are teaching or questioning a set of youths who do not know them, and do not know each other, on a large number of subjects, different in kind, and connected by no wide philosophy, three times a week, or three times a year, or once in three years, in chill lecture-rooms or on a pompous anniversary.

Nay, self-education in any shape, in the most restricted sense, is preferable to a system of teaching which, professing so much, really does so little for the mind. Shut your college gates against the votary of knowledge, throw him back upon the searchings and the efforts of his own mind; he will gain by being spared an entrance into your Babel. Few indeed there are who can dispense with the stimulus and support of instructors, or will do anything at all, if left to themselves. And fewer still (though such great minds are to be found), who will not, from such unassisted attempts, contract a self-reliance and a self-esteem, which are not only moral evils, but serious hindrances to the attainment of truth. And next to none, perhaps, or none, who will not be reminded from time to time of the disadvantage under which they lie, by their imperfect grounding, by the breaks, deficiencies, and irregularities of their knowledge, by the eccentricity of opinion and the confusion of principle which they exhibit. They will be too often ignorant of what everyone knows and takes for granted, of that multitude of small truths which fall upon the mind like dust, impalpable and ever accumulating; they may be unable to converse, they may argue perversely, they may pride themselves on their worst paradoxes or their grossest truisms, they may be full of their own mode of viewing things, unwilling to be put out of their way, slow to enter into the minds of others; —but, with these and whatever other liabilities upon their heads, are likely to have more thought, more mind, more philosophy, more true enlargement, than those earnest but ill-used persons, who are forced to load their minds with a score of subjects against an examination, who have too much on their hands to indulge themselves in thinking or investigation, who devour premise and conclusion together with indiscriminate greediness, who hold whole sciences on faith, and commit demonstrations to memory, and who too often, as might be expected, when their period of education is past, throw up all they have learned in disgust, having gained nothing really by their anxious labors, except perhaps the habit of application.

Yet such is the better specimen of the fruit of that ambitious system which has of late years been making way among us: for its result on ordinary minds, and on the common run of students, is less satisfactory still; they leave their place of education simply dissipated and relaxed by the multiplicity of subjects, which they have never really mastered, and so shallow as not even to know their shallowness. How much better, I say, is it for the active and thoughtful intellect, where such is to be found, to eschew the college and the university altogether, than to submit to a drudgery so ignoble, a mockery so contumelious. How much more profitable for the independent mind, after the mere rudiments of education, to range through a library at random, taking down books as they meet him, and pursuing the trains of thought which his mother wit suggests. How much healthier to wander into the fields, and there with the exiled Prince to find "tongues in the trees, books in the running brooks." How much more genuine an education is that of the poor boy in the Poem (Crabbe's "Tales of the Hall")—a poem, whether in conception or in execution one of the most touching in our language—who, not in the wide world, but ranging day by day around his widowed mother's home, "a dextrous gleaner" in a narrow field, and with only such slender outfit

> . . . as the village school and books a few
> Supplied,

contrived from the beach and the quay and the fisher's boat and the inn's fireside and the tradesman's shop and the shepherd's walk and the smuggler's hut and the mossy moor and the screaming gulls and the restless waves, to fashion for himself a philosophy and a poetry of his own!

JOSEPH FORT NEWTON

THE MINISTRY OF MASONRY

Joseph Fort Newton was born in Decatur, Texas, in 1876 and was ordained in the Baptist ministry in 1893. He has held pastorates in many important churches, in the Civic Temple, London, and in the Church of the Divine Paternity, New York, and is the author and editor of many books and has long been prominent in Masonic circles. The following address was delivered before the Grand Lodge of Iowa at its seventieth Annual Communication at Council Bluffs, June 10, 1913.

SOMETHING in this scene, something in the words of my dear friend, appeals to me very deeply. So gracious a greeting evokes feelings beyond my words, and I understand what Lord Tennyson must have felt when, looking out upon the sea and listening to its voices, he cried:

> I would that my tongue could utter
> The thoughts that arise in me.

Once upon a time, as my friend has said, I tried to talk to you as best I could on the mission of Masonry, its faith, its philosophy, its demand for freedom, and its plea for universal friendship.

But the more I brood over the mystery of this order, its history, its genius, its possibilities of ministry to the higher human life, the more the wonder grows, the higher the horizon, and the longer the vistas that unfold. Let me beseech you, then, to lend me your hearts while I tell you a little more of the meaning of Masonry as it has grown up in my heart. Studying Masonry is like looking at a sunrise; each man who looks is filled with the beauty and glory of it, but the splendor is not diminished. Over all alike its ineffable wonder falls, subduing the mind, softening the heart, and exalting the life.

THE MINISTRY OF MASONRY

I

The better to make vivid what lies in my heart, let me recall a scene from one of the great books of the world, "War and Peace," by Count Tolstoi—a name that should be spoken with reverence wherever men assemble in the name of good-will. He was, if we except Lincoln, the tallest soul, the most picturesque and appealing figure who walked under our human sky in the last century. This book, the greatest of its kind known to literature, makes one thing of a giant playing with mountains, tossing them to and fro as though they were toys —so powerful is it, so vast in its sweep, so vivid in its panorama. Its heroine is a whole nation—the beautiful, strange, tormented land of Russia. We see its lights and shadows, its wide expanse, and its quiet hamlets; its people at work and play, in peace and war—now hovering like a shadow on the heels of their enemies, now fleeing in terror in the glare of their burning cities. What a picture of the tumult of a nation, and the vicissitudes of life, in the light of the Napoleonic invasion!

One of the arresting figures of the story is Count Pierre Bezuhov—in whom Tolstoi has shown us one side of his own soul, as in Prince Andre he has unveiled the other. Pierre is the richest man in Russia, owning vast estates, including both the land and the serfs on the land. Like so many young noblemen of his day, he has lived a wild, sensual, dissolute life, careless alike of the rights and wrongs of his fellows. He was married to a beautiful, bewitching, sensual woman, whose paramour he has just killed in a duel. On his way to St. Petersburg he falls in with an old man, simply dressed, but with the light of a great peace in his face. The stranger addresses the Count and tells him that he has heard of his misfortune, referring to the duel resulting in the death at his hands of the lover of his wife. He is aware, too, as he goes on to say, of the wild, sin-bespattered life the Count has lived, of his way of thinking, of his pride, indolence, and ignorance. The Count listened to these severe words, he hardly knew why—perhaps because he heard in them an undertone of sympathy, the accent

20

of a great pity, and what he heard in the voice he saw in the kindly face.

On the hand of the old man the Count noticed a ring, and in it the emblem of the order here assembled. He asked the stranger if he was not a Mason. Whereupon the old man, looking searchingly into the eyes of the Count, said that he belonged to that order, in whose name he extended to him the hand of a brother man, in the name of God the Father. At the mention of the name of God a smile curled on the lips of the Count, who said:

"I ought to tell you that I don't believe in God." The old Freemason smiled as a rich man, holding millions in his hand, might smile at a poor wretch.

"Yes, you do not know Him, sir," said the stranger. "You do not know Him, that is why you are unhappy. But He is here, He is within me, He is in thee, and even in these scoffing words you have just uttered. If He is not, we should not be speaking of Him, sir. Whom dost thou deny? How came there within thee the conception that there is such an incomprehensible Being?"

Something in the venerable stranger, who spoke earnestly, as one who stood in the light of a vision, touched the Count deeply, and stirred in him a longing to see what the old man saw and to know what he knew. Abject, hopeless, haunted by an ill-spent life, with the blood of a fellow-man on his hands—his eyes betrayed his longing to know God. Though he did not speak, the kindly eyes of the stranger read his face and answered his unasked question.

"He exists, but to know Him is hard. It is not attained by reason, but by life. The highest truth is like the purest dew. Can I hold in an impure vessel that pure dew and judge of its purity? Only by inner purification can we know Him."

Finally, the old man asked the young nobleman if he would not like to look into the mysteries of Masonry. Not so much what the stranger had said as what he was—his gentle, austere, benign spirit, that had in it something of the Fatherhood of God—made the Count say, "Yes." The stranger asked him to report at a certain room in St. Petersburg, where he would be introduced to those high in authority among Freemasons.

Meanwhile, what the gently stern old man had said sank into the soul of the hitherto heedless young nobleman; and when he reported at the lodge room and was asked, as every man is asked, the one indispensable question: "Do you believe in God?"—something deeper than his doubts, something higher than his skepticism spoke within him, and he answered, "*Yes.*"

There follows a detailed description of his initiation, which those who are not Masons may be curious to read. Unfortunately, it tells them nothing of what takes place in a lodge room on such occasions; but it will show them the spirit that lives and glows on the altar of Masonry. No one but a Mason could have written it; and while the chain of evidence is not quite complete, I am safe in saying that, as with Count Pierre in the story, so with Count Tolstoi himself, it was Masonry which first lifted him out of the pit of atheism and sensualism, set his feet upon the Rock of Ages, and started him toward the city of God. Does this not suggest to us the deeper meaning of Masonry, its higher ministry, and the service it may render to the inner life of man?

II

What is Masonry? What is it trying to teach? What does it seek to do? Above all, what can it do for the man who receives it into his heart, loves it, and lives in the light of it? What profound ministry may it render to the young man who enters its temple in the morning of life, when the dew is on his days and the birds are singing in his heart? Let me try to answer these questions this summer afternoon in the spirit of Count Tolstoi, who must hereafter be numbered with those prophets and bards—with poets like Goethe and Burns, musicians like Mozart, patriots like Mazzini and Washington—who loved this historic order. Such names shine like stars in the crown of humanity, and none with truer luster than that of Tolstoi, who was a teacher of purity, pity, and peace among men.

Time out of mind Masonry has been defined as a system of morality, veiled in allegory, and illustrated by symbols. That is so far true—far enough, indeed, to describe a world-encircling fellowship and its far-ramifying influence. But it is not of the extent of Masonry that I wish to speak this afternoon, but, rather, of its depth—its service to the lonely inner life of man where the issues of character and destiny are determined for good or ill. No more worthy purpose can inspire any order than the earnest, active endeavor to bring men—first the individual man, and then, so far as possible, those united with him—to a deeper, richer fellowship with spiritual reality. Since this is the purpose of Masonry, let us inquire as to what it is, whence it came, and how it seeks to reach the souls of men where the real battles of life are fought, now with shouts of victory, now with sobs of defeat.

It is true that Masonry is not a religion, still less a cult, but it has religiously preserved some things of highest importance to religion—among them the right of each individual soul to its own religious faith. Holding aloof from separate sects and creeds, it has taught all of them to respect and tolerate each other; asserting a principle broader than any of them—the sanctity of the soul and the duty of every man to revere, or at least to regard with charity, what is sacred to his fellows. Our order is like the crypts underneath the old cathedrals—a place where men of every creed, who long for something deeper and truer, older and newer than they have hitherto known, meet and unite. Having put away childish things, they find themselves made one by a profound and child-like faith, each bringing down into that quiet crypt his own pearl of great price—

"The Hindu his innate belief in this world, and his unhesitating belief in another world; the Buddhist his perception of an eternal law, his submission to it, his gentleness, his pity; the Mohammedan, if nothing else, his sobriety; the Jew his clinging, through good and evil days, to the one God, who loveth righteousness and whose name is 'I AM'; the Christian, that which is better than all, if those who doubt it would only try it—our love of God, call Him what you will, manifested in our love of man, our love of the living, our love of the dead, our living and undying love. Who knows but that the crypt of the past may yet become the church of the future?"

There have been great secret orders, like that represented here to-day, since recorded history began; and no man may ever hope to estimate their service to our race. In every age, in every civilized land—from the priests of Isis on yonder side of the Pyramids, to the orders of Eleusis and Mithras in Greece and Rome—we trace their silent, far-reaching influence and power. The *Mysteries,* said Plato, were established by men of great genius, who, in the early ages, strove to teach purity, to ameliorate the cruelty of the race, to refine its manners and morals, and to restrain society by stronger bonds than those which human laws impose. Cicero bears a like witness to the high aim of the same mystic orders in his day. Thus in ages of darkness, of complexity, of conflicting peoples, tongues, and faiths, these great orders toiled in behalf of friendship, bringing men together under the banner of faith, and training them for a nobler moral life.

No mystery any longer attaches to what those orders taught, but only as to what particular rites, dramas, and symbols were used by them in their ceremonies. They taught faith in a God above, in the moral law within, heroic purity of soul, austere discipline of character, justice, piety, and the hope of a life beyond death. Tender and tolerant of all faiths, they formed an all-embracing moral and spiritual fellowship which rose above barriers of nation, race, and creed, satisfying the craving of men for unity, while evoking in them a sense of that eternal mysticism out of which all religions were born. Their ceremonies, so far as we know them, were stately and moving dramas of the moral life and the fate of the soul. Mystery and secrecy added impressiveness, and fable and enigma disguised in imposing spectacle the simple, familiar, everlasting laws of justice, piety, and a hope of immortality. As Cicero said, the initiates of the *Mysteries* not only received lessons which made life tolerable, but drew from their rites happy hopes for the hour of death.

Masonry stands in this tradition; and if we may not say that it is historically related to those great ancient orders, it is their spiritual descendant, and renders the same ministry to our age which the *Mysteries* rendered to the olden world. It is, indeed, no other than those same historic orders in disguise; the same stream of sweetness and light flowing in our day—like the fabled river Alpheus which, gathering the waters of a hundred rills along the hillsides of Arcadia, sank, lost to light, in a chasm in the earth, only to reappear in the fountain of Arethusa. Apart from its rites, there is no mystery in Masonry, save the mystery of all great and simple things. So far from being hidden and occult, its glory lies in its openness, its emphasis upon the realities which are to our human world what air and sunlight are to nature. Its secret is of so great and simple a kind that it is easily overlooked; its mystery too obvious to be found out.

Our age resembles in many ways the age which saw the introduction into the world of the teachings of Jesus. To one who regards mankind with tenderness, a time like this is full of hope, but full of many perils also. Men are confused, troubled, and strangely alone. Anything is possible. Forms of faith are changing, and many are bewildered—as witness the number of those running to and fro, following every wandering light, and falling, often, into the bogs of fanaticism. Oh, the pathos of it! A strange indifference has settled over the world, but underneath it there is a profound, unsatisfied hunger. There is a mood to-day which soon will utter a cry, and it will be a cry for a more vivid sense of God: that is our hope. Yet that cry may fling many a soul upon the bosom of doubt and despair: that is our fear. Amidst this peril, Masonry brings men together at the altar of prayer, keeps alive faith in the truths that make us men, seeking, by every resource of art, to make tangible the power of love, the worth of beauty, and the reality of the ideal. Who can measure such a ministry, who can describe it!

III

Let me strive to make it all more vivid by recalling a parable translated by Max Müller from the lore of the East. The gods, having stolen from man his divinity, met in council to discuss where they should hide it. One suggested that it be carried to the other side of the earth and buried; but it was pointed out that man is a great wanderer, and that he might find the lost treasure on the other side of the earth. Another proposed that it be dropped into the depths of the sea; but the same fear was expressed—that man, in his insatiable curiosity, might dive deep enough to find it even there. Finally, after a space of silence, the oldest and wisest of the gods said: "Hide it in man himself, as that is the last place he will ever think to look for it." And it was so agreed, all seeing at once its subtle and wise strategy.

Man wandered over the earth for ages, searching in all places, high and low, far and near, before he thought to look within himself for the divinity he sought. At last, slowly, dimly, he began to realize that what he thought was far off, hidden in "the pathos of distance," is nearer than the breath he breathes, even in his own heart. Here lies the deepest ministry of Masonry—that it makes a young man aware of the divinity that is within him, wherefrom his whole life takes beauty and meaning, and inspires him to follow and obey it. No hour in life is more solemn and revealing than that in which a man learns that what he seeks he has already found, else he would not be seeking it. Once a man learns that deep secret, life is new, and the old world is a valley all dewy to the dawn, aglow with beauty and athrill with melody.

There never was a truer saying than that of Thomas Carlyle when he said that the religion of a man is the chief fact concerning him. By religion he meant, as he went on to explain, not the creed to which a man will subscribe or otherwise give his assent; not that necessarily; often not that at all—since we see men of all degrees of worth and worthlessness signing all kinds of creeds. No, the religion of a man is that which he practically believes, lays to heart, acts upon, and knows concerning this mysterious universe and his duty and destiny in it. That is in all cases the primary thing in him, and creatively determines all the rest; that is his religion. It is, then, of vital importance what faith, what vision, what conception of life a man lays to heart and acts upon. It is as a man thinks in his heart whether life be worth while or not, and whether the world be luminous or dark.

Let me show you that this is so. Optimists and pessimists live in the same world, walk under the same sky, and observe the same facts. Skeptics and believers look up at the same great stars—the stars that shone in Eden and will flash again in Paradise. Thomas Hardy and George Meredith were contemporaries and friends—one looking out over a dismal, shadow-haunted Egdon heath, under a sky as gray as a tired face; the other a citizen of a world all dipped in hues of sunrise and sunset, with a lark-song over it! Clearly, the difference in all these cases is a difference not of fact, but of faith; of insight, outlook, and point of view—a difference of inner attitude and habit of thought with regard to the worth of life and the meaning of the world. By the same token, any influence which reaches and alters that inner habit and bias of mind, and changes it from doubt to faith, from fear to courage, from despair to sunburst hope, has wrought the most vital and benign ministry which a mortal may enjoy in the midst of the years.

Every man, as each of you can testify, has a train of thought on which he rides when he is alone. The dignity and nobility of his life, as well as its happiness, depends upon the direction in which that train is going, the baggage it carries, and the scenery through which it travels. If, then, Masonry can put that inner train of thought on the right track, freight it with precious baggage, and start it on the way to the city of God, what other or higher service can it render to a man? That is just what it does for any man who will give himself to it, bringing to him from afar the old wisdom-religion—that simple, pure, and lofty truth wrought out through ages of experience, tested by time, and found to be valid for the life of man. Whoso lays that lucid and profound wisdom to heart, and acts upon it, will have little to regret, and nothing to fear, when the evening shadows fall.

High, fine, ineffably rich, and beautiful is the faith and vision which Masonry gives to those who foregather at its altar. By such teaching, if they have the heart to heed it, men become wise, knowing that all evil ways have been often tried and found wanting. By it they learn how to be both brave and gentle, faithful and firm; how to renounce superstition and yet retain faith; how to keep a fine poise of reason between the falsehood of extremes; how to accept the joys of life with glee, and endure its ills with patient valor; how to look upon the folly of man and not forget his nobility—in short, how to live cleanly, kindly, calmly, opened-eyed, and unafraid in a sane world, sweet of heart and full of hope. It may not be a substitute for religion, but he who makes it a law of his life, loves it, and obeys it, will be most ready to receive the great passwords of religious faith. Happy the young man who in the morning of his years takes this simple and high wisdom as his guide, philosopher, and friend!

IV

Such is the ministry of Masonry to the individual—lifting him out of the mire and setting his feet in the long, white path marked out by the footsteps of ages; and through the individual it serves society and the state. If by some art one could trace those sweet, invisible influences which move to and fro like shuttles in a loom, weaving the net-work of laws, reverences, sanctities, which make the warp and woof of society—giving to statutes their dignity and power, to the gospel its opportunity, to the home its canopy of peace and beauty, to the young an enshrinement of inspiration, and the old a mantle of protection; if one had the pen of an angel then might one tell the story of what Masonry has done for Iowa. No wonder George Eliot said that eloquence is but a ripple on the bosom of the unspoken and the unspeakable!

What is it that so tragically delays the march of man toward that better social order whereof our prophets dream? Our age and land are full of schemes of every kind for the reform and betterment of mankind. Why do they not succeed? Some fail, perhaps, because they are imprudent and ill-considered, in that they expect too much of human nature and do not take into account the stubborn facts of life. But why does not the wisest and noblest plan do half what its devisers hope and pray and labor to bring about? Because there are not enough men fine enough of soul, large enough of sympathy, noble enough of nature to make the dream come true. So that when Masonry, instead of identifying itself with particular schemes of reform, devotes all its benign energy to refining and ennobling the souls of men, she is doing fundamental work in behalf of all high enterprises. By as much as she succeeds, every noble cause succeeds; if she fails, everything fails!

Recall what was passing before the eyes of men in this land fifty years ago to-day. What gloom, what uncertainty, what anxiety—Gettysburg less than a month away! The very life of the republic hung in the balance! Think of those first three days of July, 1863, when fifty-four thousand young men, the flower of our future, lay dead and wounded—piled in heaps of blue and gray, quivering with pain, their white faces turned to the sky! Far away in northern towns and southern hamlets, sad-faced women heard, now with shrieks, now with dumb, unutterable woe, the long roll-call of the dead! What man who has a heart, or who cares for the future of his race, does not pray that such scenes may never again be witnessed on this earth! What can prevent a repetition of the horrors of war? Nothing but the growth in the hearts of men of the spirit of justice, freedom, and friendship which Masonry seeks, quietly, to evoke and inspire! If our fathers had known each other in the sixties as we know each other to-day, there would have been no Civil War! So it will be the world over, when man comes to know his fellow men as he learns to know them and love them at the altar of this order. Then shall be fulfilled the song of those who sang of "peace on earth *among men of good-will!*"

Again, no one need be told that we are on the eve, if not in the midst, of a stupendous and bewildering revolution of social and industrial life. The questions in dispute can never be settled in an air of hostility. If they are settled at all, and settled right, it must be in an atmosphere of mutual recognition and respect such as that which Masonry strives to create and make prevail. Whether it be a conflict of nations, or a clash of class with class, appeal must be made to intelligence and the moral sense, as befits the dignity of man. Amidst bitterness and strife Masonry brings men of capital and labor, men of every rank and walk of life together as men, and nothing else, at an altar where they can talk and not fight, discuss and not dispute, and each may learn the point of view of his fellows. Other hope there is none save in this spirit of friendship and fairness, of democracy and the fellowship of man with man.

Even so it is in religion—that kingdom of faith and hope and prayer so long defamed by bigotry and distracted by sectarian feud. How many fine minds have been estranged from the altar of faith because they were required to believe what it was impossible for them to believe—and, rather than sacrifice their integrity, they turn away from the last place from which a man should ever turn away. No part of the ministry of Masonry is more beautiful and wise than its appeal, not for tolerance, but for fraternity; not for uniformity, but for unity of spirit amidst varieties of outlook and opinion. God be thanked for one altar where no one is asked to surrender his liberty of thought and become an indistinguishable atom in a mass of sectarian agglomeration. What a witness to the worth of an order that it brings together men of all faiths in behalf of those truths which are greater than all sects, deeper than all dogmas—the glory and the hope of man!

When is a man a Mason? When he can look out over the rivers, the hills, and the far horizon with a profound sense of his own littleness in the vast scheme of things, and yet have faith, hope, and courage. When he knows that down in his heart every man is as noble, as vile, as divine, as diabolic, and as lonely as himself, and seeks to know, to forgive, and to love his fellow man. When he knows how to sympathize with men in their sorrows, yea, even in their sins—knowing that each man fights a hard fight against many odds. When he has learned how to make friends and to keep them, and above all how to keep friends with himself. When he loves flowers, can hunt the birds without a gun, and feels the thrill of an old forgotten joy when he hears the laugh of a little child. When he can be happy and high-minded amid the meaner drudgeries of life. When star-crowned trees and the glint of sunlight on flowing waters subdue him like the thought of one much loved and long dead. When no voice of distress reaches his ears in vain, and no hand seeks his aid without response. When he finds good in every faith that helps any man to lay hold of higher things, and to see majestic meanings in life, whatever the name of that faith may be. When he can look into a wayside puddle and see something besides mud, and into the face of the most forlorn mortal and see something beyond sin. When he knows how to pray, how to love, how to hope. When he has kept faith with himself, with his fellow man, with his God; in his hand a sword for evil, in his heart a bit of a song—glad to live, but not afraid to die! In such a man, whether he be rich or poor, scholarly or unlearned, famous or obscure, Masonry has wrought her sweet ministry!

MEREDITH NICHOLSON

THE SUNNY SLOPES OF FORTY

Address delivered by the well-known novelist Meredith Nicholson at the public meeting of the American Academy of Arts and Letters and the National Institute of Arts and Letters held in Chicago, Nov. 15, 1913.

WE who gain the watershed of the years, no matter how humble our station or how flimsy our achievements, may be pardoned for loitering to throw out and reappraise the accumulations in our pack with a view to lightening the load for further traveling. Those who, climbing the ladder of the parallels toward the white North, pause at life's meridian to compare notes of their adventures, may still profit by criticism; whereas others who wait to cache the reflections of their senectitude in the polar ice, to be resurrected by later travelers, may commit themselves irrevocably to error. If we have gained the ridge in good spirits we are still able to fight back, and to defend ourselves from attack.

The sunny slopes of forty are those that dip down on the farther side of the Great Divide. Any one can see with half an eye that they are less precipitous than the geographers describe them. It appears from a cautious survey that by following the more deliberate streams that longest hold the heat of the sun we may delay appreciably our arrival at the polar waste. We are not of those who, having mislaid their charcoal tablets,

> In disdainful silence turn away,
> Stand mute, self-centered, stern, and dream no more.

We mean to give the official chloroformer a lively sprint before he overtakes us. We shall fool the world as long as we

Copyright by the American Academy and printed with its special permission.

can by keeping our trousers pressed and flaunting the bravest neckwear the haberdasher affords. By tacking a new collar to our spring overcoat and shaking out the moth balls we may carry it—thrown indifferently over the arm as though we never expect to use it—a long way into November.

Those of us who have reached the great watershed certainly cannot complain of the fate that launched us on our pilgrimage in the last half of the nineteenth century. The drama has never been dull and we have watched the course of many excellent players. An imaginative boy, born in the later sixties, could still hear the bugles and the clash of arms. Throughout this midwestern country every hearthside had its Iliad. Now and then, within my own recollection, there appeared at the doorstep men who, unable to redomesticate themselves after four years of camp and field, still clung to the open road. How long the faded old army overcoat hung together—and on how many shoulders it became an advertisement of valor, an asset, a plea for alms! Having been denied the thrills of war itself it was no small compensation to look upon its heroes—to observe daily in the street men who had commanded armies, to attend those gatherings of veterans that so brightly visualized for curious youth the magnitude of the great struggle of the sixties. If one's father had been of the mighty legion; if there existed in the garret a musket or a sword that he had borne in the conflict; if there remained, in a soap-box under the eaves, the roster of his company, an order or a report or a bundle of old letters, for inspection on rainy days, the luckier the lad to whom such memorabilia came as a birthright. It is inconceivable that any boy born in those times could have escaped the fascination of those heroes, whether he sat at meat with them daily in his own household, or saw them in the streets with the stamp of the drill sergeant still upon them. And nothing was so impressive as the fact that they had flung down their youth as the gage of battle.

We are none of us without our wistful tenderness for those who won "the immortal youthfulness of the early dead":

> Shelley and Keats, with laurels fresh and fair,
> Shining unwithered on each sacred head;
> And soldier boys who snatched death's starry prize,

> With sweet life radiant in their fearless eyes,
> The dreams of love upon their beardless lips,
> Bartering dull age for immortality:
> Their memories hold in death's unyielding fee
> The youth that thrilled them to the finger tips.

The historian and the philosopher have not yet exhausted those decades that immediately followed the war. The social and political conditions of the post-bellum period present phenomena as interesting as any in our history, and in spite of the dark shameful pages of reconstruction it seems still little short of a miracle that the combatants yielded themselves as readily as they did to readjustment. I remember when "The Fool's Errand" was a novel much discussed; it must have been the best seller of its day. But quite aside from its value as a criticism of life or as a protest against Ku-Klux ferocity, I recall Judge Tourgee's appearance in a Methodist pulpit in my town one Sunday morning, dashingly arrayed in evening dress.

The display of these obscene vestments, so coolly flaunted in the sanctuary, deepened my early impression of the literary life as a gay adventure against which even the terrors of a provincial Sabbath could not prevail. However, the garment oftenest in the eyes of the youth of those days was the enticingly described bloody shirt, whose pleasant appellation envisaged it in glowing scarlet and seemed to set it dancing on all the clotheslines in Christendom. It was, I fancy, from the sheer contrariness of youth that, having heard from the cradle so much of the unreconstructed and menacing character of the Southern colonels and brigadiers, I clearly resolved to identify myself with the political party whose strength lay chiefly in the states lately in rebellion. I must be pardoned if I mention this the least bit jauntily, for in dark alleys and on vacant lots safely remote from the domestic altar my irreconcilable playmates made necessary the defense of my apostasy with fists none too skillful and a frame wherein anemia threatened early extinction. My sinful leanings toward magnanimity and tolerance I shall not seek to justify on any high grounds: though perhaps there was a degree of sincerity in my feeling that the war being over it was preposterous to renew the fight every time the community was called upon to elect a constable.

Those feelings and agitations had the effect nevertheless of stimulating in most of my generation an interest in politics. The idealism that had flowered in the war not unnaturally withered and awaited a refreshening of the exhausted soil. It was with real astonishment that most of us whose youth synchronized with the complete unbroken denomination of the humbled South and who saw the spirit of military triumph revived in all political struggles, began to hear strange murmurings on our own side of the Ohio as we approached manhood. In 1876 there had been rumblings that threatened for a time to deepen into the bellowings of cannon—when it seemed that those swords that had not been beaten into plowshares but providentially stored away in the attic might be oiled and sharpened for other battles.

The limitations of time compel me to compress in a word a belief, by no means original with me, that the campaign of 1884 marked a reflowering of idealism in our political life. It seems in the retrospect that the exalted faith which has planted its bright gonfalon on the heights of so many battle-fields in the sixties had begun once more to assert itself. Not the least interesting circumstances attending Mr. Cleveland's appearance as the protagonist of a new gospel was his unconscious appeal to what may be called the academic element in our population, long scorned as an impractical body of visionaries, but which from his advent has exerted an increasingly salutary influence in public affairs. The once despised professor with his preposterous ideals, his fatuous insistence that human experience is not to be neglected in the scrutiny of present tasks and duties, has now become a force to reckon with in public matters great and small. It must be with certain grim humor that those of us who take our politics seriously glance toward Washington and see there, in the seat of the Presidents, a gentleman finely representative of the academic type—who on ceremonial occasions in the groves of academe wore so demure and cloistral an air—administering the affairs of the United States with an intelligence, a poise, a courage, that are so admirable to the majority of his countrymen, so bewildering to the hungry and thirsty among his fellow partisans.

I beg to be indulged a moment longer to reflect **a conviction** held by many that our colleges and universities are to exert more and more an influence upon our political ideals and the efficiency of governmental administration. I shall not attempt to enumerate the long list of scholars in universities who have in the past twenty years taught political morality and economic freedom, or who have not scrupled to stand on the firing line when there was work for fighting men to do; but the individual cases are not so impressive as the appearance in so many states, and notably in so many state universities, of men who, often with personal discomfort and sacrifice, are stimulating in American youth a faith in ideals and the courage to defend and support them. It is not, I believe, a fantastic notion, that within twenty years we shall find in American universities, schools for the education of men and women in all branches of municipal administration, and that towns and cities will draw upon these specially-trained students for their public servants in the same spirit in which other corporations seek the best available talent to administer their business. And manifestly there is no sane reason why any community should choose to be governed from the gutter rather than by experts with no other ambition than to serve the public honestly and efficiently.

The boy that I seem to have been in those green valleys below was not interested solely in military and political heroes, though my first literary admirations were linked in some degree to the earlier passion. I took my boyish pantheon, Emerson, Lowell, Whittier, Longfellow and Thoreau, whom I appraised as quite worthy to trail their austere robes among the military and political heroes of my adoration; and their New England, which none of my forbears had ever looked upon, became a half-mythical and fabled world. Nor can I think of them now as other than priests of high consecration who stood valiantly at their simple altars and preached the clean gospel that was in them. Democracy, as they interpreted it, became a finer thing than it had been before and fortunate are the new generations if they do not wholly neglect them.

By what transitional processes or under what guidance I gave over the concealment and perusal of trash and dipped into those deeper and cleaner currents I have no impression, but I recall that at sixteen I was the most devoted of Emersonians. Having habitually secreted innumerable copies of Beadle's most seductive romances in the lining of my waistcoat or, being more in keeping with the daring spirit of the tales themselves, tucked them into the top boots which boys wore in those days, the open display of pocket volumes of Emerson marked an advance in moral tone as well as in taste. Conceit and priggishness which dance malevolently on the ink-bottle at this point must vanish before my admission that in the case of Emerson at least, I had found and pocketed only an odd stone, as puzzling in its way as a magnet and affording the unexpected shocks of a toy battery. The very discontinuity of the essays and their allusiveness and irrelevance were well calculated to arrest and charm the young mind. And they were so amazingly plausible! Higher up on the slopes of youth I was to find the English poets, but quite likely they would have bound me less strongly if the New Englanders had not fallen in my way just when they did.

I have since learned that Emerson propounded no consistent philosophy; that he was after all only a kind of rural almanac man, the keeper of a wayside spring who handed up cold water in a rusty dipper to the passerby; and yet I have never escaped his charm; and an acquaintance with him and his contemporaries implanted in me a reverence for the New England landscape over which in my fancy they roamed, uttering wisdom and chanting songs. I speak of this only because it is fair to assume that to many thousand of us in these prairies those New England voices came as a great inspiration. In these days of literary exploitation, when a new genius is heralded every morning and eclipsed by another at sundown, when the horse power of every novelist's motor is advertised to hasten the steps of the hesitating purchaser toward the bookshop, those austere Olympians appear a trifle dingy. We are assured that Emerson was a peddler of discarded rubbish from old garrets, that Whittier piped a thin music, and that Longfellow was only a benevolent Sunday-school teacher leading his class for a picnic in the forest primeval. Lowell has been described as a dull essayist and a poet who gleaned a negligible aftermath in older fields, Hawthorne as a melancholy bore, and Holmes as a cheerful one; and yet for those of us who found them in youth, when returning travelers brought news of them from the seat of the Brahmins, they still speak with golden tongues.

We may well wonder, now that every one and every one's aunt writes a novel, whether the literary calling will ever again enjoy the dignity of those days. Authorship seems bent upon confusing itself with journalism, with which, we used to be told, it has no kinship whatever. I can recall at the moment no new shrine at a Concord, a Cambridge or a Salem, no lately discovered cottage in snow-bound Amesbury that is likely to lure the pious pilgrim. Those brooding New Englanders seem rather absurd in these roaring times when every daily newspaper boasts a staff poet and when a novelist who fails to utter two books a year is neglecting his opportunities. Where some prosperous manufacturer of salacious romance is becalmed in his motor, and dictates to his secretary while a new tire is being adjusted—there indeed may the delighted villagers pour forth to render him homage; but those who attempt to look upon the author at home are as likely as not to be whipped from the estate by the gamekeepers or drowned for my lord's entertainment in the lilied moat beneath the royal windows.

The literature of Democracy has its own path to blaze, and its opportunities for service are enormous. Certain recent tendencies toward the vulgar and vicious in fiction are disturbing and disheartening, but it is to be hoped that they are only temporary. It is hardly possible that the novel is to be linked permanently to the garbage can; that the strength of the "strong" books of which we hear lies merely in their malodorousness, or that the novel as a representation of life and manners is to be abandoned wholly to literary adventurers who combine the confectioner's trade with the fragrant calling of the scavenger. American fiction has not lacked noble servants, and there are writers still abiding with us—Howells, James and Cable, to go no further—who have carried the torch high and firmly planted it for our guidance.

We need chant no miserere as we lift our pack and look down upon our further course. We are still alive, midway of a great era, and some things of worth we have seen accomplished. A perceptible strengthening of moral fiber in our political life and an increasing patience with idealism in its many expressions we may safely jot down on our tablets.

I take it as a good omen that this society, whose purpose is the encouragement of sobriety and earnestness in all the arts, has unfolded its young banner in this teeming Chicago. As a citizen of another state no sentiment of local pride inspires my feeling that here in this great city, whose aspect is not without its terrors for the unfamiliar eye, idealism is struggling to flower with as fine a spirit as may be found anywhere in America. Nothing is more cheering than the knowledge that here at the foot of the lakes, in this great western clearing house, this huge caldron of the nations, so many greathearted and earnest men and women are addressing themselves to social betterment, to political freedom and honesty, to the dissemination of sweetness and light. The ills of Chicago may strike the unfriendly critic as appalling, but there are many wise and skilled physicians seeking to diagnose her afflictions and supply the remedies. It may be doubted whether any city of its size in the world, with any similar history, ever offered encouragement along so many lines of progress as this western capital. If to Chicagoans this tribute appear gratuitous and presumptuous, I make it nevertheless with a feeling that I should like some such expression to become a part of the record of this society. We find here not only groups of people interested in civic administration, in social uplift, and in education along broad lines, but we find a municipal spirit that we have only to know to admire. It is conceivable that here within the lives of many of us the municipal riddle shall be solved and ideals of beauty and utility so blended and standardized as to become an example to forward-looking cities everywhere. And it is a privilege and a pleasure thus to bring from a sister province and a sister city this frail wreath to hang upon the huge door, imaginably wrought of iron and somewhat battered, that stands at this western gate. The pillars may loom grim and forbidding against the unsoftened glare of the prairies, but at the top there are already tracings of "lily-work," as on the columns that Hiram lifted to the glory of Solomon.

EMMELINE PANKHURST

MILITANT SUFFRAGISTS

Mrs. Pankhurst is widely known because of her active interest in the cause of woman suffrage in England. She was the energetic leader of the militant suffragists in the campaign for "Votes for Women" and in 1913, although under a sentence of penal servitude, came to America to explain their methods and achievements. The following address was delivered on November 13, 1913, in Hartford, Connecticut.

MANY people come to Hartford to address meetings as advocates of some reform. To-night it is not to advocate a reform that I address a meeting in Hartford. I do not come here as an advocate, because whatever position the suffrage movement may occupy in the United States of America, in England it has passed beyond the realm of advocacy and it has entered into the sphere of practical politics. It has become the subject of revolution and civil war, and so to-night I am not here to advocate woman suffrage. American suffragists can do that very well for themselves. I am here as a soldier who has temporarily left the field of battle in order to explain—it seems strange it should have to be explained—what civil war is like when civil war is waged by women. I am not only here as a soldier temporarily absent from the field of battle; I am here —and that, I think, is the strangest part of my coming—I am here as a person who, according to the law courts of my country, it has been decided, is of no value to the community at all; and I am adjudged because of my life to be a dangerous person, under sentence of penal servitude in a convict prison. So you see there is some special interest in hearing so unusual a person address you. I dare say, in the minds of many of you —you will perhaps forgive me this personal touch—that I do not look either very like a soldier or very like a convict, and yet I am both.

It would take too long to trace the course of militant methods as adopted by women, because it is about eight years since the word militant was first used to describe what we were doing; it is about eight years since the first militant action was taken by women. It was not militant at all, except that it provoked militancy on the part of those who were opposed to it. When women asked questions in political meetings and failed to get answers, they were not doing anything militant. To ask questions at political meetings is an acknowledged right of all people who attend public meetings; certainly in my country, men have always done it, and I hope they do it in America, because it seems to me that if you allow people to enter your legislatures without asking them any questions as to what they are going to do when they get there you are not exercising your citizen rights and your citizen duties as you ought. At any rate in Great Britain it is a custom, a time-honored one, to ask questions of candidates for Parliament and ask questions of members of the government. No man was ever put out of a public meeting for asking a question until Votes for Women came onto the political horizon. The first people who were put out of a political meeting for asking questions, were women; they were brutally ill-used; they found themselves in jail before twenty-four hours had expired. But instead of the newspapers, which are largely inspired by the politicians, putting militancy and the reproach of militancy, if reproach there is, on the people who had assaulted the women, they actually said it was the women who were militant and very much to blame.

It was not the speakers on the platform who would not answer them, who were to blame, or the ushers at the meeting; it was the poor women who had had their bruises and their knocks and scratches, and who were put into prison for doing precisely nothing but holding a protest meeting in the street after it was all over. However, we were called militant for doing that, and we were quite willing to accept the name, because militancy for us is time-honored; you have the church militant and in the sense of spiritual militancy we were very militant indeed. We were determined to press this question of the enfranchisement of the women to the point where we were no longer to be ignored by the politicians as had been the case for about fifty years, during which time women had patiently used every means open to them to win their political enfranchisement.

Well now, let me come to the situation as we find it. We felt we had to rouse the public to such a point that they would say to the government, you must give women the vote. We had to get the electors, we had to get the business interests, we had to get the professional interests, we had to get the men of leisure all unitedly saying to the government, "Relieve the strain of this situation and give women the vote"; and that is a problem that I think the most astute politician in this meeting would find very difficult. We have done it; we are doing it every day; and I think when you take that fact into consideration you will realize why we have been attacking private property, why we have been attacking the property of men so absorbed in their business that they generally forget to vote in ordinary elections, why we have attacked the pleasures of men whose whole life is spent in a round of pleasure, and who think politics so dull and so beneath their distinguished ossification that they hardly know which party is in power. All these people have had to be moved in order to bring enough pressure to bear upon the government to compel them to deal with the question of Woman Suffrage. And now that in itself is an explanation. There is a homely English proverb which may help to clear the situation which is this: "You cannot rouse the Britisher unless you touch his pocket." That is literally true. Perhaps you now can understand why we women thought we must attack the thing that was of most value in modern life in order to make these people wake up and realize that women wanted the vote, and that things were going to be very uncomfortable until women got the vote, because it is not by making people comfortable you get things in practical life, it is by making them uncomfortable. That is a homely truth that all of us have to learn.

I don't know whether I have used the domestic illustration in Hartford, but it is a very good one; it is quite worth using again. You have two babies very hungry and wanting to be fed. One baby is a patient baby, and waits indefinitely until its mother is ready to feed it. The other baby is an impatient baby and cries lustily, screams and kicks and makes everybody unpleasant until it is fed. Well, we know perfectly well which baby is attended to first. That is the whole history of politics. Putting sentiment aside, people who really want reforms learn that lesson very quickly. It is only the people who are quite content to go on advocating them indefinitely who play the part of the patient baby in politics. You have to make more noise than anybody else, you have to make yourself more obtrusive than anybody else, you have to fill all the papers more than anybody else, in fact you have to be there all the time and see that they do not snow you under, if you are really going to get your reform realized. That is what we women have been doing, and in the course of our desperate struggle we have had to make a great many people very uncomfortable. Now, one woman was arrested on an occasion when a great many windows were broken in London, as a protest against a piece of trickery on the part of the government, which will be incredible in fifty years, when the history of the movement is read. Women broke some windows as a protest; they broke a good many shop-keepers' windows; they broke the windows of shop-keepers where they spent most of their money when they bought their hats and their clothing; they also broke the windows of many of the Clubs, the smart Clubs in Piccadilly. One of the Clubs was the Guard Club. Well the ordinary army man is not much in politics, but he very often, because of his aristocratic and social connections, has considerable influence if he would use it. One woman broke the windows of the Guard Club, and when she broke those windows she stood there quietly until the Guard hall porter came out and seized her and held her until the policemen came to take her to prison. A number of the guards came out to see the kind of woman it was who had broken their windows, and they saw there a quiet little woman. She happened to be an actress, a woman who had come into our militant movement because she knew of the difficulties and dangers and temptations of the actress's life, of how badly paid she is, what her private sorrows are and her difficulties, and so she had come into the militant movement to get votes for actresses as quickly as possible, so that through the vote they could secure better conditions. Some of the guards—I think men who had never known what it was to earn a living, who knew nothing of the difficulties of a man's life, let alone the difficulties of a woman's life—came out, and they said, "Why did you break our windows? We have done nothing." She said: "It is because you have done nothing I have broken your windows." And perhaps out of that woman's breaking of windows has come this new movement of men of my country, where we find distinguished men who fought through the Boer war are drilling now like Sir Edward Carson, in Belfast, drilling men in order to form a bodyguard to protect the militant women. Probably that broken window of the Guard Club did a good deal to rouse men to the defense of women and to the injustice of their situation.

Then, there were the shop-keepers who could not understand why we should break their windows. Why should we alienate the sympathy of the shop-keepers? Well, there is the other side of the question, gentlemen,—why should the shop-keepers alienate the sympathy of their customers by refusing to help them to get political power, some power to make the condition of the woman who helps to earn the shop-keeper's money by serving in his shop, easier than it is at the present time. Those women broke shop-keepers' windows and what was the situation? Just at the beginning of the winter season when all the new winter hats and coats were being shown, the shop-keepers had to barricade all their windows with wood and nobody could see the new winter fashions. Well, there again is an impossible situation. The shop-keeper cannot afford to quarrel with his customers, and we have to-day far more practical sympathy amongst the shop-keepers of London than we ever had when we were quiet, gentle, lady-like suffragists asking nicely for a vote.

Well, then, there were the men of pleasure, or the business men who were so busy earning money during the week that all they could think of when the week came to an end was recreation, and the great recreation in England to-day is playing golf. Everywhere on Saturday you see men streaming away into the country for the week-end to play golf. They so monopolize the golf links that they have made a rule that although the ladies may play golf all the week, the golf links are entirely reserved for men on Saturday and Sunday; and you have this spectacle of the exodus of men from London into the country to fill up the week-end with playing golf. They are not, ladies, putting their heads together thinking how best they can govern the country for you, what good laws they can make for you and for the world; they are there, all of them, getting their health, and I do not blame them for it at the week-end. Well we attacked the golf links; we wanted to make them think; and if you had been in London and taken a Sunday paper you would have read, especially if you played golf, with consternation, that all the beautiful greens that had taken years to make, had been cut up or destroyed with an acid or made almost impossible to play upon on the Friday night, when in many cases there were going to be important matches on the Saturday afternoon and Sunday.

Just to give you an illustration of the effectiveness of these methods in waking the Britisher up, in conveying to him that women want the vote and are going to get it even if we do not adopt quite the men's methods in order to do so, I was staying at a little house in the country on a golf links, a house that had been loaned to me to use whenever I could get away from my work, and several times in the course of that Sunday morning I got telephone calls from gentlemen who were prominent members of golf clubs in that vicinity. It so happened that the golf links where I was spending the week-end, had not been touched. Those links had been respected because some of the prominent women suffragettes happened to be members of the club, and those women who destroyed the greens—I don't know who they were, but it was no doubt done by women—spared the links where these women whom they admired and respected, played. Well, then, that morning I was rung up over and over again by excited gentlemen who begged that those golf links should be spared, saying: "I don't know whether your followers know that we are all suffragists, on our committee; we are entirely in favor of woman suffrage." And I said: "Well, don't you think you had better tell Mr. Asquith so, because if you are suffragists and do nothing, naturally you will only add to the indignation of the women. If you really want your golf links spared you had better intimate to Mr. Asquith that you think it is high time he put his principles into practice and gave the women the vote."

But this experience will show you that if you really want to get anything done, it is not so much a matter of whether you alienate sympathy; sympathy is a very unsatisfactory thing if it is not practical sympathy. It does not matter to the practical suffragist whether she alienates sympathy that was never of any use to her. What she wants is to get something practical done, and whether it is done out of sympathy or whether it is done out of fear, or whether it is done because you want to be comfortable again and not be worried in this way, doesn't particularly matter so long as you get it. We had enough of sympathy for fifty years; it never brought us anything; and we would rather have an angry man going to the government and saying, my business is interfered with and I won't submit to its being interfered with any longer because you won't give women the vote, than to have a gentleman come onto our platforms year in and year out and talk about his ardent sympathy with woman suffrage.

If you are dealing with an industrial revolution, if you get the men and women of one class to rising up against the men and women of another class, you can locate the difficulty; if there is a great industrial strike, you know exactly where the violence is, and every man knows exactly how the warfare is going to be waged; but in our war against the government you can't locate it. You can take Mrs. Hepburn and myself on this platform, and now, without being told, how could you tell that Mrs. Hepburn is a non-militant and that I am a militant? Absolutely impossible. If any gentleman who is the father of daughters in this meeting went into his home and looked around at his wife and daughters, if he lived in England and was an Englishman, he couldn't tell whether some of his daughters were militants or non-militants. When his daughters went out to post a letter, he couldn't tell if they went harmlessly out to make a tennis engagement at that pillar-box by posting a letter, or whether they went to put some corrosive matter in that would burn all the letters up inside of that box. We wear no mark; we belong to every class; we permeate every class of the community from the highest to the lowest; and so you see in the woman's civil war the dear men of my country are discovering this absolutely impossible to deal with it; you cannot locate it, and you cannot stop it. "Put them in prison," they said; "that will stop it." But it didn't stop it. They put women in prison for long terms of imprisonment, for making a nuisance of themselves—that was the expression when they took petitions in their hands to the door of the House of Commons; and they thought that by sending them to prison, giving them a day's imprisonment, would cause them to all settle down again and there would be no further trouble. But it didn't happen so at all: instead of the women giving it up, more women did it, and more and more and more women did it until there were three hundred women at a time, who had not broken a single law, only "made a nuisance of themselves" as the politicians say.

The whole argument with the anti-suffragists, or even the critical suffragist man, is this: that you can govern human beings without their consent. They have said to us, "Government rests upon force; the women haven't force, so they must submit." Well, we are showing them that government does not rest upon force at all; it rests upon consent. As long as women consent to be unjustly governed, they can be; but directly women say: "We withhold our consent, we will not be governed any longer so long as that government is unjust," not by the forces of civil war can you govern the very weakest woman. You can kill that woman, but she escapes you then; you cannot govern her. And that is, I think, a most valuable demonstration we have been making to the world.

Now, I want to say to you who think women cannot succeed, we have brought the government of England to this position, that it has to face this alternative; either women are to be killed or women are to have the vote. I ask American men in this meeting, what would you say if in your State you were faced with that alternative, that you must either kill them or give them their citizenship,—women, many of whom you respect, women whom you know have lived useful lives, women whom you know, even if you do not know them personally, are animated with the highest motives, women who are in pursuit of liberty and the power to do useful public service? Well, there is only one answer to that alternative; there is only one way out of it, unless you are prepared to put back civilization two or three generations; you must give those women the vote. Now that is the outcome of our civil war.

You won your freedom in America when you had the Revolution, by bloodshed, by sacrificing human life. You won the Civil War by the sacrifice of human life when you decided to emancipate the negro. You have left it to the women in your land, the men of all civilized countries have left it to women, to work out their own salvation. That is the way in which we women of England are doing. Human life for us is sacred, but we say if any life is to be sacrificed it shall be ours; we won't do it ourselves, but we will put the enemy in the position where they will have to choose between giving us freedom or giving us death.

ALFRED S. PINKERTON

SPIRIT OF ODD-FELLOWSHIP

Address by Alfred S. Pinkerton, lawyer (born in Lancaster, Pa., March 19, 1856), delivered at Richmond, Va., in his capacity as Grand Sire of the Sovereign Grand Lodge of Odd Fellows, September 17, 1900.

MR. CHAIRMAN, YOUR EXCELLENCY, MR. MAYOR, REPRESENTATIVES OF OUR ORDER, LADIES AND GENTLEMEN:—This is not the first time that I have received the greetings of a Richmond audience and been the recipient of Virginian hospitality. I know the warmth of the one, the unbounded generosity of the other, and I voice the sentiment of every member of the Sovereign Grand Lodge when I say that each of us appreciates the splendid welcome you have given, and rejoices in the privilege that is his of visiting, under such happy auspices, this beautiful and historic State.

We knew that chivalry and knightly courtesy still existed in the Old Dominion; that Southern hearts would welcome us, and Southern hands be extended in fraternal greeting. Our anticipations have been realized, and we sit among you not as strangers, but as welcome guests, as neighbors, and as friends.

Representing an Order founded in man's nobility, we gladly assemble among a people whose ancestors first proclaimed the right of the individual man to direct his own affairs and destiny.

Before Plymouth Rock felt the touch of English feet the seeds of a nation had been sown at Jamestown. On Virginian soil representative government in America was born. The colonial charter of 1621 was the first grant of self-government given by a hereditary ruler to dwellers on this continent, given to those who dared assert that English blood in Virginia meant a voice in Virginian rule.

As two centuries ago the people of England testified in behalf of those bishops who but asserted their privileges of self-respect; as then the flower of the British bar successfully pleaded for freedom of church and freedom of right; so in our fathers' time it was a country lawyer, "who spoke as Homer wrote," who in the "parsons'" cause voiced that sentiment of Virginia which afterwards flamed in syllabled fire from that old church still standing in your city; he it was who ten years before a political revolution that divided in government—but not in heart—the New World from the Old, offered the resolution by which your General Assembly declared that it alone had the right to tax Virginians. It was a Virginian who presided over the first American Congress, and from Virginian hands came another and immortal resolution, that which declared these colonies should be free and independent States.

I come from a community that has much in common with this. Sprung from the same great freedom-loving race, speaking the same language, sharing the glory of a common descent and of a common literature, one in sentiment and in aspiration, the colonies of Virginia and Massachusetts were side by side in the contest for political independence. Each called its land a "commonwealth," thus in the very title indicating the form of government under which its people lived—the *common wealth*—the home and rule of all the people—the union of all for the benefit of each—the land of equal opportunities and equal privileges. Yes, in the old days we were together. Virginia remembers—

> . . . how the Bay State, in answer to the call
> Of her old House of Burgesses spoke out from Faneuil Hall
> When, echoing back her Henry's cry, came pulsing on each breath
> Of northern winds the thrilling cry of "liberty or death."

Beneath the old elm still standing by Harvard College the first soldier of Virginia—the first American—assumed command of that army of "tradesmen, farmers, and mechanics," that in a spirit of sublime prophecy dared to called itself "Continental," that won freedom from the trained soldiery of Europe and gave visible form to a government that has made good the name its soldiers bore. Then side by side our fathers fought; then side by side our statesmen sat; and the first name that appears upon that immortal Declaration of Independence, penned by a Virginian hand, and based upon Virginia's bill of rights, is that of a Massachusetts man, President of that Congress which gave to the world and to the godlike and aspiring soul this bible of the rights of man.

Hancock and Jefferson, Adams and Mason, Otis and Henry, united those two colonies that, more than any others, gave impulse to American thought and speech and action. There was Bunker Hill; here Yorktown. Nor do we forget that mighty lawyer, born of your blood and sleeping in your soil, the great interpreter of the written Constitution of our land, nor him, of Northern birth, that Constitution's eloquent defender—Marshall and Webster—great sons of the same proud race.

It was the civilization of Jamestown and of Plymouth that made possible this Government of ours, and though for a time the clouds lowered o'er our house, thank God we are once more as of yore; as, of old, they together "encountered Tarleton's charge of fire," so again have Virginia and Massachusetts struck hands—and this time in deathless friendship; so again in the presence of a common danger, and in honor of a common flag, have our brothers touched elbows in the ranks, slept by the same camp-fires, and together offered upon the country's altar the rich libation of their blood. History is making fast. From the western hemisphere has departed every vestige of Castilian power. The starry flag has become a fixed constellation o'er Asiatic seas, but, better than all, we have learned to know our Motherland. The conquering English-speaking people have come closer together—and so have we at home. It was a good day for America when the soldier boy of New England and of the Northwest enlisted under a Virginian Lee, and when the star of Wheeler glistened upon a coat of army blue. Gone are the days of strife and bitterness and doubt; welcome the days of peace, of confidence, of lasting brotherhood.

We come to you in the closing hours of the nineteenth century, a century of wonderful development; a century of great achievements. Old empires have passed away; nations in swaddling-cloths have grown to manhood's state. Kings and czars have been born, have ruled, and been forgotten—boundaries of nations have been changed—thrones have fallen, and old dynasties been destroyed. Man everywhere is asserting the power and attributes of man. This Government of the people has shed its radiating light throughout the world. Europe, Asia, and Africa have felt its beneficent beams; individual man, under whatever government he may live, lifts his eyes higher than ever before, and while war and famine, and pestilence, and death still constitute a portion of our heritage, the path is upward, and never has God's light seemed so warm and bright to the great toiling masses of the earth as at this hour, when kingdoms and principalities and powers are but the instruments and not the destroyers of men.

Nor has the development been confined to the political world. In art, in science, in mechanics, has

> Man put forth
> His pomp, his pride, his skill,
> And arts that made fire, flood, and earth,
> The vassals of his will.

The cotton-gin, the power-loom, the sewing-machine, the rotary printing-press, the reaper, the telegraph and telephone, the binding of electricity to man's common use, the thousand and one mechanical appliances that make our burdens light, and life more worth living, are but a part of this century's tribute to the future. In letters and in literature what advances have been made! The printing-press has brought the richest thoughts of the best minds within easy reach of all, and the philosopher and the astronomer share their secrets with a thousand friends. Thought is purer than before, theology more simple and humane, religion more near the human heart and soul.

This is the age in which we live; this is the century that called into life that great humanitarian movement which we denominate Odd-Fellowship. It is the child of American spirit and life; it is a creation designed for daily food; it lives and moves among breathing men; it is for the closet and for the field; it is of practical use to a practical people; its secrets are a shield and not a sword; it believes in the royal heritage of man and in the divine right of self-advancement. Teaching loyalty to established government, and obedience to law, it holds that governments are made for man and that the citizen who controls himself, who recognizes the rights of, and has faith in, his fellow citizens is the best prop and support of such a government. It believes in truth, in honor, in temperance, in the overshadowing Fatherhood of God; in the lasting, eternal brotherhood of man; in charity in thought and charity in acts; to the cry of Cain it answers, "I am my brother's keeper," and in every hour of its existence it has blessed humanity and lessened human toil and suffering.

Bear with me for a moment. If I am correctly informed, the present total taxable valuation, real and personal, of this city is $69,215,240. Raze beautiful Richmond to the ground; convert into coin every foot of land within its corporate limits; let every stone and timber of every factory, every business block, every dwelling-house, contribute to the sum; into the crucible put your jewels and your stores of gold and silver; market the securities, bonds, and stocks of your people; and when you shall have done all this, when you shall have converted your city's soil and buildings into scrip, when you shall have stripped your citizens of all their taxable property, you will, even then, be over fifteen million dollars short of the amount of money that this Order has expended, since 1830, in brotherly relief. You will then be short a sum equal to seven-twelfths of the entire taxable valuation of the personal property here owned. At the present rate of charitable expenditure we distribute, for such purposes, the wealth of a Richmond every nineteen years; a distribution in which there is no expense account and in which every dollar finds the pocket of the beneficiary. Pardon the illustration, Mr. Mayor. We like your city too well to despoil it; we hope to come again; but the comparison made demonstrates the magnitude of this Order's silent charitable work.

Can you question the fraternal spirit of such a brotherhood? Dare you challenge its right to live? Can you define the future's bounds? It is not my purpose to enter into a discussion of the Order's principles, or to pronounce an eulogy upon its work. To-day it holds one million souls within its fond embrace. The streams of its unostentatious charity have flowed to every corner of our land; its white banner has led the march of fraternal life. To-day we salute our comrades across the seas; our flag is uplifted in the isles of the Pacific. Our faith has overleaped the barriers of States, nor has it been retarded by the artificial distinctions of society. Virginia's sons have shared our Order's struggles and its honors. They have taught its lessons on your soil, and "by their works ye shall know them."

We come to-day representing every State and Territory of this great Union in answer to Virginia's call, and in response to Richmond's welcome. With us as comrades, brothers, and friends are citizens of that northward land, with whose sons we claim kinship, whose national hymn is set to the same air as ours, and whose gentle ruler is Queen of American as well as of English hearts. Within our convention hall are clustered the flags of sixteen different lands wherein this Order dwells, and over all hangs the white flag of peace, emblazoned with the scarlet links of truth.

Such an order it is my proud privilege to represent. In its name I accept your greeting, and in its name I thank you for it. Generous as have been the spoken words, more generous has been the manner of your salutation. From the moment we entered Virginia until this hour we have been the recipients of boundless hospitality. We have traveled your beautiful valleys with delight—we have shared in a true Virginia welcome—we are glad that we have come, and we shall bear to our several homes brightest recollections of the Old Dominion and of its sons and daughters.

To your Excellency, to you, Mr. Mayor, to the several representatives of our Order, and to you who represent our gentle sisterhood, I tender the thanks and the fraternal salutations of the Sovereign Grand Lodge, and I trust that our sojourn among you may be as pleasant to you as it is profitable and enjoyable to us.

Representatives: Virginia has formally welcomed us to her heart; Richmond has opened wide her gates; our brothers and sisters, the portals of their homes; let us repay this courtesy by making this the most memorable session of our history—memorable for the good we accomplish, for the inspiration given to our brotherhood, for the assistance rendered to the weary soul. As the gates of a new century swing outward at our touch, let us lift our flag to loftier heights, and let us dedicate our Order anew to the great purposes that gave it birth.

We meet among a generous people and amid historic surroundings. Here, in more ancient days, people of our blood and kin laid the foundations of a mighty power. The history of this commonwealth is interwoven with that of this nation and of the English-speaking race. Its sons have been conspicuous in the forum and on the battlefield. Again and again has it sent forth its bravest to build up other States, and to the nation it has given rulers whose name and fame will live while centuries pass away. We know its splendid history; we have faith in its bright future, and—

> Again we hail thee
> Mother of States and unpolluted men,
> Virginia, fitly named from England's manly Queen.

WILLIAM C. REDFIELD

FIRST GET THE FACTS

William C. Redfield, born in 1858, Secretary of Commerce during the Wilson Administration, has already been represented in Volumes III and V of "Modern Eloquence." The address which follows was delivered before the Case School, Cleveland, Ohio, May 27, 1915.

THERE is connected with the Department of Commerce a remarkable institution called the Bureau of Standards. Its work is more or less familiar to you because one or more groups of students from this school have visited it at various times. I have on some occasions spoken of this bureau as the "house of accuracy," for in it in a special sense the truth is sought. We call the seeking of this kind of truth research. It may be chemical research or physical research or the act of research applied to any of the sciences that underlie our industries and public utilities. Truth is sought in this work because it is believed that the facts concerning nature are of infinite value to mankind. It is recognized that the effectiveness of our civilization rests upon facts first ascertained and then used. It is there thought faulty to proceed on the basis of incomplete truth or of undigested facts, and neither time, labor, nor expense is spared to find the facts and make them known to those who can use them.

One of the standards of the Bureau of Standards itself must be that of speaking the truth so far as it shall have become known, and men know they may depend upon what it says as expressing the truth within these limits in which it has been ascertained. To tell half of a truth if the other half were known would be thought a destructive violation of the very *raison d'être* of the service. To know the truth and not to tell it would be equally violative.

FIRST GET THE FACTS

In what has been thus far said I have described only the normal workings of the scientific mind as applied to research. The mind of science is one of high ideals. It is a modest mind for it recognizes that there are many things it does not know. It is a discriminating mind for it tests and selects or rejects as the test may tell. It is a practical mind for it aims to find the hidden things of nature and put them to use. It is an honest mind for it seeks neither to deceive nor to be deceived. It is an open mind, ready to reject the truth which seems to be in favor of that which is proven to be. The scientific mind, if it be true to itself, knows no passion nor prejudice nor predilection, unless it be the passion for the truth that is not yet known, a judgment given in advance in favor of that truth when it shall be known and a preference for any form of truth whatever, and a distaste for shams. I have a friend who said that if he did not know why he knew what he thought, he knew he wanted to know, and in this attitude of thought he expressed something of the outreach of the mind of science, which ever seeks to learn the what and the why of things.

In the business world facts are respected. This is so because facts are stubborn things and insist upon being respected. They have a way of bowling one over if one does not respect them. Enter a great mill and look about you. The machine which is nearest at hand is itself the illustration we seek. It is the embodiment of ascertained fact. As you stand and look at it and think of how it came to be you will find your mind running back through a long series of facts which one by one were gathered often through many years and which have ended in the mechanism which you see. If it were not made in accord with the facts out of which it grew it would cease to work and become a helpless thing. If it is not used in accordance with the facts which control its service it ceases to be useful and again becomes a helpless thing. It is made up not of past facts. It is working out present facts, and its product often points toward the development of facts which are to be.

We stand, you and I, whether in school or office or mill, in the midst of a constant evolution of facts and development of truth. The truth of yesterday is not that of to-day. The truth of to-day is but the parent of that which is to be to-morrow. Prejudice and truth are enemies, and truth has no finer task than that which it daily performs of destroying prejudice. Where prejudice is, truth is so far excluded, for no judgment given in advance of known truth is either sound or safe.

Let us not, however, go on as if we were paying mere verbal homage to a high ideal. Let us become practical in the matter. The relation men hold to truth, their respect for facts, their use of facts, largely determines their place and power in life. We make progress in the business world not necessarily by research for facts but at least by outreach for them and by respectful treatment of them when they are found. If the mill you are some day each of you to run is not run in accord with the facts that environ that mill it will not run long. Nay, you may find the more obvious facts that should control the mill and by conforming to them may succeed a little. The amount of success will depend a good deal upon how far your vision goes in seeing the facts that surround you and on the extent to which your practice goes in using those facts. The man of broad mind sees more facts than he who has a narrower vision. Mental near-sight is usually not profitable. To be far-sighted is at times physically inconvenient but commercially has much in its favor. It is more essential, however, that the sight whether it be far or near shall know a fact when it sees it and be ready to abandon a pseudo fact for a real one and to abide by the latter till further facts are found.

These suggestions are simple and primary yet acceptance of them is all too rare. About all of us is a penumbra shutting out many truths we would do well to know. Amid the enlightened circle, which is perhaps not of the same size for any two of us, we walk with such light as we have. This perhaps leads us normally to repeat that profound truth from Holy Writ, "If the light that is within you" (or, I may add, about you) "be darkness, how great is that darkness?"

Facts have a cruel way of substituting themselves for fancies. There is nothing more remorseless, just as there is nothing more helpful, than truth. If your head comes in contact with the moving crank-shaft of an engine, the fact as to the relative hardness of the two will be both painfully and speedily determined. Yet it would not do to argue that because the crank-shaft breaks your head it was a destroying force in the world. Sometimes the head itself is more of a destroying force than the unconscious mechanism which it has created.

It is well, therefore, to be on the right side of the facts. This means that there are certain standards by which our opinions may be judged whether they are false or true. For the truth is not affected by what men think about it. Your or my unbelief in it does not make it less the truth. It is a stern though kindly standard that thus is daily set against our judgments, and if you and I fail to meet the standard it does not hurt the standard but it does hurt us. Those are fine lines which run:

> It fortifies my soul to know
> That though I perish truth is so;
>   That howso'er I stray or range,
>   What'er I do truth does not change.
> I steadier step when I recall
> That though I slip truth does not fall.

Shall men be able to rely on you in your working life? If so, it will be because they find by experience that in word and deed you meet the test of truth. Of one man we say he is fanciful; of another that he is a dreamer; of another than he is a pessimist, and of a fourth, an optimist, and by all these things we mean certain shades of criticism whereby we detect the departure from a certain mental standard of our own as to the relation men should normally have to facts.

Prejudice then, and half truths, and narrowness of view, and obstinacy of thought, these are all weights men carry in the race of life; expensive things, bringing at times both pain and poverty into his lot who tolerates them.

I have intimated in substance that modern industry is the utilizing of certain facts or the outgrowth of them for the production of other facts; or to state it differently, that industry represents the practical application of truth to life. If one passes from the field of industry into public life there is nothing which strikes one more forcibly than the degree of absence of this relation to fact. Our scientific thought, our industrial thought, our agricultural thought, even our artistic and literary thought either pays homage to the laws of truth which govern those activities or at least panders more or less unwillingly to the recognized power of the controlling truths. This condition does not prevail to an equal degree in the discussions of public life. Nothing strikes one, leaving a business atmosphere for that of public service, more than the inaccuracy in statement and in criticism which is there found. Around the table gather the board of directors of an industrial company. As the facts concerning the company's affairs are discussed it is usual for those present to speak of the business in which they are concerned with accuracy and for the listeners to believe that they speak the truth as they know it. I mean no personal and certainly no sharp criticism when I say that this is far from being the case when men, perhaps even the same men, meet to discuss public affairs. The things which are at times currently believed by many among us on various public subjects are not infrequently things that are not so, and criticisms are based and policies commended or condemned with astonishing frequency on the basis of things which are said to be but which do not exist. It is not throwing the standards of business discussion into excessively high relief to say that our public affairs would be vastly improved if the accuracy of statement and the courtesy when differences of opinion arise common in business circles could be transferred to public ones. This is not because the facts are not available, for most of them are such as are of public record. The condition exists in spite of these existing records, and often without consulting them. On a recent occasion it was my duty to point out that in a paragraph from an address by a well known man of affairs on certain public subjects not a single correct statement was made; yet the facts concerning which the statements were made were all of them available on request and without expense.

It must not be understood, however, that I am now making either a sweeping or a specific charge of untruthfulness or of desire to misrepresent. I am dealing with a condition and not with persons and a condition in which persons of unquestioned probity and honor constantly act and speak concerning public affairs without the precise information on which they commonly act in private matters. This is not because they have ceased to be upright and truthful men but because the standards respecting facts do not seem to be quite the same nor is the same care always taken to ascertain the facts. There is no question in my mind that the gentleman whose remarks I had occasion to correct would in the management of a factory be scrupulously careful to learn the facts before he spoke concerning them to his board of directors. So far, however, as my knowledge goes, though the records concerning the facts of which he inaccurately spoke are in the Department of Commerce, no effort was made to ascertain them.

Neither must it be understood that I single any one person out or any party or locality. It has been my experience that the same separation from the normal accuracies of life has occurred with men of many varying views and of different localities when they came to speak of public matters. It seems to be a general and not a particular condition.

I once noticed when having charge of a portion of the highways of an important city that many citizens spoke as if they were intimately informed respecting the somewhat technical subject of street pavements. Possibly it is because we assume that our public affairs are easily grasped by all men without special inquiry concerning them that this habitual inaccuracy appears in conversation and criticism. So far from its being easy to know and understand our multiplex public matters I think it is true that many if not most of our citizens have but vague conceptions of what the actual detailed operations of the Government are. One is constantly requested in all good-will and sincerity to do that which is impossible or even unlawful. I received but a few days since a numerously signed petition urging that the department enter upon a line of business not only unknown to the law but which would require an amendment to the Constitution of the United States to make a law concerning it possible. Possibly the fact that we have all been taught that power lies in a democracy with the people leads some to think that anything which some individual desires is therefore both lawful and possible.

Accompanying the comments based upon absentee facts are others which deal with assumed motives having no sounder basis. It is but a few days since the unconscious act of one in no way connected with the Government was made the basis of a charge that an important service had sold itself, and was described in adjectives as lurid and abusive as they were wanting in basis.

This is, however, neither a complaint of conditions nor a plea for relief but a suggestion for helpfulness. No administrator worthy the name but welcomes candid and constructive criticism, and from many sides I have received comments and suggestions through many years that have altered methods and improved results. It is the fact of course that criticism and attack, having no basis in truth, pass by one as the idle wind which one respects not and has no result save to injure the influence of the critic who descends to such means, if it is consciously done. The problem that needs solution, however, is how to guide men who wish to speak clearly and accurately out of the all too pervading habit of doing neither when public business is concerned. It is, I believe, assumed that through the daily press we have a means of throwing light on all these things and one would be foolish to deny that much light is continually thus thrown. We must not, however, in justice to that press, forget that the nature of its service requires that what they print shall be of the day, daily, or almost of the hour, hourly; that a thing to have news value must in some degree be new or to have what is technically called "punch," must have some element more or less of the dramatic, or must have such a character as will arrest attention. Unfortunately for the public mind, much that needs to be known has neither character. The larger part of the useful and productive work of a Government department is not only nonpolitical but is continuous, developing steadily from day to day, similar in its character to the operation of a factory or a business, turning out a regular product which does not have in it always the appeal of the moment which gives it either "punch" or news value.

These things, therefore, are not and in a sense can not be grist for the mill of the daily press even though they may be more important in the way of information than that which falls more truly within the class of the said grist.

There is, therefore, something yet to be done in the way of bringing before the people who own the Government the facts respecting that Government in its daily evolution. It has been a pleasure to me in more than one city (among them this one) to speak of the work of the Department of Commerce to busy men of affairs. It has interested and enlightened me to see how keen an interest has been taken and how much surprise has at times been shown on learning the facts. There is every reason to believe that other departments than that of Commerce contain as much if not more of interest to the average man.

I should myself be guilty of inaccuracy if there is left in your minds any impression to the effect that the press in any of its forms is deemed negligent of its duty to inform the owners of the Government respecting their own affairs. This does not seem to be the case. It is rather that all the conditions are such that in a matter of grave importance to every one of us the necessary means of publicity for full knowledge by us all of our affairs is not available. We do not ignore the fact that magazines of many kinds, and frequent articles in numerous other publications, throw much light upon some of the operations of various public services, but there does not seem to be available any regular and systematic source of adequate knowledge as to what is regularly going on. Books, indeed, several of them, exist having this for their purpose, and they are good to have and read. Yet it is doubtful if any of them really fulfills its mission. Such an organization as the Chamber of Commerce of the United States continuously and with effect strives to perform for a business world the function of giving knowledge concerning the government. It maintains committees which are in more or less frequent touch with different departments; it publishes a paper of much value; yet I doubt if its able and effective officers would feel that their function lay in the way of informing the whole public on all our governmental affairs or even if they would say that they had as yet reached that state of perfection of information for their own share of our public that they themselves desire.

The truth seems to be that in a republic where a knowledge of public affairs is more or less charged upon us all by the very nature of our institutions those same institutions have grown so vast and far-reaching, so intricate in their operations, that it is, to say the least, extremely difficult for anyone to follow them. Indeed, one might talk to you for two hours on the work of a single bureau of the Department of Commerce without exhausting that subject, yet neither that bureau nor the department is among the largest there are. If to the burden thus imposed, happily without consciousness, upon the average man, there is added that of understanding his own State and municipal affairs, plus the duties of his own vocation, the responsibilities of the citizen of a republic would seem onerous indeed.

It would undoubtedly, however, be pushing our thought much too far to urge any such comprehensive view as the duty of any single man. For one such to follow the daily changes arising from the evolution of our National Government would be itself a serious task. The important thing, and the thing which unfortunately exists far too little, is to know accurately the things which we do know. How is this to be done? Each department is a great storehouse of facts which in many ways it strives to make known and to utilize. In dealing, as we in our department do, with the promotion of our foreign trade in one of our services, the problem is ever before us how to let the business world know what we are actually doing for it. Through branch offices, by use of press and platform, by the publication of a daily paper, by official reports, monographs, and such other use of the press as brings our annual total of expenditure for printing up into the hundreds of thousands of dollars per annum, we strive to inform the people. Yet we are conscious that much more needs to be done than is in fact accomplished. It is a common thing to have men say when this or that or the other thing is shown them, "I had no idea of this." Speaking not long since to a prominent manufacturer of the work in behalf of manufactures of one of our great bureaus he said he had not even heard of the bureau. I do not mean that he was to blame. The fact is, the means of informing our people on their own affairs, even in this land of printing presses and publications, either are not adequate, or if they are sufficient they do not for some reason perform their function.

Possibly some may say that official reports are not so juicy a type of literature as to afford pleasant food for the mind, and no one who has had to write such a report would argue to the contrary. Nevertheless the facts of the Government's daily work are many of them of surprising interest. The discovery of a great unknown bed of edible scallops extending hundreds of miles along the Atlantic coast, the utilization of sea mussels for food, a use common in Europe, hitherto neglected here but now springing into activity; the finding of great fishing banks close by the Oregon shore not hitherto known to exist, the maintaining of the pearl button industry by inoculating fish through a biological laboratory near the Mississippi River with a parasite which in time becomes the fresh water clam, the finding of decorative millinery in the bottom of Long Island Sound in the shape of a primitive sea animal, which becomes beautiful when both dead and dyed—these are simply part of the ordinary routine work of the Bureau of Fisheries. It would be easy to go on in this same service and tell how a certain river perch lays a mass of eggs much larger than itself and how fish exist which are good for food yet are thrown away at a time when men complain of the high cost of living. One could go on for long telling of matters of this kind. They are facts which affect daily life sometimes to the extent of altering its conditions. Here a slight change in a government specification opens a great market to American cements that were theretofore excluded; there a hint that a certain duty has been modified leads to the large exportation of coal. A few lines in print open the way to the shipment of hundreds of cases of glass abroad. The study of a ceramic chemist in the quiet of his laboratory produces a leadless glaze and destroys the evils of lead poisoning. Some work of the same man develops value out of hitherto useless clays and makes possible the production of porcelain of a kind not made here before.

It would be easy to run on. These are only faint indications of living matters of interest conducted by the public and for the public but of which the public does not get that close and intimate knowledge which it is desirable they should have.

I have not touched upon the extent to which partisanship or passion may come in to modify facts or to obscure them. I regret that it should be true that half-truths should be as common among us as they are. Let us, however, deal to-day not with matters known and controverted even though known but in part and that which is known used but partially. We have spoken rather of things of general interest that are not controversial but which in their aggregate mean the service that the people through their organized government are doing for themselves.

You will doubtless observe I have presented no remedy for the weaknesses that have been suggested. This is because I do not know of any panacea that will work any immediate or even extended cure. We are so busy in the actual doing and in striving to make the doing useful to those for whom it is done, so actively facing the difficulties of being as helpful as we desire, that we are perhaps more conscious of the struggle than prophetic of success in it. This is not a confession of defeat, for on the contrary much accomplishment is real. It is only when we measure what all of us who own our affairs would like to know and ought to know about those same affairs beside the ability to inform them of those affairs that the task seems hard.

A mental danger besets us all. It is that of parochial thinking. It is all very well for a man when he is dead to rest his bones within the quiet shade and encircling wall of some churchyard, but he needs a larger sphere while he is alive. Up to the time when a man leaves school to begin a man's job in the world I suppose it may be said, generally speaking, to be true that his mind has worked chiefly intensively. From that time on I suppose it to be true that the mind should work chiefly extensively. The point at which one method of thinking passes over into the other would be hard to trace. One can do extensive thinking in school and must do intensive work after assuming the work of life. None the less, generally speaking, I believe that the training of young manhood looks to the extension of thought in maturer life. You are not primarily going on to get facts out of books and out of the laboratory and out of the experience of others into your mind. You are to begin to take the facts which that mind has digested and to work them out into useful forms and into productive service. You have been perhaps the beneficiaries hitherto of the things which have been created and of the thoughts which others have worked out in the crucible of their own mental processes. You are now to become in a sense creators and to think both for yourselves and others. You have been one may say absorbers; you are to become producers. Your value as men depends on what the product shall be.

The country is not so greatly concerned, I venture to believe, with the amount that a man knows as it is with the use he makes of what he knows. It does not want the man who while his body may live, still keeps his mind in a mental churchyard. One of the great phrases of the Old Testament says, "Thou hast taken me and Thou hast set me in a large place"; and what the world needs is men who can think in great areas. It is necessary but it is not sufficient to get the facts. One who would do a man's job in the world must through those facts serve his fellows.

Think, if you please, what the symmetry of life should be. It should not be narrow; it should not be crooked. It should be straight and square. It should be high, to keep out of the dust and mire. It should be broad that it may rest securely. It should be deep, based on the eternal verities. It must be low, for living things grow upward into the light. I would have you question all your life long whether this or that or the other form of alleged truth which is presented to you be so or not. If it is found not to be the truth I would have you reject it without regret and without fear of inconsistency, for there is some force in the statement that consistency is the virtue of weak minds. Truth is progressively revealed and one must readjust himself in thought and action to the greater knowledge of truth that we ought continually to gain. The man who at 50 thinks as he thought at 30 has mentally ceased to grow. If one's mind is open to the light whence it may fall, if one's steps are guided by all light whitherso'er it may lead, there is little to fear either as to treading the path safely or as to the place in the world to which it shall conduct one.

SIR ALFRED ROBBINS

FREEMASONRY IN ENGLAND AND AMERICA

The following address was delivered by the Right Worshipful Brother Sir Robbins, P. G. W., president of the Board of General Purposes of the United Grand Lodge of England before the Jurisdiction of the Right Worshipful Grand Lodge of Free and Accepted Masons of Pennsylvania at a dinner given in his honor on April 10, 1924. He was introduced by the Right Worshipful Past Grand Master Brother Abraham M. Beitler who concluded his speech as follows:

"And now, brethren, let me introduce to you a man who is preëminent in his own Grand Lodge. He is practically the Prime Minister of the Grand Lodge of England; a man who has spoken and written of Masonry; a man who has held every important post in Masonry in the subordinate lodges and in the Grand Lodge; a man who is one of the important men of his country, Sir Alfred Robbins." [Applause, the brethren rising.]

RIGHT WORSHIPFUL GRAND MASTER, RIGHT WORSHIPFUL PAST GRAND MASTER, AND BRETHREN OF PENNSYLVANIA: I have only one complaint to make as to the tokens of welcome given me in your city; and it is that your Grand Master and your Past Grand Master have kept me so fully employed that I have had no time to prepare a finished oration to give in this land of finished orators. Therefore, what I say to-night—I will not say will be unpremeditated, because everything I shall say will be derived from my Masonic experience and based upon my Masonic beliefs—but it will not be quite so complete a product of speech as such a distinguished audience deserves.

I think the best way to begin is to answer the questions which instinctively will be put by every one of you: "Who are you?" "What are you?" "And what are your credentials?" As to who and what I am, I am a Mason of thirty-five years' standing, a Past Master of my Mother Lodge, at this moment Master of a great English Lodge of Research, and in the United Grand Lodge of England I have the distinction of being, as our Brother Beitler pointed out, President of the Board of General Purposes, which is equivalent to being chief of the administration of that Grand Lodge.

That is who and what I am. As for the credentials I bring, I come not only with the direct approval of the Grand Lodge of England, which has been expressed on more than one occasion, but I come with more. For the first time in the history of our organized English Freemasonry, I bring with me a direct recommendation—a letter of credit—from the Most Worshipful the Grand Master of the United Grand Lodge of England, His Royal Highness the Duke of Connaught, uncle of King George, and last surviving son of that illustrious and revered monarch, Queen Victoria.

The Duke of Connaught, in a private letter to myself, expressed the hope that my visit may be a successful one; and he wished me to bear a message from himself to the American brethren, and that message, therefore, I give in his own words. The message from the Grand Master of the United Grand Lodge of England to the Free Masons of all the jurisdictions of America is in these terms: "On the occasion of the visit of Brother Sir Alfred Robbins, Past Grand Warden and President of the Board of General Purposes, to the United States, I take the opportunity of conveying through him to the brethren of all jurisdictions in friendly association with the United Grand Lodge of England, my fraternal good wishes, and sincere desire for their continued happiness and prosperity. It is my earnest hope that the tenets of our order may assist still further to strengthen the bond of friendship and good will which so happily exists between our two nations; and I shall watch with sympathy every endeavor to promote these feelings by the development of Freemasonry in its purest and highest aspects."

That is the message to the Free Masons of America from the Grand Master of England. It is a message I bear with all my heart, because for many years, and long before I imagined I should ever have the opportunity for meeting my American brethren, both in lodge and throughout America, I have endeavored to voice my belief that, as Brother Beitler has put it to you, in the union of English-speaking Masons lies not merely the future of Freemasonry, but to a large extent the peace and welfare of the world. [Applause.]

Brethren, I was intensely interested to hear the historic account, which has just been read, of your Grand Lodge in Pennsylvania. A great deal stated in that paper I had already learned; but there were two letters included in the narrative which I had not previously seen, but which bear out a contention I have made in England and elsewhere, a contention that has never been challenged. The two letters read, one from your own Grand Lodge to the Grand Lodge of England and the reply thereto of the Grand Lodge of England in 1786, shows that the Grand Lodge of England never participated in any way in fomenting discord between these two countries. If the statesmen of England had been as prescient as the leaders of ancient Freemasonry, there would have been no need for the War of Independence. It would have sufficed that the American colonies, when they had risen from pupilage to manhood, should have been able to sever themselves quietly and amicably from the parent country, just as did your Grand Lodge from the parent Grand Lodge. That would have been because ancient Freemasonry—long before the phrase "No taxation without representation" became known as a well-accepted political maxim, long before you insisted, and rightly insisted, on a severance from the mother country—because the Grand Lodge of England had never asked a penny of taxation from these daughter Grand Lodges overseas for the support of the Masonic government at home. It is true that the Grand Lodge of England accepted from these Grand Lodges in America voluntary contributions towards funds wholly expended for benevolent purposes and in which all shared. But that was not taxation: it was a voluntary gift for charitable purposes, willingly given, thankfully received, and faithfully applied. If the Government of England had dealt in the same way with the American Colonies, there would not have come into existence those acts which brought about bloodshed. There would have been better feeling on both sides; and that which was the cause of war would not have been the cause of strife, but reason for amicable separation. In Freemasonry, we English Masons can look you

American brethren in the face, and say that, whatever may be chargeable to England with regard to the relations between the two countries one hundred and fifty years ago, it is not chargeable to Freemasonry, because at no point and in no way did Freemasonry accentuate the differences between the two countries.

Now, brethren, this is well-established, and it is right to put it before you when it is asked why we English Masons are trying to promote—I will not say a union, because that savors of treaties and alliances—why we are trying to promote a more friendly feeling, a better understanding, between English-speaking Free Masons by more full, free, and frequent intercourse among the leading brethren of the two countries.

Brother Beitler says that no Englishman—that is, no accredited representative of the Grand Lodge of England—has yet visited your Grand Lodge. But the English are a stay-at-home people, who do not wander as far afield as Americans so often do, for, as a rule, many more Americans every year visit Europe than Europeans come to America, except those who, escaping the pitfalls of Ellis Island, intend staying here for some period. But the Grand Lodge of England—and I was active on the committee associated with the occasion—five years ago when the war was over, determined to invite the Grand Masters and Grand Secretaries of every American jurisdiction to be present as the guests of the Grand Lodge of England in London for a week during the summer of 1919, to celebrate the coming of a peace which we then hoped would be a lasting and a real one. Twenty-nine of your leading brethren in America accepted that invitation, and were welcomed with all warmth, with all affection, in the greatest meeting of Freemasons it had ever been my privilege to address—a meeting of eighty-six hundred Masons in the Royal Albert Hall. We then, at least, showed that we liked to see American Masons.

I am not certain whether some of your brethren—especially those from cities not so near England as Philadelphia—whether they expected quite so warm a welcome from a people they had been told were cold-hearted. But, perhaps, I may say that, when about to visit Pennsylvania, I was warned that I would go among a cold-hearted and rather distant body of brethren, and that if I went West I would have a warmer reception. Brethren, as I have said to both your Grand Master and your Past Grand Master, if I have a much warmer reception when I go to the Middle West than I have had in Pennsylvania and other parts of the East, then of a certainty I shall be burned to a frazzle, and not return home alive.

I use that illustration because the reputation of the English as being cold and distant is like the similar reputation which Philadelphia and the State of Pennsylvania have acquired in a certain section of America. But the coldness and the distance are matters of imagination. It only means that the brethren of Pennsylvania, like the brethren of England, want to know something about the people they welcome before they are too enthusiastic in welcoming them.

Five years ago at our Grand Lodge invitation the American brethren came, they saw, they were conquered; we won the hearts of all of them; and, as a consequence, invitations were given to us to come and see America. I am the first to have the privilege of accepting that invitation. I shall not be the last, but I am the first to have been thus well received, and to hope to have deserved to be so well received. Others will follow: and if they follow, as they will, they will come to you from a Grand Lodge which is not only the parent Grand Lodge of the Freemasonry of the world, but is the strongest and most widely extended of all Grand Lodges. Under the jurisdiction of the Grand Lodge of England are thirty-nine hundred lodges in active daily work. Nine hundred of those lodges are within the boundary of London alone; over twenty-three hundred are in the provinces of England and Wales outside London; and there are some seven hundred beyond the seas. These lodges are scattered over every continent, including the continent of America—not, of course, the United States of America, because we strictly realize that the Americans have their full independence—but there are lodges even in North America which continue their allegiance to the Grand Lodge of England. The very fact of the existence of these lodges in the sparse and scattered territories of the world—in the deserts, in places where in order to attend their lodge, brethren have to ride two and three hundred miles through swamp and jungle, over mountains and plains—that very fact shows the attraction of Masonry to the men who believe in it; and these brethren come from their distant quarters once a month, after giving up four days every month, to attend their Masonic Lodges. The Masonic attraction of these lodges in distant places is a sign of civilization and of right. They inspire with self-confidence men who otherwise, dwelling as they do remote from other white men, living a silent and solitary life, would, if Freemasonry were not established in those places, break down under a nervous and a moral strain and become moral and nervous wrecks. They are sustained day by day by the knowledge that, almost every month, they will meet their fellow white men—of various countries it may be, but their fellow white men. In Masonry they find a comfort and a sustenance which buoy them up. Their self-respect is maintained; their character is strengthened; and Freemasonry, as a civilizing agent, sustains the white man in the midst of dangers to his heart and to his head as well as to his health, dangers which by Freemasonry are overcome as by no other institution in the world. Not even the strongest church has the same widespreading attraction for a white man in dark countries as has Freemasonry for the men who of necessity reside there.

Brethren, we are supporting an institution, an organization, which is world-spread in its influence—in its influence not only upon us at home but on those who are distant from our shores. The responsibility for that influence on us at home should be a very real one; and it will be real in proportion to the serious manner in which we regard our Masonic obligations. I do not wish an assembly of brethren to be dull at heart and tearful of eye. I believe that in our seriousness we can get a very great deal of cheerfulness and help. But what I feel is that, unless we take Masonry seriously; unless we rigidly regard the obligations we took at the altar of the lodge as we proceeded from degree to degree; unless we hold them close to our hearts and practice them in our daily life, our Freemasonry will gradually crumble and disappear.

In England, I am glad to say, we take our Masonry very seriously. We will not put in the minds of candidates anything which we consider might give cause to the enemy to blaspheme

—anything which might enable the world to scoff. What we say is, "We are a body of individuals joined together in great ideals for a common purpose, and that purpose the elevation of our fellow men." We believe in our fellow men, and we will try to raise them.

We hold that a Mason should not put off his Masonry with his Masonic apron—should not leave his Masonic principles with the Tyler at the door when he leaves the lodge. He should not put on his best clothes for Masonry, and, when he takes off those clothes, feel that Masonry is nothing. He should live Masonry in his daily life, in his home, in his relations with his fellow men. If he does that, he will show his fellow men that there is something real in Freemasonry, something which, after all my experience in the craft, I would not attempt to define, excepting so far as this: "I came into my lodge blindfolded. I was there admitted to light. The light came to me through a statement of certain principles with which, when I heard them, I agreed. The more I have studied them the more I have accepted them." Those principles, brethren, are founded on the eternal law, from which, if Freemasonry departs at any time, it will fall, and will deserve to fall, as nations have fallen when, because of prosperity, they have departed from righteousness. The history of the world is strewn with dead empires. The history of every country is marked by the passing of organizations which have lived, have grown, have died, because they had not soul enough to sustain them. In Freemasonry we possess that soul. For two hundred years Freemasonry, as an organized body, as an institution, has flourished. Is it to be believed that it has flourished from nothingness? If we were Freemasons simply in order to make new friends, or to push our business, or to do something which was agreeable at the moment, Freemasonry would only have had its fashionable time and then have gone its way. Freemasonry to-day is stronger than ever it was, and stronger, I believe, in this country—stronger, I know, in my own country—largely as a result of the war. The war taught us much. I am speaking for the young men whom the war taught the lesson of brotherhood, the need for brotherhood, such as they had not been taught before. It taught them that all men at heart were brothers. Many came back trying to find organizations which would allow them to preserve that feeling of fraternity they had learned while standing shoulder to shoulder in the trenches. Our Masonic Lodges in England to-day are increasingly full of younger men, all of whom will tell you that it is largely the result of their experience in the war. That experience brought them into a Craft which was carrying forward the principle of fraternity they had learned on the battlefield, where they had further learned that war was no solution of the world's difficulties.

It is easy for politicians to talk war; it is easy for journalists to teach war; it seems easy for clergymen to preach war. It is not easy for those men who day after day, and month after month, and year after year had to stand in danger of death and disability, far away from their home and friends, to talk or to think of war. These do not talk lightly of another war. I come from a country in which ninety-nine out of every hundred of our men to-day are passionately desirous of peace. When you hear about England wishing to stir up fresh strife, you have not heard the common people of England—you do not know the mothers of England. What we there do know is that, if we were threatened again to-day, as we were threatened ten years since, by any attempt upon our liberties, upon our rights, and upon our lives, every man who fought in that war on our side would be as ready to fight again as he was to fight then. But he would not fight unless he had a supreme cause for fighting; and it is the hope of these young men, it is the prayer of their mothers, that no such supreme cause will arise. And this is true not only of those who fought at the front. Does anyone imagine that we elders, who had to see our sons fighting because we were too old to fight ourselves; that we who lived in London through those terrible winters when we were under fire, when night after night we were under bombardment from the heavens, when houses were crashing around us, when our friends were being killed in the streets, when every night tens of thousands of our women and children had to take refuge in subterranean tunnels from dangers above— does anyone think we would lightly desire another war? We do not so desire; and it behooves every man among us who wishes for peace to ask himself "How can I best promote the cause?"

I believe, and believe firmly—I had the honor of saying this to your President in Washington last week—that in the union of thought and feeling between the English-speaking peoples, lies the future peace of the world. [Prolonged applause.]

And, when your President asked me—when he spoke at greater length and with more freedom to me than I am told he is accustomed to speak to the Washington politicians who occasionally call at the White House—when he inquired the mission I was engaged upon, and I told him very much in the words already stated to you—when I had told him, his reply was "Your object is a good one. Good will among nations in these times is much more a matter of peoples than of governments."

We can, by a union of hearts among Freemasons, do a very great deal in this direction. We can do it through the English-speaking nations—and, for the moment, I am not so anxious as some of the brethren seem to be to start off by getting the whole world together before they have harmonized their own differences among themselves. I want to get together the English-speaking brethren as a beginning to world peace—I want to get together the brethren who in all essentials are united.

The English-speaking brethren in the United States, in England, and throughout the British Empire alike have the same fundamentals of beliefs in Masonry. There are differences of practice among us: there are not differences in essentials. Our fundamentals are the same; and I pray they may ever remain the same. There is no problem of language, no difference of belief, between the English-speaking Masons. The same thought is animating all English-speaking Freemasons; they all agree in the great essentials of what Freemasonry stands for, in the great fundamental principles of the craft. By the free exchange of thought with each other, by more frequent intercourse between us, any difficulties that may arise can be overcome.

There have been differences of policy between our Grand Lodge and certain American Grand Lodges on the recognition of some foreign Grand Lodges, and particularly those of Latin countries. There are some American Grand Lodges which en-

MASONRY IN ENGLAND AND AMERICA 361

tertain the honest belief that it is possible to invent or improvise a formula by which the difference between the Freemasons who do believe in the existence and full recognition of the Great Architect of the Universe and those who do not can be bridged. My own Most Worshipful Grand Master and his advisers during the past few months have been giving very close attention to this question of the possibility of bridging the difficulties between the jurisdictions holding entirely different ideas as to this fundamental principle of Freemasonry. They have not discovered one single method which would not mean the forfeiture of the great position we hold, the undermining of the rock on which we stand. [Applause.]

I am not, in this statement, expressing a merely personal opinion. As I have indicated, this particular question has been very lately the subject of most serious consideration by the body of leading Freemasons of England whom the Grand Master honors with his confidence, and from whom he seeks advice; and I am charged, with the Grand Master's full assent, with this message to-night—that our position on this subject we will in no way compromise, we will not water down. We will not turn away from our belief that recognition of the Eternal is the absolute minimum we require of the candidate for initiation.

Right Worshipful Grand Master, I know there are certain American Masons who challenge even the fact that the Grand Lodge of England insists upon this recognition. A distinguished Mason in one of the southern jurisdictions has lately written a clever statement trying to show that, from the beginning of organized Freemasonry, our Grand Lodge has never insisted on the recognition of the Great Architect of the Universe as essential; and this acute reasoner has fastened upon a rather vague phrase in one of the Ancient Charges, and chosen it for his proof. Naturally, he is not as closely acquainted with the history of the Grand Lodge of England as are those of us who have worked with it for a long time, and have had to deal closely with it; and, on the point he raises, I want to put forward this as one evidence against his statement. We, as the United Grand Lodge of England, are directly descended from the original Grand Lodge of 1717. That had as its motto on its seal from the beginning the words, "In the Lord is our Trust"; and, therefore, any utterance of any particular brother stands as nothing to me against the fact that, from the very beginning, the original Grand Lodge of England proclaimed on all its documents "In the Lord is our Trust." And, when there was a rival Grand Lodge established forty years later—happily now joined in the United Grand Lodge of England—that Grand Lodge had its own rules and its own motto, and that motto was "Holiness to the Lord."

In the case of each Grand Lodge, therefore, its official documents, which went to everybody from the outset, declared to all Masons and to all non-Masons alike their belief, their absolute belief, in the Lord. And to-day, rather than purchase peace by any attempt at weakening that position, every leading man in English Freemasonry, and, I believe, ninety-nine per cent of the private lodges in England, would at once say, "We put aside a Freemasonry which is not that with which we came into the lodge. It is not that Masonry which we carried into our daily lives and hearts. It is something alien and foreign to us. And, not for the sake of peace or of increase of apparent power, will we compromise on that head."

Right Worshipful Grand Master, I ask you and the brethren to pardon me for the length at which I have spoken on this matter; but it is a matter which has been brought into controversy, and on which doubts have been expressed as to the position of the Grand Lodge of England. I, therefore, take this opportunity to say to so representative a gathering of American Freemasons that they can take my absolute assurance that the United Grand Lodge of England stands as firmly by the principle of the reverent and absolute recognition of the Eternal as it ever did, and that it was never less likely to depart from it. [Applause.]

I am asked sometimes, "Why cannot we agree to differ?"—a convenient phrase for a compromise that satisfies neither party to it. In this matter of difference, we believe, with all British Freemasons, in the principle going back to almost unknown ages, "In essentials, unity; in non-essentials, diversity; in all things, charity." We have charity towards all who disagree with us—there is no need for angry wrangling among those who are not acquiescent. On the essentials we stand firm. On non-essentials—such as the different practices I see in your lodge rooms—there is abundant room for difference of opinion, and for each to think his working the best. I am sure, indeed, that every American jurisdiction believes it has the best working in the United States, just as, when I go into lodges in England, I am assured that every lodge does better working than any other lodge near by. I do not wish, indeed, to see an absolute uniformity of crystallized working in Masonic life, as I think it would be apt to deaden part of the charm attaching to it. Stand by your own work; insist upon it being well done to the utmost of your power; but do not think that everybody is wrong who does not happen to see exactly as you do, as to how there should be controlled and how directed non-essential parts of the various ceremonies.

I, therefore, say to you that all I hope for, all I wish for, is not formal unity but fuller understanding. I do not want to see any kind of binding alliance between independent jurisdictions. I do not understand that there is a binding alliance even between the forty-nine jurisdictions of the United States of America. I am certain you will not get such an understanding among all the jurisdictions of the world; and, even if you did, the structure would become top-heavy, because the outskirts would not trust the center, having no direct voice, or vote, or influence upon that which those at the center were doing. I think it is well, therefore, to have these independent jurisdictions each doing its own work, each engaged in friendly rivalry to make itself the best governed. That is all for good. But it is equally well to have an interchange of visitations—a better knowledge of each other. By that means we can get what I am sure we all desire—a better understanding between ourselves.

In drawing these remarks to a close, I wish to express the intense gratitude I feel—and I feel it for my wife as well as for myself—at the warmth of the reception that has been given to us by the American Freemasons we have already met, a warmth never more splendidly shown than during our two days in Philadelphia. We have received every kindness, and the utmost good wishes have been shown us; and we shall carry away with us, not only from Philadelphia, but from the other great centers of American Masonry, imperishable memories of the kindness displayed on every hand. Why is this? It is because of that Masonic feeling which, inexpressible in words, is very real in fact. Believing as we do in the same grand principles, working as we do with the same inner feeling, encompassed as we are with the same Eternal hope, we go forward as a body conquering and to conquer. And I am sure that, by a better understanding between us, by a more close association of one country, of one jurisdiction, with another, we shall all realize an old ideal, and one which every Mason can attain. We shall all realize by closer companionship the great ideal of readiness to strive

> For the right that lacks assistance;
> 'Gainst the wrong that needs resistance;
> For the future in the distance;
> And the good that we can do.

[Prolonged applause, standing.]

ELIHU ROOT

SEVENTY-FIFTH ANNIVERSARY OF THE CENTURY CLUB

The Century, one of the oldest and most distinctive of American clubs, celebrated its seventy-fifth anniversary on April 22, 1922, with the Commemorative address by its president, Mr. Elihu Root. It may be interesting to compare this address with speeches included in these volumes made by William Cullen Bryant and George Bancroft on another celebration at the Century fifty-eight years earlier in 1864. Several other speeches by Mr. Root are given in Volumes III and XII.

It is seventy-five years since Gulian Verplanck, William Cullen Bryant, Henry W. Bellows, Daniel Huntington, Jonathan Sturges, Asher B. Durand, and a little group of their sympathetic friends, forty-two in all, joined in founding "The Century" for the purpose of promoting the advancement of art and literature.

They called their organization simply "The Century." Ten years later the Legislature granted them a corporate charter under the name "The Century Association." As the years passed, the demands of intimate fellowship developed the accessories and methods of a club, and the associations of friendship were preserved by the familiar scenes of a club home. For corporate purposes and by legal definition we are "The Century Association." We can probably be described best to the world at large as "The Century Club." But here, among its members, the institution is as it was in the beginning, simply "The Century"; and the meaning of the name is to be learned not from the dictionary, but only from the traditions and memories and living purpose evoked in the life of the institution by the never-ceasing stream of influence from a spiritual impulse sent forth by the great-hearted founders.

I do not think it was ever anybody's intention that The Century should perform its function of promoting the advancement of art and literature by becoming an institution for the education of others outside of its membership. It was an association to learn rather than to teach, to help each other in acquiring knowledge, appreciation, discriminating judgment, and true feeling in art and literature, through the interaction one upon the other of sympathetic and friendly natures. So the purpose of The Century has prevented it from becoming didactic or reforming towards the rest of the world, and has enabled the "authors, artists, and amateurs of letters and the fine arts," composing its constitutional membership, to live together in the unruffled harmony of modest friendship.

We are living in a different world from that in which The Century was founded. That was a quiet and leisurely world. The good Queen Victoria was in the early years of her long and serene reign. Gladstone and Disraeli were young members who had not yet found themselves, in the House of Commons. No one had yet heard of the British Empire. Louis Philippe sat on the throne of France. Germany was a multitude of petty independent states, apparently absorbed in the ponderous and trivial etiquette of opera bouffe courts. Bismarck was in that year making his first appearance in the Prussian Landtag.

Italy was a geographical expression for the region in which Austrian possessions and states of the Church and decadent principalities faintly continued ancient intrigue. The star of Cavour had not risen. Garibaldi was an unnoted exile in South America. In Austria Francis Joseph had not yet begun the long reign which was to end in such tragic disaster. In Russia a nation of serfs was chained to the soil under the iron hand of Nicholas I. The Turk ruled the Balkans. The first few treaty ports of China had just been opened for trade with the foreign devils. Japan was hermetically sealed and the Shoguns ruled within. Throughout the continent of Europe the fires of the coming revolution slumbered unnoted. Throughout South America the process of internal fermentation, which seems as necessary to the making of republics as it is to the making of beer, pursued its conventional and externally negligible course.

In the United States there was quiet, hardly disturbed by

the sideshow of the Mexican War. Webster and Ashburton had just settled the northeastern boundary. The Oregon Treaty had just been signed. California and the vast mountain regions to the east of it were Mexican territory. Individual enterprise was winning the west in family formation. Polk was leading the procession of mediocrity in Executive office. Procrastination was feebly endeavoring to avert the inevitable conflict over slavery by a succession of futile compromises. Whittier and Lowell were voices crying in the wilderness. The period of Irving and Cooper and Bryant was passing. The period of Emerson and Hawthorne and Longfellow and Holmes and Parkman was just beginning. In that very year the Brook Farm phalanx was dissolved.

Morse and Eliot and Huntington were tending the cradle of art in America. The Bessemer steel process had not yet been invented. There were but few short local railroads, not amounting to one-fiftieth part of our present railroad system, scattered throughout the country. Steam navigation was still in its feeble and experimental stage. It was less than three years since Morse had demonstrated the success of the first telegraph line in messages between Baltimore and Washington. Men were still practically in the age of the stage coach and the sailing vessel. Great corporations as we see them were unknown. Great labor organizations as we see them were unknown.

No one had realized the tremendous power of organization for peaceful enterprise. No one had realized the tremendous power of mechanical transportation and swift communication which are breaking down the physical barriers between peoples and making all the nations of the earth interdependent, and changing the community of nations from a convenient working theory of international relation to a necessity vital to national independence because vital to national life. There were no radio stations, no telephones, no telegraphs, no aëroplanes, no automobiles, no elevators, no skyscrapers, no stenographers, no typewriters. Life was lived at long hand. Farming was an occupation but not yet a business. The vast multiplication of human power to produce wealth was still in the future. The comparative poverty of mankind favored simplicity. The physical obstacles to speed of action assured opportunity and time for reflection and mature judgment. The tardy steps of news discouraged the spectacular and sensational.

The highly accelerated speed of life in these later days cannot fail to affect character. The multiplication of objectives in life, the multitude of material prizes for enterprise, the imperative need for alert perception, swift decision and sudden action, cannot fail to create new habits of thought and feeling.

How comes it that, after all, The Century is the same and the spirit of the founders of three-quarters of a century ago still remains among the associates who know them only by tradition? Good fellowship and friendship, a sane and gentle philosophy of life, sympathy in love of beauty in art and literature and character, have not been frightened away by the rude alarms and excursions of a turbulent world. I think it is because those benign spirits were seeking something of more worth than all the wealth and power of this wonderful age of material progress. They formed an association not for the purpose of doing something, but for the purpose of being something.

Many members of The Century have done fine things. Paintings and sculptures and noble buildings and books that will live and unselfish service to the community have come from them. But the test in The Century is not what it has done, but what it has become. Thousands of associations for profit and power and glory of their members, to instruct and educate others, to reform and regenerate the world, fill the air with a great noise. The Century has no such mission. Its objective is in the influence of its members on each other to care for sincerity in art and literature and in character, to achieve the liberal spirit, the habit of kindly judgment, to be unimpressed by the external displays of life, to care for our fellows because of what they are, not because of what they may achieve.

These things which make for the building of character and the growth of the spirit are what the founders of The Century sought, and from their day influence upon character has formed character, extending the influence to new generations, standards of judgment accepted have become habits of thought and feeling, memories have ripened into traditions and as the generations have passed, through the miracle of spiritual succession, the founders live and will continue to live though their names be forgotten. In that spirit The Century has kept itself simple. In an age of marble palaces and eastern magnificence it has kept itself inexpensive so that wealth should not by any means become a requisite for membership.

There is a motto: I don't know whence it came. I saw it years ago over a doorway in the office of an old-fashioned banking house in Holland. It runs like this: *"L'âge d'or est l'âge où l'or ne régnait pas."* The Century has lived in the spirit of that motto. Joseph de Maistre said: "One's country is an association upon the same soil, of the living and the dead, with all who are yet to be born." Such an alliance in The Century in a peculiarly personal sense between ourselves, the living, and all the Centurians of the past, and all who are yet to come, we celebrate upon this anniversary. As our memories drift back over the periods of our own membership in this Association, how full of feeling they must become.

We may be dimly conscious that back in the past were the founders whom we have never seen, but after Verplanck and Bryant and Bancroft we begin to remember faces and forms and we begin to fill the familiar spaces of the club with the memories of Huntington and Bigelow and Potter and Choate and Evarts and Carter and Beaman and Henry E. Howland and Loyall Farragut and Gilder and Richard Hunt and Lawrence Hutton and John La Farge and McKim and Stanford White and St. Gaudens and Frank Millet and Tom North and Stoddard and Weir and Weston. Each one of us can go on with the list according to his own special affections. What fine and noble fellows they were! How interesting and admirable! What wit, what humor, what spirit, what genius for friendship! What dear and lovable fellows they were. A blessed thing, is it not, to have the memory of them as a part of our lives! All the mines of Nevada could not buy such a thing. We are better and more human because of them. We are grateful in recognition. We are affectionate in memory. We have a feeling for the places where we knew them, and we cry "Long live The Century!"

BERTRAND RUSSELL

HOW TO BE FREE AND HAPPY

Bertrand Russell, mathematician and philosopher, has been most influential in molding the thought of his day. A member of one of the oldest and most distinguished families in England, he has never been bound by the traditions of caste and society. His visit to this country in 1924 added to his influence on American opinion through his lectures and addresses. The following lecture was delivered under the auspices of *Free Youth*, official organ of the Young People's Socialist League, at Cooper Union, New York City, on May 28, 1924.

LADIES AND GENTLEMEN: The subject upon which I am supposed to be talking to you to-night is a very modest and easy subject—"How to Be Free and Happy." I do not know whether I can give you a recipe, like a cook book recipe, which each one of you can apply. I do want, this last time that I am speaking in America, to say a few things which I believe firmly and consider, as far as my own experience goes, very important, and which I have not had much occasion, in previous talks, to say in this country.

Perhaps there may be some of you here, and certainly there are many elsewhere, who will say that the whole answer to my question "How to Be Free and Happy" is summed up in one simple sentence—"Get a good income!" [Laughter.] That is an answer which I think is generally accepted. If I put that forward I should have won the assent of every one that is not here. [Laughter.] However, I think that it is a mistake to imagine that money, that income, is a very much more important thing in producing happiness than it actually is. I have known in the course of my life a great many rich people, and I can hardly think of one of them who appears to be either

Reprinted with the permission of The Rand School of Social Sciences.

happy or free. I have known a great many people who were extremely poor—they also could hardly be happy and free. But in the intermediate realms you find most happiness and freedom. It is not great wealth or great poverty that brings most happiness.

My impression about it is this: that when you are talking of the external conditions of happiness—I am going to talk mostly of the conditions in your own mind, about the internal conditions—a person must have, of course, enough to eat and the necessaries of life and what is needed for the care of children. When you have those things you have as much as really contributes to happiness. Beyond that you only multiply cares and anxiety. So that I don't think enormous wealth is the solution. I should say, for the external conditions of happiness, that in this country, as far as the material problem of the production of goods is concerned, you have quite solved it. If the goods that are produced were distributed with any justice, that certainly would be a real contribution towards happiness. Your problem here is two-fold. It is first a political problem: to secure the advantages of your unrivaled production for a wider circle. On the other hand, it is the psychological problem of learning how to get the good out of these material conditions that have been created by our industrial age. That, I think, is where we modern people have failed most—on the psychological side, on the side of being able to enjoy the opportunities which we have created. I think that this is due to a number of causes.

I should attribute it partly to the effect of Puritanism in decay. Puritanism in its heyday was a conception of life which filled people's minds and made them in their way happy. Anything which fills people's minds makes them happy. But people nowadays don't believe in the Puritan way; they retain certain principles which are connected with Puritanism, though not perhaps quite obviously. They have, in the first place, a certain kind of moral outlook, that is, a tendency to be looking out for opportunities to find fault with others, a tendency to think that it is very important to keep up certain rules of conduct. There are a number of old, inherited taboos and rules which people don't think about but simply go on with because they always have been there. These do not touch the core of the matter. The thing that has survived most out of Puritanism is a contempt for happiness—not a contempt for pleasure, *a contempt for happiness!* You find among rebels a very great desire for pleasure but very small realization of happiness as against pleasure, and that has gone through our whole conception of pleasure and of happiness.

For ages the Puritan outlook was devoted to making people think that pleasure was a base thing, and because of that belief the people who were not base did not devote themselves to producing the better forms of pleasure, such forms as art, etc., and pleasure, therefore, became just as base as the Puritans said it was. And that evil has tended to survive. It tends to be still the case that the nations, such as yours and mine, which have gone through this Puritan phase are unable to get happiness and even to get pleasure—pleasure that is not trivial. It is only the less worthy forms of pleasure which survive in spite of that Puritan domination. I think that perhaps that is the main reason why Puritanism wherever it has existed, has proved itself so very destructive of art, because art, after all, is the pursuit of a certain kind, probably the most supreme and perfect kind, of pleasure; and if you think of pleasure as bad, art is bad. That is one thing we owe to Puritanism.

Another thing that we owe to it is the belief in work. In America I have spent most of my time in preaching idleness. I made up my mind when I was young that I would not be restrained from preaching a doctrine merely because I have not practised it. I have not been able to practice the doctrine of idleness, because the preaching of it takes up so much time. [Laughter.] I don't mean idleness in the literal sense, for most people, the great majority of us white people, don't enjoy sitting in the sun and doing nothing; we like to be busy. What I mean by idleness is simply work or activity which is not part of your regular professional job. Under the influence of this dogma, Puritanism has forced us to retain in our operative beliefs the notion that the important part of our life is work. That, at any rate, applies to the major portion of mankind: that the important part of what we do is getting on in our business, and getting a fortune which we can leave to our descendants, and they, in turn, get a larger fortune to leave to theirs. This whole business has taken the place of living for Heaven, for in the old Puritan days we tried to forego pleasures in this life in order to get to Heaven.

Heaven has disappeared, but the idea of living in order to leave a large fortune has not disappeared, and the kind of a life which is required for the one purpose is much the same that is required for the other—the foregoing of enjoyment for the sake of future benefits. That we have retained from the old Puritan outlook, and that, I think, is not in its modern form a very fine or noble thing. In the old days there was something splendid about it, but in this modern form it is not anything that we should particularly admire, and for the sake of it we do forego everything that would make life civilized, free and happy.

By the way, let me tell you what I have often noticed when I have been traveling on the continent of Europe, where there are beautiful objects of art. I have seen the middle-aged American business man being dragged about by his wife and daughter in a condition of almost intolerable boredom, because he was away from his office. It would be a better thing if, instead of getting concentrated upon work, people had larger interests. If we had a good social system we ought none of us to have to work more than four hours a day. [Applause.] Well, I am very glad to get that response from you, but when I made this remark to some other audiences in America a thrill of horror went through them and they said to me: "What on earth should we do with the other twenty hours?" I felt, after that, that this gospel very much needed preaching.

It is really a terrible thing to get the human being with all his capacities—to get him into blinkers with such a narrow outlook that he can only run along one little path. It is a disfigurement of the human being—it is something that every person who wants to see growth finds intolerable. A population of stunted human beings is growing up, shut out from the pleasures of human companionship, the pleasures of art, the pleasure from all the things that really make life worth living. Because, after all, to struggle all your days to amass a fortune is not really an end worthy of anyone.

I don't want to suggest to anyone that pleasure, mere pleasure, is an end in itself. I don't think it is, and, indeed, I think that the effect of the Puritan morality has been to emphasize pleasures at the expense of happiness, because, as base pleasures can be got more easily, they are less controlled by the censorship of official morals. We all know, of course, the sort of way in which the ordinary person who does not live up to the official morality of his time fails to do so: he seeks those ways which are most frivolous and have the least value in their own selves. That always will be the effect of a morality which is preached but not practiced.

I think the Chinese have shown their wisdom by having an official morality which can be practiced. We in the West who have adopted the opposite plan, we have prided ourselves upon the extraordinary magnificence of the morality we profess, and thought that excused us from practicing it. I think that if we are going to have a true morality, if we are going to have an outlook upon life which is going to make life richer and freer and happier, it must not be a repressive outlook, it must not be an outlook based upon any kind of restrictions or prohibitions; it must be an outlook based upon the things that we love rather than those that we hate. There are a number of emotions which guide our lives, and roughly you can divide them into those that are repressive and those that are expansive. Repressive emotions are cruelty, fear, jealousy; expansive emotions are such as hope, love of art, impulse of constructiveness, love, affection, intellectual curiosity, and kindliness; and they make more of life instead of less. I think that the essence of true morality consists in living by the expansive impulses and not by the repressive ones.

What I am saying has, I am afraid, very revolutionary consequences to which I cannot hope to win the assent of every one. There will be many who think that my deductions are not deductions to be accepted. For example, love and jealousy are—the one expansive and the other repressive. Now, in our traditional morality, when you subject it to psychological analysis and see whence it has sprung, you will all have to admit that jealousy has been the main-spring; it has been jealousy that has given rise to it. I don't myself feel that it

HOW TO BE FREE AND HAPPY

is very probable that a code rising in that way and from that source can be the best possible. It seems to me far more likely that one arising out of the positive emotions would be better than one arising out of the negative, and that such restrictions as would have to be placed on freedom should arise out of affection or kindliness for other persons, and not out of the sheer repressive emotion of jealousy. If you apply *that* principle it leads to a better development of character and more wholesome type of person, a person freed from many of the cruelties which limit the conventional moralist.

There is a very strong element of cruelty in traditional morals—part of the satisfaction which every moralist derives from his morality is that it gives him the justification for inflicting pain. We all know that the infliction of punishment is to a great many people delightful. There was once a prime minister who traveled from Constantinople to Antioch, and spent there eight hours watching his enemy being tortured. I think that the impulse towards pleasure in the suffering of others is one which arises through people thwarting their natural emotions, through the fact that they have not been able to find a free outlet for their creative impulses.

I do not positively *know* whether that is really the basis of a great deal of cruelty, but I cannot help thinking that an enormous mass of the cruelty that we see in the world is from unconscious envy. That is a very deep-seated feeling in human nature, and when you have a nice, convenient code to embody it, of course it is very popular.

I don't know whether I can quite convey to you the kind of way in which it seems to me that one can live most happily. I find things in the Gospels which illustrate the sort of thing I mean—not texts which are very often quoted, but, for example, "Take no thought what ye shall eat, or what ye shall drink, or wherewithal ye shall be clothed." If you really lived upon that principle—which, by the way, forbids all discussion of the Volstead Act—you would find life very delightful. There is a certain kind of liberation, a certain kind of care-free attitude, which, if you can once acquire it, makes you able to go through the world untroubled. The gist of the matter is to be rid of fear. Fear lies very deep in the heart of man; fear has been the source of most religions; fear has been the source of most moral codes; fear is our instincts; fear is encouraged in our youth, and fear is at the bottom of all that is bad in the world. When once you are rid of fear you have the freedom of the universe. Of course, you all know about the sort of dark superstitions of more barbarous ages, when men, women and children were sacrificed to the gods out of fear. This superstition we see to be dark and absurd, but our own superstitions do not strike us in the same light. Now, I am not prepared to say that no great disaster can ever overtake us, but I say this, that the fear of those things that might overtake us is a greater evil than the things themselves, and it would be far better to go through life not fearing, and come to some disaster, than go through life creeping, wise, and cautious, and burdened—never having enjoyed life at any moment and yet dying peacefully in your bed.

I think we want our lives to be expansive and creative, we want to live to a very great extent upon impulse; and when I say impulse I don't mean every transitory impulse of every passing moment—I mean those major impulses that really govern our lives. There are in some people great artistic impulses, in others scientific, and in others this or that form of affection or creativeness. And if you deny those impulses, provided that they do not infringe upon the liberty of another, you stunt your growth. I know, for instance, any number of men who are Socialists, and who spend their lives as journalists writing for the most conservative papers. These men may get pleasure out of life, but I don't believe that it is possible for them to get happiness. Happiness is at an end for any man who denies himself one of those fundamental impulses about which life ought to grow.

I should say precisely the same thing about the private affections. Where a really strong or powerful affection exists, the man or woman who goes against it suffers the same kind of damage—it is the same kind of inner destruction of something precious and valuable; all the poets have said so. We have accepted it when it was said in verse, because nobody takes verse seriously, but if it is said in prose and in public we think it is very dreadful.

HOW TO BE FREE AND HAPPY

I don't know why everybody is allowed to say a host of things in private that he is not allowed to say in public. I think it is about time we said the same things in public that we say in private. [Applause.] Walt Whitman, in praise of the animals, says: "They don't grunt and sweat over their condition—not one of them is respectable or unhappy throughout the whole world." I must say I have a very great affection for Walt Whitman. He illustrates what I mean—how the man who lives expansively lives in a kindly way; how he is free from cruelty, from the desire to stop other people from doing what they want.

I think it is very important to get that idea into one's head —that every artificial morality means the growth of cruelty. Of course, we cannot live like Walt Whitman's animals, because man has foresight and memory, and, having foresight, he has to organize his life into a unit. That is where we develop our superstitions. And you know quite well that it would not do if you followed each whim without a certain amount of discipline, and I don't want you to think that there is not a need of discipline. There is, but it should be that discipline that comes from within, from the realization of one's own needs, from the feeling of something which one wishes to achieve. Nothing of importance is ever achieved without discipline. I feel myself sometimes not wholly in sympathy with some modern educational theorists, because I think that they underestimate the part that discipline plays. But the discipline you have in your life should be one determined by your own desires and your own needs, not put upon you by society or authority.

Authority comes from the past and the old, and, speaking to a League of Free Youth, I suppose I need not speak, at my time of life, with that respect which I might be expected to show to it, because the old, although they are supposed to be wise, are not necessarily wise. We learn a great deal in youth and forget a great deal in age. We are at our maximum at thirty; at thirty we are at the moment when we learn at the same rate at which we forget. [Laughter.] After that we begin to forget faster than we learn; so if we do have to have authority I should have a council composed of persons of thirty, but on the whole I think we can do much better without authority in those matters which do not directly affect the rest of the world.

Of course, it is your affair if you murder someone, but it is his affair also; so you cannot object to someone coming to interfere with your murdering him. But in those acts which affect ourselves it is absurd that the State or public opinion should have any voice at all. In the private relations of life society should take no part whatsoever—that is a matter for the individual. The welfare of children is, of course, a matter in which the community is concerned. It is not at present enough concerned. About children: you want that there should be enough, but not too many; you want them to be healthy and educated. Those are the things that the State should see to. At present it sees to some and not to others. All those things are affairs for the State. But where children are not involved, it seems to me that all interference is an impertinence —the State has no business in the matter whatsoever. Now, I don't want to talk only about that issue, because there are many other directions in which the same kind of thing applies. It applies, above all, in the æsthetic side of life. We in our industrial civilization have taken over from Puritanism, from Christianity, a certain utilitarian outlook, a certain belief that our acts should not be for their own sakes, for what they are now, but for a certain distant end. Things get to be judged by their uses and not by their real values. That is death to the æsthetic side of life, for the beauty of anything consists in what the thing is in itself and not in its uses.

I admit the sphere of the utilitarian, but not in judging of artistic matters. I find that we seem to have lost not only in the world of art—that is generally admitted—but we have lost something also in human companionship, in friendship, through not having so great a sense of intrinsic quality as we used to have. A man tends to be judged by what he does, and that is quite a different thing from the intrinsic quality of him; and so you will find that when a man has become a celebrity, everybody knows that what he says is very wonderful, whereas in his youth, when he was not recognized as a celebrity, he may have said far more wonderful things without being noticed.

The excellence of a man's remarks, even if he is not famous, should be recognized, as well as vice versa.

In our private relations we all get so busy that we have not time to develop affections for others as they deserve to be developed; we have not time for sympathy, the understanding for all those things that make the beauty of human relations, because we all are so busy, and when we are not busy we are tired. [Laughter.] You have in this country, on the average, if the goods produced in this country were divided equally, much more than anybody needs for happiness, and it would be possible to live on a very much smaller amount of work and yet have enough; you could then develop and cultivate those things that make for happiness. You would have freedom. A man does not have freedom if he has to indulge all day in an activity which is not one he likes; that is as bad as a treadmill. We cannot always be doing delightful things, but we can for the greater part of the day; and I think that in the advanced industrial nations a better ideal of private happiness is probably the thing that is most wanted. More important even than political and economic reconstructions is the realization of the things that really make for human happiness.

We should not be so ready to go to war if our lives were happier. It is to my mind quite an amazing thing to see the extraordinary feebleness in the modern world of what you might call the will to live. There is a will to work, but not a will to live; you don't find that the prospect of wholesale destruction is considered intolerable. You don't find that people are willing to sacrifice money and power in order that they may be rid of the menace of war; they don't really want to be rid of it. A happy nation would not be willing to sacrifice life, health and happiness for the idle business of fighting, and possibly winning. [Applause.] This comes because our lives are too collective and too little individual. We, living as we do, forced by the mechanical mold of our civilization more and more to resemble each other, we, I say, more and more live by mass emotions and less and less by the individual, personal ones. In that way the individual gets sacrificed. A life where the individual is sacrificed is not one where the individual is going to have a strong love for life.

We imagine we want all sorts of things, such as power and wealth, which are not the sources of happiness. You will find the sources far more truly portrayed in the Gospel. I am speaking of just the sort of thing that I quoted a moment ago, about taking no thought for to-morrow. If you have a human being that you love, or a child, if you have any one thing that you really care for, life derives its meaning from that thing, and you can build up a whole world of people whose lives matter. But if you start with the nation—"Here am I; I am a member of a nation; I want my nation to be powerful"—then you are destroying the individual. You become oppressive, because whether your nation is powerful depends upon the regimentation of people and you set to work to regulate your neighbor.

It is the individual that is important. You will think that, perhaps, is an odd thing for a Socialist to say. I believe the material side of life has got to be given over to Socialistic organization, but I believe that because I think the material side of life is the least important. So long as you have not enough to keep your life tolerable, material things are all-important—in most European countries there is such dire poverty that material things are of the utmost importance. But we can now, with our capacity of technical production, totally abolish the problem of poverty, that lingers because we are perfect asses. [Laughter and applause.] And when you think of the world you will have when poverty is eliminated, you see that in such a world material things will not be the important ones. You will have to settle, in a Socialistic community, whether the community is to work an extra hour a day and have an extra motor-car for each member. In such a community as that the spiritual goods will be more important, will be worth more than the things that are got through the collective community. The collective community will give you your daily bread and your daily tasks. Your leisure you can devote, if you like, to other work, or football or movies, or whatnot.

I am sometimes asked: How can you insure that people will use their leisure well? I don't want to insure it. You are still in the realm of undue morality, of undue pressure of the community upon the individual, when you raise such a problem. As long as leisure is not used in any way to damage other people, it is a matter for the individual. Well, then, I say in the spiritual world we want individualism. It is in the material world that we want Socialism. We have Socialism now in the spiritual world and we have individualism now in the material world. [Laughter and applause.]

What you are to think, how you are to manage your emotions, are supposed to be matters for the State to settle; but whether you are to have enough to eat, that is not a matter of the State—there the sacred principle of liberty comes in. It has been put in exactly the wrong place. The thing that I am saying to you is really, after all, exactly what all great religious leaders have said, that the soul of man is the important thing. And that is the great thing to learn. The great thing is to feel in yourself that the soul, your own thoughts, your own understandings and sympathies, that is the thing that matters and that the external outward of your life is unimportant so long as you have enough to keep you going and to keep you alive. It is because we are so immersed in competitiveness that we do not understand this simple truth.

I have been talking rather lightly to you, but the thing that I mean is something immensely living and a real kind of liberation—being free in this world, free of the universe, so that things that happen to you no longer worry you, the things that occur no longer seem to matter. There is a kind of fire that can live in the soul of every man and woman, and when you have that you don't care any longer about the little things of which our lives are so full. You can live in that way—you can live freely and expansively. You will find that when you let those fears drop off you are closer to others, you can enjoy friendship in a different degree. The whole world is more interesting, more living—there is something there that is infinitely more valuable. Whoever has once tasted it knows that it is infinitely better than those things gotten by other methods. It is an old secret—it has been taught by all teachers and been forgotten by their priests; it is that secret of being in close contact with the world, of not having the walls of self so rigid that you cannot see what is beyond. The moralist is concerned to think "How virtuous I am," and he also is an egoist like the rest. It is not in that world of hard immorals that you will find the life that is happy and free. It is in the kind of life where you have lost fear because a little hurt is worth enduring—it comes from the knowledge of the fact that there is something better than the avoidance of hurt—there is the securing of a kind of intense union with the world, a kind of intense love, something glowing, warm, like a personal affection and yet universal. If you can achieve that you will know the secret of a happy life.

JOHN LANCASTER SPALDING

OPPORTUNITY

Address by Bishop J. L. Spalding, Roman Catholic Bishop of Peoria, Ill., since 1877 (born in Lebanon, Pa., 1849; died 1916), delivered at the opening of the Spalding Institute, Peoria, December 6, 1899.

How shall I live? How shall I make the most of my life and put it to the best use? How shall I become a man and do a man's work? This, and not politics or trade or war or pleasure, is the question. The primary consideration is not how one shall get a living, but how he shall live, for if he live rightly, whatever is needful he shall easily find. Life is opportunity, and therefore its whole circumstance may be made to serve the purpose of those who are bent on self-improvement, on making themselves capable of doing thorough work. Opportunity is a word which, like so many others that are excellent, we get from the Romans. It means near port, close to haven. It is a favorable occasion, time, or place for learning or saying or doing a thing. It is an invitation to seek safety and refreshment, an appeal to make escape from what is low and vulgar and to take refuge in high thoughts and worthy deeds, from which flows increase of strength and joy. It is omnipresent. What we call evils, as poverty, neglect, and suffering, are, if we are wise, opportunities for good. Death itself teaches life's value not less than its vanity. It is the background against which its worth and beauty stand forth in clear relief. Its dark form follows us like our shadow, to bid us win the prize while yet there is time; to teach that if we live in what is permanent, the destroyer cannot blight what we know and love; to urge us, with a power that belongs to nothing else, to lay the

Copyright, by A. C. McClurg. Published by permission.

stress of all our hoping and doing on the things that cannot pass away. "Poverty," says Ouida, "is the north wind that lashes men into Vikings." "Lowliness is young ambition's ladder." What is more pleasant than to read of strong-hearted youths, who, in the midst of want and hardships of many kinds, have clung to books, feeding, like bees to flowers? By the light of pine-logs, in dim-lit garrets, in the fields following the plough, in early dawns when others are asleep, they ply their blessed task, seeking nourishment for the mind, athirst for truth, yearning for full sight of the high worlds of which they have caught faint glimpses; happier now, lacking everything save faith and a great purpose, than in after years when success shall shower on them applause and gold.

"Where a man can live, he can also live well; but he may have to live in a palace," says Marcus Aurelius, implying that right life is most difficult in high places. Why, then, should we wish to dwell in a great city or to have great wealth or notoriety? These things are distractions and hindrances. They draw us from out the depths of the soul and thrust us into the midst of noise and confusion, of strife and envy, or they lead us into the pitfalls of sensuality, taking us away from ourselves to make us the sport of the mob of time-servers and idlers. To live for an hour alone with God gives us a more intimate sense of the value and sacredness of life than to dwell for years in the company of worldlings. O Highest and Best, Source of all, of all Father, Guide, and Nourisher, from out the midst of infinite mystery and suffering we look to Thee! On Thee our faith and hope and love, on Thee our need and despair still call. We cannot grasp Thy being or comprehend Thy ways. We can but know Thy truth, Thy goodness, and Thy beauty. It is enough: Thou art with us; in Thee we live. What Thou doest is eternally right; on Thee we throw the burden of our lives. Thou art, Thou hast ever been, Thou shalt be forever; Thou holdest us in Thy sight whether we live or whether we die.

The measure of the value of opportunity is its influence on religious and moral life. We are athirst for God, and finding Him not we harden to mere materialists, or sink into lethargy, or drown consciousness in the sloughs of sensuality. In the end, each one has but himself, and if God be not in that self, he is poor and wretched, though he possess a universe; for with a few spadefuls of earth on his head it will all be over, forever. The vanity, the nothingness of the individual, when his existence is thrown against the background of eternity and infinity, is appalling, but when it is lifted into the light and life of the Almighty Father, who is truth and love and righteousness, it acquires divine meaning and worth.

To throw away life is the greatest crime we can commit. It is our duty to live; therefore it is our duty to live in ever-increasing completeness of faith and love, of wisdom and power; for if we cease to grow, we begin to die. The body indeed is doomed to decay, but the soul was made to rise toward God throughout eternity. The only right opportunities, then, are those which help to make us god-like—strong, patient, active, fair, wise, benevolent, useful, and holy.

Genuine progress is spiritual. The man has higher value than the machine. Nietzsche holds that it would be right and admirable to sacrifice all men actually existing, if it were possible thereby to originate a stronger species. This, he says, would be real progress. But if there is no divine Being, no immortal life, this mightier superhuman, who would also have keener insight, would but see more clearly the misery and futility of existence. Let us rather listen to Matthew Arnold, when he declares that whatever progress may be made in science, art, and literary culture, however much higher, more general and more effective than at present the value for them may become, Christianity will be still there, as what these rest against and imply; as the indispensable background, the three-fourths of life. It is only when we walk in the spirit and follow in the footsteps of the Son of God, that we come to understand that life is opportunity, rich as earth, wide as heaven, deep as the soul.

We weary of everything,—of labor, of rest, of pleasure, of success, of the company of friends, and of our own, but not of the divine presence uttering itself in hope and love, in peace and joy. They who live with sensual thoughts and desires soon come to find them a burden and a blight; but the lowly-minded and the clean in heart, who are busy with whatsoever things are true and fair and good, feel themselves in a serene world where it is always delightful to be. When we understand that all is from God and for Him, and turn our wills wholly to Him, trouble, doubt, and anxiety die away, and the soul rests in the calm and repose that belong to whatever is eternal. He sees all and is not disturbed. Why should we be filled with apprehension because there are ripples in the little pond where our life-boat floats?

Since He has made us for everlasting bliss, He has made us to be happy now in the work that lies at our hand or in the sorrow and suffering we must bear. Whatever brings a high thought or a gentle or a generous mood is consecrated as though wafted to us from the wings of angels. Had we the power to gratify every wish and whim, human life would become impossible. God's love is as manifest when He hems us in as when He enlarges the bounds in which He permits us to move. We ask blindly for many things, when all that we need is that He guide us. "Thy will be done," is the sum of all true worship and right prayer. The rest is aside from the divine purpose, and could it be realized would make the world a chaos or a desert. We should not love the flowers if it were always spring; and our purest pleasures would pall did not pain and loss come to teach us their worth.

Life is action; but to be passive, awaiting the utterances of God, through whatever medium they may come, is often the highest wisdom. To souls that are calmly expectant, whisperings become audible, as in the silence of serene nights, which tell of diviner worlds, where it is eternally well with the gentle, the loving, and the pure of heart.

There is no worse perversion of Christian truth than to maintain that the Savior taught that to make one's self miserable here is the means of attaining future blessedness. They who follow Him walk in the way of peace and joy. They are unafraid. They dwell in a heavenly kingdom. The Omnipotent is their father, with them in death as in life. They need little, nor fear to lack that little. Suffering makes them wise and strong. They are able to be of help, for they think not of themselves. They do no evil, and therefore can suffer none. They despise not this present life, for they are conscious that even now they are with God and are immortal. Since universal love is the law of Christ's religion, they thrust forth whatever may foster the spirit of distrust and alienation. It is weakness and ignorance to imagine that to dislike those who have a creed or a country other than ours, is proof of piety and patriotism. The bitterness we cherish against others makes our own lives bitter; the wrong we do them we ourselves must suffer. We play the Pharisee when we think or believe as though we were superior to the rest of men.

The followers of the Divine Master best know that true men need not great opportunities. He himself met with no occasions which may not be offered to any one. His power and goodness are most manifest amidst the simplest and lowliest surroundings. To beggars, fishermen, and shepherds He speaks words which resound throughout the ages and still awaken in myriad hearts echoes from higher worlds. Whether He walks amid the cornfields, or sits by the well, or from a boat or a hillside speaks to the multitude; whether He confronts the elders who bring Him the guilty woman, or stands before Pilate, or hangs on the cross, He is equally noble, fair, and God-like. The lesson He teaches by word and deed is that we should not wait for opportunity, but that the secret of true life and best achievement lies in doing well the thing the heavenly Father gives us to do. He who throws himself resolutely and with perseverance into a course of worthy action will at last hear the discords of human existence die away into harmonies; for if the voice within whispers that all is well, it is fair weather, however the clouds may lower or the lightning play. What we habitually love and live by, will, in due season, bud, blossom, and bear fruit.

Whatever opportunity is favorable to genuine life, to its joy, purity, beauty, and power, is good; whatever occasion is hurtful to such life is evil. In each one's path through the world there are a thousand pitfalls, into any one of which he may step unawares. Let us take heed therefore and choose our way.

Let a man have a purpose, let him resolve and labor to make of himself a good mechanic, or merchant, or farmer, or lawyer, or doctor, or teacher, or priest; but first of all let him have the will and the courage to make of himself a true man, for else there shall be no worth in him. On the miser, the drunkard, the liar, the lecher, the thief, no blessings can fall. Our value is measured by that of the things we believe, know, love, and strenuously strive to accomplish. Make no plans, entertain no schemes. Think and do day by day the best thou art able to think and do. This is the open secret, which all might learn and which only a few know. But to them it reveals the way to the highest and the holiest.

Busy thyself not with what should be corrected or abolished; but give thyself wholly to learning, loving, and diffusing what is good and fair. The spirit of the creator is more joyful and more potent than that of the critic or reformer. Budding life pushes away the things that are dead; and if thou art a wellspring of vital force, thou shouldst not be a grave-digger. The test of a man's strength and worth is not so much what he accomplishes as what he overcomes. When circumstances favor, the lesser may do the greater work, as cowards who are armed conquer heroes who are weaponless. He who has made his own the spiritual wealth of all the ages, knows more and can do more than the mighty men of the past, who excelled him in natural endowment and in virtue. The wise therefore are not exalted in their own conceit by the advantages and opportunities they enjoy, but they are made humble rather when they remember the greater and worthier men who, lacking all save honest minds and true hearts, hewed their way through a thousand obstacles to freedom and light.

Few can utter words of wisdom, but opportunity to speak kind words is offered to every one; and they are more helpful. When we are thrown with persons who have feeble mental culture, but who are mild, simple, and true, we feel how little intellectual accomplishments contribute to form what is best in man. They who have the mother virtues are not injured by their ignorance of the objections which would discredit all virtue. The best is within the reach of all; therefore it is not to be found in great possessions or exalted position or abstruse thoughts. The reward of all right life is increase of the power of living rightly. The world can give to the hero or the saint nothing that is comparable to the growing strength and joy there is in being a hero or a saint. "To be spiritually minded is life and peace." Opportunity for many things may be lacking, but it is always possible to do what belongs to one's condition; and if it be only to wait and suffer, the right spirit will make this enough.

Whatever is inevitable or irremediable is, in so far, part of the divine purpose, and to accept it with a grave trustfulness is the only wisdom; but let us be slow to believe that a thing is inevitable or irremediable. Walk perseveringly in the light of a great purpose, and difficulties shall disappear, even as the horizon recedes before the advancing step. Have faith in thyself and in God, and thou shalt be borne upward and onward as by invisible wings fanning the ethereal element, where the soul breathes its proper atmosphere and knows nor doubt nor fear. If small things are given thee to do, do them as though they were great, since for thee their significance is infinite.

We are the slaves of our needs—the fewer they are, the freer are we; the higher they are, the nobler the masters we serve. Not independence, but interdependence, is the law of our life. It is only in ministering to one another, in bearing one another's burdens, in sharing one another's joys, that we become human and truly live. Let us draw closer together, that we may feel the pulsings of divine sympathy and love in one another's hearts. If we stand apart we shall be stranded in the great river, we shall miss the good of living, we shall lose God. Life is communion and helpfulness; death is disintegration and impotence. A spiritual empire, a heavenly kingdom can be constituted and sustained only by the moral and mental union and communion of its citizens, and this can be brought about and kept vital only by right education. When a noble faith and great thoughts strike root in the heart and mind of a people, it is held together by bonds which no catastrophe, no conquest, no dismemberment or dispersion can loosen; and without a noble faith and great thoughts neither military power nor vast territory nor wealth can give to a people a permanent place in history or a lasting influence on the progress of the race. All else passes and becomes as though it had not been, but what the world once recognizes and accepts as a vital truth, as an ideal of human perfection which cannot be outgrown, remains a possession forever to purify and enrich life.

Opportunity in the highest sense of the word is opportunity for education, for making ourselves men. This end every occasion should serve, since for this we are born. "We should, as far as it is possible," says Aristotle, "make ourselves immortal, and strive to live by that part of ourselves which is most excellent." Now, the testimony of the wise of all ages agrees that a virtuous life is the best and the happiest. Choose and follow it then though thou find it hard; for custom will make it easy and pleasant. Piety nourishes faith, hope, and love, and therefore sustains life. If thou seekest for what is new and also permanently interesting, live with the old truths, until they strike root in thy being and break into new light and power. The happenings of the day and year are but novelties, but bubbles that burst in the vacant air; that which is forever new is ancient as God. It is that whereby the soul lives. It was with the first man when first he blossomed forth from eternity; it is with thee now and shall be with all men until the end. It is the source whence thy being springs: its roots dip into infinity; its flowers make the universe glad and sweet; it is the power which awakens the soul to the consciousness of its kinship with Him who is All in All, who is Life and Truth and Love, who the more He is sought and loved doth seem to be more divine, and beautiful, and good. Learn to live with the thoughts which are symbols of His Eternal Being, and thou shalt come to feel that nothing else is so fresh or fair. As a sound may suggest light and color, a perfume recall forgotten worlds; as a view, disclosed by a turn in the road may carry us across years and oceans to scenes and friends long unvisited; as a bee weaving his winding path from flower to flower may bring back the laughter of children, the songs of birds, and the visionary clouds fallen asleep in the voluptuous sky of June; so the universe will come to utter for us the voice of the Creator, who is our Father. Nothing touches the soul but leaves its impress, and thus, little by little, we are fashioned into the image of all we have seen and heard, known and meditated; and if we learn to live with all that is fairest and purest and best, the love of it all will in the end become our very life.

EDWARD LEE THORNDIKE

EDUCATION FOR INITIATIVE AND ORIGINALITY

Address by the Professor of Educational Psychology, Teachers College, New York, November 12, 1916. Professor Thorndike, born 1874, is one of our leading psychologists and well known upon the lecture platform.

It is my office to report what recent psychology can suggest concerning training for self-reliance or independence; initiative and originality—"all from the standpoint of education in a democratic state and for the sake of efficient democratic citizenship."

Unfortunately a standard report, voicing settled doctrines of science, cannot be made. We are not agreed even concerning how far self-reliance, initiative and originality can be trained or concerning the elementary qualities which constitute them, and their mode of operation. I can therefore only report probabilities as I see them.

We may best begin with some negatives. Self-reliance, initiative and originality are not little deities of the mind which act according to caprice. They are as truly determined by natural law as the fall of a stone or the rise of the tides.

They are not intelligent slaves which hasten to act when bidden. No child becomes independent merely by being told to think for himself, or original merely by being ordered not to be a copy-cat. If every one of the half-million teachers of our country should to-morrow, and every day thereafter for a decade, order, "Be more independent, self-reliant and original

Reprinted from *Teachers College Record*, Vol. XVII, No. 5 (November, 1916). Copyrighted. This is the fifth of a series of addresses given before the staff of Teachers College.

than you have been," these billions of commands would, in and of themselves, do nothing to attain their object. Other factors than the mere commands would decide whether an increase or a decrease in these virtues would result.

Nor will indiscriminate practice make them perfect. Self-reliance, initiative and originality (which we may call the active virtues of citizenship in contrast to obedience, docility, and conformity) are specialized in their development. Self-reliance in handicraft need not imply self-reliance in thought about politics or religion. Originality in mathematics or salesmanship is consistent with the most complete conformity to social customs. Extreme expectations of all-round improvement—formal discipline—in these active virtues are as fallacious as they are elsewhere. A boy will not be made independent in general by being led to choose his own method of solving each of a thousand problems in arithmetic, any more than he will be made a good observer in general by recording the cloudiness of the sky daily for a year. Some transfer there is, but not enough to excuse the absence of special training in the special fields where the virtue is required by life to act.

Further, these virtues, in the shape in which the community or nation requires them, could not be general, ubiquitous, unfailing tendencies. The nation does not wish its citizens to rely each on himself when to rely on a physician or public-health officer or financial expert or chemist is wiser. It is folly for more than a dozen men out of a million to try to think of anything original about Newton's laws or the Napierian system of logarithms. To cultivate a general, diffuse initiative would be to become a busybody. For a man whose every thought was original we should have to go to our hospitals for the insane!

We have to cultivate these active virtues in such special lines as are important "for the sake of efficient democratic citizenship," and to guard them against misuse. We cannot simply demand them, nor give them indiscriminate exercise.

As I see it, the first and most important step toward so cultivating them is to treat them consistently as positive factors, —to think of independence, not as unreadiness to follow or obey or believe other men, but as a readiness and ability to contribute to good causes something more than is suggested by others,—to think of initiative, not as an unreadiness to wait or coöperate or be modest, but as a readiness and ability to move ahead, "speed up," lead and take promising risks, and as an attitude of expecting to create opportunities, take risks, and do ten dollars' worth of work for a dollar. Originality must not mean weakness in doing routine work in old ways, or any essential dislike of traditional knowledge or customs as such, or any paucity of fixed habits,—but strength in doing work that is new or doing it in new ways, an attitude of hoping to change knowledge or practice for the better, an organization of habits that causes their progressive modification.

This matter seems to me so important that I venture to illustrate it in the case of originality.

Once in so often some student who wishes to do work for the Doctor's degree in education writes about his ideas and adds that he knows they are original, because he has avoided reading anything on the topic! We never encourage such men to come to Teachers College.

It is my lot to read many manuscripts on psychology and education. The commonest mistake which they reveal is the painful elaboration by a man, through long years, of some intellectual result which he should have acquired in ten hours in the course of the routine work of keeping up with what has been done in his field.

It is my privilege to know a fair number of original thinkers and workers in science, medicine, the ministry, law, and business. Such men are extraordinarily competent in routine work and extraordinarily strong in mere knowledge. The most original children of my acquaintance are so not by any denial of the claims of mere lesson-learning and skill-acquiring in traditional ways. On the contrary, they could beat the pedants and hacks of equal age at their own games. Occasionally they, and like minds of older age, become justly skeptical of the past, and impatient of methods adapted to dull minds, but they never have the hopeless skepticism of the fool who does not care enough about the past even to learn its contributions.

During the past month I have been studying the ratings of sixty electrical engineers employed by the Westinghouse Company and rated by the company's officers for originality and seventeen other qualities, such as thoroughness, knowledge, industry at routine tasks, and the like. Far from there being any antagonism between originality and industry at routine tasks, or between originality and common sense, or between originality and system, there is a positive correlation, and one as close as that between industry and enthusiasm or that between thoroughness and system.

The truly independent thinker does not make less use of other men's ideas than the servile thinker, but more. The expert man of science or law or business has a thousand masters while the servile mind has but a few. The truly independent thinker does not put less faith in his masters than the servile mind. He puts more faith in them, but he chooses the right ones to put his faith in. The servile mind has faiths that seem strong only because he never questions them. His faith in Jones' liver pills or the divine right of kings is really at the mercy of any new quack or Napoleon. In fact, a good definition of intellectual independence is *"reasoned dependence."*

The truly initiating mind does not imitate less, but more. It imitates more men, in more fields, in a greater variety of conditions. But here again it is reasoned imitation; and out of multifarious reasoned imitatings comes, to him who has the capacity, the insight to discern, and the zeal to take, the profitable risk, the hopeful leap in the dark, the courageous step upward where no foothold may be found.

Nothing, then, need be lost for American independence, initiative and originality by greater emphasis on obedience to the right masters, imitation of the right models, and learning of the right facts in our schools. If it is necessary for our future as a nation that our present *laissez faire* and individualism give way to deliberate learning to do the nation's work, obey the nation's creed and live as the nation decrees, there need not be any loss in the useful self-reliance, enterprise and inventiveness of our people.

Only two conditions must be fulfilled. First, the masters,

models, facts, creeds and ideals must be right, in the sense of being impartially chosen in the light of pure reason as the best for the nation's welfare. Second, each man and woman, boy and girl, must be taught, so far as he can learn it, that he, as well as the highest of his rulers, is free to do what he can to change ideas, customs, masters, models, creeds and ideals—*for the better,* and that not the highest of the highest is free to change them otherwise.

Let us turn this somewhat abstract analysis into terms of practice. I dare to affirm that if we had a national system of education, with all private schools rigidly supervised by the state, and if the educational obligations were fixed by central authority for every future citizen, there need not be one iota less of worthy independence, initiative and originality in our population, if this central despotism was constituted by enlightened reason acting for the nation's good. Permit me to add that I do not believe in such a central organization within ten or perhaps a hundred years. If I had believed in it, Professor Dewey's address in this series would have converted me. Still less, however, do I believe that such a form of organization would necessarily weaken the active virtues which are our topic, or that if it did weaken them, it would do so by its success in inculcating obedience, fidelity, accuracy, knowledge and skill. Effective independence, initiative and originality are not the negations of dependence, imitation, and fixed habits, but are their continued organization upon a new and higher level.

Assuming that it is folly merely to demand, and wasteful to give indiscriminate, miscellaneous practice, and that we do not need to rob useful obedience, imitativeness or conformity to pay independence, initiative and originality, and would probably make no gain for the latter if we did so, what shall be done to cultivate these active virtues?

The general answer is, "Provide those situations which by the nature of *homo sapiens* call the active virtues into play; and make their exercise satisfying to the individual. Induce these tendencies to act; and reward their action." In schools, the prolongation of school life, the provision of work with things as well as with words, the use of humane and significant projects, and the encouragement of specialization have been valuable factors in replacing submissive and passive by energetic and active thinking. For they have given boys and girls more chances to be mentally independent and aggressive in useful ways. The introduction of the physical sciences and the learning of history, literature and languages in something more or less approximating the scientific spirit, have been valuable. For one article of the creed of the man of science has been to reward intellectual enterprise.

The recent movements to dignify manual and executive work in the schools, providing for the boys and girls who can manage things and men whether they can or cannot manage ideas, seem likely to be very valuable by giving a chance for useful exercise of the active virtues by pupils whose only wise act of initiative with respect to abstract linguistic and mathematical pursuits would be to drop them! Also teachers are more likely to discern and reward useful enterprise in making things or running errands than in methods of study in the abstract fields.

Still more important, probably, is the indirect rewarding of these virtues in the young by rewarding them in the world at large. We are just beginning to learn to honor our prophets or initiating classes instead of stoning them, and to pay for originality at least a small fraction of what we pay for conformity. To learn it fully and practice it will mean an enormous addition to the useful initiative and originality of our country. So long as we pay a physician $50,000 a year for following the old routine and pay nothing to the man of equal general ability for discovering a far better treatment, can we expect our medical students to try to be usefully original? The Nobel prizes since their inception have received less public attention (as measured by newspaper space) than a single prizefight. The public still pays more money to be fooled by quack advertisements and poisoned by quack drugs than it pays for the bureau of commerce and labor, schools of commerce, and all our public health service,—probably five times as much.

I recently asked one of our most successful story-writers why he chose that career. He replied, "On thinking it over

I decided that there were two things that human beings had enjoyed most since the world began—eating and drinking, and listening to lies. Having absolutely no talents as a restaurant keeper, I had my try at telling them lies." If we would only reduce the alcohol in our physical, and the lies in our intellectual, dietaries, and spend the savings in rewarding the men who use initiative and originality for the common good! To give able men and women a chance to be enterprising and reward their useful enterprises is the surest way to cultivate the active virtues.

So in schools also we have only to give boys and girls chances to be self-reliant and inventive where it is useful for them to be so and to reward their successful efforts.

The response a pupil makes to any situation is caused in large measure by his attitude or mind-set. The same intellect may absorb, or absorb and criticize, or absorb, criticize and seek to amend, a doctrine, according as it happens to be born in the fourteenth, eighteenth or twentieth century, or to attend a theological school, law school, or research institution to-day. The mere attitude of expecting to do more than one is required to do, to see more than one is shown, to try more experiments than one has seen tried, in and of itself increases the independence and aggressiveness of one's action and thought in the situation or field in question. The school teaches pupils to be self-reliant and inventive by teaching them to take independent and aggressive attitudes when and where they should.

If these principles are sound, the technique of teaching these active virtues has to reckon with two main problems. First, for any given pupil at any given stage, what shall he accept more or less blindly and what shall he prove to himself? When shall he follow and when shall he go ahead by himself? Where shall he be ruled by outside pressure and where by reasoned conviction? Second, how may he be led by the laws of his own nature, to think and act wisely for himself in those cases where he should do so? There is here obviously room for infinite ingenuity, experiment and improvement. Present practice is chaotic but hopefully open-minded and experimental.

My comments also will be chaotic, in the form of a few questions and suggestions, first about the selection of occasions for active rather than passive behavior.

Is not our present selection of occasions for the exercise of the active virtues rather indiscriminate, at times leading to improper vainglory and at times to unnecessary discouragement or sluggishness? Probably many of you have been amused in kindergartens at hearing the five-year-olds urged to independent judgment on matters of difficult fact and taste; and then later seeing them make no attempt to put on their own coats and rubbers. The high school pupil is expected to solve difficult originals in geometry, but not to keep any account of how he studies or of which methods of study serve him best.

Do we not permit or even encourage young and old to decide for themselves in many cases where they should decide whom to ask to decide for them, or should contribute facts and reasons to aid the expert in his decision, or should learn the expert's general decision and modify it to suit their special needs? On the other hand are they not often left to follow conventional customs or blind faiths where a rational decision is really well within their powers?

We have seen that, in our day and manner of life, independence consists in choosing whom to follow rather than in following one's own devices. Is not special training in judging the qualities of leaders worthy of a place in democratic education? By our theory we must not teach future citizens to follow hereditary kings or lords, or a military or priestly caste, or a landlord clan. But human beings will follow and should. Who should be followed in a democracy? I see no answer but "the impartial expert." Men and women who best know the facts in a given field and who judge the facts most impersonally seem the safest to trust. If a dozen able boys were set to studying business from sixteen to twenty-five in the same spirit and by the same methods now used in studying science and engineering, being taught to think of personal profit no more and no less than the scientist is taught to think of it, I would rather trust them to control railroads, insurance companies, and the like than trust any state legislature in our land. In a nation of a hundred million people ninety-nine per cent of the power must be given to one per cent of the people. Cannot boys and girls of the high school age be taught that the essentials for leadership are expertness and impartiality? At least, they can be taught that glorious apparel, self-esteem, prodigality, physical prowess, the "glad hand" and a silver tongue, before which man's original nature bows, are not symptoms of fitness to lead in the twentieth century. They can also be cured of the unfortunate pretense that one person is as good as another in politics, personal and public hygiene, or business management.

Do we allow sufficiently for individual differences, setting tasks for the active virtues within the individual's powers?

The fact that only a small fraction of a school class usually succeeds with tasks demanding initiative and self-direction seems to me to bear witness to their too great difficulty. Indeed, it seems to be tacitly assumed by many of those interested in encouraging self-reliance and aggressive thought, that not more than a quarter of the pupil's own shots will be hits. The common assumption is that in the active virtues it is the attempt rather than its success that counts. Is it not often considered entirely permissible for three out of four children in the class to make preposterous suggestions so long as the answer comes from somewhere in the class rather than from the teacher? Yet there is no rational justification for teaching pupils to fail in original thinking any more than in routine. It is true that a pupil may well make a hundred failures as means to eventual success, if the failures are instructive, but our toleration of failure *outright* seems a sign of improper selection of the tasks.

Do we sufficiently realize that provision by routine for all matters which do not actually demand thought may be made one of the greatest aids to self-reliance, independence and originality in those matters which do demand thought?

It would obviously be idiotic for the man who has to decide important questions of scientific truth, or legal evidence, or business policy to decide on each occasion what he shall eat, what clothes he shall wear, or whether he shall walk or ride. Ten minutes a month should establish the necessary routines.

So in school also a certain economy of initiative is desirable. A boy's originality as a writer is not checked by being given once for all a routine for the size of margin, place of heading, and the like. As we noted earlier, the dynamic opposite of originality is not efficiency in routine, but stupidity; the dynamic opposite of efficient routine is not genius, but disorder.

Finally, will it not clear the whole argument somewhat if, in our thinking about education, we replace the word "self-reliance" by *reliance on facts*, "self-direction" by *rational direction*, "initiative" by *readiness and ability to begin to think and experiment*, "independence" by *readiness to carry thought or experiment on to its just conclusions despite traditions and customs and lack of company;* and if we add to the company of these active virtues an impersonal, objective habit that scorns hopes and fears and neglects self-interest, cherishing only the naked facts of life and the zeal to control them for the common good?

Are not the active virtues of citizens in a democratic state in sum and substance the ability and readiness to think and act *impersonally,* each as nature has given him capacity, in the field where his thought and action will do the most good?

If the state is itself rational—a sincere effort to work out the best possible harmony of the conflicting wants of its members—it can command obedience, and prescribe useful habits for its citizens in school and out, with, so far as can be seen, a net increase in the power of independent thought and action. For it is the magic of reason—of impersonal thought—as of nothing else in the world, to be an essential necessary harmony. Fixed habits, chosen by reason, promote it. Obedience to laws devised by reason is a training in reasonableness, not slavery. Whatever wounds reason inflicts, reason itself can heal.

The life of reason will prevail in the nation (within the limits set by human capacity), just as fast and as far as we really wish it to prevail.

In the long run a nation, unless subject to severe external compulsion, does get as good government as it deserves, as good education as it really wishes, and as good thinking and action as it will tolerate. Nobody forces the United States to pay a million dollars a year to Miss Mary Pickford and

Mr. Charlie Chaplin. We do it because we wish to. We could have paid a million a year to Joseph Henry, the prime mover in modern electrical inventions and to Louis Pasteur, the beginner of preventive medicine, if we had chosen. It is our own fault if John L. Sullivan, the prize fighter of Boston, had a fame far outreaching Horace Mann's. Within the limits set by the capacity of the human species, we can have just as efficient citizenship in this democracy as we really crave.

It seems probable that in the decade to come the leaders of American education will strive deliberately to adapt school work more fully to the job of making our national government safe against attack from without. The clamor for military drill in schools, for example, measures a popular feeling which educational leaders should use to secure support for really valuable training in both active and passive national virtues.

Here, it seems to me, is a wonderful opportunity for you to use whatever independence, initiative, and originality you have. Is the nation with the strongest army and navy least likely to go to war? Have the successes of Germany in the present war been due to junkerdom and the slavery of military conscription or to the social and industrial reforms which have made the German workmen happy and competent? Are all wars really about money due to the childish notion that it is profitable for one nation to make money at the expense of another? Is it true that the rank and file of a nation always suffer from a war, but on the average are as well off from losing as from winning? What does each nation, as a nation, really want? If some omniscient trustee for all the nations of the world could list the actual cravings of all his wards, what would they be and which of them would conflict, and what would be the effect of this, that and the other possible war upon their realization? Do we as a nation really want to exclude a man from citizenship because he is of Japanese birth, or to trade with any nation to its disadvantage, or to drive a sharp bargain in a treaty, or to stand in the world's limelight as a boss of the world's affairs? What do we really want? What ought we to want? Just what are the dangers to our country from without? What are the dangers from weakness, conflict and corruption within?

26

Would it not be worth while for us to find out the answers to these and similar questions as a means to planning our campaign to use the schools to preserve the nation and to make the nation worth preserving? Should we not keep on going to school to the economists, historians and men of affairs, as we have been doing in these conferences, and by absorbing, imitating and following, organize our minds to creative work toward a sound national educational policy?

As a profession, we have in the past been content to leave questions of concrete national ideals in action to publicists, contenting ourselves with generalities of philosophy and ethics or detailed issues of school management and teaching. Most of you probably still believe that a board of representative men,—lawyers, business men, manufacturers, and the like,—should determine educational policy.

Whichever *should* be the case, I am convinced that just as soon as we develop men who are justly recognized as educational experts, policies as well as their execution will be left largely to them. The world is learning rapidly that when a man of ability has studied a topic scientifically and makes his judgments about that topic in the impartial, impersonal fashion of the expert, it is wise to put on him every responsibility in that limited field that he will take. Control by public opinion and legislation is giving way to control by expert administrative boards at an increasing rate. If any five of our graduates were in the minds of the country as qualified in education as, say, Doctors Welch and Flexner are in medicine, I believe they could become a national commission with power to regulate schools within ten years. It might not be for the nation's advantage that they should thus become educational dictators, responsible only to their consciences and professional ideals, but it certainly will be for the nation's advantage when five hundred men and women are qualified as experts for such work. What greater stimulus to learning and industry, initiative and originality could there be than the work of finding and training them? Teachers College must do its part in discovering and developing "educational leadership that shall concern itself not merely with the mechanics of school-keeping, but also shall rise to the heights of patriotic statesmanship."

THEODORE NEWTON VAIL

LIFE ON THE FARM

Theodore Newton Vail was born in Carroll County, Ohio, in 1845. He entered the telephone business in 1878 and was President of the American Telegraph and Telephone Co., the Western Union Telegraph Co. and the New York Telephone Co. after 1907. He died in 1920. In addition to his interests in many corporations and in public affairs, Mr. Vail always had a special interest for his Vermont farm. He often spoke at the commencement exercises of the Lyndon Agricultural School and was very much alive to the interests of the New England farmers. The present address was given at the Commencement Exercises of the Graduating Classes of Lyndon Institute and Lyndon School of Agriculture, Lyndon Center, Vermont, June, 1914.

You are now about to take up the great problems of life under your own guidance and direction, and upon your own responsibility. Heretofore you have had guidance, direction, and assistance, but no real responsibility, and while you have increased learning you have acquired no real experience or absolute knowledge.

It will be your own actions, and the experience and knowledge gained from them, that will mold you and make for you, your place as active, responsible members of society. Experience, your greatest teacher, will be a costly one unless you act with caution and forethought.

Every act, small or great, will have some influence on your future; it will have its part in the formation of your character; be careful, therefore, that each act is a rightful act, and one that will be part in the formation, for you, of a good and worthy character and reputation.

A permanent or desirable reputation is slow in coming, but once gained, while it may be temporarily obscured by misunderstanding, or misconstruction, or mistaken knowledge of your acts, no thoroughly good reputation, based on character, and on actions which have been guided by correct principles can ever be permanently destroyed except by yourself.

As you go through life you will need the assistance, credit and the confidence of your fellow men. Credit and confidence are based on reputation, and on the cumulative influence of your acts far more than they are upon any other asset you may have. Credit, confidence, and intelligent productive labor, together with coöperation, create prosperity, both of the individual and of the community.

You will also be called on to assist others. Never ask another to do for you anything that you are not ready to do for him under similar circumstances.

In your daily life and intercourse with others always have proper regard for courtesy, orderly appearance and the conventional laws of society. Conventions are the unwritten laws of society, the result of untold ages of experience and are laws of personal action for the comfort and convenience of the individual both as an individual and as a member of society.

Disregard of conventions, lack of courtesy, disorderly appearance, disagreeable bearing towards others and breach of good manners may attract attention, and when backed by extraordinary ability get you a notoriety and a questionable reputation, but can never afford you real satisfaction.

Personal appearance and bearing are good letters of introduction: they will get you a hearing, or opportunity, which you otherwise could not get.

Among the very few things which are the very "fundamentals" of success and happiness, perhaps the first is contentment and a determination not only to do your best, but to make the best of everything.

Not that thriftless, shiftless, senseless contentment that is satisfied with anything; but that healthy contentment that only comes after a consciousness that you have brought into action your best ability and applied your best efforts. Morbid discontent is the source of nine-tenths of the unhappiness of this world. In almost any condition or in almost any possession there can be found some good.

It is hard to determine or say where content or satisfaction might dull or lessen effort or ambition; that, each man must settle for himself, but be careful to settle it honestly and not to make it an excuse for inactivity or abandonment of effort.

Acquire the habits of preparation, concentration and application. Whatever you want or have to do, prepare a definite idea of what is to be accomplished, concentrate upon it, and then apply yourself to the doing of it, and do it thoroughly. In this way you will make yourself master of yourself, of your time and work, and will have opened your life to, and have time for, the proper enjoyment of the results of your efforts, as well as to the acceptance of greater opportunities. Dawdling, which is lack of application and concentration, is very ineffective. It consumes your time, accomplishes nothing, and is in every way unsatisfactory to either yourself or your employers.

Try to do whatever you undertake a little better than you have ever done it before and a little better than any one else does it. While you cannot always succeed, the effort brings its reward through its influence on your character and the satisfaction afforded you.

No matter what you may undertake, forethought and organization will help you to accomplish it better; this applies as well to your own efforts and your own labor as it does to the management and organization of the labor and efforts of thousands.

Ordinary results come from ordinary methods; the great results of the world are the results of that organization and efficiency which produce more with less effort and work than can be produced by ordinary methods.

It is the elimination and utilization of waste, waste effort, waste time and material, the minimizing of destruction and damage, wear and tear, that produce the great results in the industrial world. There is no magic in these accomplishments. The leaders in action or thought are not magicians but steady, persistent workers.

Take two lumbermen. One goes into the woods in advance, looks over the ground, lays out his plan of operation, starts his men in with definite instructions. His operating force is properly balanced so that all are equally employed. Each man knows just what to do; there is no chance or excuse for standing around discussing how and what to do or any waiting for instructions. He sees that everything is properly cared for and kept in good order and repair, and when the season's work is over, properly stored and sheltered for another season; his force is worked no harder, if as hard, and is much better cared for than those not so organized; there is a minimum of waste.

The other neglects all or part of these things. His possible profits are wasted.

The normal prices of all products are based on cost of efficient production plus a profit. The man who does not produce efficiently cuts into his profits; they have been dissipated, wasted without benefiting any one.

Whichever activity in life you undertake, do not take anything beyond your limitations, natural or acquired, and before undertaking be sure that you have a fair understanding of what you are about to undertake. Do not have over-confidence. Have just enough lack of confidence to recognize that there may be some things you do not know and that you could not accomplish and thus avoid recklessness and failure, but do not lack confidence sufficiently to kill initiative and enterprise.

Recognize and have proper deference and subservience to age, position and larger experience.

Whether it be raising chickens, farming on a large or small scale, or running a manufacturing establishment or a bank, you will need relatively as much preparation for the one as for the other. Without preparation, without a knowledge of all the little obstacles, the concealed difficulties, the peculiar intricacies of any particular work, you will be bound to make a failure.

Be patient and content while you are acquiring this knowledge. It takes time to acquire knowledge, and it is much better to give that time in your younger days, in your formative days, than later.

All the great successes of this world have been made by those who, while acquiring knowledge and experience, have also accumulated by saving at least the greater part of the capital with which to start themselves.

When you have demonstrated your ability to save, and ability to produce good work on a small scale, you will find no difficulty in getting assistance for larger work or extended efforts as fast as caution and good sense will allow you to take it.

Neither ask nor expect others to bear the expense of getting your experience and knowledge. Every man's position in this world dates back to the practically unaided efforts of the individual, and, even if part of it comes from his forebears, is only maintained and can only be maintained permanently by the individual efforts of the possessor.

Dependence upon assistance from others is apt to be like putting concentrated fertilizer on the hills of corn planted in very poor soil—it makes a splendid start but a lamentable finish. The soil in which it is planted and the preparation and cultivation makes the crop.

Everything in this life worth having is dependent upon your own efforts, either in the getting or in the maintenance. Learning and experience you cannot inherit.

These truths or rules of guidance which I have laid down are not new or original, they are but the summary of thousands of years of experience. Individuals have varied characteristics and degrees of natural capacity and ability, but within your natural limitations your successes will be measured by the completeness of your understanding and the thoroughness of the application of them to your daily life.

HENRY VAN DYKE

BOOKS, LITERATURE, AND THE PEOPLE

Address by Henry van Dyke, delivered at the first meeting of the National Institute of Arts and Letters, in Mendelssohn Hall, New York City, January 30, 1900. Other addresses by Dr. van Dyke are printed in Volumes III and IX.

THE founding of a National Institute of Arts and Letters is an affair which has its serious aspects. The invitation to speak for literature, before such a body of men, at their first public assembly appears almost like "a solemn responsibility."

It would be easy to say too much: it would be natural to say too little. Between the strict requirements of the occasion, and its large opportunities, I stand in doubt. With so many writers in the audience, technicalities would be superfluous: with so many readers, novelties would be impossible.

But fortunately the President of the Institute has already met the requirements and harvested the opportunities of this meeting with admirable skill and thoroughness, in his opening address. Following him, I am released, with a good conscience, from the oppressive duty of being instructive or original, and can give myself cheerfully to the small but useful task of gleaning a few forgotten truisms in regard to the relations of books, literature, and the people.

Let us begin by trying to distinguish between the people and the public.

The public is that small portion of the people which is in the foreground at the moment. It is the mirror of passing fashions, the court of temporary judgments, the gramophone of new tunes.

The people is a broader, deeper word. It means that great

Copyright, 1900, by John H. Finley. Published by permission.

and comparatively silent mass of men and women on which the public floats, as the foam floats on the wave. It means that community of human thought and feeling which lies behind the talk of the day.

There are many publics, for they change and pass. But the people are one.

In the realm of letters, as elsewhere, I hold to the principles of democracy. The people have inalienable rights to life, liberty, and the pursuit of happiness. The people do not exist for the sake of literature; to give the author fame, the publisher wealth, and books a market. On the contrary, literature exists for the sake of the people: to refresh the weary, to console the sad, to hearten up the dull and downcast, to increase man's interest in the world, his joy of living and his sympathy with all sorts and conditions of men.

"Art for art's sake" is heartless, and soon grows artless. Art for the public market is not art at all, but commerce. Art for the people's service, for the diffusion—

> Of joy in widest commonalty spread,

is a noble, vital, permanent element of human life.

If this Institute were composed of self-elected men, seeking merely the advancement of art and letters, without regard to the needs and the welfare of the people, it would be open to suspicion as a new kind of trust, or to ridicule as an old kind of mutual admiration society. But it stands on a totally different basis. The fact that its membership was chosen, and its organization promoted, by the American Social Science Association, is a fine birthmark.

Its life is derived from a social impulse, and must be dedicated to social service. So far as it shall have an influence in the republic of letters it must stand clearly on the human and humane side. Whatever it may do in the way of technical work for the confederation of authors (or the conversion of publishers), it must aim to do something broader and better for the welfare of the people. It must seek to strengthen, deepen, and improve the relations of American literature to the American people, that it may really enrich the common life, promote the liberty of the individual from the slavery of the superficial, and wisely guide and forward men in the pursuit of happiness.

In setting out to seek this end, let us remember that there is no advance possible without a recognition of the ground already gained. Pessimism never gets anywhere. It is a poor wagon that starts with creaking and groaning. Let us cheerfully acknowledge that the state of literature and its relations to the people are better to-day than they have ever been before in the history of the world. Freedom is a great gain. Open libraries are milestones on the path of human progress.

Books are easier of access and possession, at the present time, than any other kind of food. They have become incredibly cheap, partly through the expiration of copyrights, and partly through the reduction in the cost of manufacture. I cannot think that the loss involved for certain classes in either of these processes is to be weighed for a moment against the resulting advantage to the people. The best books are the easiest to get, and, upon the whole, they have the widest circulation. Notably this is true of the most beautiful, powerful, and precious of all books—the English Bible—which is still the most popular book in the world.

Another good thing in which we must rejoice is the liberation of books from various kinds of oppression. The *Index Librorum Prohibitorum* still exists, but it is no longer what it used to be. The only officers of the Inquisition in the modern world of letters are the librarians; and, taken all in all, they exercise their power with mildness and beneficence.

The influence of party politics on the fate of books is almost extinct. The days of literary partisanship, when the *Edinburgh Review* scalped the conservative writers while the *Quarterly* flayed the liberals, are past.

The alleged tyranny of the modern magazine editors is a gentle moral suasion compared with the despotism of the so-called patrons of art and letters in earlier times. Let any one who thinks that there is too much literary log-rolling in the present day, turn back to the fawning dedications of the Renaissance and the Age of Queen Anne, and he will understand how far authorship has risen out of base subserviency into independence and self-respect.

Certainly the condition of the realm of letters is better, its relation to the people is closer, and its influence on the world is greater than ever before.

But this does not mean that there are no evils to be removed, no dangers to be averted, and no further steps to be taken in advance.

Books are now sold in the dry-goods shops. No one can fairly object to that. But is there not some objection to dealing in books as if they were dry-goods?

A book can be bought for a nickel. There is no harm in that. But is there not considerable harm in advertising nickel-plated writing as sterling silver?

All that is necessary, at present, to sell an unlimited quantity of a new book, is to sell the first hundred thousand, and notify the public. The rest will go by curiosity and imitation. Is there no danger in substituting popularity for perfection as the test of merit?

Five thousand books are published every year in England, and nearly as many more in America. It would be a selfish man who could find fault with an industry which gives employment and support to such a large number of his fellow men. But has there not come, with this plethora of production, an anæmia of criticism? That once rare disease, the *cacoëthes scribendi,* seems to have become endemic.

The public must like it, else it would not be so. But have the people no interests which will be imperiled if the landmarks of literary taste are lost in the sea of publications, and the art of literature is forgotten in the business of bookmaking?

Every one knows what books are. But what is literature? It is the ark on the flood. It is the light on the candlestick. It is the flower among the leaves: the consummation of the plant's vitality, the crown of its beauty, and the treasure-house of its seeds.

Literature is made up of those human writings which translate the inner meanings of nature and life, in language of distinction and charm, touched with the personality of the author, into artistic forms of permanent interest. The best literature, then, is that which has the deepest significance, the most perfect style, the most vivid individuality, and the most enduring appeal to the human mind and heart.

On the last point contemporary judgment is but guess-work. But on the three other points it should not be impossible to form, nor improper to express, a definite opinion.

The qualities which make a book salable may easily be those which prevent it from belonging to literature. A man may make a very good living from his writings, without being in any sense a man of letters. He has a perfect right to choose between the enrichment of the world by writing along the best lines, and the increase of his bank account by running along the trolley-car tracks of the public imagination. He has the right to choose: but his choice places him.

On the other hand, the fact that a book does not sell is not in itself a sufficient proof that it is great. Poor books, as well as good ones, have often been unsuccessful at the start. The difference is that the poor ones remain unsuccessful at the finish. The writer who says that he would feel disgraced by a sale of fifty thousand copies, cheers himself with a wine pressed from acid grapes, and very unwholesome. There is no reason why a book which appeals only to the author should be considered better than a book which appeals only to the public.

Neither is there any reason why a publisher of popular books should go to the opposite extreme, and say that "there is no use under heaven for the critic; the man who buys the book is the real critic, and so discriminating is he that a publisher cannot sell a bad book." If this standard prevails, we shall soon hear the proud and happy publisher saying of a book in its hundredth thousand, as Gregory the Great is reported to have said of the Scripture, that "he would blush to have it subjected to the rules of grammar."

The true cause of blushing lies in the fact that criticism has been so much confused with advertisement; that so many of the journals which should be the teachers of the public have become its courtiers; that realism in its desire to be dramatic has so often turned to the theater instead of to real life, and thus has become melodramatic; that virility (which is a good word in its place) has been so much overworked, and used as a cloak to cover a multitude of sins; and that the distinction between books and literature has been so often overlooked and so largely forgotten.

The public is content with the standard of salability. The prigs are content with the standard of preciosity. The people need and deserve a better standard. It should be a point of honor with men of letters to maintain it, by word and deed.

FRANCES WILLARD

WORK FOR HUMANITY

Miss Willard (born in 1839, died in 1898) became secretary of the Women's Christian Temperance Union in 1874. As editor, author, and speaker, she was a great leader in the prohibition movement. The selection given here is the conclusion of her address before the seventeenth convention of the World's Women's Christian Temperance Union at Atlanta, Georgia, 1890.

I WISH we were all more thorough students of the mighty past, for we should thus be rendered braver prophets of the future, and more cheerful workers in the present. History shows us with what tenacity the human race survives. Earthquake, famine, and pestilence have done their worst, but over them rolls a healing tide of years and they are lost to view; on sweeps the great procession, and hardly shows a scar. Rulers around whom clustered new forms of civilization pass away; but greater men succeed them. Nations are rooted up; great hopes seem blighted; revolutions rise and rivers run with the blood of patriots; the globe itself seems headed toward the abyss; new patriots are born; higher hopes bloom out like stars; humanity emerges from the dark ages vastly ahead of what it was on entering that cave of gloom, and ever the right comes uppermost; and now is Christ's kingdom nearer than when we first believed.

Only those who have not studied history lose heart in great reforms; only those unread in the biography of genius imagine themselves to be original. Except in the realm of material invention, there is nothing new under the sun. There is no reform which some great soul has not dreamed of centuries ago; there is not a doctrine that some father of the Church did not set forth. The Greek philosophers and early Christian Fathers boxed the compass once for all; we may take our choice of what they have left on record. Let us then learn a wise humility, but at the same time a humble wisdom, as we remember that there are but two classes of men—one which declares that our times are the worst the world has seen, and another which claims our times as best—and he who claims this, all revelation, all science, all history witnesses is right and will be right forevermore.

The introspective is not the beautiful life. Suppose the eye should set out to see itself, the ear to hear itself! No, these organs are only in their normal use when applied to the outward world; and the soul is normal only when joined on to God and Humanity—its natural correlates, the atmosphere of its lungs, the air to its wings, the love for its heart. Introspective is the last infirmity of noble minds, it is repression's penalty and life's distemper; it reverses the soul's enginery and sets it grinding on itself. Let us rather fling ourselves out into the thickening battle; let us live the life of action which is the only true and happy life. Men tell us God is force—nay, He is that purposed force behind all forces, that combines head, hand and heart; God is action—let us be like God. God's word constantly sets before us images of vigor, of action, of power. Women need to study this; they need translating out of the passive into the active voice; out of aimless reverie and into resolute aim. The Women's Christian Temperance Union has no higher, holier mission than to help bring this about. The most perfect eye is the one of which its possessor is most unconscious except that he knows how well it sees. The most perfect ear is that of which its possessor is most unconscious except that he knows how well it hears. This which is true in detail is just as true in the wholeness of one's life. A morbid self-consciousness is the greatest hindrance to any heart. Man is like an engine—the greater and more perfect, the less conscious is it of its parts, but more conscious of its power. The Corliss engine swings its great levers and turns its mighty wheels a thousand times more quietly than the rattling little freight.

The most normal and the most perfect human being is the one who most thoroughly addresses himself to the activity of his best powers, gives himself most thoroughly to the world around him, flings himself out into the midst of humanity, and is so preoccupied by his own beneficent reaction on the world that he is practically unconscious of a separate existence. Introspection and retrospection were good for the cloister; but the uplook, the outlook and the onlook are alone worthy the modern Christian. To change the figure, a normal Christian stands in the midst of a great, beautiful and varied landscape. It is the landscape of beneficent work. Above him reaches the boundless skies, brilliant with the stars of God and Heaven.

Love and friendship form a beautiful rainbow over his landscape and reach up toward his sky. But the only two great environments of the soul are work for humanity and faith in God. Those wounded in love will find that affection, dear and vital as it is, comes to us not as the whole of life, not as its wide wondrous landscape of the earth, not as its beautiful vision of the sky, but as its beautiful embellishments, its rainbow fair and sweet. But were it gone there would still remain the two greatest and most satisfying pictures on which the soul can gaze—humanity and God.

WOODROW WILSON

THE COURSE OF AMERICAN HISTORY

Address by Woodrow Wilson, when he was professor of jurisprudence and politics in Princeton University, delivered before the New Jersey Historical Society. His famous War speeches are given in Volume XII and a Fourth of July address at Gettysburg in Volume XI.

GENTLEMEN:—In the field of history, learning should be deemed to stand among the people and in the midst of life. Its function there is not one of pride merely: to make complaisant record of deeds honorably done and plans nobly executed in the past. It has also a function of guidance: to build high places whereon to plant the clear and flaming lights of experience, that they may shine alike upon the roads already traveled and upon the paths not yet attempted. The historian is also a sort of a prophet. Our memories direct us. They give us knowledge of our character, alike in its strength and in its weakness; and it is so we get our standards for endeavor,— our warnings and our gleams of hope. It is thus we learn what manner of nation we are of, and divine what manner of people we should be.

And this is not in national records merely. Local history is the ultimate substance of national history. There could be no epics were pastorals not also true,—no patriotism, were there no hopes, no neighbors, no quiet round of civic duty; and I, for my part, do not wonder that scholarly men have been found not a few who, though they might have shone upon a larger field, where all eyes would have seen them win their fame, yet chose to pore all their lives long upon the blurred

Copyright, 1896, by Woodrow Wilson. By special permission of the author and his publishers, Houghton Mifflin & Co.

and scattered records of a country-side, where there was nothing but an old church or an ancient village. The history of a nation is only the history of its villages written large. I only marvel that these local historians have not seen more in the stories they have sought to tell. Surely here, in these old hamlets that antedate the cities, in these little communities that stand apart and yet give their young life to the nation, is to be found the very authentic stuff of romance for the mere looking. There is love and courtship and eager life and high devotion up and down all the lines of every genealogy. What strength, too, and bold endeavor in the cutting down of forests to make the clearings; what breath of hope and discovery in scaling for the first time the nearest mountains; what longings ended or begun upon the coming in of ships into the harbor; what pride of earth in the rivalries of the village; what thoughts of heaven in the quiet of the rural church! What forces of slow and steadfast endeavor there were in the building of a great city upon the foundations of a hamlet: and how the plot broadens and thickens and grows dramatic as communities widen into States! Here, surely, sunk deep in the very fiber of the stuff are the colors of the great story of men,—the lively touches of reality and the striking images of life.

It must be admitted, I know, that local history can be made deadly dull in the telling. The men who reconstruct it seem usually to build with kiln-dried stuff,—as if with a purpose it should last. But that is not the fault of the subject. National history may be written almost as ill, if due pains be taken to dry it out. It is a trifle more difficult: because merely to speak of national affairs is to give hints of great forces and of movements blown upon us by all the airs of the wide continent. The mere largeness of the scale lends to the narrative a certain dignity and spirit. But some men will manage to be dull though they should speak of creation. In writing of local history the thing is fatally easy. For there is some neighborhood history that lacks any large significance, which is without horizon or outlook. There are details in the history of every community which it concerns no man to know again when once they are past and decently buried in the records: and these are the very details, no doubt, which it is easier to find upon a casual search. It is easier to make out a list of county clerks than to extract the social history of the country from the records they have kept,—though it is not so important: and it is easier to make a catalogue of anything than to say what of life and purpose the catalogue stands for. This is called collecting facts "for the sake of the facts themselves"; but if I wished to do aught for the sake of the facts themselves I think I should serve them better by giving their true biographies than by merely displaying their faces.

The right and vital sort of local history is the sort which may be written with lifted eyes,—the sort which has a horizon and an outlook upon the world. Sometimes it may happen, indeed, that the annals of a neighborhood disclose some singular adventure which had its beginning and its ending there: some unwonted bit of fortune which stands unique and lonely amidst the myriad transactions of the world of affairs, and deserves to be told singly and for its own sake. But usually the significance of local history is, that it is a part of a greater whole. A spot of local history is like an inn upon a highway: it is a stage upon a far journey: it is a place the national history has passed through. There mankind has stopped and lodged by the way. Local history is thus less than national history only as the part is less than the whole. The whole could not dispense with the part, would not exist without it, could not be understood unless the part also were understood. Local history is subordinate to national only in the sense in which each leaf of a book is subordinate to the volume itself. Upon no single page will the whole theme of the book be found; but each page holds a part of the theme. Even were the history of each locality exactly like the history of every other (which it cannot be), it would deserve to be written,—if only to corroborate the history of the rest, and verify it as an authentic part of the record of the race and nation. The common elements of a nation's life are the great elements of its life, the warp and woof of the fabric. They cannot be too much or too substantially verified and explicated. It is so that history is made solid and fit for use and wear. Our national history, of course, has its own great and spreading pattern, which can be seen in its full form and completeness only when the stuff of our national life is laid before us in broad surfaces and upon an ample scale. But the detail of the pattern, the individual threads of the great fabric, are to be found only in local history. There is all the intricate weaving, all the delicate shading, all the nice refinement of the pattern,—gold thread mixed with fustian, fine thread laid upon coarse, shade combined with shade. Assuredly it is this that gives to local history its life and importance. The idea, moreover, furnishes a nice criterion of interest. The life of some localities is, obviously, more completely and intimately a part of the national pattern than the life of other localities, which are more separate and, as it were, put upon the border of the fabric. To come at once and very candidly to examples, the local history of the Middle States,—New York, New Jersey, and Pennsylvania,—is much more structurally a part of the characteristic life of the nation as a whole than is the history of the New England communities or of the several States and regions of the South. I know that such a heresy will sound very rank in the ears of some: for I am speaking against accepted doctrine. But acceptance, be it never so general, does not make a doctrine true.

Our national history has been written for the most part by New England men. All honor to them! Their scholarship and their characters alike have given them an honorable enrollment amongst the great names of our literary history; and no just man would say aught to detract, were it never so little, from their well-earned fame. They have written our history, nevertheless, from but a single point of view. From where they sit, the whole of the great development looks like an Expansion of New England. Other elements but play along the sides of the great process by which the Puritan has worked out the development of nation and polity. It is he who has gone out and possessed the land: the man of destiny, the type and impersonation of a chosen people. To the Southern writer, too, the story looks much the same, if it be but followed to its culmination,—to its final storm and stress and tragedy of the Great War. It is the history of the Suppression of the South. Spite of all her splendid contributions to the steadfast accomplishment of the great task of building the nation; spite of the long leadership of her statesman in the national counsels;

spite of her joint achievements in the conquest and occupation of the West, the South was at last turned upon on every hand, rebuked, proscribed, defeated. The history of the United States, we have learned, was, from the settlement at Jamestown to the surrender at Appomattox, a long-drawn contest for mastery between New England and the South,—and the end of the contest we know. All along the parallels of latitude ran the rivalry, in those heroic days of toil and adventure during which population crossed the continent, like an army advancing its encampments. Up and down the great river of the continent, too, and beyond, up the slow incline of the vast steppes that lift themselves toward the crowning towers of the Rockies, —beyond that, again, in the gold-fields and upon the green plains of California, the race for ascendency struggled on,— till at length there was a final coming face to face, and the masterful folk who had come from the loins of New England won their consummate victory.

It is a very dramatic form for the story. One almost wishes it were true. How fine a unity it would give our epic! But perhaps, after all, the real truth is more interesting. The life of the nation cannot be reduced to these so simple terms. These two great forces, of the North and of the South, unquestionably existed,—were unquestionably projected in their operation out upon the great plane of the continent, there to combine or repel, as circumstances might determine. But the people that went out from the North were not an unmixed people; they came from the great Middle States as well as from New England. Their transplantation into the West was no more a reproduction of New England or New York or Pennsylvania or New Jersey than Massachusetts was a reproduction of old England, or New Netherland a reproduction of Holland. The Southern people, too, whom they met by the western rivers and upon the open prairies, were transformed, as they themselves were, by the rough fortunes of the frontier. A mixture of peoples, a modification of mind and habit, a new round of experiment and adjustment amidst the novel life of the baked and untilled plain, and the far valleys with the virgin forests still thick upon them: a new temper, a new spirit of adventure, a new impatience of restraint, a new license of life,—these are the characteristic notes and measures of the time when the nation spread itself at large upon the continent, and was transformed from a group of colonies into a family of States.

The passes of these eastern mountains were the arteries of the nation's life. The real breath of our growth and manhood came into our nostrils when first, like Governor Spotswood and that gallant company of Virginian gentlemen that rode with him in the far year 1716, the Knights of the Order of the Golden Horseshoe, our pioneers stood upon the ridges of the eastern hills and looked down upon those reaches of the continent where lay the untrodden paths of the westward migration. There, upon the courses of the distant rivers that gleamed before them in the sun, down the farther slopes of the hills beyond, out upon the broad fields that lay upon the fertile banks of the "Father of Waters," up the long tilt of the continent to the vast hills that looked out upon the Pacific—there were the regions in which, joining with people from every race and clime under the sun, they were to make the great compounded nation whose liberty and mighty works of peace were to cause all the world to stand at gaze. Thither were to come Frenchmen, Scandinavians, Celts, Dutch, Slavs,—men of the Latin races and of the races of the Orient, as well as men, a great host, of the first stock of the settlements: English, Scots, Scots-Irish,—like New England men, but touched with the salt of humor, hard, and yet neighborly too. For this great process of growth by grafting, of modification no less than of expansion, the colonies,—the original thirteen States,—were only preliminary studies and first experiments. But the experiments that most resembled the great methods by which we peopled the continent from side to side and knit a single polity across all its length and breadth, were surely the experiments made from the very first in the Middle States of our Atlantic seaboard.

Here from the first were mixture of population, variety of element, combination of type, as if of the nation itself in small. Here was never a simple body, a people of but a single blood and extraction, a polity and a practice brought straight from one mother land. The life of these States was from the beginning like the life of the country: they have always shown the national pattern. In New England and the South it was very different. There some of the great elements of the national life were long in preparation: but separately and with an individual distinction; without mixture,—for long almost without movement. That the elements thus separately prepared were of the greatest importance, and run everywhere like chief threads of the pattern through all our subsequent life, who can doubt? They give color and tone to every part of the figure. The very fact that they are so distinct and separately evident throughout, the very emphasis of individuality they carry with them, but proves their distinct origin. The other elements of our life, various though they be, and of the very fiber, giving toughness and consistency to the fabric, are merged in its texture, united, confused, almost indistinguishable, so thoroughly are they mixed, intertwined, interwoven, like the essential strands of the stuff itself: but these of the Puritan and the Southerner, though they run everywhere with the rest and seem upon a superficial view themselves the body of the cloth, in fact modify rather than make it.

What in fact has been the course of American history? How is it to be distinguished from European history? What features has it of its own, which give it its distinctive plan and movement? We have suffered, it is to be feared, a very serious limitation of view until recent years of having all our history written in the East. It has smacked strongly of local flavor. It has concerned itself too exclusively with the origins and Old World derivation of our story. Our historians have made their march from the sea with their heads over shoulder, their gaze always backward upon the landing-places and homes of the first settlers. In spite of the steady immigration, with its persistent tide of foreign blood, they have chosen to speak often and to think always of our people as sprung after all from a common stock, bearing a family likeness in every branch, and following all the while old, familiar, family ways. The view is the more misleading because it is so large a part of the truth without being all of it. The common British stock did first make the country, and has always set the pace. There were common institutions up and down the coast; and these had formed and hardened for a persistent growth before the great westward migration began which was to reshape and modify every element of our life. The national government itself was set up and made strong by success while yet we lingered for the most part upon the eastern coast and feared a too distant frontier.

But, the beginnings once safely made, change set in apace. Not only so: there had been slow change from the first. We have no frontier now, we are told,—except a broken fragment, it may be, here and there in some barren corner of the western lands, where some inhospitable mountain still shoulders us out, or where men are still lacking to break the baked surface of the plain and occupy them in the very teeth of hostile nature. But at first it was all frontier,—a mere strip of settlements stretched precariously upon the sea-edge of the wilds: an untouched continent in front of them, and behind them an unfrequented sea that almost never showed so much as the momentary gleam of a sail. Every step in the slow process of settlement was but a step of the same kind as the first, an advance to a new frontier like the old. For long we lacked, it is true, that new breed of frontiersmen born in after years beyond the mountains. Those first frontiersmen had still a touch of the timidity of the Old World in their blood: they lacked the frontier heart. They were "Pilgrims" in very fact,—exiled, not at home. Fine courage they had: and a steadfastness in their bold design which it does a faint-hearted age good to look back upon. There was no thought of drawing back. Steadily, almost calmly, they extended their seats. They built homes, and deemed it certain their children would live there after them. But they did not love the rough, uneasy life for its own sake. How long did they keep, if they could, within sight of the sea! The wilderness was their refuge; but how long before it became their joy and hope! Here was their destiny cast; but their hearts lingered and held back. It was only as generations passed and the work widened about them that their thought also changed, and a new thrill sped along their blood. Their life had been new and strange from their first landing in the wilderness. Their houses, their food, their clothing, their neighborhood dealings were all such as only the frontier brings. Insensibly they were themselves changed. The strange life became familiar; their adjustment to it was at length unconscious and without effort; they had no plans which were not inseparably a part and a product of it. But, until they had turned their backs once for all upon the sea; until they saw their western borders cleared of the French; until the mountain passes had grown familiar, and the lands beyond the central and constant theme of their hope, the goal and dream of their young men, they did not become an American people.

When they did, the great determining movement of our history began. The very visages of the people changed. That alert movement of the eye, that openness to every thought of enterprise or adventure, that nomadic habit which knows no fixed home and has plans ready to be carried any whither,—all the marks of the authentic type of the "American" as we know him came into our life. The crack of the whip and the song of the teamster, the heaving chorus of boatmen poling their heavy rafts upon the rivers, the laughter of the camp, the sound of bodies of men in the still forests, became the characteristic notes in our air. A roughened race, embrowned in the sun, hardened in manner by a coarse life of change and danger, loving the rude woods and the crack of the rifle, living to begin something new every day, striking with the broad and open hand, delicate in nothing but the touch of the trigger, leaving cities in its track as if by accident rather than design, settling again to the steady ways of a fixed life only when it must: such was the American people whose achievement it was to be to take possession of their continent from end to end ere their national government was a single century old. The picture is a very singular one! Settled life and wild side by side: civilization frayed at the edges,—taken forward in rough and ready fashion, with a song and a swagger,—not by statesmen, but by woodsmen and drovers, with axes and whips and rifles in their hands, clad in buckskin, like huntsmen.

It has been said that we have here repeated some of the first processes of history; that the life and methods of our frontiersmen take us back to the fortunes and hopes of the men who crossed Europe when her forests, too, were still thick upon her. But the difference is really very fundamental, and much more worthy of remark than the likeness. Those shadowy masses of men whom we see moving upon the face of the earth in the far-away, questionable days when States were forming: even those stalwart figures we see so well as they emerge from the deep forests of Germany, to displace the Roman in all his western provinces and set up the States we know and marvel upon at this day, show us men working their new work at their own level. They do not turn back a long cycle of years from the old and settled States, the ordered cities, the tilled fields, and the elaborate governments of an ancient civilization, to begin as it were once more at the beginning. They carry alike their homes and their States with them in the camp and upon the ordered march of the host. They are men of the forest, or else men hardened always to take the sea in open boats. They live no more roughly in the new lands than in the old. The world has been frontier for them from the first. They may go forward with their life in these new seats from where they left off in the old. How different the circumstances of our first settlement and the building of new States on this side the sea! Englishmen, bred in law and ordered government ever since the Norman lawyers were followed a long five hundred years ago across the narrow seas by those masterful administrators of the strong Plantagenet race, leave an ancient realm and come into a wilderness where States have never been; leave a land of art and letters, which saw but yesterday "the spacious times of great Elizabeth," where Shakespeare still lives in the gracious leisure of his closing days at Stratford, where cities teem with trade and men go bravely dight in cloth of gold, and turn back six centuries,—nay, a thousand years and more,—to the first work of building States in a wilderness! They bring the steadied habits and sobered thoughts of an ancient realm into the wild air of an untouched continent. The weary stretches of a vast sea lie, like a full thousand years of time, between them and the life in which till now all their thought was bred. Here they stand, as it were, with all their tools left behind, centuries struck out of their reckoning, driven back upon the long dormant instincts and forgotten craft of their race, not used this long age. Look how singular a thing: the work of a primitive race, the thought of a civilized! Hence the strange, almost grotesque groupings of thought and affairs in that first day of our history. Subtle politicians speak the phrases and practice the arts of intricate diplomacy from council chambers placed within log-huts within a clearing. Men in ruffs and lace and polished shoe-buckles thread the lonely glades of primeval forests. The microscopical distinctions of the schools, the thin notes of a metaphysical theology are woven in and out through the labyrinths of grave sermons that run hours long upon the still air of the wilderness. Belief in dim refinements of dogma is made the test for man or woman who seeks admission to a company of pioneers. When went there by an age since the great flood when so singular a thing was seen as this: thousands of civilized men suddenly rusticated and bade to do the work of primitive peoples,—Europe frontiered!

Of course there was a deep change wrought, if not in these men, at any rate in their children; and every generation saw the change deepen. It must seem to every thoughtful man a notable thing how, while the change was wrought, the simples of things complex were revealed in the clear air of the New World: how all accidentals seemed to fall away from the structure of government, and the simple first principles were laid bare that abide always; how social distinctions were stripped off, shown to be the mere cloaks and masks they were, and every man brought once again to a clear realization of his actual relations to his fellows! It was as if trained and sophisticated men had been rid of a sudden of their sophistication and of all the theory of their life, and left with nothing but their discipline of faculty, a schooled and sobered instinct. And the fact that we kept always, for close upon three hundred years, a like element in our life, a frontier people always in our van, is, so far, the central and determining fact of our national history. "East" and "West," an ever-changing line, but an unvarying experience and a constant leaven of change working always within the body of our folk. Our political, our economic, our social life has felt this potent influence from the wild border all our history through. The "West" is the great word of our history. The "Westerner" has been the type and master of our American life. Now at length, as I have said, we have lost our frontier: our front lies almost unbroken along all the great coast-line of the western sea. The Westerner, in some day soon to come, will pass out of our life, as he so long ago passed out of the life of the Old World. Then a new epoch will open for us. Perhaps it has opened already. Slowly we shall grow old, compact our people, study the delicate adjustments of an intricate society, and ponder the niceties, as we have hitherto pondered the bulks and structural framework, of government. Have we not, indeed, already come to these things? But the past we know. We can "see it steady and see it whole"; and its central movement and motive are gross and obvious to the eye.

Till the first century of the Constitution is rounded out we stand all the while in the presence of that stupendous westward movement which has filled the continent: so vast, so various, at times so tragical, so swept by passion. Through all the long time there has been a line of rude settlements along our front wherein the same tests of power and of institutions were still being made that were made first upon the sloping banks of the rivers of old Virginia and within the long sweep of the Bay of Massachusetts. The new life of the West has reacted all the while—who shall say how powerfully?—upon the older life of the East; and yet the East has molded the West as if she sent forward to it through every decade of the long process the chosen impulses and suggestions of history. The West has taken strength, thought, training, selected aptitudes out of the old treasures of the East,—as if out of a new Orient; while the East has itself been kept fresh, vital, alert, originative by the West, her blood quickened all the while, her youth through every age renewed. Who can say in a word, in a sentence, in a volume, what destinies have been variously wrought, with what new examples of growth and energy, while, upon this unexampled scale, community has passed beyond community across the vast reaches of this great continent!

The great process is the more significant because it has been distinctively a national process. Until the Union was formed and we had consciously set out upon a separate national career, we moved but timidly across the nearer hills. Our most remote settlements lay upon the rivers and in the open glades of Tennessee and Kentucky. It was in the years that immediately succeeded the War of 1812 that the movement into the West began to be a mighty migration. Till then our eyes had been more often in the East than in the West. Not only were foreign questions to be settled and our standing among the nations to be made good, but we still remained acutely conscious and deliberately conservative of our Old World connections. For all we were so new a people and lived so simple and separate a life, we had still the sobriety and the circumspect fashions of action that belong to an old society. We were, in government and manners, but a disconnected part of the world beyond the seas. Its thought and habit still set us our standards of speech and action. And this, not because of imitation, but because of actual and long-abiding political and social connection with the mother country. Our statesmen,—strike but the names of Samuel Adams and Patrick Henry from the list, together with all like untutored spirits, who stood for the new, unreverencing ardor of a young democracy,—our statesmen were such men as might have taken their places in the House of Commons or in the Cabinet at home as naturally and with as easy an adjustment to their place and task as in the Continental Congress or in the immortal Constitutional Convention. Think of the stately ways and the grand air and the authoritative social understandings of the generation that set the new government afoot,—the generation of Washington and John Adams. Think, too, of the conservative tradition that guided all the early history of that government: that early line of gentlemen Presidents: that steady "cabinet succession to the Presidency" which came at length to seem almost like an oligarchy to the impatient men who were shut out from it. The line ended, with a sort of chill, in stiff John Quincy Adams, too cold a man to be a people's prince after the old order of Presidents; and the year 1829, which saw Jackson come in, saw the old order go out.

The date is significant. Since the War of 1812, undertaken as if to set us free to move westward, seven States had been admitted to the Union: and the whole number of States was advanced to twenty-four. Eleven new States had come into partnership with the old thirteen. The voice of the West rang through all our counsels; and, in Jackson, the new partners took possession of the Government. It is worth while to remember how men stood amazed at the change: how startled, chagrined, dismayed the conservative States of the East were at the revolution they saw effected, the riot of change they saw set in; and no man who has once read the singular story can forget how the eight years Jackson reigned saw the Government, and politics themselves, transformed. For long,—the story being written in the regions where the shock and surprise of the change was greatest,—the period of this momentous revolution was spoken of amongst us as a period of degeneration, the birth-time of a deep and permanent demoralization in our politics. But we see it differently now. Whether we have any taste or stomach for that rough age or not, however much we may wish that the old order might have stood, the generation of Madison and Adams have been prolonged, and the good tradition of the early days handed on unbroken and unsullied, we now know that what the nation underwent in that day of change was not degeneration, great and perilous as were the errors of the time, but regeneration. The old order was changed, once and for all. A new nation stepped, with a touch of swagger, upon the stage,—a nation which had broken alike with the traditions and with the wisely wrought experience of the Old World, and which, with all the haste and rashness of youth, was minded to work out a separate policy and destiny of its own. It was a day of hazards, but there was nothing sinister at the heart of the new plan. It was a wasteful experiment, to fling out, without wise guides, upon untried ways; but an abounding continent afforded enough and to spare even for the wasteful. It was sure to be so with a nation that came out of the secluded vales of a virgin continent. It was the bold frontier voice of the West sounding in affairs. The timid shivered, but the robust waxed strong and rejoiced, in the tonic air of the new day.

It was then we swung out into the main paths of our history. The new voices that called us were first silvery, like the voice of Henry Clay, and spoke old familiar words of eloquence. The first spokesmen of the West even tried to con the classics, and spoke incongruously in the phrases of politics long dead and gone to dust, as Benton did. But presently the tone changed, and it was the truculent and masterful accents of the real frontiersman that rang dominant above the rest, harsh, impatient, and with an evident dash of temper. The East slowly accustomed itself to the change; caught the movement, though it grumbled and even trembled at the pace; and managed most of the time to keep in the running. But it was always henceforth to be the West that set the pace. There is no mistaking the questions that have ruled our spirits as a nation during the present century. The public land question, the tariff question, and the question of slavery,—these dominate from first to last. It was the West that made each one of these the question that it was. Without the free lands to which every man who chose might go, there would not have been that easy prosperity of life and that high standard of abundance which seemed to render it necessary that, if we were to have manufactures and a diversified industry at all, we should foster new undertakings by a system of protection which would make the profits of the factory as certain and as abundant as the profits of the farm. It was the constant movement of the population, the constant march of wagon-trains into the West, that made it so cardinal a matter of policy whether the great national domain should be free land or not: and that was the land question. It was the settlement of the West that transformed slavery from an accepted institution into passionate matter of controversy.

Slavery within the States of the Union stood sufficiently protected by every solemn sanction the Constitution could afford. No man could touch it there, think, or hope, or purpose what he might. But where new States were to be made it was not so. There at every step choice must be made: slavery or no slavery?—a new choice for every new State: a fresh act of origination to go with every fresh act of organization. Had there been no Territories, there could have been no slavery question, except by revolution and contempt of fundamental law. But with a continent to be peopled, the choice thrust itself insistently forward at every step and upon every hand. This was the slavery question: not what should be done to reverse the past, but what should be done to redeem the future. It was so men of that day saw it,—and so also must historians see it. We must not mistake the program of the Anti-Slavery Society for the platform of the Republican party, or forget that the very war itself was begun ere any purpose of abolition took place amongst those who were statesmen and in authority. It was a question, not of freeing men, but of preserving a Free Soil. Kansas showed us what the problem was, not South Carolina: and it was the Supreme Court, not the slave-owners, who formulated the matter for our thought and purpose.

And so, upon every hand and throughout every national question, was the commerce between East and West made up: that commerce and exchange of ideas, inclinations, purposes, and principles which has constituted the moving force of our life as a nation. Men illustrate the operation of these singular forces better than questions can: and no man illustrates it better than Abraham Lincoln.—

> Great captains with their guns and drums
> Disturb our judgment for the hour;
> But at last silence comes:
> These all are gone, and, standing like a tower,
> Our children shall behold his fame,
> The kindly-earnest, brave, foreseeing man,
> Sagacious, patient, dreading praise not blame,
> New birth of our new soil, the first American.

It is a poet's verdict; but it rings in the authentic tone of the seer. It must be also the verdict of history. He would be a rash man who should say he understood Abraham Lincoln. No doubt natures deep as his, and various almost to the point of self-contradiction, can be sounded only by the judgment of men of a like sort,—if any such there be. But some things we all may see and judge concerning him. You have in him the type and flower of our growth. It is as if Nature had made a typical American, and then had added with liberal hand the royal quality of genius, to show us what the type could be. Lincoln owed nothing to his birth, everything to his growth: had no training save what he gave himself; no nurture, but only a wild and native strength. His life was his schooling, and every day of it gave to his character a new touch of development. His manhood not only, but his perception also, expanded with his life. His eyes, as they looked more and more abroad, beheld the national life, and comprehended it: and the lad who had been so rough-cut a provincial became, when grown to manhood, the one leader in all the nation who held the whole people singly in his heart:—held even the Southern people there and would have won them back. And so we have in him what we must call the perfect development of native strength, the rounding out and nationalization of the provincial. Andrew Jackson was a type, not of the nation, but of the West. For all the tenderness there was in the stormy heart of the masterful man, and staunch and simple loyalty to all who loved him, he learned nothing in the East; kept always the flavor of the rough school in which he had been bred; was never more than a frontier soldier and gentleman. Lincoln differed from Jackson by all the length of his unmatched capacity to learn. Jackson could understand only men of his own kind, Lincoln could understand men of all sorts and from every region of the land: seemed himself, indeed, to be all men by turns, as mood succeeded mood in his strange nature. He never ceased to stand, in his bony angles, the express image of the ungainly frontiersman. His mind never lost the vein of coarseness that had marked him grossly when a youth. And yet how he grew and strengthened in the real stuff of dignity and greatness: how nobly he could bear himself without the aid of grace! He kept always the shrewd and seeing eye of the woodsman and the hunter, and the flavor of wild life never left him: and yet how easily his view widened to great affairs; how surely he perceived the value and the significance of whatever touched him and made him neighbor to itself!

Lincoln's marvelous capacity to extend his comprehension to the measure of what he had in hand is the one distinguishing mark of the man: and to study the development of that capacity in him is little less than to study, where it is as it were perfectly registered, the national life itself. This boy lived his youth in Illinois when it was a frontier State. The youth of the State was coincident with his own: and man and State kept equal pace in their striding advance to maturity. The frontier population was an intensely political population. It felt to the quick the throb of the nation's life,—for the nation's life ran through it, going its eager way to the westward. The West was not separate from the East. Its communities were every day receiving fresh members from the East, and the fresh impulse of direct suggestion. Their blood flowed to them straight from the warmest veins of the older communities. More than that, elements which were separated in the East were mingled in the West: which displayed to the eye as it were a sort of epitome of the most active and permanent forces of the national life. In such communities as these Lincoln mixed daily from the first with men of every sort and from every quarter of the country. With them he discussed neighborhood politics, the politics of the State, the politics of the nation,—and his mind became traveled as he talked. How plainly amongst such neighbors, there in Illinois, must it have become evident that national questions were centering more and more in the West as the years went by: coming as it were to meet them. Lincoln went twice down the Mississippi, upon the slow rafts that carried wares to its mouth, and saw with his own eyes, so used to look directly and point-blank upon men and affairs, characteristic regions of the South. He worked his way slowly and sagaciously, with that larger sort of sagacity which so marked him all his life, into the active business of State politics; sat twice in the State legislature, and then for a term in Congress, —his sensitive and seeing mind open all the while to every turn of fortune and every touch of nature in the moving affairs he looked upon. All the while, too, he continued to canvass, piece by piece, every item of politics, as of old, with his neighbors familiarly around the stove, or upon the corners of the street, or more formally upon the stump; and kept always in direct contact with the ordinary views of ordinary men. Meanwhile he read, as nobody else around him read, and sought to gain a complete mastery over speech, with the conscious purpose to prevail in its use; derived zest from the curious study of mathematical proof, and amusement as well as strength from the practice of clean and naked statements of truth. It was all irregularly done, but strenuously, with the same instinct throughout, and with a steady access of facility and power. There was no sudden leap for this man, any more than for other men, from crudeness to finished power, from an understanding of the people of Illinois to an understanding of the people of the United States. And thus he came at last, with infinite pains and a wonder of endurance, to his great national task with a self-trained capacity which no man could match, and made upon a scale as liberal as the life of the people. You could not then set this athlete a pace in learning or in perceiving that was too hard for him. He knew the people and their life as no other man did or could: and now stands in his place singular in all the annals of mankind, the "brave, sagacious, foreseeing, patient man" of the people, "new birth of our new soil, the first American."

We have here a national man presiding over sectional men. Lincoln understood the East better than the East understood him or the people from whom he sprung: and this is in every way a noteworthy circumstance. For my part, I read a lesson in the singular career of this great man. Is it possible the East remains sectional while the West broadens to a wider view?—

> Be strong-backed, brown-handed, upright as your pines;
> By the scale of a hemisphere shape your designs,

is an inspiring program for the woodsman and the pioneer; but how are you to be brown-handed in a city office? What if you never see the upright pines? How are you to have so big a purpose on so small a part of the hemisphere? As it has grown old, unquestionably the East has grown sectional. There is no suggestion of the prairie in its city streets, or of the embrowned ranchmen and farmer in its well-dressed men. Its ports teem with shipping from Europe and the Indies. Its newspapers run upon the themes of an Old World. It hears of the great plains of the continent as of foreign parts, which it may never think to see except from a car window. Its life is self-centered and selfish. The West, save where special interests center (as in those pockets of silver where men's eyes catch as it were an eager gleam from the very ore itself): the West is in less danger of sectionalization. Who shall say in that wide country where one region ends and another begins, or, in that free and changing society, where one class ends and another begins?

This, surely, is the moral of our history. The East has spent and been spent for the West: has given forth her energy, her young men and her substance, for the new regions that have been a-making all the century through. But has she learned as much as she has taught, or taken as much as she has given? Look what it is that has now at last taken place. The westward march has stopped upon the final slopes of the Pacific; and now the plot thickens. Populations turn upon their old paths, fill in the spaces they passed by neglected in their first journey in search of a land of promise; settle to a life such as the East knows as well as the West,—nay, much better. With the change, the pause, the settlement, our people draw into closer groups, stand face to face, to know each other and be known: and the time has come for the East to learn in her turn; to broaden her understanding of political and economic conditions to the scale of the hemisphere, as her own poet bade. Let us be sure that we get the national temperament; send our minds abroad upon the continent, become neighbors to all the people that live upon it, and lovers of them all, as Lincoln was.

Read but your history aright, and you shall not find the task too hard. Your own local history, look but deep enough, tells the tale you must take to heart. Here upon our own seaboard, as truly as ever in the West, was once a national frontier, with an elder East beyond the seas. Here, too, various peoples combined, and elements separated elsewhere effected a tolerant and wholesome mixture. Here, too, the national stream flowed full and strong, bearing a thousand things upon its currents. Let us resume and keep the vision of that time; know ourselves, our neighbors, our destiny, with lifted and open eyes; see our history truly, in its great proportions; be ourselves liberal as the great principles we profess; and so be the people who might have again the heroic adventures and do again the heroic work of the past. 'Tis thus we shall renew our youth and secure our age against decay.

EMILE ZOLA

APPEAL FOR DREYFUS

Address by Emile Zola, novelist (born in Paris, April 2, 1840; died, 1902), delivered to the jury at his trial for libel in connection with the Dreyfus case, Paris, February 21, 1898.

In the Chamber at the sitting of January 22, M. Meline, the Prime Minister, declared, amid the frantic applause of his complaisant majority, that he had confidence in the twelve citizens to whose hands he intrusted the defense of the army. It was of you, gentlemen, that he spoke. And just as General Billot dictated its decision to the court martial intrusted with the acquittal of Major Esterhazy, by appealing from the tribune for respect for the *chose jugée,* so likewise M. Meline wished to give you the order to condemn me out of respect for the army which he accuses me of having insulted!

I denounce to the conscience of honest men this pressure brought to bear by the constituted authorities upon the justice of the country. These are abominable political maneuvers, which dishonor a free nation. We shall see, gentlemen, whether you will obey.

But it is not true that I am here in your presence by the will of M. Meline. He yielded to the necessity of prosecuting me only in great trouble, in terror of the new step which the advancing truth was about to take. This everybody knew. If I am before you, it is because I wished it. I alone decided that this obscure, this abominable affair, should be brought before your jurisdiction, and it is I alone of my free will who chose you,—you, the loftiest, the most direct emanation of French justice,—in order that France might at last know all, and give her opinion. My act had no other object, and my person is of no account. I have sacrificed it, in order to place in your hands not only the honor of the army, but the imperiled honor of the nation.

It appears that I was cherishing a dream in wishing to offer you all the proofs: considering you to be the sole worthy, the sole competent judge. They have begun by depriving you with the left hand of what they seemed to give you with the right. They pretended, indeed, to accept your jurisdiction, but if they had confidence in you to avenge the members of the court martial, there were still other officers who remained superior even to your jurisdiction. Let who can, understand. It is absurdity doubled with hypocrisy, and it is abundantly clear that they dreaded your good sense,—that they dared not run the risk of letting us tell all and of letting you judge the whole matter. They pretend that they wished to limit the scandal. What do you think of this scandal? Of my act, which consisted in bringing the matter before you,—in wishing the people, incarnate in you, to be the judge? They pretend also that they could not accept a revision in disguise, thus confessing that in reality they have but one dread, that of your sovereign control. The law has in you its entire representation, and it is this law of the people elect that I have wished for,—this law which, as a good citizen, I hold in profound respect, and not the suspicious procedure whereby they hoped to make you a derision.

I am thus excused, gentlemen, for having brought you here from your private affairs without being able to inundate you with the full flood of light of which I dreamed. The light, the whole light,—this was my sole, my passionate desire! And this trial has just proved it. We have had to fight—step by step—against an extraordinarily obstinate desire for darkness. A battle has been necessary to obtain every atom of truth. Everything has been refused us. Our witnesses have been terrorized in the hope of preventing us from proving our point. And it is on your behalf alone that we have fought, that this proof might be put before you in its entirety, so that you might give your opinion without remorse in your consciences. I am certain, therefore, that you will give us credit for our efforts, and that, moreover, sufficient light has been thrown upon the affair.

You have heard the witnesses; you are about to hear my

counsel, who will tell you the true story: the story that maddens everybody and which no one knows. I am, therefore, at my ease. You have the truth at last, and it will do its work. M. Meline thought to dictate your decision by intrusting to you the honor of the army. And it is in the name of the honor of the army that I too appeal to your justice.

I give M. Meline the most direct contradiction. Never have I insulted the army. I spoke, on the contrary, of my sympathy, my respect for the nation in arms, for our dear soldiers of France, who would rise at the first menace to defend the soil of France. And it is just as false that I attacked the chiefs, the generals who would lead them to victory. If certain persons at the War Office have compromised the army itself by their acts, is it to insult the whole army to say so? Is it not rather to act as a good citizen to separate it from all that compromises it, to give the alarm, so that the blunders which alone have been the cause of our defeat shall not occur again, and shall not lead us to fresh disaster?

I am not defending myself, moreover. I leave history to judge my act, which was a necessary one; but I affirm that the army is dishonored when gendarmes are allowed to embrace Major Esterhazy after the abominable letters written by him. I affirm that that valiant army is insulted daily by the bandits who, on the plea of defending it, sully it by their degrading championship,—who trail in the mud all that France still honors as good and great. I affirm that those who dishonor that great national army are those who mingle cries of "Vive l'armée!" with those of "A bas les juifs!" and "Vive Esterhazy!" Grand Dieu! the people of St. Louis, of Bayard, of Condé, and of Hoche: the people which counts a hundred great victories, the people of the great wars of the Republic and the Empire, the people whose power, grace, and generosity have dazzled the world, crying "Vive Esterhazy!" It is a shame the stain of which our efforts on behalf of truth and justice can alone wash off!

You know the legend which has grown up: Dreyfus was condemned justly and legally by seven infallible officers, whom it is impossible even to suspect of a blunder without insulting the whole army. Dreyfus expiates in merited torments his abominable crime. And as he is a Jew, a Jewish syndicate is formed, an international *sans patrie* syndicate, disposing of hundreds of millions, the object of which is to save the traitor at any price, even by the most shameless intrigues. And thereupon this syndicate began to heap crime on crime: buying consciences, casting France into a disastrous agitation, resolved on selling her to the enemy, willing even to drive all Europe into a general war rather than renounce its terrible plan.

It is very simple, nay childish, if not imbecile. But it is with this poisoned bread that the unclean Press has been nourishing our people now for some months. And it is not surprising if we are witnessing a dangerous crisis; for when folly and lies are thus sown broadcast you necessarily reap insanity.

Gentlemen, I would not insult you by supposing that you have yourselves been duped by this nursery tale. I know you; I know who you are. You are the heart and the reason of Paris, of my great Paris; where I was born, which I love with an infinite tenderness, which I have been studying and writing of now for forty years. And I know likewise what is now passing in your brains; for, before coming to sit here as defendant, I sat here on the bench where you are now. You represent there the average opinion; you try to illustrate prudence and justice in the mass. Soon I shall be in thought with you in the room where you deliberate, and I am convinced that your effort will be to safeguard your interests as citizens, which are, of course, the interests of the whole nation. You may make a mistake, but you will do so in the thought that while securing your own weal you are securing the weal of all.

I see you at your homes at evening under the lamp; I hear you talk with your friends; I accompany you into your factories and shops. You are all workers—some tradesmen, others manufacturers, some exercising liberal professions. And your very legitimate anxiety is the deplorable state into which business has fallen. Everywhere the present crisis threatens to become a disaster. The receipts fall off; transactions become more and more difficult. So that the idea which you have brought here, the thought which I read in your countenances, is that there has been enough of this and that it must be ended. You have not gone the length of saying, like many: "What matters it that an innocent man is at the Ile du Diable? Is the interest of a single man worth this disturbing a great country?" But you say, nevertheless, that the agitation which we are raising, we who hunger for truth and justice, costs too dear! And if you condemn me, gentlemen, it is that thought which will be at the bottom of your verdict. You desire tranquillity for your homes, you wish for the revival of business, and you may think that by punishing me you will stop a campaign which is injurious to the interests of France.

Well, gentlemen, if that is your idea, you are entirely mistaken. Do me the honor of believing that I am not defending my liberty. By punishing me you would only magnify me. Whoever suffers for truth and justice becomes august and sacred. Look at me. Have I the look of a hireling, of a liar, and a traitor? Why should I be playing a part? I have behind me neither political ambition nor sectarian passion. I am a free writer, who has given his life to labor; who to-morrow will reënter the ranks and resume his suspended task. And how stupid are those who call me an Italian;—me, born of a French mother, brought up by grandparents in the Beauce, peasants of that vigorous soil; me, who lost my father at seven years of age, who did not go to Italy till I was fifty-four. And yet, I am proud that my father was from Venice,—the resplendent city whose ancient glory sings in all memories. And even if I were not French, would not the forty volumes in the French language, which I have sent by millions of copies throughout the world, suffice to make me a Frenchman?

So I do not defend myself. But what a blunder would be yours if you were convinced that by striking me you would reestablish order in our unfortunate country. Do you not understand now that what the nation is dying of is the obscurity in which there is such an obstinate determination to leave it? The blunders of those in authority are being heaped upon those of others; one lie necessitates another, so that the mass is becoming formidable. A judicial blunder was committed, and then to hide it a fresh crime against good sense and equity has had daily to be committed! The condemnation of an innocent man has involved the acquittal of a guilty man, and now to-day you are asked in turn to condemn me because I gave utterance to my pain beholding our country embarked on this terrible course. Condemn me, then! But it will be one more fault added to the others—a fault the burden of which you will bear in history. And my condemnation, instead of restoring the peace for which you long, and which we all of us desire, will be only a fresh seed of passion and disorder. The cup, I tell you, is full; do not make it run over!

Why do you not exactly estimate the terrible crisis through which the country is passing? They say that we are the authors of the scandal, that it is lovers of truth and justice who are leading the nation astray, and urging it to riot. Really this is a mockery! To speak only of General Gillot—was he not warned eighteen months ago? Did not Colonel Picquart insist that he should take in hand the matter of revision, if he did not wish the storm to burst and overturn everything! Did not M. Scheurer-Kestner, with tears in his eyes, beg him to think of France, and save her from such a catastrophe? No! our desire has been to facilitate everything, to allay everything; and if the country is now in trouble, the responsibility lies with the power which, to cover the guilty, and in the furtherance of political interests, has denied everything, hoping to be strong enough to prevent the truth from being shed. It has maneuvered in behalf of darkness, and it alone is responsible for the present distraction of conscience!

The Dreyfus case! ah, gentlemen, that has now become a very small affair. It is lost and far-away in view of the terrifying questions to which it has given rise. There is no longer any Dreyfus case. The question now is whether France is still the France of the rights of man, the France that gave freedom to the world, and that ought to give it justice. Are we still the most noble, the most fraternal, the most generous nation? Shall we preserve our reputation in Europe for equity and humanity? Are not all the victories that we have won called in question? Open your eyes, and understand that, to be in such confusion, the French soul must have been stirred to its depths in face of a terrible danger. A nation cannot be thus upset without imperiling its moral existence. This is an exceptionally serious hour; the safety of the nation is at stake.

And when you shall have understood that, gentlemen, you

will feel that but one remedy is possible,—to tell the truth, to do justice. Anything that keeps back the light, anything that adds darkness to darkness, will only prolong and aggravate the crisis. The rôle of good citizens, of those who feel it to be imperatively necessary to put an end to this matter, is to demand broad daylight. There are already many who think so. The men of literature, philosophy, and science are rising on every hand in the name of intelligence and reason. And I do not speak of the foreigner, of the shudder that has run through all Europe. Yet the foreigner is not necessarily the enemy. Let us not speak of the nations that may be our adversaries tomorrow. Great Russia, our ally, little and generous Holland; all the sympathetic peoples of the north; those lands of the French tongue, Switzerland and Belgium,—why are men's hearts so full, so overflowing with fraternal suffering? Do you dream then of a France isolated in the world? When you cross the frontier, do you wish them to forget your traditional renown for equity and humanity?

Dreyfus is innocent. I swear it! I stake my life on it—my honor! At this solemn moment, in the presence of this tribunal, which is the representative of human justice: before you, gentlemen, who are the very incarnation of the country, before the whole of France, before the whole world, I swear that Dreyfus is innocent. By my forty years of work, by the authority that this toil may have given me, I swear that Dreyfus is innocent. By the name I have made for myself, by my works which have helped for the expansion of French literature, I swear that Dreyfus is innocent. May all that melt away, may my works perish, if Dreyfus be not innocent! He is innocent. All seems against me—the two Chambers, the civil authority, the most widely-circulated journals, the public opinion which they have poisoned. And I have for me only the ideal,—an ideal of truth and justice. But I am quite calm; I shall conquer. I was determined that my country should not remain the victim of lies and injustice. I may be condemned here. The day will come when France will thank me for having helped to save her honor.